Public Administration and Information Technology

Volume 15

Series Editor
Christopher G. Reddick, San Antonio, TX, USA

More information about this series at http://www.springer.com/series/10796

Mehmet Zahid Sobaci
Editor

Social Media and Local Governments

Theory and Practice

Springer

Editor
Mehmet Zahid Sobaci
Faculty of Economics and Administrative Sciences
Department of Public Administration
Uludağ University
Nilufer, Turkey

Public Administration and Information Technology
ISBN 978-3-319-17721-2 ISBN 978-3-319-17722-9 (eBook)
DOI 10.1007/978-3-319-17722-9

Library of Congress Control Number: 2015939177

Springer Cham Heidelberg New York Dordrecht London

Printed on acid-free paper

Springer International Publishing AG Switzerland is part of Springer Science+Business Media (www.springer.com)

Preface

Today, social media provide public institutions with new channels for rapidly spreading information, boosting transparency and accountability, self-promotion to improve their image in the public eye, methods for designing and delivering public services with citizens, improving policy making, and encouraging the cross-agency cooperation. In this context, social media can contribute to the emergence of citizen-oriented, open, and participatory public administration. Taking the advantage of the opportunities offered by social media tools is not limited to central government. These tools can be platforms to exchange views, share information, deliver public service, engage the citizens, and trigger the debate regarding social and political problems at the local level. Thus, these platforms may bring about the adaptation of a new conception of local services and the roles of local politicians and their relationship with the citizens. In this context, this book focuses on the relationship between the local governments and social media.

This edited book deals with the change that social media have caused in the organization, understanding of public service provision, and performance of local governments. In this book, the effect of social media on the relations between local governments and their partners is analyzed. Moreover, this study focuses on the impact of social media on local politics. In other words, this book tries to explicate the role that the social media tools play in local governments as the new forms of internet-based communication. This edited book supposes that the social media tools have an impact on the conception of local service provision and local politics. However, it has to be examined and analyzed whether the social media tools actually do realize their potential in local governments. Thus, this study provides evaluations of basic issues, questions, and problems related to the use of social media tools by local governments and includes case studies.

This edited book raises the following questions and issues: (1) How does the use of social media affect the organization, functions, performance, and relationships with partners of local government? (2) How are the social media adopted by local governments and local politicians? What are the factors that affect the adoption of social media tools by the local governments and the elected? (3) What are the benefits and risks of using and adoption of social media by the local governments and local politicians? (4) Does the use of social media contribute to the improvement of public services, citizen participation, and the strengthening of local democracy? (5) Can the efficiency of the use of social media tools in local governments be measured? (6) Do the social media transform the local politics and local leadership? (7) How are the social media tools used in local elections?

There are 17 chapters which are divided into six parts in this book. Each of the parts deals with an important dimension of social media in local government. Part I, *Concept, Policy and Perception*, provides an evaluation of the relationship between local governments and social media, presents social media policy for local government, and captures the perception of policymakers in local government regarding social media. Part II, *Presence and Use*, through case studies, focuses on how and to what extent local governments use social media. Part III, *Adoption and Diffusion*, analyzes factors that affect the adoption of social media tools by local governments and local politicians through case studies. Part IV, *Communication and Citizen Engagement*, investigates how social media tools are used by local governments as a communication and citizen engagement channels. Part V of the book, *Local Elections and Campaigns* includes chapters focusing on the effect of social media on local politics and election campaigns. Part VI, *Emerging Issues*, focuses on the emerging issues such as the role of the social media in city branding and in crisis communication management.

This edited book deals with social media in local government from theoretical and practical perspectives. Despite the expansion of literature on social media, there is hardly any book focusing on the relationship between the social media and local governments. In addition to theoretical discussions, this study presents cases from some countries with different political regimes, administrative structures, political and administrative culture, and socio-economical levels. Thus, I believe that this book fills in a vital gap in the relevant literature.

The book provides a good source of reference for graduate students, academicians, and researchers, in several disciplines and fields, such as information and communication technology, public administration, political science, communication studies, and public policy. Moreover, local politicians and administrators will find the book very useful. Politicians, public officials, and research centers on social media and local government around the world can use the insights from the book to guide their decisions.

This book is a product of a very intensive effort of many people. I would like to record my gratitude to them. Firstly, I would like to thank the authors of this book. They made tireless efforts to revise their chapters. This book would not be possible without the tireless work of the contributors. I am indebted to reviewers whose critical and constructive reports have contributed to the quality of the chapters. In particular, I appreciate immensely the time and effort taken by my colleague İbrahim Hatipoğlu. I express my appreciation for the proficient work done by the staff of Springer. My editorial work would not be possible without the support of them.

Finally, I want to express my particular thanks to my family especially my brothers Cihat and Faik Selim for their patience, tolerance, and moral support.

Nilufer, Turkey Mehmet Zahid Sobaci

Contents

Part I
Concept, Policy and Perception

Chapter 1
Social Media and Local Governments: An Overview

Mehmet Zahid Sobaci

Abstract Today, social media provide public institutions with new channels for rapidly spreading information, transparency, self-promotion to improve their image in the public eye, methods for designing and delivering public services with citizens. Taking advantage of the opportunities offered by social media is not limited to central government. Local governments deploy Internet-based innovative technologies that complement traditional methods in implementing different functions. However, social media tools provide opportunities as well as risk and challenges for local governments. In this context, aim of this chapter is to provide an overall evaluation of the relationship between local governments and social media.

1.1 Introduction

Social media have become an important part of the daily lives of millions of people all over the world. It has deeply impacted the way people communicate with each other, shop, entertain, and operate on a daily basis. In the digital age, all services and activities have gradually become available online. In this context, participation in social media has been increasing on a daily basis. In fact, the number of people using popular social media tools such as Facebook, Twitter, and YouTube has reached staggering levels. Facebook, which was founded in 2004 and adopted the mission of making the world more open and connected, has 1.35 billion monthly active users as of September 30, 2014 (Facebook 2014). Twitter, which was founded in 2007 and allows everyone to create and freely share their opinions and information, has 284 million active monthly users. Every day, 500 million tweets are sent (Twitter 2014). Every month, more than one billion users visit YouTube (YouTube 2014).

M.Z. Sobaci (✉)
Department of Public Administration, Faculty of Economics and Administrative Sciences, Uludağ University, Gorukle Campus, Nilufer, Bursa, Turkey
e-mail: zsobaci@uludag.edu.tr

M.Z. Sobaci (ed.), *Social Media and Local Governments*, Public Administration and Information Technology 15, DOI 10.1007/978-3-319-17722-9_1

Even though these technologies were first discovered by the private sector, social media have also attracted the attention of political actors and administrative institutions that inform citizens as a prerequisite of open and transparent administration, deliver public services, and contact stakeholders. Today social media in government has been a rising trend. Different from web 1.0, with its interactive nature, social media provide public institutions with new channels for rapidly spreading information, transparency in public administration, self-promotion to improve their image in the public eye, methods for designing and delivering public services with citizens. Additionally, social media involves stakeholders in the decision-making process. In fact, Bertot et al. (2010, p. 53) stated that "social media technologies hold great promise in their ability to transform governance by increasing transparency and its interaction with citizens."

Taking advantage of the opportunities offered by social media tools is not limited to central government. Local governments deploy Internet-based innovative technologies that complement traditional methods in implementing different functions. For instance, local governments can benefit from blogs to gather opinions and ideas from different stakeholders. Blogs can be valuable tools for local governments to detect social problems and obtain ideas for new services. Wikis may be useful for initiating discussions about corporate social responsibility activities and other projects. Local governments can disseminate certain documents (such as announcements and draft of regulations) and presentations through media sharing platforms. Moreover, social networks such as Facebook and Twitter can be used to send local service-related messages to the public and collect citizen feedback (Bonsón et al. 2012).

The use of social media tools to achieve public goals of the local governments, of course, is a choice open to local officials. Local officials may or may not use the above-mentioned opportunities for democratic local governments, better public services, and good public policies. A cost-benefit analysis, made by local officials, will be important to this decision because social media tools provide opportunities as well as risk and challenges for local governments. However, as Gibson (2010) stated, the real challenge for local governments is that there is a greater risk not to participate in than to participate in social media. Regardless of local government participation in social media dialogues, citizens will use these tools to discuss local governments and their decisions, services and policies, with an expectation that local governments will participate in the dialogue.

In the context of technological developments and citizens' expectations, there appears to be an indispensable relationship between local governments and social media. The purpose of this chapter is to provide an overall evaluation of the relationship between local governments and social media. The study begins by introducing a conceptual framework for social media. The next section includes a general analysis of local governments' reasons for deploying social media. Then, the relationship between local governments and social media is investigated as a cyclical process. The following section focuses on social media's benefits for local governments and barriers encountered by local governments when they use social media. The final section includes a literature review and recommendations for future research on social media use by local governments.

1.2 Social Media: A Conceptual Framework

It is difficult to find a commonly agreed upon definition for the concept of social media. In fact, social media and Web 2.0 are often interchangeably used. The literature provides many complicated technical definitions as well as definitions that focus on social media's purpose or practices. Therefore, defining social media is a difficult endeavor. However, to define social media, we can start with defining Web 2.0 because social media were developed based on Web 2.0 technologies.

According to O'Reilly (2007), Web 2.0 is a networked platform that gives the user control in creating, designing, improving, and sharing content and services. Collective intelligence is one of Web 2.0's fundamental features. In this context, Web 2.0 "is of the user, by the user, and, more importantly, for the user" (Chu and Xu 2009, p. 717). Web 2.0 is individual user centered. Therefore, governments will engage with citizens using the social media tools that citizens are already active users instead of setting up websites and publishing content. Web 2.0 comprises technologies such as blogs, wikis, mashup, RSS, podcast and vlog, tagging and social bookmarking, and social networking sites. Table 1.1 presents these social media types. For governments, these technologies reflect a loss of control, informality of communication, and customization to citizens, which implies that the content and services will be designed differently from the way they are currently designed (Chang and Kannan 2008).

Social media "is a group of Internet-based applications that build on the ideological and technological foundations of Web 2.0, and that allow the creation and exchange of user generated content" (Kaplan and Haenlein 2010, p. 61). In this context, the basic characteristics of social media are as follows (Mayfield 2007): (a) Participation: social media encourages contributions and feedback from all interested parties. (b) Openness: most types of social media are open to voting, feedback, comments, and information sharing. There are rarely barriers to accessing and using content. (c) Conversation: while social media provide a basis for conversation and are seen as two-way communication tools, traditional media is about broadcast, in which content is transmitted or distributed to an audience. (d) Community: social media allow communities to quickly form and effectively communicate about common interests such as political issues or favorite TV shows. (e) Connectedness: Most social media thrive on their connectedness, via links and combining different media types in one place.

From the public sector's perspective, social media are a group of Internet-based technologies that, by using the web 2.0 philosophy, allow public institutions to engage with citizens and other stakeholders (Criado et al. 2013). In public administration, these tools have been added to the existing tool kit based on one-way (unidirectional) technologies that view citizens as passive information receivers. Social media tools have elevated citizens to the content co-creator and sender positions (Mergel 2013a).

In fact, the use of social media applications in the public sector can be seen as an extension of the digitalization efforts of public administration as a new wave of

Table 1.1 Social media types

Blog	A Web log (Blog) is a Web-based interactive application that allows one to log journal entries on events, or to express opinions and make commentaries on specific topics. It is a popular content generation tool. Blogs typically consist of text, images, videos music, and/or audios
Microblogging	The process of creating a short blog that is primarily achieved through mobile devices to share information about current events or personal opinions. A well-known example is Twitter
Wiki	A Web-based collaborative editing tool that allows different people to contribute their knowledge to the content. One author's content can be modified and enhanced with another author's contribution. A well-known example of this application tool is Wikipedia
Social networking	A Web-based tool or model that allows individuals to meet and form a virtual community through socializing via different relationships, such as friendships and professional relationships, sharing and propagating multimedia information, exchange interests, and communicating
Multimedia sharing	The rich multimedia contents such as photos, videos, and audios are shared through multimedia sharing tools. Typical examples include YouTube, Flickr, Picasa, Vimeo, etc.
Mashup	An application that uses contents from two or more external data sources combines and integrates them and thus creates new value-added information. This is a reuse and repurposing of the source data by retrieving source contents with open APIs (Application Programming Interfaces) and integrating them according to the information needs, instead of navigating them sequentially
RSS	A Web application that can pull the content from sources that are structured in standard metadata format called RSS (Really Simple Syndication) feeds such that it is easy to syndicate the contents from RSS formatted documents. The RSS feeds or Web feeds can be published and updated by the authors such that the updates can be easily inserted and quickly updated in content aggregation sites. The RSS feeds (also called atoms) are annotated with metadata such as the author and date information. The RSS-based content aggregators include news headlines, weather warnings, blogs, etc. Once the source content is updated, the content aggregator sites will be updated thus always sharing the updated content
Widgets	Small applications either on the desktop, a mobile device, or the Web. The widgets bring personalized dedicated content to the user from predefined data sources
Virtual World	A virtual world is an interactive 3-D computer-simulated world where avatars, controlled and played by the users, interact with each other as inhabitants
Social bookmarking and tagging	A tagging system that allows the users to describe the content of the Web sources with metadata such as free text, comments, evaluative ratings, and votes. This human-generated collective and collaborative set of tags forms a folksonomy and helps cluster Web resources

Source: Chun et al. (2010)

e-government era. However, social media differ from previous e-government waves. (1) Social media applications are provided by third parties, thus technological features are hosted outside of public institution's direct control. (2) Compared to e-government practices, such as static websites, social media is more interactive. (3) Content is created by both public institutions and citizens. (4) Social media applications cannot replace offline services and e-government services; these applications are existing communication mechanisms (Mergel 2013b).

In this context, the use of social media in the public sector is expected to contribute to the fulfilment of such purposes as cost savings, improvement of public services and citizen satisfaction, enhancement of transparency and accountability, citizen participation, co-production, and cross-agency collaboration.

1.3 Reasons for Using Social Media in Local Governments

In this day and age, there are several factors that encourage local governments to use social media for improving democracy, encouraging participation and citizens' knowledge of political processes. These factors can be discussed from economic, political, administrative, and social context frameworks. Economic and financial crises may increase the local government's social media use. Currently, countries all over the world have experienced severe economic and financial crises. These crises emerged in a globalized economic structure, and, like previous crises, upset many states' economic and financial balances. Local government's financial conditions are not immune to the financial disruptions faced by countries. Therefore, several recent studies have focused on the global crises' impact on local governments (United Cities and Local Governments 2009; Council of European Municipalities and Regions 2009; Commonwealth Secretariat 2010; Local Government and Public Service Initiative 2009). The global economic crisis negatively impacted local government's financial structure. Because of a sharp decrease in revenues (both tax revenues and central government financial transfers), economic activity recessions, and increased unemployment, local governments have experienced increased spending and budget deficits (Paulais 2009; Council of European Municipalities and Regions 2009).

Local governments that have to rationally use resources may be more sensitive to efficient and productive working and rational resource use during crisis periods. Social media may offer important opportunities to rationally allocate resources by determining citizen's priorities and needs; to make more acceptable policies by gathering citizen's ideas and opinions; and to provide citizen-oriented, efficient, and productive public services. These opportunities may encourage local governments to use social media tools.

Participatory democracy and new political understandings may also encourage local governments to use social media tools. Today, there is significant discontent with functioning of democracy. Low voter turnout and confidence crises in political institutions are seen as the symptoms of this disappointment (Putnam 1995; Berman 1997). Coleman and Gøtze (2001) asserted that many developed democracies experienced a loss of confidence in traditional democratic government models. To prevent and end the democratic legitimacy and accountability crisis, there is a need for a new type of relationship between citizens and governance institutions. In this context, representative democracy is criticized, and there are increases in participatory democracy. Although the idea that information and communication technologies (ICTs) have the potential to improve democracy is not new, there has been a rise in current expectations from Internet-based technologies such as social media to materialize participatory democracy.

Moreover, a growing, new understanding of politics may also play an important role for use of social media by local governments. Today, Internet-based technologies have become an integral part of election campaigns, political communication, and political marketing practices. In fact, politicians cannot be indifferent to developments in ICTs. However, politicians at the national and local levels intensively use opportunities offered by social media tools in an attempt to organize and mobilize supporters and communicate messages to the public. Of course, the use of the social media by important elected figures such as mayors and council members may encourage the local governments to open official institutional accounts on social media.

Emerging alternative approaches to public service delivery and changing social expectations make social media use at the local level a prerequisite. Today, public service improvement constitutes a vital part of countries' administrative reforms. Because governments have questioned the traditional conception of public service delivery, in the context of New Public Management (NPM), alternative approaches regarding public service delivery have been introduced. However, although they provide gains in efficiency, these alternative mechanisms have also been strongly criticized, as they have failed to account for citizens perceptions in public service improvement. It has been argued that mechanisms introduced by NPM failed to meet expectations for improving citizen satisfaction, trust and participation (OECD 2011). In fact, post-NPM debates, such as collaborative governance (Ansell and Gash 2007), new public governance (Osborne 2006), and public value (Moore 1995), directly or indirectly focus attention on this problem. Today, citizens expect public institutions to not only provide public services in an efficient way, but to also provide them in a participatory and accountable manner. In fact, it is believed that the involvement of citizens in every stage of public service design and delivery, as an innovative approach, can help improve public services through better understanding of citizens' changing priorities and accumulating citizen's information and ideas (OECD 2009).

The literature discusses this innovative approach as the concept of "co-production" (Bovaird 2007; Brandsen and Pestoff 2006; Cassia and Magno 2009; OECD 2011). "This new conception towards public services alters the role of the citizens and elevates them from the passive recipients of public services to the position of partner and contributor. The views, expectations, and demands of the citizens are considered as a vital input in improving the public services" (Sobaci and

Karkin 2013, p. 418). This innovative concept for public service delivery is compatible with philosophy of social media. Therefore, this innovative concept and the citizen's changing expectations may encourage the local governments to use social media tools.

1.4 The Local Government - Social Media Relationship: A Cyclical Process

The relationship between local governments, stakeholders, and social media can be considered as a cyclical process. In fact, this cyclical process provides a simple road map for local government's social media use. I introduce a road map for deploying social media tools by local governments. I developed this road map based on the Young Foundation's framework for the use of social media by local governments. While the Young Foundation framework is composed of three steps, I have developed the local government and social media relationships cyclical process in five steps. These steps include: making decisions to deploy and choosing tools; listening; participation; transformation; and evaluation.

The first step in the cyclical process is to make a decision and choose a tool. Local governments may deploy social media tools for various purposes (such as making them aware of decisions or services; being visible; self-promotion; developing personnel recruitment; promoting local tourism; developing the policy-making process; or problem solving). Accordingly, the first step of the process for the local governments is to decide to partake in the social media world and choose the appropriate social media tool. Local governments have to fulfil their public goals and conduct certain functions to meet these goals. In principle, an initial awareness must emerge about how social media could contribute to the realization of public goals and a decision must be made to take advantage of these innovative technologies. As explained above, every social media tool has unique features. Therefore, local governments may deploy different social media tools for different goals and functions. Moreover, the target group or social segment may vary depending on local government activities. Thus, it is crucial to choose the correct purpose-compatible social media tool. For instance, if a local government seeks to promote the local economy by attracting tourists to the city, it would be appropriate to deploy video and photo sharing sites. A local government that wishes to produce policies for young people should use the social media tools that young people most use and the local governments get into contact with them.

The second step in this cyclical process, specifically when the target is the improvement of policy-making process and solving certain local problems, is to listen to social media users and their conversations about local problems. It is fairly easy for local governments to start to listen to social media users and does not pose any risk. In this way, local governments may first build an understanding of who talks and what they are talking about. Listening to these online conversations is important because this step may help obtain unfiltered ideas and opinions on local issues. Moreover, listening to citizens in social media supports the first step of the process as it helps determine the best channels for reaching citizens and different segments of society (Young Foundation 2010).

After listening to stakeholders in the social media, the most appropriate reaction to stakeholder's sharing (such as posts, tweets, and comments) would be to participate in social media conversations. In general, this method is at no cost for local governments. There is no cost because local governments will not establish new websites or platforms to create online communities but will join into preexisting communities, such as Facebook and Twitter. In the participation stage, citizens will make judgments based on the online behavior of local governments: Do local governments respond in a constructive way and provide timely feedback? Do the local governments really listen? Or do they just react? (Young Foundation 2010).

Thus, local governments should be cautious in the participation stage and restructure social media participation around five key activities: Dialogue (having conversations with the citizens via social media); Energize (providing citizens an issue that they can support and mobilize); Support (providing platforms for people); Involve (involving citizens in the decision-making process); Measure (being informed about the impact of social media) (Young Foundation 2010).

The next step in local governments' relationship with social media is transformation (Young Foundation 2010). Local governments should implement transformation by using the local knowledge that was obtained in the listening and participation stages as input in the problem solving, decision-making, public service improvement, and altering working methods processes.

The last stage of the cyclical relationship is evaluation. It is necessary to measure and evaluate the real contribution that social media makes in reaching predetermined social, political, organizational, and financial aims or resolving a problem. As with all social phenomena, it is difficult to measure and evaluate the impact or contribution of social media. However, social media performance and impact on the results should be evaluated with several tools (analysis of social media-based indicators; network analysis; citizen surveys). In this way, it is possible to understand whether the correct social media tools have been selected and appropriately used throughout the process.

1.5 The Benefits of Social Media to Local Governments

One of the questions to be answered to understand the significance of social media for local governments is how social media can make a contribution to local governments. In other words, in what areas do social media provide opportunities for local governments? In fact, the literature has discussed the benefits of social media use in the public sector (Bertot et al. 2010; Mergel 2013b; Picazo-Vela et al. 2012; Mossberger et al. 2013). However, given unique features of local governments, it is possible to outline the opportunities offered by deploying social media for local governments in several areas:

Improving Efficiency and Productivity: In a period when public administration faces challenges in terms of resources, social media may contribute to fulfilling many functions with little resources (Freeman and Loo 2009; Landsbergen 2010; Kuzma 2010). The use of social media by local governments may play a complementary role for traditional methods in many activities or services they organize and save resources, money, and time. For instance, via social media tools such as Facebook and Twitter, local governments may more quickly and cost-effectively contact citizens and other stakeholders. Similar to the private sector, local governments may take advantage of social media tools such as LinkedIn, specifically for personnel recruitment. Local governments may share council meetings via YouTube. Similarly, sharing platforms, such as YouTube or Pinterest, can be used to promote historical and cultural places and improve the city's tourism potential. In addition, as Landsbergen (2010) stated, local governments may benefit from social media, not only for finding resources that are out of their control but also as creative and innovative tools for mobilizing resources to fulfil the public purposes.

Improving Local Public Services: Social media tools allow local governments, as institutional actors or political actors (including the mayor or council members), to more frequently and comprehensively interact with citizens. Social media allow almost everyone to easily communicate opinions, recommendations, and criticisms to local officials, including those who do not often have their voices heard. In other words, social media include several channels for citizens to report problems they faced. At the same time, social media allow local governments to use the feedback they obtained from citizens as input in improving public services. In this way, social media pave the way for local governments to co-produce public services and mediate citizens' satisfaction in public services. For instance, mayors may use blogs or Twitter as a channel for collecting citizen's opinions and complaints.

Improving Policy Making: Local governments may start interactive and powerful dialogues with citizens about local issues via social media tools and involve them in the decision-making process. Social media tools provide new opportunities for involving citizens in problem-solving, community engagement, crowdsourcing, consultation, and cooperation processes. Thus, social media tools may lead to more rational and legitimate decision-making based on local knowledge and community preferences. A good example of policy improvement via social media is from England and is called "Help a London Park." This was a simple competition that was run by the Mayor of London and allowed people in London to vote for parks that would receive £400,000 for improvement. This project allowed Facebook groups to be set up and created YouTube videos, Flickr photos and countless blog articles. More than 110,000 votes were cast in this consultation project (Gibson 2010).

Strengthening the Local Democracy: There is a very close relationship between local governments and democracy. This is because the most appropriate scale for democracy is local scale. Local governments make decisions that directly impact citizen's lives. Because local governments are closest to citizens, it is easier for citizens to inspect and hold local governments accountable. Providing information to the citizens about decisions and services may enhance transparency and accountability.

Involving citizens and other stakeholders in the decision-making process may increase trust in local governments. Social media can improve local democracy by enhancing transparency, accountability, trust in government, and participation at the local level.

Moreover, as Gibson (2010) stated, social media tools provide new opportunities to engage people in elections. For instance, the Derbyshire County and Newcastle City Councils in England used Twitter and Facebook to provide information about local elections and announce election results.

Collaboration and Knowledge Management: Strengthening intra- or cross-agency cooperation is one of the fundamental objectives of public administration reforms. It is necessary to remove the "silo effect" that negatively impacts organizational efficiency and productivity. Fragmentation has a negative impact, especially in emergencies and disasters. Social media tools can be deployed in the public sector to join government and provide cross-agency cooperation (Osimo 2008). Thus, they also contribute to knowledge management. According to Chun et al. (2010, pp. 4–5), "These social network systems allow large scale distributed collaboration, information sharing and creation of collective intelligence in government areas at all levels from local to federal."

1.6 Risks and Barriers for Local Governments

There is some skepticism about using social media in the public sector (Kingsley 2009; Zavattaro and Sementelli 2014). In general, critics emphasize the intrinsic risks of social media use and barriers to social media adoption. In this context, it is not clear if social media is an opportunity or a threat (Spurrell 2012). However, it is possible to say that there is in general a dominant optimistic point of view. There are few studies that identify barriers to social media use and make suggestions to remove them in the relevant literature (Bertot et al. 2012; Picazo-Vela et al. 2012; Zheng 2013; Landsbergen 2010; Meijer et al. 2012; CIO Council 2009; Tappendorf 2012). These studies use social, political, legal, organizational, technological, and information-related categories to understand barriers for the use of social media in public sector (Picazo-Vela et al. 2012; Zheng 2013). The barriers to public sector social media use are related to leadership, lack of resources, privacy, security, public records management, perceptions, social inclusion, and governance (Bertot et al. 2012; Landsbergen 2010; Dadashzadeh 2010; Meijer et al. 2012).

It is beneficial to briefly review contextual factors that may impact local government's social media use before discussing the barriers that local governments have encountered in practice. As has been seen in prior e-government practices, the most important barrier to social media in the public sector is not the innovative technology itself, but public institution's adoption of Internet-based applications. Thus, the first requirement is a mind-set change. In other words, by abandoning traditional functioning, the adoption of social media by public institutions requires awareness, collective belief, and consensus about the opportunities offered by social media for public institutions.

In this context, as with any innovative organizational initiative, leadership is an important factor for local governments to take advantage of social media applications in an efficient way to achieve specific objectives (transparency, accountability, participation, and cooperation). A powerful leadership that does not see using social media as a waste of time can facilitate social media use in local government. In other words, one potential barrier to local government's social media use is a lack of powerful leadership.

Another contextual factor that may influence local government's social media use is culture. Here, culture can be classified into two categories: Organizational culture and political culture. Organizational culture is a decisive factor in an institution's adoption of a change and ability to keep up with ongoing changes. In this context, a local government's culture that does not resist social media applications is closely related to being an open system and sensitive to environmental changes in the local government.

For political culture, it is necessary for citizens to have an active role so that these technologies can contribute to transparency, participation, and cooperation. The nature of social media predicts a two-way relationship and dialogue between the governing and the governed. When local governments adopt social media applications, there is a need for citizens to use these technologies for political and administrative purposes to achieve the above-mentioned objectives. In other words, citizens are required to be active and participatory political actors. The political culture in a country decides if this type of citizen can emerge and be nurtured by the democratic climate. In addition, even if the political culture of a country paves the way for an active and participatory citizen to emerge, citizens still must have the skills to use the social media tools. Therefore, the e-maturity of the society has an indirect impact on local government's social media use.

The other contextual factor is digital divide. For expected benefits from social media to emerge at the local level, disabled and socioeconomically disadvantaged people need to have access to social media tools. In other words, there is a need to overcome the problem of digital divide.

Having briefly explicated contextual factors above, we can explain the risks and barriers that local governments encounter while using social media in the following section:

Resources: One main barrier to local government social media use is a lack of sufficient resources. The problem of resources can be addressed in three ways: technological, personnel, and time. In the technological dimension, local governments need to have the required broadband to support streaming videos; security measures to protect their institution's network from viruses and malware-rich social media software; and to have sufficient disk space to support certain applications (Center for Technology in Government 2009). Local governments are faced with various challenges in terms of personnel. The use of social media by local governments requires that personnel have certain new and different skills. Thus, local governments should hire a person responsible for the management of social media or set up a team that will be responsible for social media relations. Moreover, all institutional personnel should know how to use social media tools, which raises personnel training and development questions. For local governments to effectively use and implement best practices in social media, they need to train their personnel on social media. In addition, allocated time is needed to respond to citizen's posts, partake in conversations with citizens on behalf of the institution, and follow ongoing discussions and activities in the social media. Indeed, empirical studies that have focused on local government's social media use confirm that the lack of sufficient resources is a significant barrier raised by local officials (Howard 2012; Purser 2012; Center for Technology in Government 2009).

Legal Issues: The use of social media by local governments highlights many legal concerns on which officials need to attentively focus. These legal issues comprise the following concerns: compatibility with laws of open records laws or sunshine laws (such as the obligation of the council meeting being open to the public and retaining records); monitoring personnel's appropriate use of social media (the potential impact of social media use on productivity, inappropriate online activity on agency computers); posting inaccurate information in the agency's name and the resulting liability for consequences resulting from misinformation; employer–employee relationships (employer requests for social media passwords); posts causing copyright issues; and concerns of discrimination based on digital divide (Center for Technology in Government 2009; Hennessy 2012; Tappendorf 2012; Hrdinová et al. 2010; Kingsley 2009).

Security: Security concerns are one of the most fundamental barriers to local governments social media use. Security concerns include risks, such as malware software targeting institutions' networks or cyber-attacks by hackers and leaking secret information. The use of social media by local governments has introduced new methods (information scraping, spear phishing, social engineering, spoofing, and web application attacks) for these risks (Oxley 2011; CIO Council 2009; Center for Technology in Government 2009). In fact, empirical studies that have focused on the use of social media by local government have shown that officials consider security to be one of the main barriers (Howard 2012; Purser 2012; Center for Technology in Government 2009).

Information and Content Concerns: Content management is another important issue in local government's social media use. In this context, determining the sender of information on behalf of the institution and ensuring the correct content is crucial. If these issues are not clearly determined by the institution, many personnel may post inaccurate information on behalf of the institution. In addition, sensitive information may be leaked. Moreover, because the institution does not have full control of the content, the institution may falsely seem to approve opinions and advertisements published on its social media site or from other social media sites (Center for Technology in Government 2009). Additionally, institutional personnel may share opinions and comments on social media tools that differ from the local government's official social media accounts. There may be a false perception that these opinions and comments were approved by the local government (Hrdinová et al. 2010). Finally, when citizens are informed by the local government through different sources via social media tools, there may be an abundance of information. Thus, the important messages of the institution may drown in the sea of information (Center for Technology in Government 2009). All these problems are in the list of barriers for using social media in empirical studies (Purser 2012; Howard 2012; Hrdinová et al. 2010); thus, local governments should take measures against those risks.

Reputation Management: Posts sent on social media spread very quickly. While this provides local governments with opportunities for disseminating information, it may also generate adverse consequences. Because local governments do not have control over their own messages in the social media world, there may be extensive negative statements or defamation about local government. This raises the issue of reputational risk. In other words, local governments should preserve their online reputations as social assets. Concerns about reputational risks are extensively articulated by local officials (Purser 2012; Howard 2012; Gibson 2010; Ben-Yehuda 2012).

1.7 Literature Review and Future Studies

Because social media have significant impacts on political and social life, it is an academically worthwhile endeavor to focus on and examine social media. In fact, the literature on the use of social media by the political and administrative institutions has recently expanded. However, there have been few studies on the relationship between social media and local governments, and the locally elected. For example, there are hardly any books focused on the relationship between social media and local governments. Research on local government's or politician's social media use includes very few articles published in core journals and some conference papers. Each article and paper focuses on a particular aspect of the relationship between social media and local government. Moreover, it is also possible to talk about some guides and reports focusing on the relationship between local government and social media (Gibson 2010; IDeA 2010; Hrdinová et al. 2010; Howard 2012; Purser 2012). Table 1.2 presents the studies focused on the relationship between local governments or politicians and social media.

Given the literature review on the use of social media by local governments, the following suggestions can be made:

Increasing the Number of and Enriching the Content of Studies: There is a need for more research on local government's or politician's social media use in terms of each subject specified in Table 1.2. Existing studies are often from the USA, England, and Australia. Thus, there is a need for studies that investigate the use of social media by local governments in other countries. Studies of social media in local governments could specifically focus on the experiences of underdeveloped or developing countries, countries with different political and administrative traditions, and those in different geographies (Middle-East and Asia). Moreover, there are few comparative studies. In this context, it is important to compare and analyze social media practices in different countries.

Table 1.2 Literature review on the relationship between local governments and social media

Focus	Academic studies (countries and social media tools)
Presence and use	Vaccari (2013) (Italy-Facebook, YouTube, Twitter); Avery and Graham (2013) (USA-Social media in general); Scullion (2013) (England-Twitter and Facebook); Larsson (2013) (Sweden-Facebook, Twitter, YouTube and Flickr); Mainka et al. (2014) (Various Countries-Social media in general); Panagiotopoulos and Sams (2012) (UK-Twitter); Panagiotopoulos and Sams (2011) (UK-Twitter)
Adoption and diffusion	Zheng (2013) (China-Microblog); Mundy and Umer (2012) (UK-Twitter); Omar et al. (2012) (Australia-Social media in general); Ma (2014) (China-Microblog); Oliveira and Welch (2013) (USA-Social media in general); Reddick and Norris (2013) (USA-Social media in general); Sharif et al. (2014) (Australia-Social media in general)
Communication and citizen engagement	Agostino (2013) (Italy-Facebook, Twitter and YouTube); Bonsón et al. (2013) (European Countries-Facebook); Ellison and Hardey (2013) (England-Facebook, Twitter and YouTube); Graham and Avery (2013) (USA-Facebook and Twitter); Hofmann et al. (2013) (Germany-Facebook); Lovari and Parisi (2012) (Italy-Facebook); Mossberger et al. (2013) (USA-Social media in general); Rustad and Sæbø (2013) (Norway-Facebook)
Transparency, accountability, and participation	Schellong and Girrger (2010) (Germany-Social media in general); Bonsón et al. (2012) (European Countries-Social media in general); Ellison and Hardey (2014) (England-Facebook, Twitter and YouTube); Mambrey and Dörr (2011) (Germany-Twitter); Sobaci and Karkin (2013) (Turkey-Twitter)
Local election, campaign, and politics	Segaard and Nielsen (2013) (Norway-Blog); Segaard (2012) (Norway-Blog); Lev-On (2012) (Israel-YouTube); Ozdesim Ikiz et al. (2014) (Turkey-Twitter); Criado and Martinez-Fuentes (2010) (Spain-Blog); Criado et al. (2012) (Spain-Twitter); Skogerbø and Krumsvik (2014) (Norway-Facebook and Twitter); Yannas et al. (2011) (Greece-Social media in general); Effing et al. (2013) (Holland-Social media in general); Raynauld and Greenberg (2014) (Canada-Twitter)
City planning	Evans-Cowley (2010) (USA, England and Canada-Facebook); Evans-Cowley and Hollander (2010) (USA-Facebook and Second Life); Fredericks and Foth (2013) (Australia-Facebook and Twitter); Williamson and Parolin (2013) (Australia-Social media in general)
Emergency	Panagiotopoulos et al. (2014) (England-Twitter); Tyshchuk and Wallace (2013) (USA-Social media in general)

Most existing studies focused on Facebook and Twitter. Researchers often analyze these tools because they are popular and have many users around the world. However, future studies should analyze opportunities or risks from other social media tools for local governments.

Moreover, in addition to presenting statistical findings on which tools are most frequently used and by whom, more theory-based studies on the applicability of social media tools in local governments may significantly contribute to the relevant literature in the future. Future studies may benefit from administrative reform theory, political and administrative culture discussions, policy diffusion theory, self-organizing, new institutionalism, and socio-technic systems approach.

Demand and Supply Side of Social Media Use in Local Governments: Future studies should analyze citizen's and local official's perceptions about social media. What are the factors motivating citizens to use social media in their relationship with local governments? Do citizens consider the use of social media by local governments an opportunity for efficient public service, democracy and cooperation, or a waste of time? What are the basic characteristics of citizens who contact local governments via social media? Which users are interested in specific decisions that local governments have made and, in which policy areas? What are the local politicians' and officials' perceptions of social media? Can local governments and local officials be categorized by social media use? In order for the local governments to make more legitimate and rational policies and fulfil their public goals by benefiting from social media tools, researchers should focus on these and similar problems.

Local Democracy and Participation: Given the significance of local governments, especially for democracy and efficient public service delivery, there is a need for empirical studies that analyze social media tools' potential for enhancing of transparency, accountability, and participation at the local level. When this need is met, we see whether the commitments of the social media are realized. In the past, there have been debates that previous e-government waves have failed in terms of two-way relationships, participation, and strengthening democracy.

Detailed Analysis of Barriers and Recommendations: Barriers for use of these technologies in local governments are scarcely considered and categorized in the relevant literature. At this stage, researchers should specify each and every barrier encountered by the local governments as an independent topic of study and analyze it in detail.

Measuring the Impact of Social Media on Local Governments: It is important to measure the impact of the use of social media in local governments. These innovative technologies may have organizational, political, financial, and social impacts on local governments. It is an important topic of research to measure the real impact of social media use because social media may contribute to cost saving, transparency, participation, improving the policy-making process, and cooperation. What is the reality? Have social media tools contributed to these gains? Future studies may answer these questions through case studies.

References

Agostino, D. (2013). Using social media to engage citizens: A study of Italian municipalities. *Public Relations Review, 39*, 232–234.

Ansell, C., & Gash, A. (2007). Collaborative governance in theory and practice. *Journal of Public Administration Research and Theory, 18*, 543–571.

Avery, E. J., & Graham, M. W. (2013). Political public relations and the promotion of participatory, transparent government through social media. *International Journal of Strategic Communication, 7*(4), 274–291.

Ben-Yehuda, G. (2012, Fall/Winter). Road hazards: Recognizing the risks of social media. *The Business of Government Magazine*, 68–70.
Berman, E. M. (1997). Dealing with cynical citizens. *Public Administration Review, 57*(2), 105–112.
Bertot, J. C., Jaeger, P. T., Munson, S., & Glaisyer, T. (2010). Social media technology and government transparency. *Computer, 43*(11), 53–59.
Bertot, J. C., Jaeger, P. T., & Hansen, D. (2012). The impact of polices on government social media usage: Issues, challenges, and recommendations. *Government Information Quarterly, 29*(1), 30–40.
Bonsón, E., Royo, S., & Ratkai, M. (2013). *Analysis of European municipalities' Facebook channels activity and citizens' engagement*. In XVII Congreso AECA 'Ética y emprendimiento: valores para un nuevo desarrollo', Pamplona, Spain. Retrieved from http://www.aeca1.org/pub/on_line/comunicaciones_xviicongresoaeca/cd/84g.pdf
Bonsón, E., Torres, L., Royo, S., & Flores, F. (2012). Local e-government 2.0: Social media and corporate transparency in municipalities. *Government Information Quarterly, 29*(2), 123–132.
Bovaird, T. (2007). Beyond engagement and participation: User and community coproduction of public services. *Public Administration Review, 67*(5), 846–860.
Brandsen, T., & Pestoff, V. (2006). Co-production, the third sector and the delivery of public services. *Public Management Review, 8*(4), 493–501.
Cassia, F., & Magno, F. (2009). Public services co-production: Exploring the role of citizen orientation. *International Journal of Quality and Service Sciences, 1*(3), 334–343.
Center for Technology in Government. (2009). *Exploratory social media project: Phase I—Identifying benefits and concerns surrounding use of social media in government*. Retrieved from http://www.ctg.albany.edu/publications/reports/social_media/social_media.pdf
Chang, A., & Kannan, P. K. (2008). *Leveraging web 2.0 in government* (E-Government/technology series). Washington, DC: IBM Center for the Business of Government.
Chu, H., & Xu, C. (2009). Web 2.0 and its dimensions in the scholarly world. *Scientometrics, 80*(3), 717–729.
Chun, A. S., Shulman, S., Sandoval, R., & Hovy, E. (2010). Government 2.0: Making connections between citizens, data and government. *Information Polity, 15*, 1–9.
CIO Council. (2009). *Guidelines for secure use of social media by federal departments and agencies*. Retrieved from https://cio.gov/wp-content/uploads/downloads/2012/09/Guidelines_for_Secure_Use_Social_Media_v01-0.pdf
Coleman, S., & Gøtze, J. (2001). *Bowling together: Online public engagement in policy deliberation*. London: Hansard Society.
Commonwealth Secretariat. (2010). *The global financial crisis and local government*. Commonwealth Secretariat, Discussion Paper No. 9.
Council of European Municipalities and Regions. (2009). *The economic and financial crisis: The impact on local and regional authorities*. Paris: Author.
Criado, J. I., & Martinez-Fuentes, G. (2010). Mayors' usage of blogs in local election campaign: The Spanish case study. *International Journal of Electronic Governance, 3*(4), 395–413.
Criado, J. I., Martinez-Fuentes, G., & Silvan, A. (2012). Social media for political campaigning: The use of Twitter by Spanish mayors in 2011 local elections. In C. G. Reddick & S. K. Aikins (Eds.), *Web 2.0 technologies and democratic governance* (pp. 219–232). New York: Springer.
Criado, J. I., Sandoval-Almazan, R., & Gil-Garcia, J. R. (2013). Government innovation through social media. *Government Information Quarterly, 30*(4), 319–326.
Dadashzadeh, M. (2010). Social media in government: From eGovernment to eGovernance. *Journal of Business & Economics Research, 8*(11), 81–86.
Effing, R., Van Hillegersberg, J., & Huibers, T. W. C. (2013). Social media participation and local politics: A case study of the Enschede council in the Netherlands. In M. A. Wimmer, E. Tambouris, & A. Macintosh (Eds.), *Electronic participation* (pp. 57–68). Heidelberg, Germany: Springer.
Ellison, N., & Hardey, M. (2013). Developing political conversations? Social media and English local authorities. *Information, Communication & Society, 16*(6), 878–898.

Ellison, N. R., & Hardey, M. (2014). Social media and local government: Citizenship, consumption and democracy. *Local Government Studies, 40*(1), 21–40.

Evans-Cowley, J. (2010). Planning in the age of Facebook: The role of social networking in planning processes. *GeoJournal, 75*(5), 407–420.

Evans-Cowley, J., & Hollander, J. (2010). The new generation of public participation: Internet-based participation tools. *Planning Practice & Research, 25*(3), 397–408.

Facebook. (2014). Retrieved from http://newsroom.fb.com/company-info/

Fredericks, J., & Foth, M. (2013). Augmenting public participation: Enhancing planning outcomes through the use of social media and web 2.0. *Australian Planner, 50*(3), 244–256.

Freeman, R. J., & Loo, P. (2009). *Web 2.0 and e-government at the municipal level.* Paper presented at 2009 World Congress on Privacy, Security, Trust and the Management of e-Business, August 25–27, 2009, New Brunswick, NJ, pp. 70–78.

Gibson, A. (2010). *Local by social: How local authorities can use social media to achieve more for less*. London: IDeA.

Graham, M., & Avery, J. E. (2013). Public relations and social media: An analysis of the perceptions and trends of social media use at the local government level. *Public Relations Journal, 7*(4), 1–21.

Hennessy, K. S. (2012, February). Are city governments and social media a good match? *Quality Cities Magazine*, 16–19.

Hofmann, S., Beverungen, D., Räckers, M., & Becker, J. (2013). What makes local governments' online communications successful? Insights from a multi-method analysis of Facebook. *Government Information Quarterly, 30*(4), 387–396.

Howard, A. (2012). *Connecting with communities: How local government is using social media to engage with citizens*. Sydney, New South Wales: ANZSOG Institute for Governance at the University of Canberra and Australian Centre of Excellence for Local Government.

Hrdinová, J., Helbig, N., & Stollar Peters, C. (2010). *Designing social media policy for government: Eight essential elements*. New York: Center for Technology in Government.

IDeA. (2010). *Connected councillors: A guide to using social media to support local leadership*. London: Author.

Kaplan, A. M., & Haenlein, M. (2010). Users of the world, unite! The challenges and opportunities of social media. *Business Horizons, 53*, 59–68.

Kingsley, C. (2009). *Making the most of social media: 7 lessons from successful cities*. Fels Institute of Government. Retrieved from http://www.fels.upenn.edu/sites/www.fels.upenn.edu/files/PP3_SocialMedia.pdf

Kuzma, J. (2010). Asian government usage of web 2.0 social media. *European Journal of ePractice, 9*, 69–81.

Landsbergen, D. (2010). Government as part of the revolution: Using social media to achieve public goals. *Electronic Journal of e-Government, 8*(2), 135–147.

Larsson, A. (2013). Bringing it all back home? Social media practices by Swedish municipalities. *European Journal of Communication, 28*(6), 681–695.

Lev-On, A. (2012). YouTube usage in low-visibility political campaigns. *Journal of Information Technology & Politics, 9*(2), 205–216.

Local Government and Public Service Initiative. (2009). *The impact of the economic downturn on local government: What is happening and what can be done about it?* Report by OSI/LGI to the Council of Europe.

Lovari, A., & Parisi, L. (2012). Public administrations and citizens 2.0: Exploring digital public communication strategies and civic interaction within Italian municipality pages on Facebook. In F. Comunello (Ed.), *Networked sociability and individualism: Technology for personal and professional relationships* (pp. 238–263). Hershey, PA: IGI Global.

Ma, L. (2014). Diffusion and assimilation of government microblogging: Evidence from Chinese cities. *Public Management Review, 16*(2), 274–295.

Mainka, A., Hartmann, S., Stock, W. G., & Peters, I. (2014). *Government and social media: A case study of 31 informational world cities*. In R. H. Sprague (Ed.), *Proceeding of the 47th Hawaii International Conference on System Sciences* (pp. 1715–1724), Waikoloa, HI: CPS.

Mambrey, P., & Dörr, R. (2011). Local government and social networking technologies in Germany: The example of Twitter. In P. Parycek, M. J. Kripp, & N. Edelmann (Eds.), *Proceedings of the International Conference for e-Democracy and Open Government (CeDEM11)* (pp. 249–259). Krems an der Donau, Austria: Edition Donau-Universitat Krems.

Mayfield, A. (2007). *What is social media*. Retrieved from http://www.iCrossing.com/ebooks

Meijer, A., Koops, B., Pieterson, W., Overman, S., & ten Tije, S. (2012). Government 2.0: Key challenges to its realization. *Electronic Journal of e-Government, 10*(1), 59–69.

Mergel, I. (2013a). *Social media in public sector: A guide to participation, collaboration and transparency in networked world*. San Francisco: Jossey-Bass.

Mergel, I. (2013b). A framework for interpreting social media interactions in the public sector. *Government Information Quarterly, 30*(4), 327–334.

Moore, M. H. (1995). *Creating public value: Strategic management in government*. Cambridge, MA: Harvard University Press.

Mossberger, K., Wu, Y., & Crawford, J. (2013). Connecting citizens and local governments? Social media and interactivity in major U.S. cities. *Government Information Quarterly, 30*(4), 351–358.

Mundy, D., & Umer, Q. (2012). United Kingdom Local Authority Challenges in the use of Twitter and other social media. In *SOTICS 2012: The Second International Conference on Social Eco-Informatics*, October 21–26, 2012, Venice, Italy.

O'Reilly, T. (2007). What is web 2.0: Design patterns and business models for the next generation of software. *Communications & Strategies, 65*(1), 17–37.

OECD. (2009). *Focus on citizens: Public engagement for better policy and services*. Paris: OECD.

OECD. (2011). *Together for better public services: Partnering with citizens and civil society* (OECD public governance reviews). Paris: OECD.

Oliveira, G. H. M., & Welch, E. W. (2013). Social media use in local government: Linkage of technology, task, and organizational context. *Government Information Quarterly, 30*(4), 397–405.

Omar, K., Scheepers, H., & Stockdale, R. (2012). Adoption of social media in Victorian local governments. In *23rd Australasian Conference on Information Systems*, December 3–5, 2012, Geelong, Victoria, Australia.

Osborne, S. P. (2006). Editorial: New public governance. *Public Management Review, 8*(3), 377–387.

Osimo, D. (2008). *Web 2.0 in government: Why and how?* Luxembourg: European Communities.

Oxley, A. (2011). *A best practices guide for mitigating risk in the use of social media*. Washington, DC: IBM Center for The Business of Government.

Ozdesim Ikiz, O., Sobaci, M. Z., Yavuz, N., & Karkin, N. (2014). Political use of Twitter: The case of metropolitan mayor candidates in 2014 local elections in Turkey. In *ICEGOV 2014*, October 27–30, 2014, Guimaraes, Portugal.

Panagiotopoulos, P., Bigdeli, A. Z., & Sams, S. (2014). Citizen–government collaboration on social media: The case of Twitter in the 2011 riots in England. *Government Information Quarterly, 31*(3), 349–357.

Panagiotopoulos, P., & Sams, S. (2011). Twitter in local government: A study of Greater London Authorities. In *2011 Pre-ICIS Workshop: Open Innovation in eGovernment*, Shanghai, China.

Panagiotopoulos, P., & Sams, S. (2012). An overview study of Twitter in the UK local government. In *Transforming Government Workshop*, May 8–9, 2012, Brunel University, London.

Paulais, T. (2009). *Local governments and the financial crisis: An analysis*. Washington, DC: Cities Alliance.

Picazo-Vela, S., Gutiérrez-Martínez, I., & Luna-Reyes, L. F. (2012). Understanding risks, benefits, and strategic alternatives of social media applications in the public sector. *Government Information Quarterly, 29*, 504–511.

Purser, K. (2012). *Using social media in local government: 2011 survey report*. Sydney, New South Wales: Australian Centre of Excellence for Local Government, University of Technology.

Putnam, R. (1995). Bowling alone: America's declining social capital. *Journal of Democracy, 6*(1), 65–78.

Raynauld, V., & Greenberg, J. (2014). Tweet, click, vote: Twitter and the 2010 Ottawa municipal election. *Journal of Information Technology & Politics, 11*(4), 412–434.

Reddick, C. G., & Norris, D. F. (2013). Social media adoption at the American grass roots: Web 2.0 or 1.5? *Government Information Quarterly, 30*(4), 498–507.

Rustad, E., & Sæbø, Ø. (2013). How, why and with whom do local politicians engage on Facebook? In M. A. Wimmer, E. Tambouris, & A. Macintosh (Eds.), *Electronic participation* (pp. 69–79). Heidelberg, Germany: Springer.

Schellong, A., & Girrger, P. (2010). *Government 2.0 in betaphase—An analysis of eparticipation and web 2.0 applications of Germany's 50 largest cities and 16 federal states* (Policy paper series). Wiesbaden, Germany: CSC.

Scullion, J. (2013). *Old rules for new technologies: Institutional responses to social media use by local councilors*. Paper presented at European Consortium for Political Research Conference, September 4–7, 2013, Bordeaux, France.

Segaard, S. B. (2012). Local election campaign on social media—Horizontal or vertical conversation? In *ECPR Joint Sessions of Workshops*, April 10–15, 2012, Antwerp, Belgium.

Segaard, S. B., & Nielsen, J. A. (2013). Local election blogs: Networking among the political elite. *Information Polity, 18*(4), 299–313.

Sharif, M. H. M., Troshani, I., & Davidson, R. (2014). Adoption of social media services: The case of local government. In Z. Sun & J. Yearwood (Eds.), *Handbook of research on demand-driven web services: Theory, technologies, and applications* (pp. 287–303). Hershey, PA: IGI Global.

Skogerbø, E., & Krumsvik, A. H. (2014). Newspapers, Facebook and Twitter: Intermedial agenda setting in local election campaigns. *Journalism Practice*, 1–17.

Sobaci, M. Z., & Karkin, N. (2013). The use of twitter by mayors in Turkey: Tweets for better public services? *Government Information Quarterly, 30*(4), 417–425.

Spurrell, D. (2012). An opportunity or a threat? How local government uses social media today. *The Guardian*. Retrieved February 7th Tuesday, 2012, from http://www.theguardian.com/local-government-network/2012/feb/07/local-government-social-media-today

Tappendorf, J. A. (2012). Social media. In *IMLA 2012 Annual Conference*, October 21–24, 2012, Austin, TX.

Twitter. (2014). https://about.twitter.com/company

Tyshchuk, Y., & Wallace, W. (2013). The use of social media by local government in response to an extreme event: Del Norte County, CA response to the 2011 Japan Tsunami. In T. Comes, F. Fiedrich, S. Fortier, J. Geldermann, & T. Müller (Eds.), *Proceedings of the 10th International ISCRAM Conference* (pp. 802–811), Baden, Germany.

United Cities and Local Governments. (2009). *The impact of the global crisis on local governments*, Barcelona, Spain.

Vaccari, C. (2013). City hall 2.0? Italian local executive officials' presence and popularity on web 2.0 platforms. In P. Nixon, R. Rawal, & D. Mercea (Eds.), *Politics and the Internet in comparative context: Views from the cloud* (pp. 169–185). London: Routledge.

Williamson, W., & Parolin, B. (2013). Web 2.0 and social media growth in planning practice: A longitudinal study. *Planning, Practice & Research, 28*(5), 544–562.

Yannas, P., Kleftodimos, A., & Lappas, G. (2011). Online political marketing in 2010 Greek local elections: The shift from web to web 2.0 campaigns. In G. Panigyrakis, P. Theodoridis, & A. Panopoulos (Eds.), *Proceeding of the 16th International Conference on Corporate and Marketing Communications* (pp. 38–50), Athens, Greece.

Young Foundation. (2010). *A social media framework for local government: A local 2.0 think-piece*. London: Author.

YouTube. (2014). http://www.youtube.com/yt/press/

Zavattaro, S. M., & Sementelli, A. J. (2014). A critical examination of social media adoption in government: Introducing omnipresence. *Government Information Quarterly, 31*(2), 257–264.

Zheng, L. (2013). Social media in Chinese government: Drivers, challenges and capabilities. *Government Information Quarterly, 30*, 369–376.

Chapter 2
Designing Social Media Policy for Local Governments: Opportunities and Challenges

Özer Köseoğlu and Aziz Tuncer

Abstract This study aims to contribute to the newly developing social media policy literature through examining the process of designing social media policy particularly for local governments, and analyzing opportunities and challenges that local governments face in implementing them. We underline the importance of creating a cultural shift in local governments through the help of a transformational leadership as a necessity for an effective social media policy in local governments. As a conclusion, we argue that the main principles of "social media governance" can be adopted into local governments. In such a model, local governments should design their own social media policy and guidelines with regard to the broader central government policy, incorporation with local government's other policies, and considering audiences' needs and expectations.

2.1 Introduction

Social media tools, in the first phase, have transformed people's traditional communication and interaction practices. Proliferation of flexible technological devices such as notebooks, tablet PCs, and smartphones have facilitated and thus accelerated the usage of social media among different groups of people, specifically the young. Corporations that focus on customer demands and seek alternative ways to gain commercial advantages could not disregard social media.

In a more recent period, governments and public agencies have tended to use social media for not just as a communication tool, but also for enhancing service operations, internal employee coordination, public engagement, emergency management, policy feedback, and so on. Government agencies utilize social media not solely to connect and share with constituents, but also to help carry out better quality services through social media (Hansen-Flaschen and Parker 2012). Agencies have also begun adopting mini applications with dynamic content and services provided in a web page such as widgets, modules, snippets, and plugins (Bertot et al. 2012).

Ö. Köseoğlu (✉) • A. Tuncer
Department of Politics and Public Administration, Faculty of Political Science,
Sakarya University, Esentepe Campus, Sakarya 54187, Turkey
e-mail: ozerk@sakarya.edu.tr; atuncer@sakarya.edu.tr

M.Z. Sobaci (ed.), *Social Media and Local Governments*, Public Administration and Information Technology 15, DOI 10.1007/978-3-319-17722-9_2

At regional and local level, social media has rapidly been disseminated among local authorities who recognize the benefits and advantages of Web 2.0 tools. Among them, local governments, as well as their central counterparts, popularly use specific social media sites such as Facebook and Twitter for the aims of information exchange, better-quality services, and public engagement (Bertot et al. 2012). Types of social media tools have become more diversified and sophisticated, and employment of social media for personal and professional aims by council members, local elected managers, and other public employees have increased—which have brought the need for designing social media policy to the local governments' agenda. Designing social media policy for both public and private sector organizations is relatively a new issue. Magro (2012) contends that interest in social media policy emerged strongly in 2009 and has remained as a constant theme since.

Social media policy can be seen as a component of government's regulatory function. As Klang and Nolin (2011) argue, designing social media policy is one of the elements of a polycentric regulatory effort that includes laws such as individuals' rights, employment law, administrative law and criminal law, as well as user norms, social norms, and affordances. Therefore, a multitude of local governments, in line with broader government policies in such areas of transparency, privacy, security, and governance, develop or have an intention to develop social media policies depending on various instruments that consist of strategy documents, guidelines, protocols, standards, and other alternative techniques.

Social media policy, in this chapter, is defined as "the prescribed principle of action or practice relating to an online channel, space or environment in which people engage and converse" (Cadell 2013, p. 4). In this regard, we aim to contribute to the newly developing social media policy literature through examining the process of designing social media policy particularly for local governments, and analyzing opportunities and challenges that local governments face in implementing them.

The study primarily starts with highlighting the impacts of social media on local policy-making. After asking the question of why local governments need a social media policy in Sect. 2.3, we have analyzed the process of designing social media policy for local governments in the following section. In Sect. 2.4, challenges that local governments face during the process of designating social media policy are investigated with a focus on organizational culture and leadership issues.

2.2 Integrating Social Media to Policy-Making in Local Governments

Social media tools have restructured interpersonal communications, first and foremost, by providing almost instant access to a wider range of opinions and issues. Secondly, social media has stronger connectivity between users, which facilitates sharing breaking news, broaching a social issue, and exchanging opinions in real time to a massive audience. Thirdly, social media has reduced online anonymity (Park et al. 2011). Through social media, citizens connect to a global community, proceed conversations, share ideas and information, and collaborate on the projects that attract their interest (Mergel and Greeves 2013). In essence, passive web surfers of the Internet world have become active content creators by social media (Dadashzadeh 2010).

Social media has not solely affected the interpersonal relations, but they also have led to striking changes in the public policy-making environment. Social media offers a body of opportunities for public policy-making processes of government bodies including local governments: (1) increasing citizen participation and engagement in the processes of policy development and implementation; (2) promoting transparency and accountability, and reducing corruption; (3) co-production of public services through developing and designing public services jointly with the participation of public officials and the public; (4) using public knowledge and experience to develop innovative solutions to complex societal problems (Ferro et al. 2013).

In practice, users of social media can find information relevant to a public policy through content on microblogging and media sharing sites dedicated to politics and policy. Agenda setting has become more group-led in that citizens have a chance to start a public policy debate or attend a deliberation on a specific policy issue. Additionally, governments can adopt citizens' ideas in proposing policy alternatives and making decisions, as well as evaluate policy outcomes through public hearings via social media. Moreover, a vast number of people can participate in the policy process by providing information to the government and other formal policy-makers via social network services (Park et al. 2011; Auer 2011). All in all, Web 2.0 provide opportunities for local governments to build a participative culture by engaging citizens in local public decision-making, and improving government-to-citizen and citizen-to-government relations (Bonsón et al. 2012).

2.3 The Necessity of Social Media Policy for Local Governments

While social media apps such as Twitter and Facebook provide opportunities for both private and public organizations, the social and extremely public nature of these services also bring potential hazards. Therefore, organizations including local governments are developing policies on the proper use of social media for their stuff and users (Kroski 2009). In essence, traditional workplace policies that government agencies follow do not align with the characteristics of social media (Phillips and Tremaine 2012). The new conflicts and ambiguities that come up for government agencies on the basis of using Web 2.0 tools require new solutions that embrace designating social media policies.

Social media policy helps local governments to avoid potential hazards such as posting inappropriate content, handling public comments in an unprofessional manner, and posting redundant or inaccurate information (Hansen-Flaschen and Parker 2012). Beyond fighting the predicted or unpredicted hazards, social media policies also reinforce confidence (Cadell 2013) for those using Web 2.0 tools within local governments and help to build trust relations between elected and bureaucratic officials and their constituents.

Additionally, social media policy is an effective way for developing certain principles and rules for public officials regarding their online activities in a time that the distinction between personal and professional realms is fading and seemingly everyone has a Facebook or Twitter profile. It is also a reminder that even in the personal usage of these apps the content they post is not always private and may ultimately reflect on the organization (Kroski 2009). Policies that regulate the users of social media apps for personal, professional, and organizational reasons can, therefore, create clarity for public officials, as well as provide direction for organization on how to deal with possible legal and regulatory issues (Hrdinová et al. 2010).

If there is a broader government policy on adoption and use of social media, government agencies and particularly local governments will need to design their own policy. For instance, in the USA, there is a range of legal arrangements including laws, memos, and orders that are directly or indirectly related to the adoption and usage of social media by government agencies, which thus, in turn, impel local governments to design their own social media policies depending on instruments such as guidelines to clarify and reify the broader policy (Bertot et al. 2012).

2.4 Designing Social Media Policy for Local Governments

2.4.1 Setting Goals, Objectives, and Measurement Criteria

Developing a social media policy for local governments is a part of a comprehensive regulatory policy that requires reckoning a line of factors such as legal restrictions, organizational strategies, aims and objectives, and social norms. Considering these factors, a social media policy should be modeled to ensure alignment of objectives and policy. For instance, if a local government aims to improve citizen engagement and two-way communication with its constituents, then designing a policy that does not allow external comments on the social media pages would not be convenient for achieving its strategic goal of engagement (Hrdinová et al. 2010).

As a starting point, local managers should define why they need to design a policy for social media usage in their organization and identify the goals, targets, and indicators for evaluating further accomplishments of the policy. Setting concrete goals and targets are important for future evaluations of the outcomes. Klang and Nolin (2011) identify an inventory of 18 goals that municipalities in Sweden have regarding their social media policy. These goals are complementing to traditional Web sites, disseminating information, marketing, testing new forms of reaching target groups, reaching target groups that are not otherwise reached, engaging with target groups, receiving input, improving service to target groups, creating dialogue, attracting and recruiting new civil servants, creating goodwill, strengthening brand, networking, exchanging experiences, environmental changing, aggregating traffic to municipality Web site, being able to respond to what is written about us, and improving access. The list given above demonstrates the diversity of possible goals that should be reckoned with in determining the proper social media policy for local governments.

2.4.2 Formulating Social Media Policy

In the formulation stage of social media policy, a team of experts from the legal, communication, technology, human resources, and program units (Hrdinová et al. 2010) can analyze requirements of a local government for the policy, examine alternative policies and strategies that best fit to the goals and objectives of the organization, and propose an effective policy and strategy to their clients. As Hrdinová et al. (2010) remark this team should also settle on that proposed social media policy and its implication for public officials are not in contradiction to local government's existing policies and procedures.

Empirical evidence derived from US cities indicate that searching for best practices in social media policies will be a useful starting point for formulating a social media policy (Hansen-Flaschen and Parker 2012). Local managers should recognize that best practices are only suggestions and inherent in the organizational context that is practiced. Even local governments perform almost similar duties and have mostly the same authorities and responsibilities, every local government is unique and the needs of every organization will be varied. As a result, their social media utilization policies will be unique as well.

Local governments can formulate their social media policy in various forms including strategy documents, codes, guidelines, protocols, or standards. Regardless of the regulation type, successfully formulated social media policies should include the following items (Hansen-Flaschen and Parker 2012): (1) the purpose of the policy, (2) the local government's goals for social media, (3) a list of the social media platforms that the local government approves and utilizes, (4) laws that the sites must comply with, (5) the procedure for launching and terminating a social media page (account management), (6) explanation of which employees have what level of access to the sites, (7) announcement of guidelines on acceptable and proper use by professional and personal use, (8) examples of the type of content to be posted, (9) concerns over security, specifically in terms of password protection, virus scans, and protection against hackers, (10) explanation of how social media is handled during emergencies and by whom.

Additionally, designated social media policy should operate sequentially with the local government's other policies. As a starting point, Staab (2014) states, "social media policy can be incorporated into a standing confidentiality policy, code of ethics or trustee manual." Clarifying expectations in social media policies can help public officials to use their work time as effectively as possible. It may also be stated that social media policies should be clear on how public officials will be held accountable and what circumstances they will have to deal with if they do not meet expectations (Angelotti 2013).

As it is underlined in several empirical research reports, mostly used social media policy tools in local governments are strategy documents, guidelines, standards, and recently developing alternative instruments like Elgg platform. All these instruments that help to regulate social media policy are examined in the following section.

2.4.3 Policy Alternatives for Regulation of Social Media in Local Governments

As the use of social media in local governments increase, the need for rules, regulations, and standardization has grown as well. Local governments are increasingly documenting their need for organization-specific rules for the management of their various social media accounts in forms of social media handbooks, social media strategy, policy for the use of social media, or linking strategy (Mergel and Greeves 2013). These kind of documents that represent the official social media policy of an organization explain how to govern the use of social media by employees in local governments (Hrdinová et al. 2010), but they also often extend beyond the official use of social media to build awareness that address the responsible and professional use of social media (Mergel and Greeves 2013). In this section, the policy tools that are commonly adopted by a range of local governments in different countries have been addressed.

2.4.3.1 Strategy Documents

In some cases, strategy documents are preferred to reveal social media strategies and handle the use of the social media in a professional and responsible way. A properly designated social media strategy should be based on the mission of the organization. As a first step, the strategic communication and interaction objectives should be identified, and secondly, the divergent audiences of the organization should be defined (Mergel and Greeves 2013). Following these steps it should be noted that local governments interact with various types of constituencies and provide access and information to many different stakeholders. Therefore, aligning the social media and communication objectives with local government's mission is a difficult task that local managers must deal with. However, clearly identified social media objectives will enable putting effective measurement criteria and further evaluation of the success of the strategy as well as the related policies and tactics.

Strategy documents should support local governments' use of social media as an integrated communication platform vis-à-vis citizens and business, and guide them to cope with challenges that social media policies have to deal with such as accessibility and usability in relation with security and privacy issues, assigning roles and responsibilities of public employees, and ensuring trust and credibility when commercials appear in the context of public information (Hellman 2014).

For designing a successful social media strategy, Mergel (2010) underlines five significant points: (1) Forming a team of specialists who are compatible with Web 2.0 to socialize the organization's strategy, (2) utilizing social media as a testing field for new ways of interaction between citizens and public, (3) designing social media strategy around the organization's mission and target constituencies, (4) for measuring the achievements of organizational social media policy and strategy not just focusing on the pure number of Twitter followers or Facebook fans, and (5) realizing the fact that the use of social media tools such as Twitter and Facebook have the highest increase rates in the age group of +35 years old.

2.4.3.2 Guidelines, Protocols, and Standards

When talking about designing an internal social media policy, different types of applications such as blogs, Facebook, and other social networks, and microblogging services like Twitter can be addressed (Kroski 2009). Guidelines, generally, "provide advice on how to best use social media tools to achieve a desired result, such as eliciting citizen engagement or providing suggestions for creating interesting content" (Hrdinová et al. 2010, p. 3). Policies and guidelines can also include a protocol for social media use by government agencies, and their employees (Khan et al. 2014).

Social media policy for local governments has at least two parties: (1) Elected managers, councilors, or appointed public officials and (2) generic users. Elected and appointed public officials use social media both personally and for organizational activities. In this regard, "a social media policy can help clear guidelines for staff members who are posting on behalf of the organization as well as employees with personal social media accounts" (Kroski 2009, p. 45). Public officials use social media in three distinct ways (Hrdinová et al. 2010): (1) For expressing organization's broad interests or specific policy interests, (2) for the purpose of furthering their specific job responsibilities and professional duties through the ways such as engaging with other professionals in a community,[1] and (3) for personal interests. Each type of use has different security, legal, and managerial implications and governments

[1] A distinguished example of professional uses of social media among local government managers is MuniGov, a collaborative social network that enables collaboration and communication on the topic of social media implementation within government (Mergel et al. 2011, p. 4).

at all level seek for a balance between using social media for solely organizational interests and allowing all officials access for personal and professional interests. On the other hand, users can be defined as people who have a personal account of a social media tool such as Twitter and Facebook, or who post content on local government's blogs. As Kroski puts (2009, p. 245), "[t]here are also standards being created for users, letting them know what's acceptable to post to an organization's blog and community pages."

Social media tools enable informal communication and in addition to the formal flow of knowledge they provide opportunities for public officials to interact with service users. Due to the implicit roles and responsibilities in the interaction process through social media, confusion arises for public officials and managers. For instance, whom does the public official or manager represent if the communication takes place through Twitter at 9 p.m.—herself/himself as a private person, or her/his local government as a public body? As this problem increases, the need for social policy guidelines arises (Hellman 2014). Regarding this problem, guidelines that are firstly employed in private companies have progressively been adopted by local governments.

Klang and Nolin (2011) have separated four types of guidelines that local governments use in regard to their empirical analysis of 26 Swedish municipalities. *Homogenous guidelines* are general guidelines that appropriate for YouTube, Wikipedia, and Facebook, and *heterogeneous guidelines* are specific guidelines that refer to a number of different applications in character. *Problem oriented guidelines* take social media as an administrative problem that needs to be disciplined and *resource oriented* guidelines are used as an opportunity for engaging in new practices.

There are several contradictory cases that local governments encounter while they manage social media in their organization. For instance, who or how many employees will be allowed access to social media sites? Or will there be a limitation of sites that are approved for employee access? Therefore, a social media policy guideline should include a body of essential policies or strategies on employee access, social media account management, acceptable use of social media sites for personal use while at work, ethical social media conduct for public officials, posting content on official social media sites, security concerns, legal issues, and code of conduct for citizens that refer to limitations such as offensive language, inciting violence, or promoting illegal activity (Hrdinová et al. 2010).

2.4.3.3 Alternative Tools

Problems that drive local governments to design social media policy depending on strategy documents or guidelines such as accessibility and usability, trust and credibility, and commercial content can be dealt with alternative technology platforms. Elgg platform, for instance, provides a solution to the issue of commercialization and enable advertisement-free social media (Hellman 2014). Elgg is a social networking engine that delivers the building blocks that enable businesses, schools, universities, and local governments to create their own fully featured social networks and applications (http://elgg.org, Elgg 2014). In essence, as alternative platforms may offer features which are important for public bodies in general and local governments in particular for accessibility and credibility reasons, it is actually not necessary to use Facebook or Twitter (Hellman 2014).

2.4.4 *Implementation of Policy*

In the implementation stage, the previously designated social media policy is put into practice by local government's liable departments and officials. Reworking and piloting policies before implementing across the local government's various departments will be very helpful for easily understanding and adopting the policy by employees (Hansen-Flaschen and Parker 2012).

Social media policies are not helpful for employees to use social media properly if they are designated in forms of broad rules and principles. To improve the effectiveness of the designated social media policy in the implementation stage, local governments can create social media training programs to show their employees how social media tools can be used for governmental activities, and even to improve performance and efficiency. As Meister (2012) implies companies like Dell, Intel, and IBM have positive feedbacks from their social media training programs. Local governments can adapt social media training programs that are carried out successfully by private sector companies.

2.4.5 *Evaluation of Policy Achievements*

As with any other policy, social media policies should also be reviewed periodically to ensure that they continue to reflect local government's changing strategy and priorities (Hrdinová et al. 2010). The accomplishments of the policy, that is to say, should be evaluated with qualitative and quantitative techniques. Indicators defined in the first stage of the social media policy as well as embedded in the activity plan are used for evaluating specific activities that are related to the policy. Following this, the activities may either be revised for further improvement or terminated.

There are two facts on social media tools that affect the measures of what a local government prefers: (1) each social media site has its own way of collecting and storing data and (2) a wide range of formats including text, photo, video, and sound that exist within each social media site. Despite the measurement challenges, a local government will probably begin measuring social media by primarily using baseline indicators like website statistics and search engine measures, followed by more sophisticated measures like affect analysis or social network analysis (Deschamps 2012b).

Evaluation of achievements of the social media policy is probably the weakest part of the general process, in that measurement tools and methods are mostly immature. In a study conducted by Hansen-Flaschen and Parker (2012), it is asserted that majority of the local governments are uncertain about how to gauge the effectiveness of social media activities, and they mostly track the accomplishments by monitoring the number of followers, “likes,” comments, YouTube views, number of shares, and re-posts or retweets. In most cases local governments do not systematically evaluate their social media policy, instead they provide informal updates and information when it is asked. At this point it should be stressed that a measurement strategy should focus not just on the quantitative data such as the number of followers or shares, but also aim to measure engagement in the content that is posted by local government and whether the content is influencing the conversation.

Engagement measures focus on usability of the application and the extent of engagement. Local governments can use tools provided by firms such as MeasureMap and BlogBeat to measure many applications such as blogs. There are also firms like Web Analytics and Google Analytics that ensure measurement of direct engagement of citizens in terms of their session lengths, comments, uploads, invitations to others, and so on. Moreover, if a local government intends to evaluate effectiveness of its social media policy, it should use measures such as posting comments and interacting to the quality of decision-making, citizen satisfaction with the process, increase in citizen trust and loyalty (Chang and Kannan 2008).

2.5 Engagement of Social Media Policy into Local Governments: Problems and Prospects

Some of the considerable problems that occur in both designing and implementing social media policy in local governments are mentioned above: intertwined policy goals and targets, difficulty in choosing the essential policy tool that complies with the needs of local government, and inadequate measurement systems for evaluating the accomplishments. Additionally, as Midyette et al. contend (2014), social media policy development process raises many important issues related with privacy, appropriate usage, content, responsibilities, and reach. In this section, among the many divergent issues, depending on the importance for local governments, “culture” and “leadership” have been focused on as critical dynamics for effective social media policy.

A certain degree of cultural understanding will be a necessity for local governments that intend to adopt social media for their service producing, policy-making, and citizen engagement activities. Adopting social media into local government practices requires a divergent insight more so than those that have been experienced in the past. Developing a person-to-person trust relationship between local government and personal user is significant for an effective usage of social media in local policy-making processes. In essence, social media is not solely a potential tool for dealing with policy problems, but also a policy problem itself (Deschamps 2012a). Therefore, it can be asserted that designing policies, norms, and standards for social media users for local authorities will be a useful way to enhance person-to-person trust. For that, because it provides a long range sight, developing a Web 2.0 strategy seems to be a requirement for creating a social media culture that depends on trust relations between citizens and governments. This kind of strategy should describe how to use local government's website and the wider Web 2.0 tools to accomplish its mission, reach new audiences, engage the public, and include resources needed to accomplish these goals.

Leadership is a prerequisite for building an organizational culture that depends on transparency, trust, collaboration, engagement, and effectiveness through e-governance and social media. Various open government reform reports highlight the necessity for a strong leadership from the top to make important cultural shifts (Phillips and Tremaine 2012). Local governments should also adopt and realize their own social media policy in light of the broader government strategy under a supportive leadership that is required for a cultural change in line with principles and values of open government.

It is important to stress that one of the essential characteristics of social media is being a dynamic and rapidly shifting field, which leads local government decision-makers in the process of designing their official social media policy to focus not only the commonly used social media tools such as the Facebook and Twitter but also new apps and tools that have potential to be epidemic in the future.

2.6 Conclusion

In the beginning, government managers responded to the social media challenge in a negative manner like their counterparts in the private sector. Usage of social media apps in the workplace during regular work hours were banned even for employees who wanted to benefit from Web 2.0 tools for service issues (Staab 2014). However, undeterred dissemination of social media not only for personal usage but for numerous governmental services, opportunities that social media offer for governmental agencies, and problems that raise in official usage of social media have led governments to regulate social media, and designate policies and strategies for more open, accountable, and participative government.

In this context, governments especially in Anglo-Saxon countries undertook a body of reforms in recent years: the Canadian government released "Open Government Action Plan" in 2011, the Australian government installed "Government 2.0 Taskforce" in 2009, and president Obama announced the "Open Government Declaration" immediately following his inauguration (Phillips and Tremaine 2012). As local authorities are the closest tier of government to citizens, they face challenges driven by social media more fiercely. A conclusion can be drawn from abovementioned developments: designing a social media policy, on one hand, seems compulsory for local governments where there is a general government regulation, and on the other hand, even where there is not a comprehensive public policy for social media usage in public bodies, local governments should formulate their own social media policy to ensure the proper usage for both personal and professional aims. Additionally, it is worth mentioning that there is no "one-single-way" of designing a social media policy in local governments—it is a combination of central government's strategies, local government's own requirements, and residents' expectations.

This study contributes to the social media literature in respect to focusing on a rarely studied level of government (local governments) and newly raised issue (social media policy) in social media studies. It reveals the policy options for local managers who aim to designate a social media policy. The study underlines the importance of creating a cultural shift in local governments through the help of a transformational leadership as a necessity for an effective social media policy in local governments.

Another conclusion this study draws is the requirement for local governments to broaden their perspective of designing social media policy. Local governments should actually adopt what Zerfass et al. (2011) conceptualized, "social media governance," transferring the term "governance" to the field of social media communication. The original concept refers to "the formal or informal frameworks which regulate the actions of the members of an organization within the social web" (Zerfass et al. 2011, p. 3) and encompasses a collection of policies, procedures, and educational resources (Absaldo 2012). Main principles of social media governance (Zerfass et al. 2011) can be adapted to local governments: designing social media policies and guidelines for staff in relation to social media, monitoring of social media content relevant to the local government, training of elected and appointed staff engaging in social media, and measurement and evaluation of social media activities. In such a model, local governments should design their own social media policy and guidelines with regard to the broader central government policy, incorporation with local government's other policies, and considering audiences' needs and expectations.

References

Absaldo, M. (2012). *5 components of a social media governance model*. PC World. Retrieved November 15, 2014, from http://www.pcworld.com/article/250043/4_components_of_a_social_media_governance_model.html

Angelotti, E. (2013). *How to create effective social-media guidelines*. Retrieved October 12, 2014, fromhttp://www.poynter.org/how-tos/digital-strategies/217139/how-to-create-effective-social-media-guidelines/

Auer, M. R. (2011). The policy sciences of social media. *Policy Studies Journal, 39*(4), 709–736.

Bertot, J. C., Jaeger, P. T., & Hansen, D. (2012). The impact of policies on government social media usage: Issues, challenges, and recommendations. *Government Information Quarterly, 29*, 30–40.

Bonsón, E., Torres, L., Royo, S., & Flores, F. (2012). Local e-government 2.0: Social media and corporate transparency in municipalities. *Government Information Quarterly, 29*, 123–132.

Cadell, L. (2013). Socially practical or practically unsociable? A study into social media policy experiences in Queensland cultural heritage institutions. *Australian Academic and Research Libraries, 44*(1), 3–13.

Chang, A., & Kannan, P. K. (2008). *Leveraging web 2.0 in government*. IBM Center for Business of Government, E-Government/Technology Series.

Dadashzadeh, M. (2010). Social media in government: From eGovernment to eGovernance. *Journal of Business & Economics Research, 8*(11), 81–86.

Deschamps, R. (2012a). Introduction. In K. McNutt (Ed.), *Social media & government 2.0*. University of Regina, Graduate School of Public Policy. Retrieved October 11, 2014, from http://www.schoolofpublicpolicy.sk.ca/resources/Government/Environmental%20Scan%20on%20Social%20Media%20in%20the%20Public%20Sector/Social%20Media%20and%20Government%20Final_2012.pdf

Deschamps, R. (2012b). Evaluating social media. In K. McNutt (Ed.), *Social media & government 2.0*. University of Regina, Graduate School of Public Policy. Retrieved October 11, 2014, from http://www.schoolofpublicpolicy.sk.ca/resources/Government/Environmental%20Scan%20on%20Social%20Media%20in%20the%20Public%20Sector/Social%20Media%20and%20Government%20Final_2012.pdf

Elgg. (2014). Retrieved November 11, 2014, from http://elgg.org

Ferro, E., Eurupidis, N. L., Charalabidis, Y., & Osella, M. (2013). Policy making 2.0: From theory to practice. *Government Information Quarterly, 30*, 359–368.

Hansen-Flaschen, L., & Parker, K. P. (2012). *The rise of social government: An advanced guide and review of social media's role in local government operations*. Fels Institute of Government. Retrieved October 11, 2014, from http://www.fels.upenn.edu/sites/www.fels.upenn.edu/files/fels_promising_practices_the_rise_of_social_media_website_final.pdf

Hellman, R. (2014). *The cloverleaves of social media challenges for e-governments*. Retrieved August 27, 2014, from http://medialt.no/the-cloverleaves-of-social-media-challenges-for-e-governments/1127.aspx

Hrdinová, J., Helbig, N., & Peters, C. S. (2010). *Designing social media policy for government: Eight essential elements*. Centre for Technology in Government. Retrieved October 30, 2014, from http://www.ctg.albany.edu/publications/guides/social_media_policy/social_media_policy.pdf

Khan, G. F., Yoon, H. Y., & Park, H. W. (2014). Social media communication strategies of government agencies: Twitter use in Korea and the USA. *Asian Journal of Communication, 24*(1), 60–78.

Klang, M., & Nolin, J. (2011). Disciplining social media: An analysis of social media policies in 26 Swedish municipalities. *First Monday, 16*(8). Retrieved October 19, 2014, from http://journals.uic.edu/ojs/index.php/fm/article/view/3490/3027

Kroski, E. (2009). Should your library have a social media policy? *School Library Journal, 55*(10), 44–46.

Magro, M. J. (2012). A review of social media use in e-government. *Administrative Sciences, 2*, 148–161.

Meister, J. (2012). Social media training is now mandatory: Five ways to make sure your company does it right. *Forbes*. Retrieved November 12, 2014, from http://www.forbes.com/sites/jeannemeister/2012/10/31/social-media-training-is-now-mandatory/

Mergel, I. A. (2010). Gov 2.0 revisited: Social media strategies in the public sector. *PA TIMES Online*. Retrieved November 12, 2014, http://patimes.org/gov-2-0-revisited-social-media-strategies-in-the-public-sector/

Mergel, I. A., Gerdner, M., Broviak, P., & Greeves, W. (2011). MuniGov 2.0, A new residency requirement: Local government professionals in second life. *Journal of Virtual Worlds Research, 4*(1), 3–28.

Mergel, I., & Greeves, B. (2013). *Social media in the public sector field guide*. San Francisco: Jossey-Bass.

Midyette, J. D., Youngkin, A., & Snow-Croft, S. (2014). Social media and communications: Developing a policy to guide the flow of information. *Medical Reference Services Quarterly, 33*(1), 39–50.

Park, J., Choi, H., & Park, S. M. (2011). Social media's impact on policy making. *SERI Quarterly*, 125–129.

Phillips, J., & Tremaine, S. (2012). Government 2.0. In K. McNutt (Ed.), *Social media & government 2.0*. University of Regina, Graduate School of Public Policy. Retrieved October 11, 2014, from http://www.schoolofpublicpolicy.sk.ca/resources/Government/Environmental%20Scan%20on%20Social%20Media%20in%20the%20Public%20Sector/Social%20Media%20and%20Government%20Final_2012.pdf

Staab, A. E. (2014, May 14–20). 6 tips for creating a social media policy. *Benefits Magazine*.

Zerfass, A., Fink, S., & Linke, A. (2011). *Social media governance: Regulatory frameworks as drivers of success in online communications*. Paper presented at the annual international public relations research conference, March 9–12, Miami, FL.

Chapter 3
Policymakers' Perceptions on the Citizen Participation and Knowledge Sharing in Public Sector Delivery

Manuel Pedro Rodríguez Bolívar

Abstract Public agencies are being pressured for innovation, driving service delivery towards a more personalized, outcome-driven, participative, efficient, and collaborative model. In this regard, social media has been told to be a potential powerful tool to support public engagement, intended as the improvement of public services and the establishment of relationships between government and citizens based on information sharing and dialogue. This chapter captures the perception of policymakers responsible of strategies for e-government in local governments with the aim at analyzing the following research questions: (a) Do policymakers think that Web 2.0 technologies promote the effective involvement of citizens in the improvement of public sector services? (b) Do policymakers think that Web 2.0 technologies promote the technological innovation in public services? and (c) Do policymakers think that Web 2.0 technologies promote the sharing knowledge needed to improve public sector services? To answer these research questions, an e-survey was sent to policymakers responsible of strategies for e-government in large Spanish local governments. Findings indicate that policymakers are prone for using Web 2.0 technologies to engage citizens in the process of public services delivery, but only making suggestions through consultations. No co-production or technological innovation is expected from citizens because they are expected to play a passive role more than an active one.

3.1 Introduction

Public agencies are now moving to scenarios in which citizens use public e-services to perform complex transactions with government authorities (Asgarkhani 2005) and in which the performance and the efforts of the government to deliver public services should be more efficiently (El-Haddadeh et al. 2013) with the aim at raising levels of accountability.

M.P.R. Bolívar (✉)
Department of Accounting and Finance, Faculty of Business Studies, University of Granada, C/ Campus Universitario de Cartuja, s/n, Granada 18071, Spain
e-mail: manuelp@ugr.es

M.Z. Sobaci (ed.), *Social Media and Local Governments*, Public Administration and Information Technology 15, DOI 10.1007/978-3-319-17722-9_3

To achieve this aim governments have incorporated social media technologies into the governmental workplace, which have been seen as effective tools to promote public goals (Rowe and Frewer 2005). The implementation of these technologies are changing the roles played by citizens, who will no longer be mere "end-users," but will become partners and co-creators of information and services (Johnston and Hansen 2011; Huijboom et al. 2009), which promotes to put citizens into the heart of the value chain (Tuomi 2002), and expecting them to provide insight and knowledge and thus improve public services. In fact, in the Web 2.0 era, users have become important actors in almost all aspects of online services (Huijboom et al. 2009) and are expected to provide insight and intelligence that will improve public services.

Nonetheless, despite the great significance of the future implementation of Web 2.0 technologies in public agencies and calls for studies to analyze the impact of legal, institutional, and political challenges regarding the use of IT in local governance (Sandoval-Almazan and Gil-Garcia 2012; Criado et al. 2013), little research has been conducted in the field of public administration to examine the use of these technologies to reform public service delivery.

Therefore, this chapter seeks to investigate three main research questions related to the implementation of Web 2.0 technologies in the process of public services delivery: (a) Do policymakers think that Web 2.0 technologies promote the effective involvement of citizens in the improvement of public sector services? (b) Do policymakers think that Web 2.0 technologies promote the technological innovation in public services? and (c) Do policymakers think that Web 2.0 technologies promote the sharing knowledge needed to improve public sector services? To answer these research questions, a questionnaire has been designed and sent to policymakers responsible of strategies for e-government in local governments in order to collect their opinions about the research questions mentioned before.

This analysis is especially relevant in local governments because they are mostly concerned with the daily life of people (Cegarra Navarro et al. 2012), provide a wide variety of services (Saiz 2011), and they are an important subject for the study of social media and interactivity because of traditions of citizen participation at the local level (Berry et al. 1993; Oakerson 1999). In addition, the study is focused on the Spanish local governments' context due to the managerial devolution process implemented in Spain in the 1990s (Bastida and Benito 2006; Gallego and Barzelay 2010) and the rapid introduction of new technologies by these local governments, which has been fostered with the promulgation of e-services legislation in Spain in the last decade. Finally, policymakers have been selected because they are considered key actors in the introduction of Web 2.0 technologies in public agencies taking into account not only their significant role in the policymaking process within local government, but also their direct involvement in the possible implementation of Web 2.0 technologies in public sector delivery.

The remainder of this chapter is structured as follows. Section 3.2 discusses the opportunities that Web 2.0 and social media tools offer for the co-production of public services in local governments. Section 3.3 describes the methodology of our study and the results of the research. Finally, the discussion and conclusions bring the chapter to an end.

3.2 Web 2.0 Technologies and the Co-production of Public Services

Public agencies have implemented reforms to enhance information transparency and management (Schillemans et al. 2013; Relly and Sabharwal 2009). These governmental reforms were initially focused on automating internal, often manual, routines, using only a government perspective in mind (Holgersson and Karlsson 2014). Nonetheless, a recent demand-side survey performed by the European Commission (2013) has put emphasis on the need to address the needs and concerns of citizens as well as on the need of more communicative actions to inform those that are unaware of what public services are available on line.

Indeed, most local governments are urged to provide efficient and effective e-government information and services, for the sake of increased accountability and performance management (Shackleton et al. 2004). Nonetheless, e-government initiatives over the past decade have been based mainly on first-generation web-based resources (including web sites, pages, and services), which were based on HTML, a relatively primitive, static page markup technology that simply outlines what a page should look like onscreen.

The advent of social media using Web 2.0 technologies has opened up unprecedented new possibilities for engaging the public in government work and has changed public expectations about how government work should be done (Chun et al. 2010; Lathrop and Ruma 2010; McDermott 2010). With the help of the advance in information technology, e-government should customize services based on personal preferences and needs (Ho 2002), which would largely enable users' needs to be met (Bonham et al. 2001). This way, knowledge of citizens' needs and skills is seen as essential for successful public e-service development (Verdegem and Verleye 2009).

In addition, the growing participation in social networking sites is altering the nature of social relations (Christofides et al. 2009) and changing the nature of political and public dialogue (Osimo 2008). These new developments put pressure on government organizations to innovate in their dealings with citizens, introducing new competition for "nodality" in social and informational networks (Escher et al. 2006; Hood and Margetts 2007) and offering the potential for "co-production" and even "co-creation" of government services (Margetts and Dunleavy 2013). Therefore, governments must now strengthen their capacity to assess the needs of users and involve user groups through the use of second generation web technologies in order to listen, to engage users in the design of services and in the production of policies, and to forge collective initiatives and interaction (OECD 2010).

Accordingly, local governments are increasingly embracing Web 2.0 technologies to encourage the use of means of bidirectional communication to change how they interact with stakeholders and to become more efficient in their response to stakeholders' demands, thus providing the greater accountability demanded (Redell and Woolcock 2004; Leighninger 2011). Nonetheless, having a social media icon on a webpage does not demonstrate usage and recent research has indicated that city managers are nowadays using social media mainly for disseminating information (Oliveira and Welch 2013; Mergel 2013; Mossberger et al. 2013).

But social media applications provide channels not just for mass dissemination but also for mass production and collaboration (Benkler 2006), playing an important role in implementing open government and in rendering online public services (Noveck 2009). The use of Web 2.0 technologies for the delivery of public sector services has the potential to change the roles played by citizens, who will no longer be mere "end-users," but will become partners and co-creators of information and services (Huijboom et al. 2009), which promotes to put citizens into the heart of the value chain (Tuomi 2002), and expecting them to provide insight and knowledge and thus improve public services.

Such potential should be welcome to policymakers looking for public service cuts and could lead to new interest in Digital Era Government type models (Margetts and Dunleavy 2013). In fact, with public spending reductions squeezing public services at all levels, the strategies adopted by public agencies have been aimed at achieving higher levels of online service uptake and at developing public e-services (Queensland State Archives 2010; Reggi and Scicchitano 2011), as well as obtaining the anticipated cost efficiencies (Taylor 2012).

In this regards, a push towards government co-production of services with citizens has been very clear in behavioral public policy fields, the "nudge" territory of changing life choices (Thaler and Sunstein 2009), where even more interventionist European governments acknowledge that government-only interventions are unlikely to be successful (Margetts and Dunleavy 2013). Indeed, the implementation of Web 2.0 tools by government is about recognizing that conventional governments are unable to address society's challenges alone.

Thus, while the potential impact of social media technologies on the functioning of government is expected to be "profound," it will come with "challenges in the areas of policy development, governance, process design, and conceptions of democratic engagement" (Bertot et al. 2010c). Nonetheless, whether or not citizens actually participate online, a municipal presence on social networks may convey the message that government is more responsive, open, and democratic, by allowing citizens to express their views via this channel (Hibbing and Theiss-Morse 2002).

In addition, according to the second eGovernment Action Plan (2011–2015), governments will use eGovernment to increase their efficiency and effectiveness and to constantly improve public services in a way that caters for users' different needs and maximizes public value, thus supporting the transition of Europe to a leading knowledge-based economy (European Commission 2010). In this regard, Web 2.0 technologies have the potential to share knowledge and experiences in delivering public sector services that could help governments to improve their internal productivity and interoperability.

Various popular Web 2.0 technologies, such as social networking (Facebook, MySpace), wikis, blogs, microblogs (Twitter), mashup, and multimedia sharing (YouTube, Flickr), facilitate interactive information sharing, interoperability, and collaboration (United Nations 2010) and can promote open, user-driven governance (Bertot et al. 2010a, b, c; Millard 2009). Furthermore, social media technologies, such as Twitter and Facebook, enable two-way communication and rich data exchange among members for purposes of communication to the network, knowledge exchange, and problem solving (Welch 2012).

Despite previous comments, little is known about the use of Web 2.0 technologies by government for technological innovation purposes in public services (improvement of services quality, design of public services, etc.), and, also, little is known about how Web 2.0 technologies can affect knowledge sharing purposes. Therefore, it would be interesting to know if policymakers think that Web 2.0 technologies could be a relevant tool for improving innovation in public services and in sharing knowledge. Investigating these issues through a survey of local government policymakers, we ask several questions about the use of social media:

RQ1: Do policymakers think that Web 2.0 technologies promote the effective involvement of citizens in the improvement of public sector services?
RQ2: Do policymakers think that Web 2.0 technologies promote the technological innovation in public services?
RQ3: Do policymakers think that Web 2.0 technologies promote the sharing knowledge needed to improve public sector services?

3.3 Policymakers' Perceptions on Web 2.0 Implementations and its Potential for Citizen Engagement, Improvement of Technological Innovation and Knowledge Sharing in Public Sector Services Delivery

3.3.1 Sample Selection

Local government is an important subject for the study of social media and interactivity because of traditions of citizen participation at the local level (Berry et al. 1993; Norman 2010) and the tradition of these governments to use more mechanisms that permit direct citizen involvement, in part because they are more manageable at that scale (Peters 2001) as well as they provide a wide variety of services (Russell and Bobko 1992). It has made social networks to become relevant in the local government context (Gibson 2010), especially in the largest cities because they have generally been at the forefront in the adoption of e-government innovations (Moon 2002; Ho 2002; Scott 2006).

This chapter focuses on Spanish local governments in view of the managerial devolution process implemented in Spain in the 1990s (Bastida and Benito 2006; Gallego and Barzelay 2010) and the rapid introduction of new technologies by these local governments, which has been fostered with the promulgation of e-services legislation in Spain in the last decade. In addition, according to recent studies, the e-services provided by local administrations in Spain account for 66 % of all public services (Orange Foundation 2014) and the 79 % of Internet users in Spain use some type of social network (IAB Spain Research 2014) mainly as a means to chat with friends or organizations as well as to generate content—this figure is over the mean of European Union (57 %)—(Orange Foundation 2014).

Municipalities with relatively large populations are examined in this chapter because they are usually among the first to adopt new technologies (Bonsón et al. 2012) with the aim at providing efficient services to the public (Cegarra Navarro et al. 2012) and their delivery of services is more complex (Torres et al. 2005) and comparable. Under this rationale, a sample of large Spanish municipalities has been selected (those with a population of over 50,000 inhabitants). In total, 148 Spanish municipalities meet these conditions, and account for over 50 % of the total population of Spain (Spanish National Statistics Institute (SNSI) 2014).

Data were obtained by sending a link to perform an e-survey and it was sent to the policymakers of all the local authorities studied, via email. The contact details were obtained from the Spanish central government's website. Of the 148 municipalities that comprised the survey sample, seven of them stated that the municipality had not yet introduced communication channels such as social networks, and thus neither had experience of Web 2.0 nor dedicated human resources to this area. Therefore, the questionnaire was sent to 141 local governments and 46 complete replies were received from policymakers (thus there were 107 incomplete responses to the questionnaire). To date, therefore, the minimum response rate is 32.62 %. Nonetheless, some policymakers of local governments have responded some items without finishing the full e-survey. In consequence, for some questionnaire items, the response rate exceeded the above-mentioned minimum (see Tables 3.2, 3.3 and 3.4 in Appendix). This sample size is reasonable; according to Roscoe (1975), a sample size between 30 and 500 is considered satisfactory. Data were compiled over the research period utilizing an appropriate sampling technique.

3.3.2 *Methodology of Research*

A questionnaire was designed and sent to all policymakers responsible of e-government of sample municipalities in order to capture their perceptions on the issues that are analyzed in this chapter. The questionnaire was made up of 15 questions covering the role that implementation of Web 2.0 technologies can play in local governments regarding citizen engagement, technological innovation, and knowledge sharing in public sector services (see Table 3.1 in Appendix).

Policymakers responsible of strategies for e-government of sample municipalities were addressed in this survey taking into account not only their significant role in the policymaking process within local government, but also their direct involvement in the possible implementation of Web 2.0 technologies in public sector delivery. Before the e-survey was sent out, every policymaker in the sample population was contacted and asked to participate in the study, after being informed of the study goals and of what was required by the questionnaire. They were also assured of its strictly scientific and confidential nature, and of the global, anonymous treatment of the data to be obtained.

A two-phase process was followed to design and pretest the questionnaire items of our study. First, the research team drafted a preliminary version based on the conclusions of previous work in the field of Web 2.0 technologies (Oxley 2011; Picazo-Vela et al. 2012; Gomes and Sousa 2012; Smith 2004; Dunleavy and Margetts 2010; Linders 2012). Based on this analysis, 15 items have been selected to analyze the role of Web 2.0 technologies in improving citizen engagement, technological innovation, and knowledge sharing for public services delivery (5 items for each one of the issues) (see Table 3.1 in Appendix). Second, the initial text was presented to two specialists on Web 2.0 technologies and to ten policymakers, to ascertain their opinions on (a) the understandability of the questionnaire; (b) the clarity of the questions posed and possible ambiguities; and (c) the possible inclusion of other questions relevant to the study aims. The comments and suggestions made were analyzed and, when considered appropriate, incorporated into the text of the questionnaire.

Then, the link to the second version of the questionnaire was provided to the policymakers of each local government in our sample. Policymakers were offered the possibility of clarifying any remaining doubts before completing the questionnaire. Thus, some e-mails were received concerning the exact meaning of some items; these questions were answered, and thus we may be reasonably sure that the questions measured the intended constructs.

Based on prior studies on attitude analysis (Collison et al. 2003; Emerson et al. 2007), the questionnaire was designed in which respondents were asked to describe their degree of agreement with each statement on a five-point Likert scale (ranging from strongly disagree, "1" to strongly agree, "5").[1] After the questionnaire was completed, each item was analyzed separately. Unlike in other methods, in Likert scaling, data obtained from responses could not be analyzed using the mean to comparing results between questions due to scale problems (Bertram 2007). By contrast, the analysis of the central tendency summarized by median and the

[1] Although the Likert scale has some limitations for research (Russell and Bobko 1992; Hodge and Gillespie 2003; Orvik 1972), these limitations do not invalidate conclusions about the numbers (Norman 2010) and Likert scale is suitable for attitude studies—measures simple to administer, quantify and code (Spector 1992), reliable and valid results (Matell and Jacoby 1971; Li 2013) and statistical inference is "robust" when used for parametric statistics (Norman 2010).

mode of the responses has been proved to be useful in order to analyze data obtained using Likert scale (Bertram 2007).

3.3.3 Analysis of Results

RQ1: Do policymakers think that Web 2.0 technologies promote the effective involvement of citizens in the improvement of public sector services?

According to our results, policymakers think that Web 2.0 technologies could foster the collaboration of citizens in delivering public sector services. In fact, they think that these technologies can stimulate the creation of communities (see item 1.1. in Appendix, Table 3.2) and can facilitate citizens to be involved in the delivery of public services through the co-production of these services as well as the generation of content and information about them (see items 1.2. and 1.5. in Appendix, Table 3.2).

Nonetheless, policymakers generally think that Web 2.0 technologies can improve citizen engagement in public sector delivery, but they think that the involvement of citizens must be more passive than active, because only consultation seems to be a main outlet for the implementation of Web 2.0 technologies to improve citizen engagement (see items 1.3 and 1.4 in Appendix, Table 3.2). Indeed, the co-production of services or the generation of content and information about public services, although relevant, do not achieve a high score and the standard deviation is high (see items 1.2 and 1.5 in Appendix, Table 3.2).

In addition, results indicate that the involvement of citizens in the generation of content and information about public services is the lowest score of our survey in this section of the study (median score: 3; mode score: 4), although responses have not been very homogeneous (this item presents the highest standard deviation). This result could indicate that policymakers could have expressed concern about the possible inappropriate use of Web 2.0 technologies by citizens, because comments or content uploaded onto social networks by stakeholders could damage the image of the politicians and local governments responsible for delivering public services.

Also, the involvement of citizens in the co-production of services is an item that has obtained a low score and high standard deviation (see item 1.2. in Appendix, Table 3.2). Perhaps this result could mean the fear that policymakers could feel when they give up significant control over public services or over the way in which communications and relationships with stakeholders are handled. Up to now, local governments have not had any experiences, or only a few of them, in the co-production of public services. This result could also indicate that policymakers in Spain believe local governments should play the role of commissioner (executor) rather than that of co-producer or facilitator.

Finally, results seem to indicate that Web 2.0 technologies could be a main tool for communication between citizens and government. According to the results, Web 2.0 technologies can stimulate the creation of communities and can improve the communication and collaboration of citizens in the public service delivery (see items 1.1, 1.2 and 1.4 in Appendix, Table 3.2). Nonetheless, previous comments regarding the perception of policymakers about the possibility of citizens to be involved in the generation of content and information about public services seem to indicate that Web 2.0 technologies could be only used by governments as communication channels for broadcasting public services with the information provided by them.

RQ2: *Do policymakers think that Web 2.0 technologies promote the technological innovation in public services*?

Table 3.3 in Appendix presents the results regarding the role of Web 2.0 technologies in the promotion technological innovation in public services. The results indicate that, in accordance with the perceptions of sample policymakers, the mashups or wikis technologies are not relevant for technological innovation in public services (see items 2.3 and 2.5 in Appendix, Table 3.3). Indeed, although these Web 2.0 applications are popular between young people for communication and participation (Orange Foundation 2014), policymakers seem not to be prone to use them into the field of public services.

The first one (mashups) are applications that take data and combine it either with other data or other web services to create something new and it is being used by government to take data about the location of government services (Bonsón et al. 2012). The second one (wikis) are large-scale knowledge-sharing projects that seek a communal pooling of knowledge (McNutt 2012), which has made these applications to be used by governments to engage citizens to contribute with ideas and suggestions in public services (Nam and Sayogo 2011). In any case, as noted previously, up to now, policymakers do not seem to associate great relevance to these technologies in delivering public services.

On the other hand, policymakers think that Web 2.0 technologies are not appropriated as a space where users can test new public services online before they are made available to the public (see item 2.1 in Appendix, Table 3.3). This result could indicate that governments think that other different forms should be used for testing public services (if any). Else, policymakers could be prone to implement new services and to collect feedback from users and, then, to improve that service.

By contrast, policymakers think that Web 2.0 technologies could be a relevant tool for gathering suggestions from users regarding the quality of public services and for making public services more user centered (see items 2.2 and 2.4 in Appendix, Table 3.3). Thus, this result confirms the comment noted previously in the first research question of our empirical research. It means that policymakers seem to think only in using Web 2.0 technologies for collecting information from citizens, but not for their involvement in the delivery process of public services.

RQ3: Do policymakers think that Web 2.0 technologies promote the sharing knowledge needed to improve public sector services?

Regarding this section of our study, results indicate that policymakers are aware of the potential of Web 2.0 technologies in creating a benchmark process to improve public sector services (see item 3.3 in Appendix, Table 3.4), in sharing knowledge of government, infrastructure, and other public goods (see item 3.5 in Appendix, Table 3.4) and, mainly, in creating a network for discussion of local public services in a continuous way (see item 3.4 in Appendix, Table 3.4).

Therefore, policymakers seem to be prone for using Web 2.0 technologies to achieve best practices between public agencies more than for increasing the engagement of citizens in the delivery of public services. In fact, although Web 2.0 technologies could foster effective collaboration between citizens and the government (see median for item 1.4 in Appendix, Table 3.2), policymakers recognize that local governments are not taking advantage of the skills, talents, and knowledge of citizens to solve problems in the implementation of public services (see median for item 3.1 in Appendix, Table 3.4). This finding could be a result of that previously mentioned in RQ1, because policymakers do not think relevant the involvement of citizens in the generation of content and information about public services (see median for item 1.5 in Appendix, Table 3.2).

Also, results indicate that policymakers think that standards for interoperability of public documents should be debated in other different means to those proposed by the Web 2.0 technologies (see median for item 3.2 in Appendix, Table 3.4). Perhaps this finding is produced by the public administration style in Spain, which is characterized by administrative law (Rodríguez Bolívar et al. 2006). In this regards, policymakers could think that it is better that interoperability matters must be regulated by law and not leaving this issue to be debated into digital spaces with citizens.

3.4 Discussions

As noted previously, results indicate that sample policymakers are interested in implementing Web 2.0 technologies for consultation purposes but not for participatory decision-making or co-production purposes. These results confirm prior research which demonstrated that local government still represents the Achilles heel of Spanish society as regards the advancement of e-government (Cegarra Navarro et al. 2012) due to the possible resistance of policymakers to maintain a parallel structure of working simultaneously with old-fashioned practices and with digital structures in public services delivery (Criado et al. 2013) and citizen engagement (Blank and Reisdorf 2012).

In addition, this result is produced by the public administration style in Spain, which is based on the "Weberian/Bureaucratic Model" of production characterized by administrative law which decisively influences the content, logic, and institutional autonomy of the public administration (Kickert 1997; Rouban 1997). Under the "Bureaucratic Model" of governance, the interaction among public agencies is facilitated and local governments are placed in the leading role for public services delivery under the Web 2.0 technologies framework.

Public administrators emphasize internal productive efficiency, functional rationality and departmentalization, hierarchical control and rule-based management (Bozeman 2000). In fact, our results indicate that policymakers seem to have a wish to retain a predominant role in the implementation of Web 2.0 technologies for the delivery of public services, monitoring and managing directly the Web 2.0 technologies, and they are less favorable to the inclusion of citizens in the generation of content and information. This model of Web involvement could also indicate that social media services are by no means immune to government censorship or government-sponsored censorship (MacKinnon 2008, 2009).

On the other hand, prior research has indicated that not everything written in wikis is accurate, vandalism is not uncommon, and copyrighted materials may be used in an unauthorized manner (Boulos et al. 2006). Also, the Web 2.0 technologies are new tools to be used for delivering public services which is something not controlled completely by governments. These risks related to the use of these tools could have made sample policymakers to express that Web 2.0 technologies such as mashups and wikis are not relevant for technological innovation. Perhaps, with the experience of using these new technologies in the future, policymakers will be more prone to involve citizens in the collaboration to deliver public services and they will be more prone for a more active role to be played by citizens. Indeed, some governments are increasingly using Web 2.0 technologies for that purpose (for example, security forces in countries like The Netherlands).

3.5 Conclusions

Our study is focused on the perception of policymakers regarding the influence of Web 2.0 technologies on the participation and involvement of stakeholders in the co-creation of public services, and on the knowledge sharing and technological innovation in the public service delivery. To achieve this aim, a questionnaire has been designed and sent to policymakers of local governments in order to collect their opinions about the citizen participation in public service and in the technological innovation and knowledge sharing produced in public services under the Web 2.0 era.

As noted previously, a main finding of the empirical study indicates that policymakers think that citizens must play a more passive role in the co-production of public services than an active one. Sample policymakers think that citizens must be involved in the process of public sector delivery, but only making suggestions through consultations made from local governments, but no active roles must be played by citizens in the execution of public sector services. Indeed, results indicate that the involvement of citizens in the generation of content and information about public services and the promotion of the co-production of services are not well scored by policymakers in our survey.

This finding is interesting because it could mean that policymakers seek to manage and monitor the implementation of Web 2.0 technologies in providing public services. The existence of a clear regulatory framework for the activities related to social networks or the establishment of a process to combat unauthorized or fraudulent postings could mitigate this risk and could make policymakers to be more prone to the effective involvement of citizens in the co-production of public services in the future. So, future research could test differences between countries regarding the use of Web 2.0 technologies for public services delivery according to the level of development of regulatory frameworks.

Regarding the role of Web 2.0 technologies in technological innovation in public services delivery, our findings indicate that policymakers only think that Web 2.0 technologies could be a relevant tool for gathering suggestions from users regarding the quality of public services and for making public services more user centered. This result confirms the previous one and it indicates the relevance in the use of Web 2.0 technologies, but only as a means to collect information from citizens but not to add knowledge for the innovation of public services. Indeed, tools for creating knowledge for the improvement of public services, such as wikis, are not considered relevant perhaps due to the risks involved in the use of these technologies. Regulation about the use of these technologies and training for employees to use and monitor Web 2.0 technologies could be relevant aspects to solve these problems. Therefore, future research could analyze different levels of training in public employees and the level and content of the use of Web 2.0 technologies for public sector delivery.

Finally, findings seem to indicate that policymakers are prone for using Web 2.0 technologies to achieve best practices between public agencies more than for increasing the involvement of citizens in the delivery of public services. This result could indicate the bureaucratic model of governance existent in Spanish local governments. Future research could collect the perception of other policymakers in different contexts and countries. Perhaps the administrative culture of the country could be a factor to explain possible differences regarding the opinion of this group of key stakeholders.

In brief, policymakers think that Web 2.0 can improve collaboration of citizens in delivering public sector services, but they have shown their intention to manage and to monitor them. Therefore, future research should analyze if policymakers have taken advantages of these technologies or they have been doomed to be only another channel of communication. The latter should be the death of Web 2.0 technologies in its application to public sector services and it would only serve as an innovative channel for government online representation and for broadcasting of government information about public services via social media sites (The White House 2009).

Acknowledgement This research was carried out with financial support from the Regional Government of Andalusia (Spain), Department of Innovation, Science and Enterprise (Research project number P11-SEJ-7700).

3.6 Appendix

Table 3.1 Questionnaire

Questionnaire	
RQ1. Citizen engagement in the improvement of public sector services	
1.1.	Web 2.0 technologies stimulate the creation of public/private communities
1.2.	Web 2.0 technologies improve communication between government and stakeholders to promote the co-production of public services
1.3.	Web 2.0 technologies facilitate consultation on implementation or transformation of public services to the community
1.4.	Web 2.0 technologies foster effective collaboration between citizens and the government in public service delivery
1.5.	Web 2.0 technologies promote the involvement of citizens in the generation of content and information about public services
RQ2. Role of Web 2.0 technologies in technological innovation in public services delivery	
2.1.	Allows the development and promotion of tools and spaces where users can test new public services online before they are made available to the public
2.2.	Allows the gathering of suggestions from the users to enhance public services quality and the information disclosed about them
2.3.	Wikis allow knowledge in several areas and the creation of knowledge for the improvement of public services
2.4.	Allows the design of public services directly aimed at satisfying citizens
2.5.	Mashups allow the creation of new public services and improving technological innovation in public services
RQ3. Role of Web 2.0 technologies in knowledge sharing in public services delivery	
3.1.	The local government is taking advantage of the skills, talents, and knowledge of citizens to solve problems in the implementation of public services
3.2.	Web 2.0 technologies provide digital spaces for consultation and exchange in order to develop standards for interoperability of public documents
3.3.	Web 2.0 technologies create a network that allows the transfer of best practice between public agencies is provided
3.4.	Web 2.0 technologies facilitate discussion of local public services in a continuous way
3.5.	Web 2.0 technologies allow openly share knowledge of government, infrastructure, and other public goods

Source: Own elaboration

Table 3.2 Results for items related to citizen engagement using Web 2.0 technologies in providing public services

Questionnaire	Frequency	Response rate	Median	Mean	Mode	Standard deviation	Maximum	Minimum
RQ1. Citizen engagement in the improvement of public sector services								
1.1. Web 2.0 technologies stimulate the creation of public/private communities	53	37.59 %	4	3.58	4	0.97	5	1
1.2. Web 2.0 technologies improve communication between government and stakeholders to promote the co-production of public services	53	37.59 %	4	3.38	4	1.06	5	1
1.3. Web 2.0 technologies facilitate consultation on implementation or transformation of public services to the community	54	38.30 %	4	3.98	4	0.92	5	2
1.4. Web 2.0 technologies foster effective collaboration between citizens and the government in public service delivery	54	38.30 %	4	3.67	4	0.95	5	1
1.5. Web 2.0 technologies promote the involvement of citizens in the generation of content and information about public services	53	37.59 %	3	3.15	4	1.20	5	1

Source: Own elaboration

Table 3.3 Results for items related to role of Web 2.0 technologies in technological innovation in public services delivery

Questionnaire	Frequency	Response rate	Median	Mean	Mode	Standard deviation	Maximum	Minimum
RQ2. Role of Web 2.0 technologies in technological innovation in public services delivery								
2.1. Allows the development and promotion of tools and spaces where users can test new public services online before they are made available to the public	52	36.88 %	3	2.75	3	1.10	5	1
2.2. Allows the gathering of suggestions from the users to enhance public services quality and the information disclosed about them	53	37.59 %	4	3.96	5	1.14	5	1
2.3. Wikis allow knowledge in several areas and the creation of knowledge for the improvement of public services	51	36.17 %	3	3.24	4	1.07	5	1
2.4. Allows the design of public services directly aimed at satisfying citizens	49	34.75 %	4	3.71	4	1.08	5	1
2.5. Mashups allow the creation of new public services and improving technological innovation in public services	46	32.62 %	3	3.09	3	1.03	5	1

Source: Own elaboration

Table 3.4 Results for items related to role of Web 2.0 technologies in knowledge sharing for public services delivery

Questionnaire	Frequency	Response rate	Median	Mean	Mode	Standard deviation	Maximum	Minimum
RQ3. Role of Web 2.0 technologies in knowledge sharing in public services delivery								
3.1. The local government is taking advantage of the skills, talents, and knowledge of citizens to solve problems in the implementation of public services	54	38.30 %	3	3.13	4	1.20	5	1
3.2. Web 2.0 technologies provide digital spaces for consultation and exchange in order to develop standards for interoperability of public documents	49	34.75 %	3	3.16	4	1.05	5	1
3.3. Web 2.0 technologies create a network that allows the transfer of best practice between public agencies is provided	50	35.46 %	4	3.70	4	0.99	5	1
3.4. Web 2.0 technologies facilitate discussion of local public services in a continuous way	54	38.30 %	4	3.72	5	1.12	5	1
3.5. Web 2.0 technologies allow openly share knowledge of government, infrastructure, and other public goods	55	39.01 %	4	4.20	4	0.85	5	2

Source: Own elaboration

References

Archives, Q. S. (2010). *Recordkeeping and web 2.0. survey report*. Sunnybank Hills, QLD, Australia: Author.

Asgarkhani, M. (2005). The effectiveness of e-service in local government: A case study. *The Electronic Journal of e-Government, 3*(4), 157–166.

Bastida, F. J., & Benito, B. (2006). Financial reports and decentralization in municipal governments. *International Review of Administrative Sciences, 72*(2), 223–238.

Benkler, Y. (2006). *The wealth of networks: How social production transforms markets and freedom*. New Haven, CT: Yale University Press.

Berry, J., Portney, K., & Thomson, K. (1993). *The rebirth of urban democracy*. Washington, DC: Brookings Institution Press.

Bertot, J. C., Jaeger, P. T., Munson, S., & Glaisyer, T. (2010). Social media technology and government transparency. *Computer, 43*(11), 53–59.

Bertot, J. C., Jaeger, P. T., & Grimes, J. M. (2010a). Crowd-sourcing transparency: ICTs, social media, and government transparency initiatives. In S. A. Chun, R. Sandoval, & A. Philpot (Eds.), *Proceedings of the 11th Annual International Conference on Digital Government Research* (pp. 51–58). Puebla, Mexico: Digital Government Society of North America.

Bertot, J. C., Jaeger, P. T., & Grimes, J. M. (2010b). Using ICTs to create a culture of transparency: E-government and social media as openness and anti-corruption tools for societies. *Government Information Quarterly, 27*(3), 264–271.

Bertram, D. (2007). *Likert scales*. Department of Computer Science, The University of Calgary. Retrieved June 28, 2014, from http://poincare.matf.bg.ac.rs/~kristina/topic-dane-likert.pdf

Blank, G., & Reisdorf, B. C. (2012). The participatory web: A user perspective on Web 2.0. *Information, Communication & Society, 15*(4), 537–554.

Bonham, G., Seifert, J. and Thorson, S. (2001). The Transformational Potential of E-government: The Role of Political Leadership. Paper Presented at the *Electronic Governance and Information Policy (Panel 9-1), 4th Pan European International Relations Conference of the European Consortium for Political Research*, University of Kent, Canterbury.

Bonsón, E., Torres, L., Royo, S., & Flores, F. (2012). Local e-government 2.0: Social media and corporate transparency in municipalities. *Government Information Quarterly, 29*(2), 123–132.

Boulos, M. N. K., Maramba, I., & Wheeler, S. (2006). Wikis, blogs and podcasts: A new generation of Web-based tools for virtual collaborative clinical practice and education. *BMC Medical Education*. Retrieved November 8, 2012, from http://www.biomedcentral.com/1472-6920/6/41.#B68

Bozeman, B. (2000). *Bureaucracy and red tape*. Upper Saddle River, NJ: Prentice Hall.

Cegarra Navarro, J. G., Córdoba Pachón, J. R., & Moreno Cegarra, J. L. (2012). E-government and citizen's engagement with local affairs through e-websites: The case of Spanish municipalities. *International Journal of Information Management, 32*(5), 469–478.

Christofides, E., Muise, A., & Desmarais, S. (2009). Information disclosure and control on Facebook: Are they two sides of the same coin or two different processes? *Cyberpsychology and Behavior, 12*(3), 3411–3450.

Chun, S., Shulman, S., Sandoval-Almazan, R., & Hovy, E. (2010). Government 2.0: Marking connections between citizens, data and government. *Information Polity, 15*(1–2), 1–9.

Collison, D., Lorraine, N., & Power, D. (2003). An exploration of corporate attitudes to the significance of environmental information for stakeholders. *Corporate Social Responsibility and Environmental Management, 19*(4), 199–211.

European Commission. (2010). *The European eGovernment Action Plan 2011–2015. Harnessing ICT to promote smart, sustainable & innovative Government*. Communication from the Commission to the European Parliament, the Council, the European Economic and Social Committee and the Committee of the Regions. Brussels, Belgium: European Commission.

Criado, J. I., Sandoval-Almazan, R., & Gil-Garcia, J. R. (2013). Government innovation through social media. *Government Information Quarterly, 30*(4), 319–326.
Dunleavy, P., & Margetts, H. Z. (2010). *The second wave of digital era governance*. Paper presented at the American Political Science Association conference 2010 annual meeting papers, September 2–5, Washington, DC.
El-Haddadeh, R., Weerakkody, V., & Al-Shafi, S. (2013). The complexities of electronic services implementation and institutionalization in the public sector. *Information and Management, 50*(4), 135–143.
Emerson, T. L. N., Conroy, S. J., & Stanley, W. (2007). Ethical attitudes of accountants: Recent evidence from a Practitioners' Survey. *Journal of Business Ethics, 71*(1), 73–87.
Escher, T., Margetts, H., Petricek, V., & Cox, I. (2006). *Governing from the centre? Comparing the nodality of digital governments*. Annual Meeting of the American Political Science Association, 31 August–4 September 2006, Philadelphia, PA.
European Commission. (2013). *Public services online: 'Digital by default or by detour'—Assessing user centric eGovernment performance in Europe–eGovernment Benchmark 2012*. Retrieved from http://ec.europa.eu/digital-agenda/sites/digital-agenda/files/eGov%20Benchmark%202012%20insight%20report%20published%20version%200.1%20_0.pdf
Foundation, O. (2014). *eEspaña 2014 Informe anual sobre el desarrollo de la Sociedad de la Información en España*. Madrid, Spain: Fundación Orange.
Gallego, R., & Barzelay, M. (2010). Public management policymaking in Spain: The politics of legislative reform of administrative structure, 1991–1997. *Governance, 23*(2), 277–296.
Gibson, A. (2010). *Local by social: How local authorities can use social media to achieve more for less*. London: NESTA.
Gomes, R., & Sousa, L. (2012). Contributions to the development of local e-government 2.0. *Future Internet, 4*(4), 882–899.
Hibbing, J. R., & Theiss-Morse, E. (2002). *Stealth democracy: Americans' beliefs about how government should work*. Cambridge, England: Cambridge University Press.
Ho, A. T. K. (2002). Reinventing local governments and the e-government initiative. *Public Administration Review, 62*(4), 434–444.
Hodge, D. R., & Gillespie, D. (2003). Phrase completions: An alternative to Likert scales. *Social Work Research, 27*(1), 45–55.
Holgersson, J., & Karlsson, F. (2014). Public e-service development: Understanding citizens' conditions for participation. *Government Information Quarterly, 31*(3), 396–410.
Hood, C., & Margetts, H. (2007). *The tools of government in the digital age*. Basingstoke, England: Palgrave.
Huijboom, N., Van den Broek, T., Frissen, V., Kool, L., Kotterink, B., Nielsen, M., & Millard, J. (2009). *Public services 2.0: The impact of social computing on public services*. Institute for Prospective Technological Studies, Joint Research Centre, European Commission. Luxembourg: Office for Official Publications of the European Communities.
Johnston, E., & Hansen, D. (2011). Design lessons for smart governance infrastructures. In D. Ink, A. Balutis, & T. Buss (Eds.), *American governance 3.0: Rebooting the public square?* Washington, DC: National Academy of Public Administration.
Kickert, W. (1997). Public management in the United States and Europe. In W. Kickert (Ed.), *Public management and administrative reform in Western Europe* (pp. 15–38). Cheltenham, England: Edward Elgar.
Lathrop, D., & Ruma, L. (2010). *Open government: Collaboration, transparency, and participation in practice*. Sebastopol, CA: O'Reilly.
Leighninger, M. (2011). *Using online tools to engage—And be engaged by—The Public*. Washington, DC: IBM Center for The Business of Government.
Li, Q. (2013). A novel Likert scale based on fuzzy sets theory. *Expert Systems with Applications, 40*(5), 1609–1618.
Linders, D. (2012). From e-government to we-government: Defining a typology for citizen co-production in the age of social media. *Government Information Quarterly, 29*(4), 446–454.

MacKinnon, R. (2008). Flatter world and thicker walls? Blogs, censorship and civic discourse in China. *Public Choice, 134*(1/2), 31–46.
MacKinnon, R. (2009). China's censorship 2.0: How companies censor bloggers. *First Monday, 14*(2), Retrieved from http://firstmonday.org/htbin/cgiwrap/bin/ojs/index. php/fm/article/viewArticle/2378/2089
Margetts, H., & Dunleavy, P. (2013). The second wave of digital-era governance: A quasi-paradigm for government on the Web. *Philosophical Transactions of the Royal Society A: Mathematical, Physical and Engineering Sciences, 371*, 1–17.
Matell, M. S., & Jacoby, J. (1971). Is there an optimal number of alternatives for Likert scale items? study I: Reliability and validity. *Educational and Psychological Measurement, 31*(3), 657–674.
McDermott, P. (2010). Building open government. *Government Information Quarterly, 27*(4), 401–413.
McNutt, K. (2012). *Social media & government 2.0.* Saskatoon, SK, Canada: University of Saskatchewan and University of Regina.
Mergel, I. (2013). Social media adoption and resulting tactics in the U.S. federal government. *Government Information Quarterly, 30*(2), 123–130.
Millard, J. (2009). Government 1.5: Is the bottle half full or half empty? *European Journal of ePractice, 9*(1), 35–50.
Moon, M. J. (2002). The evolution of e-government among municipalities: Rhetoric or reality? *Public Administration Review, 62*(4), 424–433.
Mossberger, K., Wu, Y., & Crawford, J. (2013). *Connecting citizens and local governments? Social media and interactivity in major U.S. cities*. Paper presented at Public Management Research Conference, June 21, 2013, Madison, WI
Nam, T., & Sayogo, D. S. (2011). Government 2.0 collects the wisdom of crowds. In A. Datta, S. Shulman, B. Zheng, S. Lin, A. Sun, & E. Lim (Eds.), *Proceedings of the Third International Conference on Social Informatics* (SocInfo 2011) (pp. 51–58). Berlin, Heidelberg: Springer-Verlag.
Norman, G. (2010). Likert scales, levels of measurement and the "laws" of statistics. *Advances in Health Sciences Education, 15*(5), 625–632.
Noveck, B. (2009). *Wiki government: How technology can make government better, democracy stronger, and citizens more powerful*. Washington, DC: Brookings Institutions Press.
Oakerson, R. J. (1999). *Governing local public economies: Creating the civic metropolis*. Richmond, VA: ICS Press.
OECD. (2010). *Denmark: Efficient e-government for smarter service delivery.* Paris: OECD Publishing. Retrieved from http://dx.doi.org/10.1787/9789264087118-en
Oliveira, G. H. M., & Welch, E. W. (2013). Social media use in local government: Linkage of technology, task, and organizational context. *Government Information Quarterly, 30*(4), 397–405.
Orvik, J. M. (1972). Social desirability for individual, his group, and society. *Multivariate Behavioral Research, 7*(1), 3–32.
Osimo, D. (2008). *Web 2.0 in Government: Why? and how?* Institute for Prospective Technological Studies, Joint Research Centre, European Commission. Luxembourg: Office for Official Publications of the European Communities.
Oxley, A. (2011). *A best practices guide for mitigating risk in the use of social media*. Washington DC: IBM Center for The Business of Government.
Peters, B. G. (2001). *The future of governing*. Lawrence, KS: University Press of Kansas.
Picazo-Vela, S., Gutiérrez-Martínez, I., & Luna-Reyes, L. F. (2012). Understanding risks, benefits, and strategic alternatives of social media applications in the public sector. *Government Information Quarterly, 29*(4), 504–511.
Redell, T., & Woolcock, G. (2004). From consultation to participatory governance? A critical review of citizen engagement strategies in Queensland. *The Australian Journal of Public Administration, 63*(3), 75–87.
Reggi, L., & Scicchitano, S. (2011). *European regions financing public e-services: The case of EU Structural Funds*. Working Papers 1110, Rome: University of Urbino Carlo Bo.

Relly, J. E., & Sabharwal, M. (2009). Perceptions of transparency of government policymaking: A cross-national study. *Government Information Quarterly, 26*(1), 148–157.
Rodríguez Bolívar, M. P., Caba, M. C., & López Hernández, A. M. (2006). Cultural contexts and governmental digital reporting. *International Review of Administrative Sciences, 72*(2), 269–290.
Roscoe, J. T. (1975). *Fundamental research statistics for the behavioural sciences*. New York: Holt, Rinehart and Winston.
Rouban, L. (1997). The administrative modernisation policy in France. In E. Kickert (Ed.), *Public management and administrative reform in Western Europe* (pp. 141–156). Cheltenham, England: Edward Elgar.
Rowe, G., & Frewer, L. (2005). A typology of public engagement mechanisms. *Science, Technology and Human Values, 30*(2), 251–290.
Russell, C. J., & Bobko, P. (1992). Moderated regression analysis and Likert scales: Too coarse for comfort. *Journal of Applied Psychology, 77*(3), 336–342.
Saiz, M. P. (2011). La Ley de Economía Sostenible: La sostenibilidad financiera del Sector Público. *Revista de Contabilidad y dirección, 13*, 21–42.
Sandoval-Almazan, R., & Gil-Garcia, J. (2012). Are government internet portals evolving towards more interaction, participation, and collaboration? Revisiting the rhetoric of e-government among municipalities. *Government Information Quarterly, 29*(Supplement 1), 72–81.
Schillemans, T., Van Twist, M., & Vanhommerig, I. (2013). Innovation in accountability. Learning through interactive, dynamic, and citizen-initiated forms of accountability. *Public Performance and Management Review, 36*(3), 407–435.
Scott, J. K. (2006). "E" the people: Do U.S. municipal government web sites support public involvement? *Public Administration Review, 66*(3), 341–353.
Shackleton, P., Fisher, J., & Dawson, L. (2004). E-government services: One local government's approach. In H. Linger, J. Fisher, W. Wojtkowski, W. G. Wojtkowski, J. Zupancic, K. Vigo, & J. Arnold (Eds.), *Constructing the infrastructure for the knowledge economy: Methods and tool: Theory and Practice* (pp. 581–592). Melbourne, VIC, Australia: Kluwer Academic/Plenum.
Smith, K. A. (2004). Voluntary reporting performance measures to the public: A test of accounting reports from U.S. cities. *International Public Management Journal, 7*(1), 19–48.
IAB Spain Research. (2014). *V Estudio Anual de Redes Sociales*. Madrid, Spain: IAB.
Spanish National Statistics Institute (SNSI). (2014). Retrieved June 1, 2014, from http://www.ine.es/inebmenu/mnu_padron.htm
Spector, P. E. (1992). *Summated rating scale construction: An introduction*. Newbury Park, CA: Sage.
Taylor, J. A. (2012). The information polity: Towards a two speed future? *Information Polity: The International Journal of Government & Democracy in The Information Age, 17*(3/4), 227–237.
Thaler, M., & Sunstein, C. (2009). *Nudge: Improving decisions about health, wealth and happiness*. London: Penguin.
The White House. (2009). *The open government initiative*. Retrieved from http://www.whitehouse.gov/open
Torres, L., Pina, V., & Acerete, B. (2005). Gauging e-government evolution in EU municipalities. *Journal of Systemics, Cybernetics and Informatics, 3*(6), 43–54.
Tuomi, I. (2002). *Theory of innovation: Change and meaning in the age of internet*. Oxford, England: Oxford University Press.
United Nations. (2010). *E-Government survey. Leveraging e-government at a time of financial and economic crisis*. New York: United Nations.
Verdegem, P., & Verleye, G. (2009). User-centered e-government in practice: A comprehensive model for measuring user satisfaction. *Government Information Quarterly, 26*(3), 487–497.
Welch, E. W. (2012). The rise of participative technologies in government. In M. A. Shareef, N. Archer, Y. K. Dwivedi, A. Mishra, & S. K. Pandey (Eds.), *Transformational government through eGov practice: Socioeconomic, cultural, and technological issues* (pp. 347–367). Bingley, England: Emerald.

Part II
Presence and Use

Chapter 4
Facebook Use in Western European Local Governments: An Overall View

Enrique Bonsón, Melinda Ratkai, and Sonia Royo

Abstract The objective of this chapter is to provide an initial assessment of Facebook use by Western European municipalities considering two aspects: citizens' engagement and municipalities' activity. The sample for this study comprises the 15 earliest member countries of the EU represented by the five largest cities of each. Thus, data on 75 local governments are employed to test the following research questions: (1) How are Western European municipalities using Facebook? and (2) How are citizens engaging with their local government by using Facebook? In order to answer these questions, a set of metrics will be used that can help governments interpret and understand their impact in the use of social media. The answers to these questions will help to determine whether the use of social media is indeed increasing citizen participation in local governance. Results show that the use of Facebook by some of the biggest Western European local governments has become commonplace. Thus, the availability of a Facebook page is confirmed as a symbol of modernity and responsiveness, which may be perceived as particularly necessary for political legitimacy, especially in times of crisis. The audiences of the official Facebook pages of Western European municipalities are rather high. But a high number of fans does not automatically mean an engaged audience and citizen engagement, in general, is still low. Therefore, these findings suggest that the interest is limited on the part of citizens in terms of engaging in conversations with local governments.

E. Bonsón • M. Ratkai (✉)
Faculty of Business Administration, Universidad de Huelva,
Plaza de la Merced 11, 21071 Huelva, Spain
e-mail: bonson@uhu.es; melinda.ratkai@sc.uhu.es

S. Royo
Faculty of Economics and Business, Universidad de Zaragoza,
Gran Vía 2, 50005 Zaragoza, Spain
e-mail: sroyo@unizar.es

M.Z. Sobaci (ed.), *Social Media and Local Governments*, Public Administration and Information Technology 15, DOI 10.1007/978-3-319-17722-9_4

4.1 Introduction

E-government is a "flagship" of both the European Union (EU) and the USA, and it is causing an overall change in governmental communication and openness. The Internet now serves as a major new linkage between society and government (Thomas and Streib 2005) and has emerged as a driving factor for citizen participation initiatives because of its potential for informing, educating, and empowering citizens. However, previous studies have shown that the use of the Internet in the public sector for external purposes has been directed predominantly at the provision of public services and information to citizens and other stakeholders, neglecting the citizen participation dimension (Brainard and McNutt 2010; Coursey and Norris 2008; Musso et al. 2000; Norris and Reddick 2013; Royo et al. 2014; Torres et al. 2006).

Recent developments on e-government include the use of social media tools (Bonsón et al. 2012; Mergel and Bretschneider 2013; Snead 2013; Zavattaro 2013). Social network sites allow people to reach a common goal via an online interactive collaboration. Social media (SM) "are technologies that facilitate social interaction, make possible collaboration, and enable deliberation across stakeholders" (Bryer and Zavattaro 2011, p. 327). The most popular examples of SM are blogs, Twitter (microblog), YouTube, Facebook, LinkedIn, etc. On these sites people usually share their opinions and comment on the news. Besides private use for leisure purposes, SM can be used to support or criticize companies, products, and public or private services.

The popularity of SM has not only reached the world of business, but also governments and municipalities. With the rapid explosion of SM, it is not surprising that public organizations are following the trend and deploying sites to reach people where they are. As of August 2012, 66 % of US adults online use Facebook, 16 % use Twitter, and 20 % use LinkedIn (Pew Internet Research Centre 2013a). Nowadays, moving toward the network society and engaging with constituents is recognized as a critical element of political legitimacy (Schellong and Girrger 2010). The use of mobile technology, combined with SM in the e-government arena, presents exciting opportunities. With strategic planning, effective management, and realistic expectations, social computing can drive the next stage of e-government growth and interactivity (Joseph 2012). However, according to Zavattaro (2013), more research is needed to investigate the role that SM technologies will play in the future of public administration.

In this study, we have focused on Facebook use by Western European local governments. Facebook has been chosen from SM because of its popularity among citizens and SM users. Facebook is on the first place among SM sites according to Alexa rankings (Alexa.com 2014). Furthermore, Facebook has the highest levels of engagement among SM users, with 63 % of Facebook users visiting the site at least once a day and 40 % doing so multiple times throughout the day (Pew Internet Research Center 2013b). According to Ellison and Hardey (2013), among all the available SM, Facebook offers the clearest possibilities for more sustained interaction between citizens and their local authority.

Facebook offers local governments the possibility to know their citizens "personally." A two-way conversation can be maintained, whereas traditional media such as television, radio, and print media only offer the possibility of one-way communication. Through dialogue, realized on the Internet, municipalities can derive many benefits, collecting feedback, ideas, and opinions which help to improve public policies and public services. Municipalities can obtain useful advice and gain more trust from citizens. Thanks to the direct interaction, citizens can acquire a deeper knowledge of the workings of the local government. In this way, local governments can gain reputation and trust, while reducing costs and spending on marketing.

Most research on SM use by local governments has been carried out in the USA, where 22.1 % of Facebook visitors are located according to Alexa rankings. The use of Facebook in European countries is under investigated, in spite of the fact that five out of the top ten countries in the number of visitors to Facebook are Western EU countries (Germany, UK, Italy, France, and Spain) and that ten of the EU countries analyzed in this study represent at least 17.8 % of Facebook visitors.[1] In this context, the objective of this chapter is to provide an initial assessment of Facebook use by Western European municipalities in order to answer the following research questions: (1) How are Western European municipalities using Facebook? and (2) How are citizens engaging with their local government by using Facebook? In order to answer these questions, a set of metrics will be used that can help governments interpret and understand their impact in the use of SM. The answers to these questions will help to determine whether SM are indeed increasing citizen participation in local governance.

The rest of this chapter is organized as follows. The next section presents some background ideas about government–citizen collaboration and the role of SM. Section 4.3 presents the sample, research design, and methods. The results are presented in Sect. 4.4 and Sect. 4.5 discusses the findings. Finally, the conclusions are presented in Sect. 4.6.

4.2 Government–Citizen Collaboration: The Role of Social Media and Related Challenges

One of the main issues for the government-to-citizen relationship is trust, which can be gained by promoting transparent and effective activities. Several strategies dealing with distrust have been investigated. One of the most popular definitions of distrust is the deficit in trust that can be made up by a greater public participation in decision making (Yetano et al. 2010). The focus on individual citizen engagement in

[1] According to Alexa rankings (Alexa.com 2014), the percentage of Facebook visitors that comes from Western European countries is as follows: Belgium (0.7 %), France (2.6 %), Germany (3.2 %), Greece (0.8 %), Italy (2.9 %), Netherlands (1 %), Portugal (0.5 %), Sweden (0.5 %), Spain (2.4) and the UK (3.2 %). No data are provided for Austria, Denmark, Finland, Ireland and Luxembourg, which are the smallest countries in our sample.

public life is part of a wider trend in public administration toward reimagining the role of the public administrator. The role of the public administrator is shifting from that of a neutral expert toward becoming a facilitator of individual and grassroots participation and engagement (Brainard and McNutt 2010). In this scenario, public administrators create opportunities to engage with citizens and use those opportunities to educate, organize, and mobilize citizens to participate in a larger public sphere and act as advocates on their own behalf. On the other hand, it also means that public administrators should engage with citizens to identify and define problems in collaboration, and implement solutions for the problems detected. As a result of this process, government-to-citizen relationships are expected to become more deliberative and dialogic rather than regulative and authority based (Brainard and McNutt 2010). In this context, the advent and rapid diffusion of Internet-related applications have been heralded as having the potential for increased democratic engagement, increased access, and greater opportunities to reduce the democratic deficit.

The use of SM tools has favored the emergence of citizen-created content that enriches sociopolitical debates, increasing the diversity of opinions expressed, and that provides the free flow of information and self-expression (Bonsón et al. 2012). SM provide new platforms where communities can easily be reached and where stakeholders can express their preferences on an ongoing basis. Interactions on SM platforms are bidirectional, affording frequent communication and feedback between government representatives and the public. The Obama administration, with the 2009 Open Government Initiative, has led the way in this regard, placing great emphasis on using SM to increase transparency, public participation in government, and improve public access to government information (Snead 2013).

According to Bonsón et al. (2012), the main benefits that SM offer to public sector entities are the enhancement of transparency and citizen participation. These benefits can be obtained by increasing government's visibility, sharing data and insights into decision-making processes in order to become more transparent, becoming more engaging, open and participatory, and offering the possibility to all stakeholders to become involved in collaborative processes (Mergel and Bretschneider 2013). SM offer chances for coproduction, crowd-sourcing solutions, transparency and accountability, and real-time information updates (Bertot et al. 2010).

Thus, SM use in the public sector must be understood as part of a larger, ongoing paradigmatic shift towards greater citizen empowerment and participation through government transparency, accountability, and open collaboration. For Snead (2013), the adoption of SM by public sector entities is a reaction to declining citizen trust and confidence in government (Tolbert and Mossberger 2006), and also declining citizen engagement with government activities and democratic processes. In this context, SM offer an opportunity for direct interaction with an audience and provide an innovative channel for participation, information dissemination, and education that a traditional, static website cannot provide (Mergel and Bretschneider 2013). SM applications offer public sector entities the opportunity to integrate information and opinions in the policy-making process in several innovative ways. Furthermore, they confer increased transparency through information sharing and collaboration with the public in preparing decisions and/or searching for solutions to government problems (Mergel 2013).

However, in spite of all these possible positive benefits, we have to bear in mind that not everything is positive with technology (Farazmand 2012; Joseph 2012). According to Farazmand (2012, p. 489), "technology is both enabler and destroyer, a tool both of opportunity and repression, freedom and tyranny, democracy and despotism, and progress and degeneration." Furthermore, both SM and Facebook can also be used in the same way as a traditional website, primarily for pushing information in a broadcasting mode without allowing direct interaction of the parties.

Mergel (2013) has distinguished three SM tactics for public sector entities based on their existing communication and interaction style: (1) a push strategy that represents formal government information on SM as additional channels of communication; (2) a pull strategy that engages and includes information from stakeholders; and (3) a networking strategy that includes both push and pull activities, with a highly interactive and bidirectional responsiveness that produces reciprocal feedback cycles.

Meijer et al. (2012) discuss three key success factors for the realization of Government 2.0: leadership in government, incentives for citizens, and mutual trust. Leadership in government is crucial since governments need to be willing to shift their interaction patterns from formal interactions with representatives of interest groups to informal information exchanges with individuals in networks. Incentives for citizens are key components as there are government initiatives that have not been taken up by citizens and thus have had no further effect. Thus, citizens' willingness to participate in these networks is crucial. Finally, mutual trust needs to be established in these government-to-citizen interactions to make the networks viable and robust.

Dialogic communication via SM helps to increase the transparency and engagement that can lead to greater trust. Local governments' use of SM means acknowledging that citizens are active agents of local democracy. They are sources of ideas and initiatives that provide a mutual enrichment (Michel 2005) and answer the citizens' demand for greater transparency and participation. The role of SM in municipalities can be analyzed in relation to two different perspectives as illustrated in Fig. 4.1.

The first perspective places greater emphasis on local governments and their strategies, activity levels, online offers, goals, etc. The second perspective is focused on the stakeholders/citizens, their activities and engagement levels, communication style, mood, satisfaction, and so on. As described in the next section, these two perspectives will be used for the empirical analysis, as both local governments' activity and citizens' engagement are the focus of this research.

Despite the growing discussion about SM technologies (whether they have the potential to enhance citizen engagement), there is still little evidence on SM adoption and usage. A study (Purser 2012), carried out in Australia, shows that although most local governments use SM in some way, the majority consider that they have just started to use these channels and they are in the initial stages of gaining experience. Only a quarter of them have a formal evaluation process in place to measure the effectiveness of the SM they use. Similarly, a recent study in the USA (Norris and Reddick 2013) shows that the use of SM by US municipalities is mostly one-way communication from the governments outward (60.6 %).

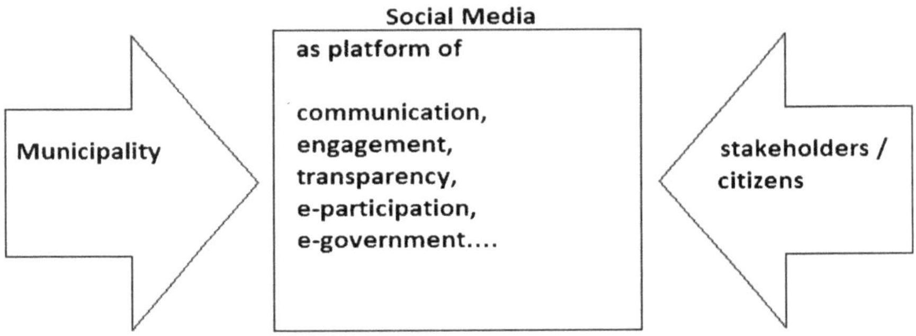

Fig. 4.1 The role of SM in municipalities

Different measures of engagement with SM platforms have been proposed by previous research. Paek et al. (2013) measured engagement with items on a Likert-type scale adapted from a prior study of Calder et al. (2009). The only pitfall of this kind of measurement is that surveys are needed to obtain the necessary data on engagement. Agostino (2013) measured citizen engagement on Facebook pages by using the number of "talking about." This metric represents the number of unique users interacting with a page (like the page; like, comment on, or share a page post; answer a question, respond to an event, mention or tag the page) over a 7-day period. This measure has two main disadvantages. First, it is an aggregated index of engagement which adds many different types of activities that cannot be individually analyzed. Second, if a fan leaves more than one comment or both likes and shares a post within the 7-day period it adds only one point to the number of "talking about." Additionally, Bonsón and Ratkai (2013) and Bonsón et al. (2014) proposed a set of metrics that are also valid to identify the dimensions of engagement with social media platforms as regards the number of comments, shares, and likes. These metrics are also valid to measure citizen engagement and they are publicly available. Therefore in this research these metrics and the aggregated index of engagement were adapted as described below.

4.3 Sample, Research Design, and Methods

The sample for this study comprises the 15 earliest member countries of the EU represented by the five largest cities of each; thus, a total of 75 EU local governments have been analyzed (see Table 4.A1 in Appendix). The observation of the 75 local governments was carried out for October 2012. Larger-sized local governments in each country were chosen because they are usually more innovative in the adoption of new technologies (Rogers 1983) and they have lower relative costs for the implementation of the new Web 2.0 tools (Bonsón et al. 2012). Furthermore, larger-sized local governments have greater disclosure needs since the distance between the governors and the governed is greater. SM are particularly effective in these circumstances, as information can be efficiently disseminated to a large, dispersed audience, providing increasing opportunities for citizen participation. A larger group of potential users usually implies more pluralistic demands and expectations for information and services, which leads to more pressure for innovative ideas and programs to address different needs in a community (Ho and Ni 2004). Lastly, larger cities have stronger incentives to enhance their reputation and public image as they are more publicly visible.

Several authors (European Institute 2012; The Economist 2011) have argued that there are North–South differences in the EU. Since the debate about globalization has arisen, we may talk about the North/South divide in relation to various aspects. The differences go beyond economic status, extending to culture, questions of responsibility, and stereotypes. Chorianopoulos (2002) found that they are different forms of urban governance and industrialization patterns in North and South Europe, which is maybe behind the lagging competitiveness of cities in Southern Europe. Previous studies characterize Northern European countries as leaders with regards to citizen participation, while Southern European countries usually lag behind (Yetano et al. 2010; Royo et al. 2014). Additionally, Neirotti et al. (2014) found that economic development (among others) is likely to influence a city's digital path. Furthermore, the present financial, economic, and social crises have had a greater impact in Southern European countries than in Northern Europe. In this study, this North–South division is also analyzed in order to establish whether it has an impact on Facebook usage by municipalities. In order to answer the first research question, the use of Facebook by each municipality was examined. The same method was applied in all cases. First of all, the official website of the municipality was checked for a direct link to the Facebook platform. If a link was found, the linked platform was accepted as the official one. For the rest of the cases, the presence of the municipality on this platform was checked by using its official name, the link to its official website, and/or the official e-mail address. A binary code (1/0) was applied to register whether a municipality had an official Facebook account or not.

Data on municipalities' activity and the number of fans were collected by using observational methods for each official Facebook account. Channel activity was calculated according to the number of posts by municipality and working day. This figure was obtained by counting the total number of posts in the examined month and dividing the total by the number of working days in each month. The number of fans (amount of people who have liked the examined page) reflects the audience of the channel.

For the second research question, three Facebook corporate metrics (P, C, and V) and an aggregated index of engagement (E) were used (see Table 4.1) as defined by Bonsón and Ratkai (2013) and Bonsón et al. (2014). These Facebook corporate metrics are calculated by using publicly available data and they reflect different types of engagement. In the rest of this study we will refer to these metrics as popularity (P), commitment (C), virality (V), and engagement (E), respectively.

Table 4.1 Metrics for stakeholder engagement

Popularity	P1	Number of posts liked/total posts	Percentage of posts that have been liked
	P2	Total likes/total number of posts	Average number of likes per post
	P3	(P2/number of fans) × 1,000	Average number of likes per post per 1,000 fans
Commitment	C1	Number of posts commented/ total posts	Percentage of posts that have been commented
	C2	Total comments/total posts	Average number of comments per post
	C3	(C2/number of fans) × 1,000	Average number of comments per post per 1,000 fans
Virality	V1	Number of posts shared/total posts	Percentage of posts that have been shared
	V2	Total shares/total posts	Average number of shares per post
	V3	(V2/number of fans) × 1,000	Average number of shares per post per 1,000 fans
Engagement	E	P3+C3+V3	Stakeholder engagement index

Source: Bonsón et al. (2014)

Finally, Pearson correlations (among the activity and engagement variables) were computed in order to see whether there is a relationship between municipalities' channel activity and citizens' engagement.

Western European countries were classified into Northern and Southern ones (European Institute 2012). In our sample Northern countries are the Netherlands, Germany, Austria, Luxembourg, Finland, Denmark, France, Belgium, the UK, Sweden, and Ireland. And Southern countries are Italy, Spain, Portugal, and Greece. This distinction can be understood as a proxy of the culture of transparency and participation embedded within the governance system (Royo et al. 2014.)

Possible differences between Northern and Southern countries have been analyzed by using the *t*-test of difference of the means between these two groups of countries.

4.4 Analysis of Results

Almost three in four (73 %) of the analyzed European municipalities had an official Facebook page in October 2012. The use is higher among Southern countries (80 % vs. 71 % in Northern countries), but 9 % difference is not so significant in this context. Table 4.2 shows these results.

Table 4.3 reports on Facebook activity levels, number of fans and different engagement levels (including popularity, commitment, and virality) among Western EU local governments. The difference in the average activity level of municipalities

Table 4.2 Rate of adoption of Facebook by EU local governments

	N° municipalities	N° with Facebook
North	55	39 (70.9 %)
South	20	16 (80.0 %)
Total	75	55 (73.3 %)

Table 4.3 Measuring activity, audience, popularity, commitment, virality, and engagement

	Mean	Median	Maximum	Min.	Std. Dev.	Obs
Activity						
North	1.8618	1.6522	7.2609	0	1.4538	39
South	4.0815	2.5870	21.6087	0	5.2522	16
Total	2.5075	1.8261	21.6087	0	3.1914	55
Audience						
North	98,523	2,135	1,957,191	77	339,191	39
South	14,248	3,856	120,926	163	29,663	16
Total	74,007	2,322	1,957,191	77	287,572	55
Popularity (P3)						
North	6.3001	2.6243	38.6625	0	8.4312	39
South	6.5942	2.1841	60.3893	0	14.9671	16
Total	6.3857	2.5633	60.3893	0	10.5956	55
Commitment (C3)						
North	0.6071	0.3025	3.4180	0	0.8164	39
South	1.8394	0.2093	19.4007	0	4.9215	16
Total	0.9656	0.2377	19.4007	0	2.7416	55
Virality (V3)						
North	0.8691	0.3509	6.4046	0	1.3130	39
South	1.3704	0.6545	9.9917	0	2.4500	16
Total	1.0149	0.5000	9.9917	0	1.7127	55
Engagement						
North	7.7764	3.3347	42.3197	0	9.7064	39
South	9.8040	3.0195	62.9581	0	17.0114	16
Total	8.3662	3.3347	62.9581	0	12.1470	55

is very significant because Southern local governments are twice as active as Northern ones (4.0814 vs. 1.8618). On average, the municipalities posted 2.5 times per working day, but as indicated by the *Maximum*, *Minimum*, and *Standard Deviation* figures, high heterogeneity in the average number of posts has been found, especially among Southern countries, where the standard deviation is 5.2522.

Considering the audience (number of fans), it can be concluded that Northern municipalities have a significantly higher number of fans (98,523), almost seven times higher than in Southern countries (14,248), on average. However, higher levels of heterogeneity also exist in Northern cities (standard deviation figure of

339,191). So, on average, the stakeholders'/citizens' basis of communication is larger in Northern than in Southern municipalities, but among Northern municipalities there is a greater variation in the number of fans of the official Facebook account of the municipality.

Table 4.3 also includes the Facebook corporate metrics of P3, C3, V3 (which are used to construct the engagement index). As can be seen, the average value of popularity (6.3857) is significantly higher than commitment (0.9656) and virality (1.0149). The mean values of these metrics are higher in Southern than in Northern cities, especially in the cases of commitment (North: 0.6071, South: 1.8394) and virality (North: 0.8691, South: 1.3704). The standard deviation figures, in general, are also significantly higher among Southern cities.

The statistics of the elaborated index of engagement (E) seem to confirm a higher engagement within Southern municipalities, since the average engagement level was significantly higher in Southern countries (North: 7.7764, South: 9.8040). As stated above, the same happened to activity levels and Facebook corporate metrics (popularity, commitment, and virality).

The complete set of metrics related to commitment (C1, C2, C3), popularity (P1, P2, P3), and virality (V1, V2, V3) are provided in Table 4.4. As can be seen from this table, liking is the most common activity performed by citizens. The percentage of the posts that were liked (P1) was 81 %, whereas the average number of likes per post (P2) was 244. Commenting on posts requires a higher level of engagement from citizens, and this activity was less common among the users of Western European local government official Facebook pages. The percentage of posts that received comments (C1) was 42 %. However, the average number of comments per post (C2) was 10. The percentage of shared posts (V1) was 49 %, and the average number of shares per post (V2) was 37. Descriptive statistics show no clear patterns in regards to North–South differences in Facebook engagement levels by citizens, but still some regularity was detected. Indicators P2, C2, and V2 (average number of likes, comments, and shares per post) were significantly higher in Northern countries (around 4 and 6 times higher than the same metrics in Southern countries, on average), which seems logical as the number of fans is significantly higher in Northern municipalities. However, these differences completely disappear when looking at the metrics deflated by the number of fans (P3, C3, and V3), and in the case of commitment and virality, citizens in Southern cities even show higher levels of engagement.

Table 4.5 presents the results of the correlation analyses among the activity and engagement variables. As can be seen, only one of the correlations was found to be significant at the 10 % level. So, these results indicate no relationship between municipalities' levels of activity and engagement levels by citizens. Therefore, more frequent posting or raising the activity of a channel is not necessarily related to a higher level of activity on the part of citizens and consequently a higher engagement level.

Table 4.6 presents the results of the *t*-tests for activity and engagement levels among Northern and Southern cities. These results confirm the previous findings,

Table 4.4 Set of metrics of popularity (P1, P2, P3), commitment (C1, C2, C3), and virality (V1, V2, V3)

	P1	P2	P3	C1	C2	C3	V1	V2	V3
North									
Mean	0.7867	322.977	6.3001	0.4159	13.0498	0.6071	0.4209	49.507	0.8691
Median	0.8714	7.9611	2.6242	0.3220	1.2727	0.3024	0.3103	0.8	0.3509
Maximum	1	5,540	38.6624	1	179.4286	3.4179	1	978.648	6.4046
Minimum	0	0	0	0	0	0	0	0	0
Std. Dev.	0.2461	1,043	8.4311	0.3284	36.0243	0.8164	0.3348	174.985	1.3130
Observations	39	39	39	39	39	39	39	39	39
South									
Mean	0.8587	52.0572	6.5942	0.4216	3.9768	1.8394	0.6464	6.5628	1.3704
Median	0.9655	10.6641	2.1841	0.4203	1.7274	0.2093	0.4902	3.5107	0.6545
Maximum	1.0000	546.5833	60.3893	0.8596	24.1539	19.4007	3.6923	17.4039	9.9917
Minimum	0	0	0	0	0	0	0	0	0
Std. Dev.	0.2657	134.2861	14.9671	0.2645	6.2679	4.9215	0.8678	6.5604	2.4500
Observations	16	16	16	16	16	16	16	16	16
Total									
Mean	0.8076	244.164	6.385	0.4176	10.410	0.9655	0.4864	37.0141	1.0149
Median	0.8888	8.111	2.563	0.375	1.4444	0.2377	0.3720	1.3174	0.5000
Maximum	1	5,540	60.389	1	179.428	19.400	3.6923	978.648	9.9917
Minimum	0	0	0	0	0	0	0	0	0
Std. Dev.	0.2516	886.67	10.595	0.3087	30.682	2.7415	0.5466	148.144	1.7126
Observations	55	55	55	55	55	55	55	55	55

Table 4.5 Pearson correlations among activity and engagement levels

	Activity		
	North	South	Total
P3	−0.273*	−0.214	−0.204
C3	−0.154	−0.209	−0.120
V3	−0.101	−0.112	−0.055
E	−0.264	−0.265	−0.213

Note: *Significant at the 10 %

Table 4.6 Differences between activity, audience, and engagement in Northern and Southern countries

	Activity	P3	C3	V3	E
Mean North	1.8618	6.3001	0.6071	0.8691	7.7764
Mean South	4.0815	6.5942	1.8394	1.3704	9.8040
t-Test	−2.449**	−0.093	−1.533	−0.986	−0.559

Note: **Significant at the 5 %

indicating that the differences in activity levels are statistically significant, being higher in Southern countries. However, the differences in engagement levels were not statistically significant for any of the metrics that form the aggregated index of engagement.

4.5 Discussion

The proliferation of social computing and SM is here for the long haul. As previous research about the USA shows (Mergel 2013), the overwhelming reason for participation in SM platforms can be summarized by one main goal: representation of the entity on all potential interaction channels, i.e., to be present where the people are. Local government, referring to the closest level of government to citizens, needs to harness potential opportunities through effective use of SM. Having a Facebook page can be considered a symbol of modernity and responsiveness, which may be perceived as a must for political legitimacy, especially in times of crisis. Our results show that there is a high presence in the usage of Facebook within the examined European municipalities (73 %). Previous research carried out in 2010 found that 17 % of these local governments had an official Facebook page (Bonsón et al. 2012), evidencing important advances in Facebook presence in a 2-year period. It seems that Western European municipalities are increasingly using Facebook in order to reach their citizens.

However, simply attaining a Facebook page is not enough. Local governments must define their strategy and allow for frequent communication and feedback among government representatives and the public. This is the only way in which government-to-citizen relationships can significantly be improved and trust be gained. Communication between a local government and a citizen must be frequent, but without overwhelming the audience. Guidelines on SM use by public sector entities suggest a minimum of two and a maximum of ten tweets/posts per working day (Cabinet Office 2009). Our results on Facebook use by Western EU local governments have found low average levels of activity: 2.5 messages per working day in 2012. However, we have to bear in mind that high levels of heterogeneity exist in the sample. In terms of the audiences of the official Facebook pages of Western municipalities, on average the number of fans was rather high, although high levels of heterogeneity among cities have also been detected.

But, are fans engaging with their municipalities? As indicated by Mergel (2013), a key question concerning SM use in the public sector is whether SM are really increasing citizen participation in government. Notwithstanding, our results still show limited levels of engagement among citizens, as the main activity is simply clicking the "like" button. When the participation of citizens involves greater effort, e.g., by selecting "friends" with whom to share the post, or commenting on the posts, levels of engagement decrease. These findings are consistent with previous studies indicating that interaction on SM tends to be limited (Hansard Society 2009; Wright 2009). The fact that most of the posts were liked (81 %) is evidence that citizens find local government posts interesting and useful, but they show less interest for sharing the information with friends or by engaging in a dialogue by commenting on them (only around 41 % of the posts are shared or commented on; the average number of comments per post is around 10 and the average number of shares per post is 37). An interesting finding is that shares are more widely used than comments, so it seems that citizens tend to share relevant content published by municipalities.

The results show that there is no apparent relationship between municipalities' activity and engagement levels by citizens. This suggests that merely raising the activity level of a channel (that is, promoting a more frequent communication flow) does not necessarily result in higher levels of activity on the part of citizens.

Our findings seem to be consistent with previous research indicating that active presence in SM depends on the special circumstances of each local government and on the political will and personal attitudes of public sector managers (Bonsón et al. 2012; Hansard Society 2009). Our results suggest that due to the greater effect of the present financial and economic crises, Southern local governments feel more pressure to be transparent, open and accountable and to promote citizen participation in policy formulation. Southern municipalities have been detected to have a higher activity on Facebook than their Northern counterparts. In general, Southern municipalities in today's Europe are in a weaker economic and financial situation, and therefore openness and transparency here seems to be more important to build trust. SM in general and Facebook in particular can be useful tools to reach this goal.

From the cases examined, it seems that channel activity is more an attitude or a decision on the part of local governments than a consequence of citizen demand or a dialogic communication with citizens. But we have to bear in mind that this study has not investigated the content of the messages/posts and their impact on engagement. Certain contents can be more important to citizens than others and generate higher engagement levels. This is an interesting area that deserves further investigation.

Significant opportunities exist, particularly with new web 2.0 technologies, to harness online media in ways that engage, rather than just communicate with constituents. Previous research has shown the importance of "perceived value" in explaining the participation continuance intentions and behavior of Facebook users (Al-Debei et al. 2013). That is, Facebook users will not risk committing time and effort to it continually without being sure of the benefits and value they can derive from participation continuance. Thus, local governments should clearly establish the main purpose of their Facebook page (to inform, capture feedback, engage) in order to avoid frustration on the part of citizens that can lead to distrust.

We do not want to bring this section to an end without indicating the limitations of this study and highlighting the areas for further research. This chapter is based on the analysis of five local governments per country in the 15 earliest EU member countries. Future studies should broaden the number of cases studied per country, the range in the sizes of the local governments analyzed, and also include geographical areas other than Western Europe. Furthermore, future studies should also analyze what are the drivers of activity levels and citizen engagement (for example, demographic and socioeconomic characteristics, ICTs penetration, level of development of e-government, and so on). We have analyzed the official corporate Facebook account, but some councils may have several official accounts on Facebook covering a "spectrum" of specific topics such as tourism, libraries, sports, cultural activities, and youth, for example. In this study we have used particular metrics to measure SM use and activity, both on the part of citizens and local governments. Future studies should also analyze the nature of activity in these platforms and the content of the posts—that is, whether the activity being promoted by local governments reflects primarily unidirectional information distribution, bidirectional exchange/transaction, or discussion, dialogue, and collaboration. This type of analysis will be particularly useful in order to see what topics attract and engage more citizens on SM platforms. Fostering participation in SM platforms is an issue that continues to present challenges for researchers and practitioners alike (Al-Debei et al. 2013; Lee and Kwak 2012). Investigating this matter in terms of the public sector's SM platforms is an area that requires further research as the continuous usage and engagement of citizens on these platforms are key success factors.

4.6 Conclusions

The use of Facebook by Western European local governments has become commonplace, with important advances in Facebook presence in recent times. SM in general and Facebook in particular can be useful tools to promote openness, transparency, citizen engagement, and collaboration. In this way, local governments can gain reputation and trust, while reducing costs and marketing spending. It seems that European municipalities are increasingly using Facebook in order to reach citizens, especially in Southern countries. As the impact of the present financial and economic crises has been greater in Southern municipalities, they feel more *urgency* to have a Facebook official page to communicate with citizens. Thus, the availability of a Facebook page is confirmed as a symbol of modernity and responsiveness, which may be perceived as particularly necessary for political legitimacy, especially in times of crisis.

The audiences of the official Facebook pages of Western European municipalities are rather high. But a high number of fans do not automatically mean an engaged audience. Unfortunately, citizen engagement in general can be considered as low. Pushing the "like" button is the most popular form of engagement, but when the participation of citizens involves greater effort, by sharing posts or commenting on them, levels of engagement decrease. The fact that most of the posts were liked is evidence that they are considered interesting and useful. But somehow people do not show any further interest in sharing the information with friends or engaging in a dialogue by means of comments. Therefore, these findings suggest that the interest is limited on the part of citizens in terms of engaging in conversations with local governments. However, we have to bear in mind that this chapter has not analyzed the content of the posts of local governments and that it is very likely that in the early stages of SM adoption, Facebook is only an additional channel to replicate information that is published through the standard ICT channels, rather than using the medium for social interactions (Mergel and Bretschneider 2013).

Our results show high levels of heterogeneity in Facebook activity. No usage patterns or relationship between municipalities' activity and engagement levels by citizens were found. It seems that channel activity is more an attitude or a decision on the part of local governments than a consequence of citizen demand or a dialogic communication with citizens. Developments of this field seem rather chaotic, taking into account both the local governments and citizens; therefore, predicting future developments in this area seems somewhat risky.

Acknowledgement This study has been carried out with the financial support of the Spanish National R&D Plan through research projects ECO2010-17463 and ECO2011-28267 (ECON-FEDER).

Appendix

Table 4.A1 List of municipalities

	Country	City	Official name	Web
1	Austria	Vienna	Magistrat der Stadt Wien	www.wien.gv.at
2		Graz	Magistrat Graz	www.graz.at
3		Linz	Magistrat Linz	www.linz.at
4		Salzburg	Stadt Salzburg	www.stadt-salzburg.at
5		Innsbruck	Stadt Innsbruck	www.innsbruck.at
6	Belgium	Antwerpen	Stad Antwerpen	www.antwerpen.be
7		Gent	Stad Gent	www.gent.be
8		Charleroi	La Ville de Charleroi	www.charleroi.be
9		Liège	Ville de Liège	www.liege.be
10		Brussels	City of Brussels	www.brucity.be
11	Denmark	Copenhagen	København Kommune	www.kk.dk
12		Aarhus	Arhus Kommune	www.aarhuskommune.dk
13		Aalborg	Aalborg Kommune	www.aalborgkommune.dk
14		Odense	Odense Kommune	www.odense.dk
15		Esbjerg	Esbjerg Kommune	www.esbjergkommune.dk
16	Finland	Helsinki	Helsingin kaupunki	www.hel.fi
17		Espoo	Espoon kaupunki	www.espoo.fi
18		Tampere	Tampereen kaupunki	www.tampere.fi
19		Vantaa	Vantaan kaupunki	www.vantaa.fi
20		Turku	Turun kaupunki	www.turku.fi
21	France	Paris	Mairie de Paris	www.paris.fr
22		Marseille	Mairie de Marseille	www.marseille.fr
23		Lyon	Mairie de Lyon	www.lyon.fr
24		Toulouse	Mairie de Toulouse	www.toulouse.fr
25		Nice	Mairie de Nice	www.nice.fr
26	Germany	Berlin	Stadt Berlin	www.berlin.de
27		Hamburg	Stadt Hamburg	www.hamburg.de
28		Munich	Stadt Munchen	www.muenchen.de
29		Köln	Stadt Koln	www.stadt-koeln.de
30		Frankfurt	Stadt Frankfurt	www.frankfurt.de
31	Greece	Athens	Δήμος Αθηναίων	www.cityofathens.gr
32		Thessaloniki	Δήμος Θεσσαλονίκης	www.thessaloniki.gr
33		Patras	Δήμος Πατρέων	www.patras.gr
34		Heraklion	Δήμος Ηρακλείου	www.heraklion-city.gr
35		Volos	Δήμος Βόλου	www.volos-city.gr
36	Ireland	Dublin	Dublin City Council	www.dublincity.ie
37		Cork	Cork City Council	www.corkcorp.ie
38		Galway	Galway City Council	www.galwaycity.ie
39		Limerick	Limerick City Council	www.limerickcorp.ie
40		Waterford	Waterford City Council	www.waterfordcity.ie

(continued)

Table 4.A1 (continued)

	Country	City	Official name	Web
41	Italy	Rome	Comune di Roma	www.comune.roma.it
42		Milan	Comune di Milano	www.comune.milano.it
43		Naples	Comune di Napoli	www.comune.napoli.it
44		Turin	Comune di Torino	www.comune.torino.it
45		Palermo	Comune di Palermo	www.comune.palermo.it
46	Luxembourg	Luxembourg	Ville de Luxembourg	www.luxembourg-city.lu
47		Esch-sur-Alzette	Administration Communale de la Ville d'Esch-sur-Alzette	www.esch.lu
48		Differdange	Mairie de Differdange	www.differdange.lu
49		Dudelange	Administration de la Ville de Dudelange	www.dudelange.lu
50		Pétange	Administration Communale de Pétange	www.petange.lu
51	Netherlands	Amsterdam	Gemeente Amsterdam	www.amsterdam.nl
52		Rotterdam	Gemeente Rotterdam	www.rotterdam.nl
53		The Hague	Gemeente Den Haag	www.denhaag.nl
54		Utrecht	Gemeente Utrecht	www.utrecht.nl
55		Eindhoven	Gemeente Eindhoven	www.eindhoven.nl
56	Portugal	Lisbon	Cámara municipal de Lisboa	www.cm-lisboa.pt
57		Oporto	Cámara municipal do Porto	www.cm-porto.pt
58		Vila Nova de Gaia	Cámara municipal de Gaia	www.cm-gaia.pt
59		Amadora	Cámara municipal de Amadora	www.cm-amadora.pt
60		Braga	Cámara municipal de Braga	www.cm-braga.pt
61	Sweden	Stockholm	Stockholms Stad	www.stockholm.se
62		Göteborg	Göteborgs Stad	www.goteborg.se
63		Malmö	Malmo Stad	www.malmo.se
64		Uppsala	Uppsala kommun	www.uppsala.se
65		Linköping	Lidköpings kommun	www.lidkoping.se
66	Spain	Madrid	Ayuntamiento de Madrid	www.munimadrid.es
67		Barcelona	Ayuntament de Barcelona	www.bcn.es
68		Valencia	Ajuntament de Valéncia	www.valencia.es
69		Sevilla	Ayuntamiento de Sevilla	www.sevilla.org
70		Zaragoza	Ayuntamiento de Zaragoza	www.zaragoza.es
71	UK	London	London City Council	www.london.gov.uk
72		Birmingham	Birmingham City Council	www.birmingham.gov.uk
73		Glasgow	Glasgow City Council	www.glasgow.gov.uk
74		Leeds	Leeds City Council	www.leeds.gov.uk
75		Manchester	Manchester City Council	www.manchester.gov.uk

References

Agostino, D. (2013). Using social media to engage citizens: A study of Italian municipalities. *Public Relations Review, 39*(3), 232–234.

Al-Debei, M. M., Al-Lozi, E., & Papazafeiropoulou, A. (2013). Why people keep coming back to Facebook: Explaining and predicting continuance participation from an extended theory of planned behaviour perspective. *Decision Support Systems, 55*(1), 43–54.

Alexa.com. (2014). Retrieved April 24, 2014, from http://www.alexa.com/siteinfo/facebook.com

Bertot, J. C., Jaeger, P. T., & Grimes, J. M. (2010). Using ICTs to create a culture of transparency: E-government and social media as openness and anti-corruption tools for societies. *Government Information Quarterly, 27*(3), 264–271.

Bonsón, E., & Ratkai, M. (2013). A set of metrics to assess stakeholder engagement and social legitimacy on a corporate Facebook page. *Online Information Review, 37*(5), 787–803.

Bonsón, E., Royo, S., & Ratkai, M. (2014). Facebook practices in Western European municipalities: An empirical analysis of activity and citizens' engagement. *Administration and Society.* doi:10.1177/0095399714544945

Bonsón, E., Torres, L., Royo, S., & Flores, F. (2012). Local e-government 2.0: Social media and corporate transparency in municipalities. *Government Information Quarterly, 29*(2), 123–132.

Brainard, L. A., & McNutt, J. G. (2010). Virtual government–citizen relations: Informational, transactional, or collaborative? *Administration & Society, 42*(7), 836–858.

Bryer, T. A., & Zavattaro, S. M. (2011). Social media and public administration. *Administrative Theory & Praxis, 33*, 325–340.

Cabinet Office. (2009). *Template Twitter strategy for government departments.* London: Government Cabinet Office.

Calder, B. J., Malthouse, E. C., & Schaedel, U. (2009). An experimental study of the relationship between online engagement and advertising effectiveness. *Journal of Interactive Marketing, 23*, 321–331.

Chorianopoulos, I. (2002). Urban restructuring and governance: North-South differences in Europe and the EU URBAN initiative. *Urban Studies, 39*, 705–772. doi:10.1080/0042 0980220119534.

Coursey, D., & Norris, D. F. (2008). Models of e-government: Are they correct? An empirical assessment. *Public Administration Review, 68*(3), 523–553.

Ellison, N., & Hardey, M. (2013). Developing political conversations? *Information, Communication & Society, 16*(6), 878–889.

Farazmand, A. (2012). The future of public administration: Challenges and opportunities—a critical Perspective. *Administration & Society, 44*(4), 487–517.

Hansard Society. (2009). *MPs online: Connecting with constituents.* London: Hansard Society.

Ho, A., & Ni, A. N. (2004). Explaining the adoption of e-government features: a case study of Iowa county treasurers' offices. *American Review of Public Administration, 34*(2), 164–180.

Joseph, R. C. (2012). E-Government meets social media: Realities and risks. *IT Professional, 14*(6), 9–15.

Lee, G., & Kwak, Y. H. (2012). An open government maturity model for social media-based public engagement. *Government Information Quarterly, 29*(4), 492–503.

Meijer, A., Koops, B. J., Pieterson, W., Overman, S., & ten Tije, S. (2012). Government 2.0: Key challenges to its realization. *Electronic Journal of e-Government, 10*(1), 59–69.

Mergel, I. (2013). Social media adoption and resulting tactics in the U.S. federal government. *Government Information Quarterly, 30*(2), 123–130.

Mergel, I., & Bretschneider, S. I. (2013). A three-stage adoption process for social media use in government. *Public Administration Review, 73*(3), 390–400.

Michel, H. (2005). E-Administration, e-Government, e-Governance and the learning city: A typology of citizenship management using ICTs. *The Electronic Journal of e-Government, 3*(4), 213–218.

Musso, J., Weare, C., & Hale, M. (2000). Designing web technologies for local governance reform: Good management or good democracy? *Political Communication, 17*(1), 1–19.

Neirotti, P., De Marco, A., Cagliano, A. C., Mangano, G., & Scorrano, F. (2014). Current trends in smart city initiatives: Some stylised facts. *Cities, 38*, 25–36.

Norris, D. F., & Reddick, C. G. (2013). Local e-government in the United States: Transformation or incremental change? *Public Administration Review, 73*(1), 165–175.

Paek, H. J., Hove, T., Jung, Y., & Cole, R. T. (2013). Engagement across three social media platforms: An exploratory study of a cause-related PR campaign. *Public Relations Review, 39*, 526–533.

Pew Internet Research Center. (2013b). Social media update 2013. Retrieved from http://www.pewinternet.org

Pew Internet Research Centre. (2013a). The demographics of social media users—2012. Retrieved February 2, 2013, from http://www.pewinternet.org/~/media//Files/Reports/2013/PIP_SocialMediaUsers.pdf

Purser, K. (2012). *Using social media in local government: 2011 Survey report*. Sydney, NSW, Australia: University of Technology, Australian Centre of Excellence for Local Government.

Rogers, E. M. (1983). *Diffusion of innovations*. New York: Free Press.

Royo, S., Yetano, A., & Acerete, B. (2014). E-participation and environmental protection: Are local governments really committed? *Public Administration Revie, 74*(1), 87–98.

Schellong, A., & Girrger, P. (2010). *Government 2.0 in betaphase a analysis of eParticipation and web 2.0 applications of Germany's 50 largest cities and 16 federal states (Policy Paper Series)*. Wiesbaden: CSC.

Snead, J. T. (2013). Social media use in the U.S. executive branch. *Government Information Quarterly, 30*(1), 56–63.

The Economist. (2011). *Latitude*. Retrieved March 22, 2013, from http://www.economist.com/blogs/dailychart/2011/11/euro-zone-economies

The European Institute. (2012). Europe's North South divide—A stubborn chasm. Retrieved March 22, 2013, from http://www.europeaninstitute.org/EA-August-2012/europes-north-south-dividea-stubborn-chasm.html

Thomas, J. C., & Streib, G. (2005). E-Democracy, e-commerce, and e-research: Examining the electronic ties between citizens and governments. *Administration & Society, 37*(3), 259–280.

Tolbert, C. J., & Mossberger, K. (2006). The effects of e-government on trust and confidence in government. *Public Administration Review, 66*(3), 354–369.

Torres, L., Pina, V., & Acerete, B. (2006). E-Governance developments in European Union cities: Reshaping government's relationship with citizens. *Governance: An International Journal of Policy and Administration, 19*(2), 277–302.

Wright, S. (2009). Political blogs, representation and the public sphere. *Aslib Proceedings, 61*(2), 155–169.

Yetano, A., Royo, S., & Acerete, B. (2010). What is driving the increasing presence of citizen participation initiatives? *Environment and Planning C: Government and Policy, 28*(5), 783–802.

Zavattaro, S. M. (2013). Social media in public administration's future: A response to Farazmand. *Administration & Society, 45*(2), 242–255.

Chapter 5
Social Media and Local Government in Canada: An Examination of Presence and Purpose

Anatoliy Gruzd and Jeffrey Roy

Abstract The objective of this chapter is to undertake a critical examination of social media usage by local or municipal governments in Canada in terms of both presence and purpose. By presence, we mean the existence of social media channels linking municipal actors (administrative and political) to their local citizenry. By purpose, we mean the objectives sought by municipal actors in leveraging social media as either an informational and communications tool on the one hand, or as a platform for consultation and engagement on the other hand, or some combination of both. Based upon a wider review of social media government practices in Canada and a specific examination of four municipalities, we, therefore, seek to respond to the following key questions: (1) to what extent are local and predominantly urban governments in Canada making use of social media; (2) what is the balance between providing information and communications vs. seeking more interactive and collaborative forms of public engagement (and how is this balance reflected in both municipal intent and actual public participation); (3) what is the balance between administrative and political actors in social media deployment and public participation; and (4) what are the most significant and identifiable opportunities and challenges for municipalities in both widening and improving public engagement capacities through social media?

A. Gruzd
Ted Rogers School of Management, Ryerson University,
350 Victoria Street, Toronto, ON, Canada M5B 2K3
e-mail: gruzd@ryerson.ca

J. Roy (✉)
School of Public Administration, Dalhousie University, Rowe Building,
3rd floor, 6100 University Avenue, Halifax, NS, Canada
e-mail: roy@dal.ca

M.Z. Sobaci (ed.), *Social Media and Local Governments*, Public Administration and Information Technology 15, DOI 10.1007/978-3-319-17722-9_5

5.1 Introduction

A convergence of social media, mobility, big data, and cloud computing are four dimensions of a digital transformation of the state that has termed as Gov 2.0 (Gartner 2012). With some estimates suggesting that nearly five billion people worldwide now have access to social media, resulting in one and a half billion content pieces being created hourly, this growing wave is one that governments at all levels cannot ignore (Rees 2013). Nonetheless, any such transformation also fosters significant tension between traditional government structures and representational democracy on the one hand, and new and more participative forms of governance both administratively and politically on the other hand (Lips 2012; Harrison et al. 2012; Roy 2013).

One conceptualization of the latter is an escalation of both opportunity and complexity across four stages that culminate in the realization of "ubiquitous engagement" (Lee and Kwak 2011). While most all governments are experimenting with reforms associated with the first and second of these stages (data transparency and improved participation), the most significant potential of Gov 2.0 lies in the latter stages (three and four) and an emphasis on collaborative governance mechanisms and genuine public engagement. Indeed, there is growing evidence that governments at all levels in most all parts of the world are committed to the trajectory and principles of Gov 2.0 despite the complexities in doing so (World Economic Forum 2011; Mergel and Greeves 2013; Roy 2014).

Within such contest, the objective of this chapter is to undertake a critical examination of social media usage by local or municipal governments in Canada in terms of both presence and purpose. By presence, we mean the existence of social media channels linking municipal actors (administrative and political) to their local citizenry. By purpose, we mean the objectives sought by municipal actors in leveraging social media as either an informational and communications tool on the one hand, or as a platform for consultation and engagement on the other hand, or some combination of both.

The limited scholarly research undertaken in Canada within the realm of social media usage suggests that (1) many local governments rival their provincial and federal counterparts in terms of social media deployment and usage, particularly for engagement-oriented pursuits; (2) local governments nonetheless remain in a largely exploratory mode in doing so, often viewing social media as an extension of their communications apparatus more so than a novel vehicle for more direct forms of engagement within municipal governance systems either administratively or politically (Roy 2013; Riarh and Roy 2014). Rather than assess or evaluate early municipal efforts in this regard, the aim of this chapter is twofold: first, to build on these previous works—and related undertakings in like-minded democratic countries, and better understand the patterns of social media usage by local governments in Canada; and secondly, to identify some of the main opportunities and challenges for municipalities in forging innovative, genuine, and ultimately effective mechanisms for online engagement via social media.

5.2 Literature Review: Gov 2.0, Participative Governance and Social Media

At the heart of Gov 2.0 are notions of collective intelligence stemming from more open, flexible, and collaborative forms of governance associated with the Internet as a platform for not only communicating but also generating content and engaging with one another (Shirky 2008; Maier-Rabler and Huber 2011; Roy 2013). Governments are seeking to respond in kind (World Economic Forum 2011; Lips 2012; Reddick and Aikins 2012; Gruzd and Roy 2014). The Australian State of Victoria, for example, has articulated a Gov 2.0 Action Plan premised on the following principles: leadership, participation, transparency, and performance. Batorski and Hadden (2010) echo the importance of such principles to a paradigm shift in leadership as an essential enabler of effective organizational change and value creation in government:

> The key difference in the era of Government 2.0 for leaders is in the need to engage with others, to convert value from the network into meaningful products and services and knowledge, and to identify practical solutions to challenges. Leaders also need the facility to operate within multiple networks. Networks of customers, partners, employees, and citizens create compelling organizational value (Batorski and Hadden 2010, p. 3).

Research of US municipalities demonstrates a widening set of experiments underway by local authorities to link social media usage with engagement-oriented purposes and objectives (Mossberger and Wu 2012). The key distinction here lies in moving beyond a traditional communications mindset and to not only seek input and feedback in a consultative manner, but also link such participation to decisions and outcomes via "good conversations":

> Of course the public should play a central role in deciding what represents value for money in public services, but the current approach is unlikely to foster any meaningful deliberation or empowerment. What we need more of is public debate, or "good conversations" between professionals and communities to avoid officials losing touch in the first place. The appropriate place to achieve this is local government because circumstances vary in different parts of the country (Viitanen 2010).

This quote thus incites a reflection as to which level of government is best placed to lead participative engagement via social media—since national level entities often have greater fiscal resources and digital visibility, whereas local authorities benefit from closer proximity to community constituents and are better able to blend online and offline processes. Indeed, emphasizing these localized advantages, Carr-West (2009) outlines a basis for proceeding with social media through localized models of experimentation and collaborative and open innovation involving four directions: freeing people to innovate; trying new ideas; embracing openness; and organically allowing good ideas to emerge that may nonetheless disrupt traditional structures and cultures (Carr-West 2009).

In Canada, as examples of bottom up experimentation with Gov 2.0 reforms, one can point to Mayor Nenshi of Calgary—a strong proponent of social media usage and a leading politician nationally in terms of his online following (the City of

Calgary is examined in more detail below). Further north within the same Province, the City of Edmonton for its pioneering efforts in open data and a community "apps" competition underpinned by a municipal infrastructure increasingly gravitating to cloud systems and mobility-inspired governance principles. Across the country's demographic heartland, the Province of Ontario, nearly one half of all municipal governments had embraced some form of social media usage by 2012 (primarily Facebook and Twitter), an increase of nearly 700 % in a mere 2 years (Timoshenko and Demers 2012).

Trends elsewhere are similar in terms of a growing appetite for social media usage by local governments. One 2011 survey of Australian local governments found just over two-thirds of all councils using social media (Facebook and Twitter are the most widely used, followed by YouTube and LinkedIn). Yet nearly 40 % of those using social media characterized themselves as being at a very early stage of development, with only 6 % self-identifying as a leader (BDO 2013). A more recent British survey found nearly 90 % of local councils making use of social media in some manner (Jellinek 2012). A separate British local government survey undertaken in 2013 revealed similarly widespread usage—as well as the cautiousness of many in doing so, with nearly all councils using social media for communication purposes but only a small minority doing so for more interactive forms of engagement (BDO 2013).

This latter distinction merits additional attention as it is central to distinguishing between presence and various purposes in deploying social media. On the one hand, social media may be viewed as a platform for pushing information, messaging, and branding (central elements of customer service in both private and public sectors alike); on the other hand, social media is invoked as a platform for social and public engagement. The following distinction underscores this duality of form and purpose between expressive and collaborative forms of social media:

- Expressive social media enables people to express themselves by sharing with others text, picture, video, and music. Facebook, MySpace, Twitter, YouTube, and Flickr are examples of this type of social media.
- Collaborative social media enables people to work together to achieve common goals. Wikis and Google Docs are examples of this type of social media (Lee and Kwak 2011, p. 9).

The traditional government service and communications mindset is more aligned with expressive social media in this regard, whereas devising strategies and platforms for genuine engagement is rarer and more complex (as underlined by evidence presented both above and below). Increasingly, conversations will occur online—and outside of the confines of traditional government websites and service processes, in particular via social media platforms. In a Web 2.0 environment, for instance, government-housed feedback surveys and response forums are unlikely to garner the sorts of insights and intelligence that exist elsewhere across a myriad of social media venues and the interactive patterns of users in terms of both expressive and collaborative types of social media activity.

Such is the emerging and more participatory context shaping interactions between governments and citizens. Accordingly, Government of Singapore has formally adopted the language of "co-creating public value" between government and its citizens (Roy 2014). Owing much to President Obama's inaugural Openness Directive introduced in 2009 that emphasized three dimensions of open government (transparency, participation, and collaboration), for example, the US federal government's usage of social media has begun to fundamentally alter the culture of the public sector and the expectations of the citizenry: "the more government agencies engage on social media, the more citizens will expect responsiveness and real-time information sharing in their future interactions with government" (Mergel 2012, p. 333). A related study of various American public sector initiatives stemming from the Obama directive further seeks a framework of escalating levels of public involvement toward what the authors define as the realization of "ubiquitous engagement", a level thus far unachieved but nonetheless consistent with the participative contours of Gov 2.0 (Lee and Kwak 2011).

5.3 Methodology: An Examination of Presence and Purpose

Our methodology builds upon the preceding literature review and seeks to both better explain the advent of Gov 2.0 and the specific impacts of social media on the public sector within such a context: in addition we have identified some recent surveys specifically examining local government usage of social media in like-minded democracies, notably Great Britain, Australia, and the USA. First, we undertook an online examination of the available offerings of social media channels across 25 of the largest local governments in Canada (the top three communities in terms of population size in each of the ten provinces with a minimum population level of 100K). Secondly, we have selected four specific locales in order to undertake a more detailed examination of social media usage and content provided by local governments during the first quarter of 2014. Thirdly and beyond these four locales (Halifax, Ottawa, Regina, and Calgary), selected as a set of comparable mid-sized Canadian cities from different regions of the country, we also draw examples from other jurisdictions in order to further illuminate the discussion. As discussed further in the conclusion, it is our hope that this largely qualitative examination of Canadian municipalities, situated within a wider comparative context, shall yield some fresh insights into the governance complexities of social media deployment, thereby setting the stage for subsequent and more targeted research efforts in the future.

In a similar vein to survey findings elsewhere, our own review of 25 of the largest local governments in Canada revealed widespread social media usage with all deploying more than one channel: in line with the Australian study referenced above, by far the most common platforms being Facebook, Twitter, and YouTube. In fact, more than three quarters of these municipalities demonstrated some presence on all three of these channels. Accordingly, one can say, as a generalized premise and point of departure for a more detailed examination of presence and purpose, that there is a nearly ubiquitous presence of local government on social media in the most populated and urbanized portions of the country.

How this presence is organized nonetheless varies significantly across jurisdictions, a likely reflection of the Australian sentiment reported above in terms of early stage experimentation and the novelty of the field. Of the four jurisdictions examined in detail (Halifax, Ottawa, Regina, and Calgary[1]), it bears noting that on their main websites or homepages, respectively, the offering of social media channels varies widely: in one case (Halifax), only Twitter is immediately evident (with live tweets on display), and in another case (Calgary) there are no social media channels linked from the main page due to the unique splash page format organized around Google search (entering social media into the search derives a link to the City's social media page). By contrast, Ottawa and Regina both offer icon-stylized links to various social media channels on their main pages. Across all four municipalities either on the home page or on separate social media pages there are links to Facebook, Twitter, and YouTube (as well as various other links to blogs and separate local organizations such as policing).

The subordination of social media to the search engine (in the case of Calgary) and more traditional website functions in the other three locales, namely informing, communications, and service transactions, suggests that social media is viewed predominantly through an expressive prism by local authorities. To be clear, each City offers opportunities for engagement (some examples provided further below), in some cases with social media elements, but the overall look and feel of website home pages and the positioning of social media links as subordinate to more traditional home page functions may limit the awareness and appeal of social media channels for local residents who, in fairness to the municipalities, are more often than not coming to the municipal site seeking information of one sort or another (we further examine the channel mix of information inquiries below).

Accordingly, municipal governments clearly feel compelled to be present on social media, no doubt in large measure due to the growing proportion of Canadians (and thus local residents) making use of such platforms. Yet the overall presentation of social media channels suggests that the purpose is to provide expressive extensions of traditional website functionality to wider audiences, rather than to fundamentally alter the online presence and ultimately behaviour of the municipality within an increasingly virtual and networked context. Such an observation, however, based purely on the presentation of social media channels, necessitates a closer examination of how social media channels are being deployed.

In terms of purpose, findings from our own review are highly consistent across jurisdictions in that local governments are primarily focused on pushing information outward to constituents—with the communication of information and events by far the most common usage of social media observed. For example, of the four jurisdictions examined in detail, only Calgary made regular usage of social media as a medium to stimulate wider public engagement by inviting feedback and

[1]The respective homepages for these municipalities are: www.halifax.ca; www.ottawa.ca; www.regina.ca; and www.calgary.ca.

viewpoints and seeking to direct the public toward local consultative initiatives of one sort or another. In the other jurisdictions, various consultative efforts provided various opportunities for involvement both offline and online, but in the latter realm they were housed and presented within traditional website home pages rather than via social media. The administrative and political contexts shaping public engagement via social media are examined further below but first we consider the service delivery apparatuses of local government and the extent to which social media has made an impact.

5.3.1 Service Delivery: Social Media as Informing

With respect to service delivery, given the rising prominence of social media within customer service models across both the public and private spheres, at first blush it is perhaps surprising to find that municipalities have thus far shied away from viewing social media as a significant driver of service innovation and cost savings (BDO 2013). Instead, in a manner not unlike indirectly promoting engagement opportunities elsewhere, social media is largely deployed as a communications vehicle for service availability and unusual updates (often arising from specific events such as weather-related emergencies) while the vast majority of service encounters continue to exist via traditional channels, namely telephony and in-person facilities.

By way of useful comparative context, a 2013 survey of British local authorities found that while nearly all used social media in some communicative capacity, just less than one-half had embraced social media as an interactive medium for responding to public inquiries (ibid.). Moreover, only about one-third of authorities expressed a belief that telephone call volumes were decreasing as a result of their social media presence, with this figure declining to one quarter for face-to-face service encounters (ibid.). Comparative figures in Canada do not exist and it bears noting that the four jurisdictions examined in detail for this study do not readily provide performance figures by service channels online in an easily accessible format. By contrast, the City of Toronto showcases its own figures which illustrate the huge proportion of service inquiries that continue to flow to city operations via the telephony channel: almost 90 % of the total contacts received by the municipality (including both service requests and general inquiries) came via the telephone.[2] This trend is perhaps not surprising given the fact that in recent years many municipal governments in Canada (including Calgary, Ottawa, and Halifax in addition to Toronto) have devised "311" integrative call centres designed to simplify service inquiries via a single number.

Although 311 also exists online, in none of the jurisdictions examined in our study is social media used to receive or formally reply to service inquiries (instead

---

[2] For detailed reporting of the City of Toronto's service inquiries via channel please see: http://www1.toronto.ca/wps/portal/contentonly?vgnextoid=108bfbfa98491410VgnVCM10000071d60f89RCRD.

service requests or comments must be registered on a webpage hosted by the municipal site). While examples are commonplace of municipal staffers responding to social media posts, such responses typically inform citizens about the avenues for seeking information or assistance via traditional online channels or options for contacting the municipality to seek resolution. In this regard, the four Canadian municipalities examined here exhibit evidence of experimentation within the first and second of three levels of social media usage for customer service—namely passiveness, selectively active, but largely falling short of genuine engagement (passive, active, and engaged being a typology adopted by the Hamilton City Council in New Zealand[3]).

A similar set of observations emerges in terms of formalized mechanisms for measuring public satisfaction in customer service—with many municipalities continuing to rely upon traditional polling survey methodologies such as Calgary's Annual Citizen Satisfaction Survey.[4] Although social media affords new opportunities for local governments to seek feedback in novel ways (so-called social listening techniques, such as Washington DC's local service report card that tracks and analyzes social media discussions pertaining to City services[5] or a like-minded effort by the London Borough of Hounslow to analyze nearly 80,000 social media conversations pertaining to the Borough, Rees 2013), there is no evidence of Canadian municipalities acting in kind.

In fairness, it must be noted that the traditional polling technique such as that of Calgary can be quite modest in terms of financial costs (estimated to be 35K by Calgary officials according to their published information online), but the wider and more strategic dimensions of social media deployment pertain to the timeliness of information gathered rather than one-off surveys, and the potential to impact the channel mix which itself drives operational costs of the municipal customer service apparatus to a significant degree (BDO 2013; Rees 2013). By contrast, at present there is every reason to believe that rather than a driver of efficiency savings, social media channels represent for most municipalities an additional cost to their customer service and technological apparatus. Until social media becomes a platform to facilitate (1) growth in the completion of general information inquiries online without the involvement of municipal staff (typically handled at present via the telephone call centre) and (2) new opportunities for learning and feedback from citizens that can, in turn, drive service innovation in terms of both design and delivery, the value proposition for social media usage in service delivery will remain extremely limited.

---

[3] For additional details pertaining to this particular local framework please see: http://www.algim.org.nz/Documents/Symposium%20CS/2013%20CS%20Symposium/Speaker%20Presentations/Jason%20Dawson%20Hamilton%20CC.pdf.

[4] For more details on the survey and its findings please see: http://www.calgary.ca/CS/CSC/Documents/2013%20Citizen%20Satisfaction%20Survey%20Backgrounder.pdf.

[5] Source: http://grade.dc.gov/.

5.3.2 *Political vs. Administrative Usage and How They Are Linked*

At the local level, in Canada or elsewhere, there exists little research as to the prevalence of social media channels and their usage across administrative vs. political entities: by the former, we mean specific municipal organizations such as departments and agencies, whereas the latter refers to elected officials seeking avenues to better connect to their constituents (for either communication or engagement purposes). In a rare effort to distinguish between political and administrative usage of social media by local government authorities, a British study undertaken by The Guardian newspaper of 32 councils in the West Midlands region found that overall "elected members are far more ready to use social media than senior officers, with 85 % of councils having social media-connected councillors compared to just 32.5 % having a senior officer using a networking site like Twitter" (Britton 2013). Both the willingness of elected officials to deploy social media and the nature of such deployments in terms of purpose are likely to impact the overall contours of social media usage by local governments since elected officials are ultimately accountable for how a municipality conducts itself and for providing direction to appointed officials.

In Canada the uptake of social media channels by elected officials at the local level has been highly uneven. A case in point is the City of Toronto, Canada's largest municipal unit with an elected council of 44 members (plus a Mayor). Whereas the administration itself offers a number of social media channels comparable to any major city, and at a time when the antics and controversies of the Mayor have attracted considerable attention in traditional media venues and major entertainment channels (in turn, generating, visibility and traffic on social media as well), it is notable that considerable variance exists amongst Councillors with respect to social media usage. Midway through 2014, for example, less than 6 months away from local elections slated for November of this same year, approximately one half of all elected officials did not have any social media links present on their official City of Toronto home pages. Among the one half of Councillors exhibiting some social media presence, furthermore, there exists considerable variance between those actively using such channels and those with largely stagnant accounts.

With respect to the four jurisdictions examined in detail for this chapter, the proportions of elected officials with a social media presence are as follows (the figures given are for those on Facebook and Twitter, respectively, as of April 2014): Halifax (37.5 and 68.75 %); Ottawa (43.5 and 95.6 %); Regina (10 and 80 %); and Calgary (50 and 85.7 %).

The consistently higher preponderance of Twitter usage across the four municipalities is perhaps not surprising when one considers the large number of constituents served by each elected officials in these urbanized settings, and the traditional contours of representative democracy that tend to reinforce the importance of communications and messaging as politicians seek to inform the public as to their activities and sources of value added for communities and constituencies (Roy 2013).

Viewed through such a prism, Twitter is an ideal platform for quick and regularized updates on matters and events impacting the locale and showcasing the presence of the elected official.

Although it bears noting that in the previous section, Facebook is actually categorized as an expressive form of social media (Lee and Kwak 2011), we would instead suggest that Facebook is potentially more conducive to community building and thus more participative and collaborative forms of engagement that politicians at all levels have thus far largely subsumed in favour of more traditional, outward, and communications-oriented purposes online. While the limited presence on Facebook is only one indicator of this assertion, the relative and seemingly growing enthusiasm for Twitter by comparison reinforces this viewpoint. Furthermore, recent American research reveals comparable usage rates of Facebook and Twitter amongst local governments (a sign of Twitter's growth given its relative youth as a platform), while at the same time both platforms are predominantly deployed for information and communications purposes with only a small minority exhibiting interactive forms of engagement (Graham and Johnson-Avery 2013).

The presence and enthusiasm for social media demonstrated by elected officials, and their relative penchant for communicating vs. engaging, is also likely to be one important determinant of the digital investments and sophistication of the municipality as a whole (since budgets and operations are approved by elected Councils). Nowhere is this truer than with the elected position of Mayor, the only elected official with a jurisdiction-wide mandate and corresponding degree of public visibility and political capital (the latter nonetheless tempered by a non-partisan Council structure assigning one vote to each elected member).

In Calgary, Mayor Nenshi was first elected in a manner that was viewed by many observers as a microcosm of the Obama 2008 campaign in terms of the importance of online technologies and social media to voter interest and mobilization (as Nenshi would emerge victorious his 2010 campaign in a manner that surprised many pundits given the presence of other more established candidates). Subsequently in office, Mayor Nenshi has been dubbed Canada's "social media Mayor" by at least one major news outlet, and has been a prominent proponent of leveraging digital platforms for greater transparency and citizen involvement in the governance of the City. This political impetus may explain the relatively higher levels of social media presence displayed by Calgary Councillors in comparison to other municipalities, and similarly we can see a more frequent usage of social media by appointed officials within the municipal administration to invite the public to provide feedback and become more engaged in the various engagement outlets offered both online and offline by municipal authorities.

A similar, albeit less pronounced dynamic may be occurring in Halifax where a first term Mayor (Mike Savage) was elected in 2012 (Check) in a relatively uncompetitive race (and with a high political profile from past service at the federal level) that nonetheless featured strong commitments to infuse municipal governance with digital innovations for greater transparency and citizen involvement. During Savage's first mandate, there have been efforts to develop open data and a like-minded apps competition and experiments in participatory budgeting designed to involve the public online in at least an indirect dialogue that would accompany and inform Council's deliberations and decisions. Despite this visibility and direction, Mayor Savage by midway 2014 had opted only for a Twitter account, thus far having shunned Facebook, suggesting perhaps a more traditional stance of online communications and visibility or a relative preference to encourage the public to participate in social media channels offered more directly by municipal authorities (or some combination of both logics).

Indeed, it is interesting to observe that of the four jurisdictions examined here, only two Mayors possess active Facebook accounts (Calgary and Ottawa), whereas three of the four Mayors have personal Twitter accounts (Regina being the exception where the Mayor instead provides a link to both Facebook and Twitter accounts for the City Administration). Calgary's Mayor Nenshi easily dwarfs all other Mayors in terms of Facebook likes—with approximately 85,000, a number that surpasses by a wide margin most every other elected official in the country at any level (with the exception of the Prime Minister and the federal Leader of the Liberal Party).

As noted above, it seems reasonable to postulate that the enthusiastic social media usage by Calgary's Mayor Nenshi impacts, in turn, the local administration's embracement of such channels as not only a means of communication but also a vehicle for alternative forms of online engagement with the local citizenry. For example, of the four jurisdictions examined in detail, Calgary was the only local government to provide an introductory video on social media usage by the City with some context around what it hopes to accomplish by deploying such channels (the Mayor of Halifax page, by contrast, provides a welcome video profiling the individual and the City whereas the other two Mayor of Ottawa and Regina rely on more traditional mixes of photos and text).

Calgary was also by far the most extensive user of social media channels to invite citizens to provide feedback and to participate in various civic forums—ones either hosted by the City itself online or via third parties. An example of the latter would be a link between the Mayor's Advisory Committee on Civic Engagement and a civic initiative, "Three Things for Calgary",[6] which mixes community-based actions with online promotion and dialogue to instigate public volunteerism for public interest purposes. While the impacts of this initiative appear to be modest thus far, attracting just over 1,000 likes on its Facebook page and nearly 3,000 Twitter followers, it is also indicative of how social media enables a local government to embed itself within a wider civic network of actors and conversations.

Similarly, of the four jurisdictions examined Calgary was the most aggressive user and promoter of participatory budgeting mechanisms designed to encourage the public to learn more about City finances and convey their preferences as to trade-offs and choices impacting Council's budget deliberations. While Halifax undertook a similar experiment in 2014, there was no evidence of this experiment on social media (rather it was hosted on the main City sites), a situation likely ascribable to the fact that Halifax was undertaking such a pilot for the first time

[6] Source: http://www.3thingsforcalgary.ca/.

whereas Calgary had been doing so for the past several years under Mayor Nenshi's tenure. Although these participatory budgeting experiments have thus far proven to be extremely modest in impacting Council's final budgeting exercises in Calgary and elsewhere, they suggest a growing appetite on the part of municipalities for facilitating greater transparency and at the very least, opportunities for engagement.

5.4 Discussion and Lessons Learned: Opportunities and Challenges

The evidence presented above, from Canada and elsewhere, suggests that local governments from countries across the democratic world are increasingly embracing social media channels as new elements of their digital government presence. Two significant opportunities stand out for municipalities looking ahead: first, leveraging social media as a driver of cost savings from self-service inquiries and information requests that remain largely directed to traditional government websites and—more so, telephony channels; and secondly, developing new capacities for listening and new forms of social and collective intelligence.

The first opportunity is the most mechanical in terms of updating service architectures and strategies in response to the widening embracement of social media channels and mobile devices that are fundamentally altering the preferences for how growing segments of the population interact with their governments. In Canada, moreover, there is much evidence from provincial and federal governments of insufficient efforts by service agents to incentivize online channels and lessen the burden on more traditional ones, namely in person facilities and telephony options (Auditor General of Canada 2013; Auditor General of Ontario 2013; Kernaghan 2013). Indeed, as we have seen above, the telephone remains by far the preferred channel for the highest proportion of the public—and it is here over the past decade where municipalities have arguably been most strategic and aggressive in integrating call centre operations and simplifying usage of this channel accordingly.

Going forward, many of the inquiries made of municipal resources via telephone can instead by responded to via self-service inquiries online—a process that can be more aggressively encouraged on social media, and one that can also be aided by citizens themselves through peer-to-peer networking and conversational ties about their encounters and engagements with local governments. One examination of the impacts on social media, for example, points to such forums as early warning systems of service system failures—as social media provides and outlet and a voice form outside of the public sector confines (Leavey 2013).

Fully maximizing the potential from this first opportunity depends on the second, namely devising capacities for "social intelligence" that realize not only cost savings from channel management but also greater and more enriched forms of public value by extracting feedback and learning from social media that can, in turn, improve the workings of municipal governance either in terms of service delivery or policy formulation. Examples previously noted above include the London Borough of Hounslow social listening exercise and the Washington DC service report card that seeks online feedback outwardly via social media channels.

With the growing number of low cost options and tools to track social media traffic this frontier denotes a crucial and growing source of learning for municipalities. It also requires a strategic and cultural reorientation of public engagement efforts that have traditionally sought to invite citizens and stakeholders to send input into government-housed channels and venues (either online or via other outlets). Social intelligence, in turn, is premised about a more outward and networked presence by municipal authorities, one akin to the third level of social media usage (engagement) presented by New Zealand's Hamilton City Council, and one also akin to Lee and Kwak's realization of "ubiquitous engagement" referenced earlier on in this chapter.

One of the most significant hurdles in leveraging social media's transformational potential is the engrained mindset of local governments to view digital channels through a primarily communicative and expressive lens rather than one more interactive and participatory. Such resistance is not exclusive to local government but rather typical of the public sector more widely (Borins et al. 2007; Bermonte 2011; Lips 2012; Roy 2013; Clarke 2013). In our own review above, we see much evidence of social media deployments for communicative purposes and far fewer examples of genuine experimentations for public engagement via social media, and indeed a very primitive exploration of social media frontiers in proactive rather than responsive manners.

Political leadership matters here, as underscored by Calgary's Mayor Nenshi and Halifax's Mayor Savage. Moreover, a growing cadre of younger elected officials (and candidates) well-versed in social media realities can potentially lead to an expansion of municipal interest and openness in exploring more participatory governance practices.[7] At the same time, however, many City Councils (as per the case of Toronto noted above) feature many long-time representatives well established in their local constituent boundaries (often termed as wards in the Canadian system): for many of these candidates, social media can also denote mainly an extension of their visibility and informing capacity that can contribute to their likelihood of re-election (as such candidates need merely to mobilize a majority of their local electorate likely to vote, typically one third of their local constituency although this figure can vary considerably across large and small jurisdictions).

The same countervailing pressures can exist administratively, where it has been shown that more experienced and thus aging senior managers are, on the whole, more resistance to 2.0-stylized work practices than younger workers (Bermonte 2011).

[7]There is no comprehensive data source publicly available on municipal elected officials in Canada. However, we do see the average age of a Canadian Mayor trending downward in recent years (Mayor Nenshi is 42 years of age whereas his Edmonton counterpart is just 34; see the Wikipedia page reference for a listing of the youngest Mayors across the country): http://en.wikipedia.org/wiki/List_of_the_youngest_mayors_in_Canada.

In Canada at least, this risk is accentuated by the limited fiscal capacity of local governments relative to provinces and the federal government, and the propensity of these latter, senior-order governments to invest first and foremost into their own digital infrastructures rather than bolstering those of their municipal subordinates (as local governments in Canada formally fall under the domain of provincial authority, and many provinces are struggling with tighter fiscal restraint than is the case for the federal government).

5.5 Conclusion

The preceding evidence and analysis suggests growing enthusiasm for local government usage of social media on the one hand and a stronger emphasis on communication and information provision vs. interactive forms of public engagement on the other hand. Such a characterization may well stem partly from the infantile stages of social media deployments at which governments (and most all organizations) find themselves at present. Yet it also stems from the traditional contours of representational democracy and administrative hierarchy historically more suited to viewing social media through a communicative prism. Beyond merely the technological platforms, embracing new forms of participatory processes premised on engagement is a complex social, organizational, managerial, and political undertaking (Lee and Kwak 2011). At a minimum, both administratively and democratically, local governments need to invest financial and discursive resources into social media strategies that account for the sorts of opportunities and challenges sketched out above.

In line with the participatory logic of social media and Gov 2.0 more widely, there is also an imperative to devise ways to formulate such strategies in an open manner—infusing them with public input and involvement that can lead to a shared sense of ownership and accountability. In doing so, delineating between administrative and political roles with respect to online channels and social media functionality and usage is also essential, while also acknowledging and addressing the unavoidable fluidity that exists in a networked paradigm of democratic governance within which the boundaries between public managers, elected officials, and citizens are becoming more porous and complex (Roy 2013). From a research perspective, better understanding of these boundaries and how they are managed represent fertile terrain for additional research. For instance, who manages the social media apparatuses for municipal governments, how do such individuals navigate both administrative and political dimensions to online activity, and what are the implications for the resulting emphasis on communications vs. engagement in terms of objectives and outcomes?

Also from a research perspective, we intend to undertake a more sophisticated mapping and analysis of social media networks encompassing municipal actors—in order to attempt to measure the relative influence of social media contributions such as Tweets and Facebook posts, as well as potentially other social media channels embraced by local governments. In line with some of our argumentation put forth above, it is also worthwhile to consider whether and how different social media platforms—particularly Facebook vs. Twitter—may shape the form and objectives of social media usage along a communicative vs. engagement continuum going forward. Additionally, analyzing social media presence and usage of all elected officials vs. Mayors can yield insights into whether and how social media is altering the balance of power and influence of both sets of actors in terms of the service and policy priorities of the municipality, as well as the extent to which one can link the digital literacy of elected officials with the overall digital sophistication and performance of the municipality. Lastly, devising comparative methodologies to examine social media presence and usage across various government levels within a country is an important area to investigate in order to ascertain whether local governments are destined to emerge as vessels of innovation and reform in terms of social media and Gov 2.0 initiatives, or instead whether they risk being overshadowed by the actions and resources of more senior-order governments also embracing social media for their own purposes (and how such competitive and/or collaborative intergovernmental dynamics shape the evolution of the public sector as a whole).

References

Auditor General of Canada. (2013). *Access to online services (chapter two)*. Ottawa, ON, Canada: Office of the Auditor General. Retrieved from http://www.oag-bvg.gc.ca/internet/English/parl_oag_201311_02_e_38796.html

Auditor General of Ontario. (2013). *Service Ontario (chapter three)*. Ottawa, ON, Canada: Office of the Auditor General. Retrieved from http://www.auditor.on.ca/en/reports_en/en13/2013ar_en_web.pdf

Batorski, M., & Hadden, D. (2010). *Embracing government 2.0: Leading transformative change in the public sector*. Alexandria, VA: Grant Thornton.

BDO. (2013). *Local councils embrace social media but are yet to fully see full financial benefit*. BDO United Kingdom. Retrieved from http://www.bdo.co.uk/sectors/public-sector/local-government/our-research/social-media-within-local-authorities

Bermonte, A. (2011). Senior leaders' use of web 2.0 and social media in the Ontario public service. *Theses and dissertations*. Toronto, ON, Canada: Ryerson University. Retrieved from http://digitalcommons.ryerson.ca/dissertations/680

Borins, S., Kernaghan, K., Brown, D., 6, P., & Thompson, F. (2007). *Digital state at the leading edge*. Toronto, ON, Canada: University of Toronto Press

Britton, J. (2013). *Councils reach out through social media but lack guidelines on how to use it. The guardian (online)*. Retrieved from http://www.theguardian.com/local-government-network/2013/jul/26/councils-trust-training-social-media-use

Carr-West, J. (2009). From e-democracy to 'here comes everybody' a short history of government and the internet. In A. Sawford (Ed.), *Local Government 3.0: How councils can respond to the New Web Agenda* (pp. 4–9). London: Local Government Information Unit.

Clarke, A. (2013). Exploiting the web as a tool of democracy: New ways forward in the study and practice of digital democracy. In *World forum for Democracy 2013 issues paper.* Strasbourg, England: Council of Europe. Retrieved from http://www.coe.int/t/dg4/cultureheritage/news/wfd/study_en.pdf

Gartner. (2012). *The nexus of forces*. Retrieved from https://www.gartner.com/doc/2049315

Graham, M., & Johnson-Avery, E. (2013). Government public relations and social media: an analysis of the perceptions and trends of social media use at the local government level. *Public Relations Journal, 7*(4), 1–21.
Gruzd, A., & Roy, J. (2014). Investigating political polarization on Twitter: A Canadian perspective. *Policy and Internet, 6*(1), 28–45.
Harrison, T. M., Guerrero, S., Burke, B. G., Cook, M., Cresswell, A., Helbig, N., Hrdinova, J., & Pardo, T. (2012). Open government and e-government: Democratic challenges from a public value perspective. *Information Polity, 17*(2), 83–97.
Jellinek, D. (2012). *Nine in ten councils embrace social media*. E-Government Bulletin. Retrieved from http://www.headstar.com/egblive/?p=1118
Kernaghan, K. (2013). Changing channels: Managing channel integration and migration in public organizations. *Canadian Public Administration, 56*(1), 121–141.
Leavey, J. (2013). *Social media and public policy: What is the evidence? Alliance for useful evidence*. Retrieved from http://www.alliance4usefulevidence.org/assets/Social-Media-and-Public-Policy.pdf
Lee, G., & Kwak, Y. (2011). *An open government implementation model: Moving to increased public engagement*. Washington, DC: IBM Center for The Business of Government.
Lips, M. (2012). E-government is dead: Long live public administration 2.0. *Information Polity, 17*(3–4), 239–250.
Maier-Rabler, U., & Huber, S. (2011). "Open": the changing relation between citizens, public administration, and political authority. *JeDEM: Journal of Democracy, 3*(2), 182–191.
Mergel, I. (2012). The social media innovation challenge in the public sector. *Information Polity., 17*(3–4), 281–292.
Mergel, I., & Greeves, B. (2013). *Social media in the public sector field guide*. San Francisco: Jossey-Bass.
Mossberger, K., & Wu, Y. (2012). *Civic engagement and local e-government: Social networking comes of age*. Chicago, IL: UIC Institute for Policy and Civic Engagement.
Reddick, C. G., & Aikins, S. K. (Eds.). (2012). *Web 2.0 Technologies and democratic governance: political, policy and management implications*. New York: Springer.
Rees, D. (2013). *Social Intelligence: realising the value of social media in local government. Local government Chronicle*. Retrieved from http://www.lgcplus.com/briefings/social-intelligence-realising-the-value-of-social-media-in-local-government/5063277.article
Roy, J. (2013). *From machinery to mobility: Government and democracy in a participative age*. New York: Springer.
Roy, J. (2014). *Mobility and government: Opportunities and challenges for service delivery and information management*. Toronto, ON, Canada: Institute for Citizen-Centred Service.
Riarh, K. & Roy, J. (2014). *The impacts of social media on government and democracy: An examination of municipal Usage in nova scotia, canada*. Public Administration and Information Technology, Open Government 4:85–99.
Shirky, C. (2008). *Here comes everybody: The power of organizing without organizations*. New York: Penguin Group.
Timoshenko, L., & Demers, J. (2012). *Social media use among Ontario municipalities is growing fast*. Toronto, ON, Canada: Redbrick Communications, Inc.
Viitanen, J. (2010). *Does transparency erode trust?* Retrieved from http://www.theguardian.com/commentisfree/2010/oct/03/transparency-trust-public-sector
World Economic Forum. (2011). *The future of government: Lessons learned from around the world*. Geneva, Switzerland: World Economic Forum's Global Agenda Council on the Future of Government.

Chapter 6
Social Media in Local Governments in Mexico: A Diffusion Innovation Trend and Lessons

Rodrigo Sandoval-Almazán and David Valle-Cruz

Abstract Academic research about how local governments use social media platforms are scarce. Most of the research is focused on services, comparative perspectives, or assessment. Little is known about the impact of Twitter and Facebook on communication means or strategic use for promoting a conversation with citizens. Despite these facts, the majority of local governments implement social media into their web sites and communications without any strategy or knowledge about their advantages or perils. Also scholars are blind-folded of what kind of research has to be done on social media and governments to understand this phenomenon and capitalize its use on public service. The purpose of this chapter is to identify new trends and lessons on social media use in local governments. Analyzing a data collection of Twitter and Facebook from the 32 Mexican local governments from 2010 to 2014, we discovered a behavior pattern very similar to the diffusion and innovation theory proposed by Rogers (Diffusion of innovations. Simon and Schuster, New York, 1995). We analyzed our data from this focus and provide five lessons to understand local governments' use of social media.

6.1 Introduction

The current trend of web 2.0 in public administration has reached local governments. The main interaction of citizens with governments is having a transformation: from the use of online formats, forums, chats, and virtual assistants into a more direct relationship using posts on Facebook or tweets over the Twitter platform to communicate with government officials (Sandoval-Almazán and Gil-García 2012).

R. Sandoval-Almazán (✉)
Political Sciences Faculty, Universidad Autónoma del Estado de México
(Autonomous University of the State of Mexico), Toluca de Lerdo, Mexico
e-mail: rsandovala@uaemex.mx

D. Valle-Cruz
Accounting and Management Faculty, Universidad Autonóma del Estado de México
(Autonomous University of the State of Mexico), Toluca de Lerdo, Mexico
e-mail: davacr@uaemex.mx

M.Z. Sobaci (ed.), *Social Media and Local Governments*, Public Administration and Information Technology 15, DOI 10.1007/978-3-319-17722-9_6

However, most of the local governments are using social media platforms without any knowledge or strategy to foster communication and conversation with citizens over their networks (Sandoval-Almazán et al. 2011). Backtalk is more related to neutralizing bad comments, diminishing claims or concerns, and reacting to bad publicity for the ruling political party (Askanius and Uldam 2011; Effing et al. 2013).

Some government portals use web 2.0 tools to promote health services, traffic warnings, or to increase tax collection (Götsch and Grubmüller 2013; Abdelsalam et al. 2013). Very few of them are using these tools to make the portal the center of the government interaction that becomes citizen-driven (Sandoval-Almazán and Gil-García 2012).

Very little research has been done on the impact of social media on local governments (Sandoval-Almazán et al. 2011; Sandoval-Almazán and Gil-García 2011). However, most of the research is related to the organizational impact or the normative challenges facing web 2.0 platforms on government requirements. Research topics such as government-user interaction and policy-making impact through social media have not been broadly studied.

Despite this lack of theoretical background to use social media in local governments, most of them are using the web 2.0 (Grossklags et al. 2011; Karantzeni and Gouscos 2013; Lerman 2007). Some applications of web 2.0 in developing countries are used to mediate citizen participation (Koothoor et al. 2012) as a new channel of interaction, constituting important innovations for government agencies (Ferro et al. 2013). Social Media tools are becoming a new communication channel for citizen communication (Josefsson and Ranerup 2003; Magnusson et al. 2012).

For this reason, the purpose of this chapter is to identify the main gaps on social media implementation from local governments as a starting point for future research on this field. To achieve such a goal, we used the diffusion innovation theory (Rogers 1995) in order to frame our research and to provide a systematic understanding. We collected data from government social media accounts from the 32 local governments in Mexico, from the years 2010 to 2014 that are analyzed with statistical methods to understand their impact.

This chapter is organized in five sections. The first section is an introductory section which describes the use of social media by federal and local governments. The second section is a literature review of the diffusion innovation theory, social media in governments, and local governments' innovations. The third section describes the methodology to collect and analyze data from social media used by local governments and the background of the Internet and social media use in Mexico. The fourth section presents the findings of the quantitative research. The fifth and last section discusses some of the achievements using the literature review, but provides some recommendations and guidelines for improving social media use in local governments.

6.2 Literature Review

The first step to understand the Diffusion Innovation Theory is to visualize the innovations adopted by different channels in time and inside a social particular system (Rogers 1995). Rogers argues that individuals are classified in different levels of disposition to adopt innovations. Members of each category have distinctive features: innovators, early adopters, early majority, late majority, and laggards. One of Rogers' interpretations (1995) is when the adoption curve is viewed as a cumulative percentage curve which draws an "S." This curve represents the adoption rate of innovation in a population.

Nowadays, local governments using technology need to innovate new strategies in order to encourage interaction with citizen and a better delivery of services (G2C); but the adoption of technology is gradual.

The use of technology in local governments has always been presented in different forms or levels; however, it has only been analyzed recently. Two surveys that assess the impact of technology adoption, effects, or consequences have been measured since 2001 (West and Berman 2001; Wolf et al. 2001). Ho (2002) analyzed the one-stop shopping strategy in different local governments that started using technology. Ho linked socioeconomic factors with organizational relationships.

Ho's research (2002) on local governments' impact on technology was divided later into several paths: (1) Technology: Holden et al. (2003) and Odendaal (2003) analyzed the impact of information and communication technology on emerging economies using the case of South Africa. (2) The impact of trust on local governments' technology implementation has been researched by Tolbert and Mossberger (2006). (3) The analysis of the UK implementation of ICT in local governments as a way to transformation (Panagiotopoulos et al. 2011).

On the other hand, implementation of online services in local governments started with the research of Hoogwout (2002) and Asgarkhani (2005) and the idea of introducing enterprise services in governments was developed by Shackleton et al. (2006). Also the Italian service delivery developed by Italian governments is an interesting contribution for this area (Nasi 2009; Nasi et al. 2011). An important contribution of online service delivery at local level was developed by Veenstra and Zuurmond (2009) who found that an externally oriented management strategy in place, adopting enterprise architecture, aligning information systems to business, and sharing activities between processes and departments, is positively related to the quality of online service delivery. Candiello et al. (2012) introduced the monitoring of services regarding quality and impact. More scholars have done research on the e-services perspective: Attoura and Longhi (2009), Mahadeo (2009), and Tudor et al. (2009).

An important contribution to understand local governments' use of technology comes from the research of Norris and his team in 2004. It was the first attempt to understand the use of technology in America. The next survey used previous results from Holden et al. (2003) and Moon and Norris (2005) along with focus groups on municipal web sites in order to understand the impact on e-government. The next step of this longitudinal study was made in 2005 by Moon and Norris (2005), in which they found that e-government adoption at the grassroots is progressing rapidly (if measured solely by deployment of web sites). However, the movement toward integrated and transactional e-government is progressing much more slowly (Norris and Moon 2005). A complementary research on this study was held by Scavo (2007) who complemented previous surveys from Norris on the U.S. The most recent paper of this longitudinal study found that e-governments have not produced the results they predicted (Norris and Reddick 2013).

A pioneer work using collaboration technology and e-commerce related to local governments was made by Reddick (2005), who surveyed the Texas County finding an improved customer service, but also a barrier for transactions.

Another area of research is to understand how local governments transform into e-governments, developing capabilities or solving problems. A pioneer research was made by Streib and Willoughby (2005), in which they found out some hurdles and advantages for e-government implementation. Another research was performed by Torres et al. (2005), analyzing 47 regional and local governments. A complementary path was developed by Cotterill and King (2007), who introduced the concept of partnership in public sectors and the idea of the social network study.

More research has been done about the description and use of technology by local governments. The study of Wohlers (2007) analyzes sophistication and trends at local level. He found that local e-government sophistication increases for municipalities governed by professional managers, endowed with more organizational resources, characterized by higher socioeconomic levels, and increasing the number of users.

Nevertheless, the assessment perspective of local e-government has been scarce in the early years of e-government implementation in local governments; much research has been done since 2010. Research from Sandoval-Almazán and Gil-García (2010) evaluates more than 100 municipalities in Mexico in order to understand their lacks and problems. A similar research has been performed by Andersen et al. (2011) in New Zealand and Australia. A complementary perspective related to assessment was developed by Ahn (2011) who used several sources and statistical methods to understand different viewpoints of the municipal perspective of the U.S.

With this same assessment perspective, the seminal work from Luna-Reyes et al. (2011) focuses on developed groups in several Mexican municipalities, which allows researchers to understand the way Mexican users interact with their government. Sandoval-Almazán et al. (2011) complement this research assessing local government portals in Mexico. He found a strong relationship between the development of web sites and citizens' interactions.

There are at least three different streams of research in the assessing of government web sites: e-citizen; web site development; and web 2.0. The first stream has been studied by different scholars such as Manoharan and Carrizales (2011); the e-citizens perspective by Sandoval-Almazán and Gil-García (2012) and finally assessment of the use of the web 2.0 on local e-government web sites by Almazán et al. Another related research reveals four patterns of social media use by local governments such as: "social media for dissemination, social media for feedback on service quality, social media for participation and social media for internal work collaboration" (Oliveira and Welch 2013, p. 397).

From the comparative perspective, we can find studies that compare the local e-government from the U.S. and Germany (Wohlers 2009). Royo et al. (2011) compares the German and Spanish local government using the citizen perspective as a comparison framework. Other comparisons are the administrative discretion analysis in Egypt (Reddick et al. 2011) and the Norwegian study of digital divide and local government geographical challenges (Sorensen and Munoz 2011).

Some ideas rise from this literature review about local e-government. For example, most research focuses on describing infrastructure, but less in understanding the organizational impact. There is important quantitative research—descriptions, surveys—about assessing technologies, software, and applications. Also there is a strong association between local and municipal governments. For some scholars, the limits between these two different levels of government are very narrow or inexistent. Finally, some research is oriented to the new trend of smart cities.

This literature review reveals the scarce amount of research on social media in municipalities. The lack of studies is the main argument for introducing a qualitative data collection, which is complemented with a quantitative analysis retrieved from 4 consecutive years of social media data. The purpose of this mixed research is to provide new insights and encourages further research for this topic.

There are four studies, which are very similar to this one. The first one is from Bonsón et al. (2012) who researched on Spanish municipalities getting to the conclusion that the social media use is still on its "infancy." In the second study from Hofmann et al. (2013), a multi-method analysis was used to examine 15,941 posts and 19,290 comments on Facebook pages in 25 of the largest German cities. They described the use of Social Network Sites (SNS) and how they promote communication between governments and citizens. Another research analyzed the use of Twitter in Turkey. Other scholars' findings revealed that this platform is used mostly for self-promotion and political marketing (Sobaci and Karkin 2013). Finally, there is the research from Mossberger et al. (2013), who examined the use of social networks in 75 of the largest U.S. cities between 2009 and 2011. During this period, they found that the adoption of Facebook skyrocketed from just 13 % of the cities in 2009 to nearly 87 % in 2011, and similarly, the use of Twitter increased from 25 to 87 %.

In Mexico, the use of social media started in 2010. More and more governments have been adopting this technology to interact with citizens (Sandoval-Almazán and Gil-García 2012). Research from Sandoval and Gil García (2013) analyzed Twitter and Facebook accounts of local governments in Mexico from 2010 to 2012 and presented a content analysis of two cases—Sinaloa and Yucatán—stating the emerging condition of social media implementation in local governments. These two studies are the direct antecedent of this study, which includes a statistical analysis and the theoretical perspective of the Diffusion Innovation Model.

6.3 Methodology

Internet research, especially regarding social media, is difficult because of the characteristics of this technological phenomenon: rapid evolution of the platforms, changing capacity, and constant innovation on software and hardware. However, the use of the traditional method (Creswell 2009) will help to understand the limitations and paradigms of e-research (Estalella and Ardevol 2011). This research is part of the longitudinal study of social media data in Mexico for which we collected data from different levels of governments since 2010. This research has three main stages:

1. Validation of social media platforms.
2. Data collection on specific periods of time.
3. Data analysis using different statistical methods.

At the first stage, we monitored Twitter and Facebook local governments' accounts from a universe of 32 local web sites. For the second stage, we have been collecting data during March, June, and October of each year since 2010. For the purpose of this chapter, we also collected data during August 2014. Data collected from Twitter are tweets, lists, number of followers, and number of following. Data from Facebook is only the number of likes received. These variables allow us to find the increased use of social media in each local government. No data were collected on June 2012, but it was possible to collect in June 2013. However, this does not affect the behavior of the data collected or the study.

For the third stage, we run a descriptive and a correlational analysis. The descriptive analysis was useful to explain the behavior of the adoption of the social media by citizens in each local government and we also ran a correlational analysis to find a relation between social media variables that could explain the citizens' behavior.

For the fourth stage, we transformed average data to a normal form for each period to homogenize the units of each variable trying to find singular data behaviors based on the use of technology and its ad option by citizens. Followers are sufficient to understand the increase of users (citizens) of Twitter and "likes" is only studied in order to understand the Facebook user trend.

Finally, we made a regression of the normalized data using a polynomial trend line fourth grade to interpolate all data trying to draw a constant soft curve. This data was compared and analyzed. We found that users' behavior is similar to the one shown by the Diffusion of Innovations Theory (Rogers 1995).

6.4 Findings and Discussion

6.4.1 Findings

The general user behavior of the sample is shown in Fig. 6.1. The most notable increase can be seen in followers, likes and tweets. Generalizing this trend, we can say that government use of social media is increasing in Mexico by the time of our

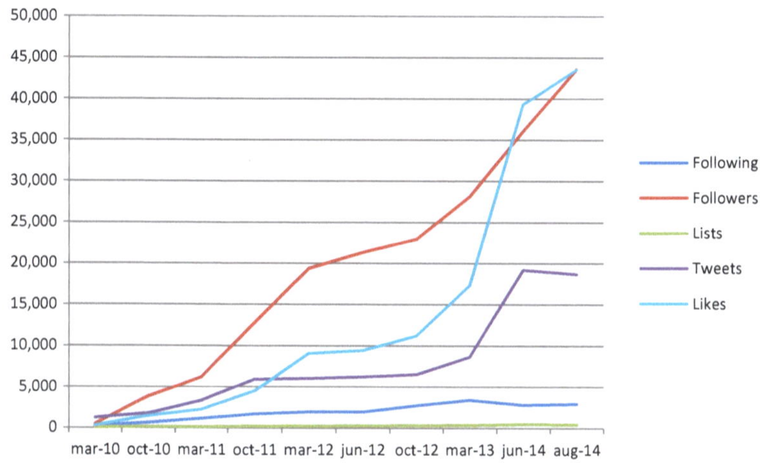

Fig. 6.1 Data collected from 2010 to 2014

study. Local governments are making efforts to use social media to provide services and communicate with users which is consistent with our literature review.

Data supports the idea that citizens and governments increased their interaction using social media tools through the consistent increase of Twitter and Facebook. The numbers of "likes" and followers reveal an increasing trend through time (see Fig. 6.1).

Figure 6.2 shows the transformed data of the normal distribution $z = \frac{x - \mu}{\sigma}$, although we don't have the population's average and standard deviation. They are estimated with the sample ones' (we have 32 cases). This is a better way to compare all the variables because they are in the same scale and distribution. A similar behavior can be seen on every variable which increased consistently, for example, the variables of lists and followers (see Fig. 6.2).

The variables of followers from Twitter and "likes" from Facebook are described on Fig. 6.3 that shows the polynomial trend line of fourth grade. This is a quantitative behavior of the data which represents an "S" curve, similar to the one described by the Diffusion of Innovations Theory (see Figs. 6.3 and 6.4).

Rogers (1995) argues that the diffusion of innovations is the process by which innovation is communicated by certain channels. The categories of adopters are: innovators, early adopters, early majority, late majority, and laggards.

According to this theory, innovators are people who are willing to take risks. Initially there were few, but by the time there is an acceptance of new technology and more people adopt more diverse technology. For the correlation test, only those important ones with a level of significance of 0.05 and 0.01 are discussed here.

A highly significant relationship between the number of followers and lists in each sampling period prevails in the correlation test (see the Appendix). This relationship can be explained due to the fact that having more followers implies the

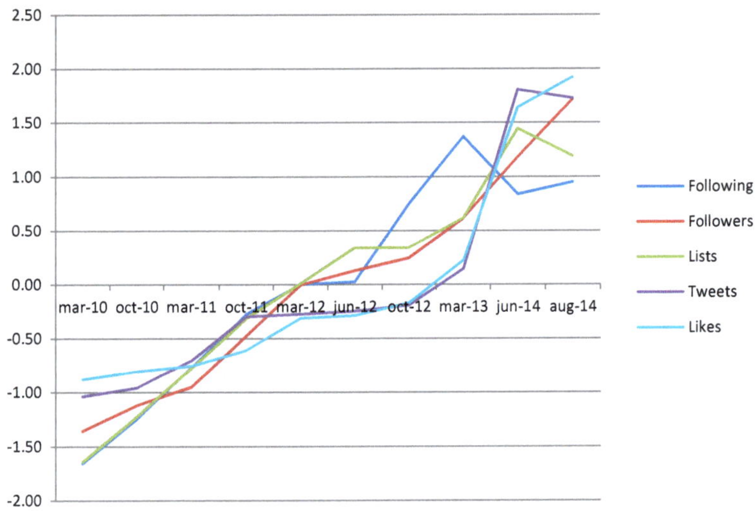

Fig. 6.2 Normalized data social media on local governments 2010–2014

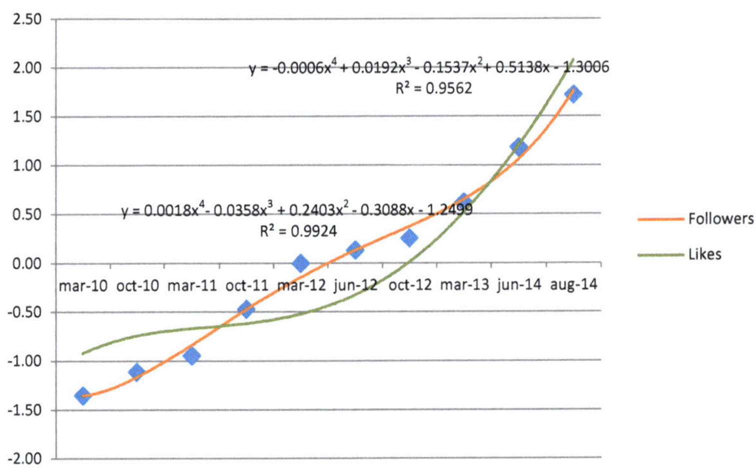

Fig. 6.3 Polynomial trend-line fourth grade

necessity of classifying them into different categories and also because the increase of lists in the local government social media tools implies more followers who will be attracted to follow that social network.

An interesting case occurred during the period of March 2010 where there was a high correlation between the number of followers and following (see Table 6.A1 in the Appendix). An explanation for this could be that a massive use of Twitter as a social network in the government started during that year.

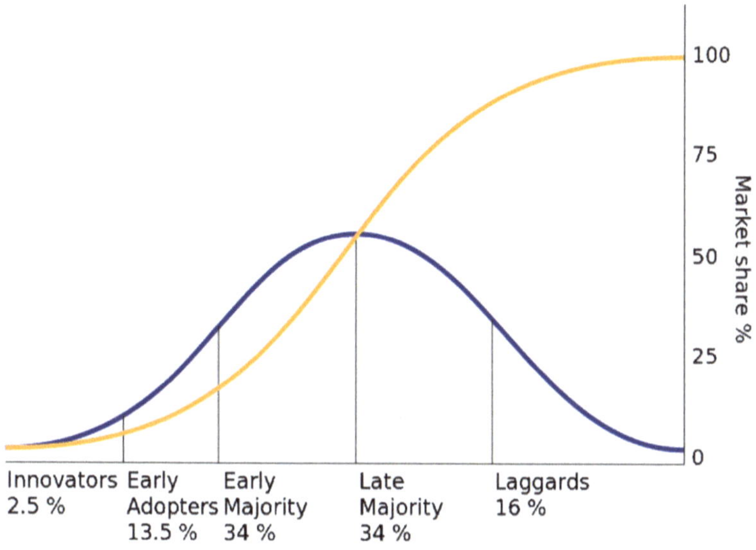

Fig. 6.4 Market share in diffusion of innovation theory (S curve)

A different case occurred in October 2010 and March 2011. There was a medium-high relationship between the "likes and following" in governments' social networks (see Tables 6.A2 and 6.A3 in the Appendix). Also, a medium relation between followers, tweets, and lists can be seen in October 2011 (see Table 6.A4 in the Appendix).

The first relation found in October 2011 is also found in March 2012 and June 2012 (see Tables 6.A4, 6.A5 and 6.A6 in the Appendix). In October 2012, March, June, and August 2014, there were no other important relationships among variables, only the ones mentioned before (see Tables 6.A7, 6.A8, 6.A9 and 6.A10 in the Appendix). An explanation for this kind of relationship among variables and their increases could be found in the diffusion of social networks among citizens and government users. Different uses for these technologies could augment their numbers.

The contribution of these findings is that the pattern followed by citizens adopting the use of technology in local governments in Mexico is very similar to the pattern of the model of diffusion of innovations. The social media behavior of local governments in Mexico is very similar to the innovators and early adopters, and nowadays, some of them can also be considered laggards.

Another finding is the increase of people adopting networking technologies which could be related to the interaction and use of social media tools and public officers. However, this possible relationship will create some difficulties if we intend to measure or forecast some data related to social media in the long term, because the level of interaction will be unknown.

In the early stages of this study, we found relations among variables because there were few and similar users. In recent periods, we can't find significant relations anymore because of the different kinds of users of social media tools used by local governments.

6.4.2 Discussion

Accordingly to our findings, we discovered five main gaps that can be used for further research in this area.

1. Lists vs. Followers.
2. Finding a relationship during 2013 and 2014 was more difficult because data became more heterogeneous.
3. There is relation cycle among more tweets—more followers—more lists. What is relevant? The number of messages—tweets—or the quality of the message?
4. The intense use of Facebook more than Twitter.
5. The Technology Diffusion Theory and the evolution of the social media implementation.

We found a relationship between the variables "lists" and "followers" in the first gap. This could be explained because of the larger number of followers who can increase the lists. However, this assumption could be wrong. The web masters of the government Twitter account will not necessarily create more lists having no direct effect in this relationship. However, these kinds of assumptions lead us to think up some more questions for further research: Will the content analysis from tweets change the relationship between followers and lists? Is the increase of users related to the quality of tweets or to any other contextual factors?

The second gap is related to a more complex issue: users' diversity. Users became so diverse during 2013 and 2014 that we could not group them on a similar path. This also means an important increase in the number of users of all local government accounts. With that amount of users' characteristics, it seems impossible to try to analyze them with a single method or strategy. This problem unfolds new kinds of research possibilities for the understanding of users of social media in local governments. Following the Rogers Diffusion Theory: Is an early adopter user still using social media in local government? How to interact, to send messages or to produce engagement with different types of users? Is it still valid to consider Twitter as a single communication channel or has it become a complex relations network for governments?

The third gap is related to the modeling of the use of social media in government communication. We found evidence that supports this cycle (tweets-followers-lists). However, we should do some more research to validate this with other measures—municipal or national social media platforms. Furthermore, this kind of model allows us to produce other models that can be used to understand the relationship between cost, strategy, and uses of social media in governments.

The fourth gap can easily be explained. Facebook access is wider and older than Twitter. But also other factors such as mobile access, usability, type of messages, frequency of use, etc. can determine which platform could be more efficient depending on the purpose. Nowadays, the use of Twitter and Facebook occurs with the same proportion; nevertheless, we do not know which platform could be more efficient for government purposes such as engagement, information, or crises situations. This gap opens the discussion about differentiating the use of both platforms for government efficiency and a coordinated strategy for social media.

And finally, the fifth gap, the validation of the diffusion theory of social media used by local governments for citizen in Mexico is an unexpected contribution. Our graphs and analysis match with this theoretical technology adoption framework. Once our framework is validated, we should address the following questions: Which social media strategy should be considered as for laggard members? Which local government strategy has a more innovative strategy capturing early adopters' attention? Is there any strategy to move faster into another stage of the diffusion theory? Are Facebook and Twitter different strategies which could have a differentiated aspect in the diffusion theory?

6.5 Conclusions and Recommendations

The main purpose of this chapter is to introduce some new research ideas or paths to analyze social media in local governments. We found five gaps that could be used as a preliminary approach to understand the use of social media in local governments. More research—qualitative research—is needed to support some of these gaps and to solve some of the questions related to it.

Previous research on Facebook' posts found that the relationship with government officials is still weak (Hofmann et al. 2013). Other research focuses more on single studies (Sobaci and Karkin 2013). This research describes a 4-year data collection (2010–2014), which allows us to analyze, interpret, and describe these potential gaps of research.

There are important limitations for our approach. It is mostly based on quantitative data that was collected directly from the social media platforms of each local government. This data is always changing. Our data does not consider new users on Twitter and Facebook which were generated by automatic bots. This could artificially increase the data that some states show without being aware of it. More research has to be done to validate real users in each case and also it is really important to search about content analysis to discover what kind of conversation, information exchange, or collaboration is being used by government and citizens (followers) on the social media.

Another limitation is the aggregated data of the platforms—Twitter and Facebook. It would be helpful to disaggregated data in order to place local governments into a category of the theoretical framework—innovators, laggards, early adopters.

Further research on the social media use in local governments must address several concerns. For example, the problem of personal users' information privacy or other concerns when interacting with social media tools used by governments. This is an important topic to be considered. Also, the security of the government information is another aspect that must be under subject of research to avoid hackers or the misuse of important information for decision-making.

Another important aspect regarding social media use for local governments is the internal regulations that the local CIO responsible for the Twitter and Facebook account needs to have in order to know which government information has to be released and which one to be kept or handled in a different way. These regulations could change accordingly to local constitutions or open government strategies.

The strategy of engaging citizens and government information is another issue that has to be considered by the CIO of the local government who is in charge of the social media platforms. There are some improvised decisions and reactions about the use of Twitter and Facebook. There is too little research in order to understand the best practices or pitfalls on social media use for government. It could be very helpful to provide some ideas about this topic.

The last research idea is to understand the bureaucratic changes caused by the social media tool use in government organizations. Researches about changes, adapting strategies, and cost reductions are important in order to assess the indirect impact caused by Facebook and Twitter government accounts. How are stakeholders, public officials, and politicians related before disclosure of some information for citizens using these channels?

All of these concerns relate to: privacy of information, security, internal regulations, engagement strategies, and organizational changes. All of them are related to social media in local governments. Our research is embedded in the assessment and metrics concern to understand the impact of social media. One purpose of our findings is to reduce the learning curve on measuring social media and provide a different insight into the theoretical approach to this practical field.

Appendix

Table 6.A1 Correlation test for March 2010

March 2010	Following	Followers	Lists	Likes
Following	1			
Followers	.853**	1		
Lists	.800**	.991**	1	
Likes	.473**	.350*	.371*	1

**Correlation is significant at 0.01 (bilateral)
*Correlation is significant at 0.05 (bilateral)

Table 6.A2 Correlation test for October 2010

October 2010	Following	Followers	Lists	Tweets	Likes
Following	1				
Followers	.493**	1			
Lists	.451**	.792**	1		
Tweets	.402*	.505**	.499**	1	
Likes	.668**	.463**	.417*	.602**	1

**Correlation is significant at 0.01 (bilateral)
*Correlation is significant at 0.05 (bilateral)

Table 6.A3 Correlation test for March 2011

March 2011	Following	Followers	Lists	Tweets	Likes
Following	1				
Followers	.399*	1			
Lists	.322	.791**	1		
Tweets	.338	.532**	.482**	1	
Likes	.615**	.402*	.403*	.527**	1

**Correlation is significant at 0.01 (bilateral)
*Correlation is significant at 0.05 (bilateral)

Table 6.A4 Correlation test for October 2011

October 2011	Following	Followers	Lists	Tweets	Likes
Following	1				
Followers	.360*	1			
Lists	.336	.711**	1		
Tweets	.244	.523**	.531**	1	
Likes	.267	.494**	.149	.088	1

**Correlation is significant at 0.01 (bilateral)
*Correlation is significant at 0.05 (bilateral)

Table 6.A5 Correlation test for March 2012

March 2012	Following	Followers	Lists	Likes
Following	1			
Followers	.306	1		
Lists	.129	.593**	1	
Likes	.125	.275	.358*	1

**Correlation is significant at 0.01 (bilateral)
*Correlation is significant at 0.05 (bilateral)

Table 6.A6 Correlation test for June 2012

June 2012	Following	Followers	Lists	Tweets	Likes
Following	1				
Followers	.287	1			
Lists	.271	.828**	1		
Tweets	.124	.560**	.435*	1	
Likes	.126	.284	.288	.348	1

**Correlation is significant at 0.01 (bilateral)
*Correlation is significant at 0.05 (bilateral)

Table 6.A7 Correlation test for October 2012

October 2012	Following	Followers	Lists	Tweets	Likes
Following	1				
Followers	.210	1			
Lists	.198	.856**	1		
Tweets	.091	.383*	.356*	1	
Likes	.414*	.266	.322	.018	1

**Correlation is significant at 0.01 (bilateral)
*Correlation is significant at 0.05 (bilateral)

Table 6.A8 Correlation test for March 2013

March 2013	Following	Followers	Lists	Tweets	Likes
Following	1				
Followers	.127	1			
Lists	.132	.925**	1		
Tweets	.010	.319	.321	1	
Likes	.228	.306	.336	.009	1

**Correlation is significant at 0.01 (bilateral)
*Correlation is significant at 0.05 (bilateral)

Table 6.A9 Correlation test for June 2014

June 2014	Following	Followers	Lists	Tweets	Likes
Following	1				
Followers	.254	1			
Lists	.116	.865**	1		
Tweets	.023	.257	.329	1	
Likes	–.120	–.178	–.117	–.299	1

**Correlation is significant at 0.01 (bilateral)
*Correlation is significant at 0.05 (bilateral)

Table 6.A10 Correlation test for August 2014

August 2014	Following	Followers	Lists	Tweets	Likes
Following	1				
Followers	.123	1			
Lists	.152	.949**	1		
Tweets	.083	.386*	.374*	1	
Likes	−.148	−.099	−.114	−.296	1

**Correlation is significant at 0.01 (bilateral)
*Correlation is significant at 0.05 (bilateral)

References

Abdelsalam, H. M., Reddick, C. G., Gamal, S., & Al-shaar, A. (2013). Social media in Egyptian government websites: Presence, usage, and effectiveness. *Government Information Quarterly, 30*, 406–416.

Ahn, M. J. (2011). Adoption of e-communication applications in US municipalities: The role of political environment, bureaucratic structure, and the nature of applications. *The American Review of Public Administration, 41*, 428–452.

Andersen, K. N., Medaglia, R., Vatrapu, R., Zinner Henriksen, H., & Gauld, R. (2011). The forgotten promise of e-government maturity: Assessing responsiveness in the digital public sector. *Government Information Quarterly, 28*(4), 439–445.

Asgarkhani, M. (2005). The effectiveness of e-service in local government: A case study. *Electronic Journal of e-Government, 3*(4), 157–166.

Askanius, T., & Uldam, J. (2011). Online social media for radical politics: Climate change activism on YouTube. *International Journal of Electronic Governance, 4*(1/2), 69–84.

Attoura, A., & Longhi, C. (2009). *Local innovation policies in services: The role of local governments in the implementation of e-administration*. Reading, UK: Academic.

Bonsón, E., Torres, L., Royo, S., & Flores, F. (2012). Local e-government 2.0: Social media and corporate transparency in municipalities. *Government Information Quarterly, 29*, 123–132.

Candiello, A., Albarelli, A., & Cortesi, A. (2012). Quality and impact monitoring for local eGovernment services. *Transform Government: People, Process, Policy, 6*, 112–125.

Cotterill, S., & King, S. (2007). *Public sector partnerships to deliver local e-government: A social network study*. Berlin, Germany: Springer.

Creswell, J. W. (2009). *Research design qualitative, quantitative and mixed methods approaches*. Thousand Oaks, CA: Sage.

Effing, R., Hillegersberg, J. van & Huibers, T. W. C. (2013). Social media participation and local politics: A case study of the Enschede Council in the Netherlands. In M. A. Wimmer, E. Tambouris, & A. Macintosh (Eds.), *Electronic Participation: 5th IFIP WG 8.5 International Conference, ePart 2013* (pp. 57–68). Berlin, Germany: Springer.

Estalella, A., & Ardevol, E. (2011). E-research: Challenges and opportunities for social sciences. *Convergencia Revista de Ciencias Sociales, 18*, 87–111.

Ferro, E., Loukis, E., Charalabidis, Y., & Osella, M. (2013). Analyzing the centralised use of multiple social media by government from innovation diffusion theory perspective. In M. A. Wimmer, E. Tambouris, & A. Macintosh (Eds.), *Electronic Participation: 5th IFIP WG 8.5 International Conference, ePart 2013* (pp. 95–108). Berlin, Germany: Springer.

Götsch. K., & Grubmüller, V. (2013). *Web 2.0 for local policy and decision making support*. Research & Development Results from the ICT Project UniteEurope.

Grossklags, J., Appel, L., & Bridges, F. (2011). Young adults and online political participation: search strategies and the role of social media. In S. A. Chun, L. Luna-Reyes, & V. Atluri (Eds.)

Proceedings of the 12th Annual International Digital Government Research Conference (dg.o 2011) (pp. 302–306). New York: ACM.
Ho, A. T. K. (2002). Reinventing local governments and the e-government initiative. *Public Administration Review, 62*, 434–444.
Hofmann, S., Beverungen, D., Räckers, M., & Becker, J. (2013). What makes local governments' online communications successful? Insights from a multi-method analysis of Facebook. *Government Information Quarterly, 30*, 387–396.
Holden, S. H., Norris, D. F., & Fletcher, P. D. (2003). Electronic government at the local level: Progress to date and future issues. *Public Performance & Management Review, 26*(4), 325–344.
Hoogwout, M. (2002). Organizing for online service delivery: The effects of network technology on the organization of transactional service delivery in Dutch local government. In R. Traunmüller & K. Lenk (Eds). *Electronic Government* (pp. 33–36). Lecture Notes in Computer Science. Berlin, Germany: Springer. Retrieved November 08, 2014, from http://link.springer.com/chapter/10.1007/978-3-540-46138-8_5
Josefsson, U., & Ranerup, A. (2003). Consumerism revisited: The emergent roles of new electronic intermediaries between citizens and the public sector. *Information Polity: The International Journal of Government & Democracy in the Information Age, 8*(3/4), 167–180.
Karantzeni, D., & Gouscos, D. G. (2013). eParticipation in the EU: Re-focusing on social media and young citizens for reinforcing European identity. *Transforming Government: People, Process and Policy, 7*(4), 477–500.
Koothoor, P., Pichandy, C., Padmanabhan, T., Jayaseelan, R., & Munusamy, N. (2012). An empirical analysis of the diffusion, adoption and the future of ICT mediated egovernance in Kerala: The FRIENDS Project—A critical review. In *9th International Conference on E-Governance (ICEG 2012)* (pp. 226–238), Cochin, India.
Lerman, K., (2007). User participation in social media: Digg study. In *Proceeding of the 2007 IEEEWICACM International Conferences on Web Intelligence and Intelligent Agent Technology-Workshops* (pp. 255–258). Washington, DC: IEEE Computer Society.
Luna-Reyes, L. F., Gil-Garcia, J. R., & Celorio Mansi, J. A. (2011). Citizen-centric approaches to e-government and the back-office transformation. In S. A. Chun, L. Luna-Reyes, & V. Atluri (Eds.), *Proceeding of the 12th Annual International Conference of Digital Government Research Conference: Digital Government Innovation in Challenging Times (dg.o' 2011)* (pp. 213–218). New York: ACM.
Magnusson, M., Bellström, P., & Thoren, C., (2012). Facebook usage in government—A case study of information content. In *AMCIS 2012 Proceedings*. AMCIS, Seattle, WA: aisnet. Retrieved from http://aisel.aisnet.org/amcis2012/proceedings/EGovernment/11
Mahadeo, J. D. (2009). *Towards an understanding of the factors influencing the acceptance and diffusion of e-government services*. Reading, UK: Academic.
Manoharan, A., & Carrizales, T. J. (2011). Recent trends in e-government: States' and local governments' utilisation of websites. *International Journal of Electronic Governance, 4*, 283–303.
Moon, M. J., & Norris, D. F. (2005). Does managerial orientation matter? The adoption of reinventing government and e-government at the municipal level. *Information Systems Journal, 15*, 43–60.
Mossberger, K., Wu, Y., & Crawford, J. (2013). Connecting citizens and local governments? Social media and interactivity in major U.S. cities. *Government Information Quarterly, 30*, 351–358.
Nasi, G. (2009). E-government and local service delivery: The case of Italian local governments. In C. G. Reddick (Ed.), *Handbook of research on strategies for local e-government adoption and implementation: Comparative studies* (pp. 735–751). Hershey, PA: Information Science Reference.
Nasi, G., Frosini, F., & Cristofoli, D. (2011). Online service provision: Are municipalities really innovative? The case of larger municipalities in Italy. *Public Administration, 89*, 821–839.
Norris, D. F., & Moon, M. J. (2005). Advancing e-government at the grassroots: Tortoise or hare? *Public Administration Review, 65*, 64–75.

Norris, D. F., & Reddick, C. G. (2013). Local e-government in the United States: Transformation or incremental change? *Public Administration Review, 73*, 165–175.

Odendaal, N. (2003). Information and communication technology and local governance: Understanding the difference between cities in developed and emerging economies. *Computers, Environment and Urban Systems, 27*(6), 585–607.

Oliveira, G. H. M., & Welch, E. W. (2013). Social media use in local government: Linkage of technology, task, and organizational context. *Government Information Quarterly, 30*, 397–405. doi:10.1016/j.giq.2013.05.019.

Panagiotopoulos, P., Elliman, T., & Fitzgerald, G. (2011). How can public sector ICT transformation be institutionally-enabled? A UK local government study. In *European Conference on Information Systems (ECIS 2011)* (pp. 2561–2567).

Reddick, C. G. (2005). Government e-commerce adoption: A study of Texas counties. *Journal of E-Government, 2*, 45–73.

Reddick, C. G., Abdelsalam, H. M., & Elkadi, H. (2011). The influence of e-government on administrative discretion: The case of local governments in Egypt. *Public Administration and Development, 31*, 390–407.

Rogers, E. M. (1995). *Diffusion of innovations*. 4th ed. New York: Simon and Schuster. Retrieved from http://www.amazon.com/Diffusion-Innovations-Fourth-Edition-Everett/dp/0029266718

Royo, S., Yetano, A., & Acerete, B. (2011). Citizen participation in German and Spanish local governments: A comparative study. *International Journal of Public Administration, 34*, 139–150.

Sandoval-Almazan, R., & Gil Garcia, J. R. (2013). Social media in state governments: Preliminary results about the use of Facebook and twitter in México. In Z. Mahmood (Ed.), *E-government implementation and practice in developing countries* (pp. 128–146). Hershey, PA: IGI Global.

Sandoval-Almazan, R., & Gil-Garcia, J. R. (2010). *Assessing local e-government: An initial exploration of the case of Mexico*. New York: ACM.

Sandoval-Almazan, R., & Gil-Garcia, J. R. (2011). The role of the CIO in a local government IT strategy: The case of Merida, Yucatán Mexico. *Electronic Journal of E-Government, 9*(1), 1–14.

Sandoval-Almazan, R., & Gil-Garcia, J. R. (2012). Are government internet portals evolving towards more interaction, participation, and collaboration? Revisiting the rhetoric of e-government among municipalities. *Government Information Quarterly, 29*(Sup 1), 72–81.

Sandoval-Almazán R., Murillo G. D., Gil-Garcia R, Luna-Reyes, L., and Luna-Reyes, D. (2011). Web 2.0 on the Mexican State sites: An overview. In M. Klun, M. Decman and T. Jukić (Eds.) *Proceeding of the 11th European conference on e-government (ECEG 2011)* (pp. 491–501). Reading, UK: Academic.

Scavo, C. (2007). Development and use of the world wide web by U.S. local governments. In A. V. Anttiroiko & M. Mälkiä (Eds.), *Encyclopedia of digital government* (pp. 296–300). Hershey, PA: Idea Group Reference.

Shackleton, P., Fisher, J., & Dawson, L. (2006). E-government services in the local government context: An Australian case study. *Business Process Management Journal, 12*, 88–100.

Sobaci, M. Z., & Karkin, N. (2013). The use of twitter by mayors in Turkey: Tweets for better public services? *Government Information Quarterly, 30*, 417–425.

Sorensen, K. H., & Munoz, L. L. (2011). Norwegian local governments electronically out of step? From social to geographical digital divides. *Etikk Praksis, 5*, 67–86.

Streib, G. D., & Willoughby, K. G. (2005). Local governments as e-governments: Meeting the implementation challenge. *Public Administration Quarterly, 29*, 77–109.

Tolbert, C. J., & Mossberger, K. (2006). The effects of e-government on trust and confidence in government. *Public Administration Review, 66*, 354–369.

Torres, L., Pina, V., & Royo, S. (2005). E-government and the transformation of public administrations in EU countries: Beyond NPM or just a second wave of reforms? *Online Information Review, 29*, 531–553.

Tudor, A. T., Blidisel, R., & Popa, A. (2009). *E-financial reporting within the Romanian public sector governance*. Reading, UK: Academic.

van Veenstra, A. F., & Zuurmond, A. (2009). Opening the black box: Exploring the effect of transformation on online service delivery in local governments. In M. A. Wimmer, H. J. Scholl, M. Janssen, & R. Traunmüller (Eds.), *Electronic Government: 8th International Conference EGOV 2009* (pp. 234–244). Berlin, Germany: Springer.
West, J. P., & Berman, E. M. (2001). The impact of revitalized management practices on the adoption of information technology: A national survey of local governments. *Public Performance & Management Review, 24*, 233–253.
Wohlers, T. E. (2007). Comparative e-government: Trends and sophistication at the local level. *Systemics, Cybernetics and Informatics, 6*(3), 49–55.
Wohlers, T. E. (2009). The digital world of local government: A comparative analysis of the United States and Germany. *Journal of Information Technology & Politics, 6*, 111–126.
Wolf, S. G., McDonough, J. P., & Bollhauer, R. G. (2001). Survey of local government use of emerging technologies. *Law Technology, 34*, 42–53.

Chapter 7
Social Media Adoption and Use by Australian Capital City Local Governments

Wayne Williamson and Kristian Ruming

Abstract This chapter explores social media adoption and use by Australian capital city local governments. Despite digital communication with the community being an integral part of modern local government functions, the types of digital communication being used are not commonly monitored or analyzed in the Australian context. This chapter provides an investigation of the types of social media being employed by local governments and a sentiment analysis of Twitter accounts from a sample of local governments in Sydney. The results suggest that social media is being used in a variety of forms according to the size and function of the local governments and is influenced by the level of Twitter activity undertaken by the mayor.

7.1 Introduction

Modern society has become reliant on online services and its influences on the way in which people communicate with one another (Wellman and Haythornthwaite 2002). Many of us conduct a significant part of our lives online paying bills, ordering groceries, booking travel, biding on auctions, and catching up with long lost friends. Social media has built on the communication capabilities of the Internet to play a significant role in changing the way people communicate with each other and with organizations. Information and communications technology has tremendous administration potential in that it can aid organizations with interconnectivity, service delivery, efficiency and effectiveness, transparency, and accountability (Yildiz 2007). One of the outcomes of this growth in online interaction has been the establishment of e-government. E-government was originally defined as the utilization of the Internet to deliver government information and services to citizens. E-government definitions have since been extended by the emergence of Web 2.0. O'Reilly (2005) coined the term Web 2.0 to distinguish Internet technologies that feature the

W. Williamson (✉) • K. Ruming
Department of Geography and Planning, Macquarie University, North Ryde, NSW, Australia
e-mail: wayne.williamson@students.mq.edu.au; kristian.ruming@mq.edu.au

M.Z. Sobaci (ed.), *Social Media and Local Governments*, Public Administration and Information Technology 15, DOI 10.1007/978-3-319-17722-9_7

generation of content by the user. Examples of Web 2.0 relevant for citizen participation include wikis, blogs, open data portals, and crowd sourcing ideas (Brabham 2009; Robinson et al. 2010; Smith 2010). E-government 2.0 adopts Web 2.0 characteristics by placing an emphasis on participation through a two-way communications model.

Despite its potential, e-government literature has been characterized by over-optimism and hype regarding its adoption, while also lacking balance in considering the negative or unintended impacts on government processes and structures (Heeks and Bailur 2007). Norris and Reddick (2013) claim that local governments are using e-government more than ever before and are experiencing fewer barriers. However, local government use remains primarily about delivering information and services along with some transactions—it remains a one-way form of communication. Notwithstanding the slow adoption of e-government 2.0, Norris and Reddick (2013) found the adoption of social media has been much faster than e-government principals and technologies as a whole and represents a significant new opportunity for engaging local residents.

Social media can be thought of broadly as an extension of Web 2.0 as it builds on Web 2.0 technologies to promote content generation by the users and facilitates the sharing and diffusion of information through social linking and interactions among people (Boyd and Ellison 2008). Social media services, such as Facebook, Twitter, LinkedIn, YouTube, Pinterest, Instagram, and Flickr, are all designed to provide a platform to create online communities, to connect people and to share information. Unlike traditional media types, social media provides the means for "many-to-many" interactions (Bertot et al. 2010). There has been strong arguments that social media contributes to transparency, participation, and communications to improve public services (Bertot et al. 2010; Bonsón et al. 2012). Many local governments are using social media to enhance transparency, but in general the concept of corporate dialog through the use of web 2.0 is still in its infancy at the local government level (Bonsón et al. 2012).

Although Australia ranks second in the latest UN e-government surveys (United Nations 2014), little literature exists exploring e-government adoption factors or the use of social media by local governments in Australia. This chapter addresses these issues by, firstly, providing a snapshot of social adoption levels in capital city local governments and, secondly, identifying how factors such as local government functions, geographic area, and mayor adoption of social media influence local government adoption. To these ends, this chapter directly addresses the following research questions:

RQ1: What is the level of social media adoption by local governments in Australian capital cities?

RQ2: What is the level of activity and influence of the Twitter accounts of local governments in Australian capital cities?

RQ3: What is the level of activity and influence of the Twitter accounts of local governments in Australian suburban cities?

RQ4: Does community functions and the geographic area impact on the use of Twitter?
RQ5: Does mayor presence on Twitter impact on the use of Twitter by Australian local governments?

Before addressing each of these questions in turn, the chapter begins by reviewing Australian and international literature on e-government before investigating the adoption of social media by international local governments. The bulk of the chapter is dedicated to answering the research questions by analyzing the social media adoption by 127 local governments in Australian capital cities, before exploring in detail the Twitter activity and sentiment of a sample of capital city local governments. A longitudinal comparison of six Sydney suburban local government Twitter accounts is also provided. The results suggest that social media is being used in a variety of forms according to the size and function of the local governments and is influenced by the level of Twitter activity undertaken by the mayor.

7.2 Literature Review

7.2.1 E-Government Adoption in Australian Local Governments

Initial e-government research in Australia focused on early adopters and the differences between public and private online delivery of information and services. Government services are different to private companies as they are focused on profits, while government is a universal service provider, not based on a customer's willingness to pay (Teicher and Dow 2002). Shackleton et al. (2006) provided further insights by looking at government web site maturity measurements using a linear model: Internet presence through to provision of online information and finally the provision of online payment services. Government does not follow this model as it focuses on the provision of information for local communities with little focus on e-commerce. Local governments also focus on public decision making, such as strategic planning (Shackleton et al. 2006). Furthermore, local governments see electronic services delivery as a series of independent projects, rather than an organization-wide strategy (Shackleton et al. 2006). In a review of Western Sydney local government web sites, Fan (2011) concluded that the majority were employed for information and one-way communications, with very few advanced tools for participation and joint decision making.

Research also focused on the functionality and responsiveness of e-government. Teicher and Dow (2002) found that government services are based on "life events", such that specific services are grouped so the community does not need to track down different services across multiple government departments. Gauld et al. (2009) found Australian governments promote electronic service delivery underpinned by concepts of responsiveness and participation. To test this concept, Gauld et al. (2009) tested both Australian and New Zealand Government agencies to find that email responsiveness is not as good as verbal communications via telephone. In order to maintain a higher level of responsiveness through e-government, Shi (2006) advises that regular reviews of web site content and accessibility testing are integral to the sustainability of e-government. Furthermore, accessibility testing should be undertaken as a key performance indicator and legal foundations are required to address equal rights for those with disabilities (Shi 2006).

Australian researchers also focused on adoption issues. As would be expected in the early 2000s, digital divide issues such as Internet access in regional and rural areas were identified by Teicher and Dow (2002), while Shackleton et al. (2006) identified costs and lack of experience with technology as impacts on adoption. More recently, Fan (2011) found that management and leadership affect fulfillment of e-government promises and suggests that successful e-government is drawn from clear coordination of goals with policies and processes. Notwithstanding the identifiable adoption issues, Teicher and Dow (2002) concluded that e-government provides a quantum leap for service quality, new services, and cost reductions; however, results are modest and not well distributed geographically.

While the majority of literature concentrated on the local government supply of e-government services, Gauld et al. (2010) focused on the demand side. Gauld et al. (2010) asserted that Australian local governments make the assumption that once technology is in place, costs and efficiency benefits will automatically follow, leading to greater accountability, transparency, improved government process, and participation. However, Gauld et al. (2010) found less than 50 % of respondents visit government web sites and up to 70 % of respondents said they prefer non-digital contact with government, particularly older community members. Notably, income and gender were not significant indicators of e-government use. According to Gauld et al. (2010), local communities are generally supportive of e-government, but also reluctant to use sophisticated transactions. Thus, the full potential of e-government remains largely unrealized in Australia.

7.2.2 E-Government 2.0 Adoption and International Local Governments

Echoing e-government research in Australia, literature from other countries raises similar adoption issues. In a longitudinal study from the United States (US), Norris and Reddick (2013) found a lack of funding to be the most common barrier for e-government adoption; however, survey responses have dropped since 2004, which suggests experience has overcome this issue to some extent. Also, fewer responses identified a lack of management support as an adoption barrier. Conversely, Norris and Reddick (2013) found saving money and citizen participation as the primary reasons for adopting e-government.

Additionally, Sandoval-Almazan and Gil-Garcia (2012) looked at government web portals in Mexico and found they are mainly information-based, with few opportunities for interaction and no participation. Sandoval-Almazan and Gil-Garcia (2012) suggest that open government is a powerful new trend that is clearly related to citizen participation and collaboration. Furthermore, web portals could support objectives of open government to facilitate communications. New technologies are relatively cheap and motivations exist to adopt it, which could make e-government adoption a reality.

In exploring e-government adoption in the US, Norris and Reddick (2013) characterize public administration as incremental. Essentially, change comes in small increments as public administration muddles through each year. Rarely are there fundamental shifts or changes in public administration. But on a positive note, Norris and Reddick (2013) advise that local governments in the US are offering more e-government tools than ever before, are experiencing fewer barriers, and usage reports are mostly positive. Nevertheless, one-way combination continues to prevail as e-government remains primarily about delivering information and services along with some transactions.

To gain an understanding of the role of leadership in e-government adoption, Reddick and Norris (2013) explored senior management support for technology adoption in local governments. They concluded that citizen demand was the main factor for elected officials to take e-government seriously. This finding is quite logical as elected officials are sensitive to their constituent's feedback. Bonsón et al. (2012) suggest the introduction of e-government without the corresponding changes in leadership, policy, and governance is unlikely to result in a more collaborative, participatory, consultative, and transparent government.

In contrast to e-government adoption issues, Norris and Reddick (2013) ascertained from their 2011 survey that US local government adoption of social media has been significantly faster. In fact, they found two thirds of local governments had adopted at least one form of social media, with Facebook being the most common platform. Reflecting international trends, Mossberger et al. (2013) found that over a 2-year period between 2009 and 2011, adoption for some social media platforms, especially Twitter, increased by over 60 %.

7.2.3 Social Media Adoption by Local Governments

There has been strong arguments that social media contribute to transparency, participation, and communications to improve public services (Bertot et al. 2010; Bonsón et al. 2012). This positive attitude towards the use of social media is manifest in a study by Kavanaugh et al. (2012), who found the rapid response to emergency matters, such as natural disasters, is a clear benefit of social media. Social media also provides a means for identifying influential community members and communicating with them directly (Kavanaugh et al. 2012). Conversely, Bonsón et al. (2012) argues that steps have been taken by local governments in the European

Union to adopt social media; however, usage is lagging behind citizens. Only half of local governments have any form of active presence in social networks. Bonsón et al. (2012) argue the adoption of social media and web 2.0 by local governments predictably corresponds to the previous adoption rates seen in e-government. It does not seem like web 2.0 tools will lead a significant revolution in government to citizen relationships. Furthermore, Kavanaugh et al. (2012) argue that citizens do not engage with local governments, as public servants lack the skills necessary to use social media to interact in an effective manner. Mergel (2013b) asserts local governments' willingness to adopt social media and engage with citizens is highly dependent on their existing communications strategy. Furthermore, Mergel (2013b) argues that traditional market mechanisms do not seem to play a role in social media adoption and suggests the key to the rapid diffusion of social media by local governments can be attributed to the free and open nature of social media, and the fact that practices of others can be openly observed and emulated.

To address the adoption of social media by local governments, Mergel (2013a) proposes a three-stage adoption model: Stage 1—early experimentation outside the formal organizational rules; Stage 2—introduction of first standards; and, Stage 3—realization of centralized organizational institutions. The model is based on the observation that, in many cases, social media usage occurs as a bottom-up adoption process that is driven by experiments and the willingness to take the risks associated with the use of social media, such as increasing mistrust of government and losing control of the message (Picazo-Vela et al. 2012).

Mergel (2013a) also developed a three-stage typology of push, pull, and networking social media strategies. Depending on a government's existing communications strategy, agencies may take on three social media tactics: the push strategy to represent formal government information as an additional communications channel, the pull strategy to engage and include information from the public, and the network strategy, which includes both push and pull activities (Mergel 2013a). Using Mergel's (2013a) three-stage typology, Mossberger et al. (2013) case studies found local governments' use of social media is primarily using the push strategy; however, there was some evidence of using pull and networking strategies. The primary social network site being used was Twitter and interactions were taking place in either the parks department or the mayor's office. This confirms Mergel (2013b) observations that citizen behavior drives adoption in government. Essentially, government reacts to observations of stakeholders changing preferences for using social media to receive information and news.

Recent social media case studies by Hofmann et al. (2013) and Sobaci and Karkin (2013) are firstly utilizing publically available data to understand how local governments are using social media, and secondly, making suggestions of how local governments could better utilize these tools. Hofmann et al. (2013) found that German Government departments are using Facebook to provide up to date information, often with URLs to external content; however, they do not use Facebook to market their services. Also, German Government rarely uses pictures or videos in their posts and infrequently uses Facebook calendar or events data types, and as such, are not using all functionality available (Hofmann et al. 2013).

In the Hofmann et al. (2013) study, the most frequently used tags were external advertisements, photos, external events, sports, and leisure activities. Comments added to government posts of this nature were mostly positive or slightly negative. Hofmann et al. (2013) discovered that pictures and videos increase citizen interactions, especially when they are dealing with events and leisure activities; on the contrary, posts regarding government reports and information on current political situations were least popular. Likewise, Sobaci and Karkin's (2013) study of mayors in Turkey found their use of Twitter was mostly to promote their own operations and actions under the guise of information sharing about public services. Hence, Twitter use involves self-promotion and political marketing, with very little attempt to improve local public services (Sobaci and Karkin 2013).

The primary factors that negatively influence e-government and social media adoption are costs and lack of experience with technology (Shackleton et al. 2006), management and leadership (Norris and Reddick 2013; Fan 2011), older community members (Gauld et al. 2010), public servants lacking the skills (Kavanaugh et al. 2012) and existing communications strategies (Mergel 2013b). While non-significant adoption factors for e-government and social media adoption include income and gender (Gauld et al. 2010). Norris and Reddick (2013) found that cost savings and citizen behavior as the primary reasons for adopting e-government; moreover, Mergel (2013a) suggests the free and open nature of social media and the fact that practices of others can be openly observed and emulated are reasons for adopting social media.

7.3 Local Government in Australia

The remainder of this chapter explores social media use by local governments in state capital cities (Fig. 7.1). A more detail analysis is provided for Sydney. Australia is characterized by a three-tiered system of government. The Australian Government, referred to as the Commonwealth or Federal Government, was established by the Australian Constitution in 1901 and covers all of Australia. The Federal Government meets in Australia's capital city of Canberra and discusses legislation and makes laws for the benefit of the entire nation (Australian Government 2014). Australia has six states being: Queensland (Qld), New South Wales (NSW), Victoria (Vic), South Australia (SA), Western Australia (WA), and Tasmania (Tas). Each state has its own constitution and may pass laws related to any matter that is not controlled by the Federal government (Australian Government 2014). All Australian states have established a third tier of government, known as local governments or local councils.[1]

[1] This chapter does not include the Australian Capital Territory and the Northern territory, because the Australian Capital Territory does not have local governments and the Northern Territory has a different government structure and functions to the states.

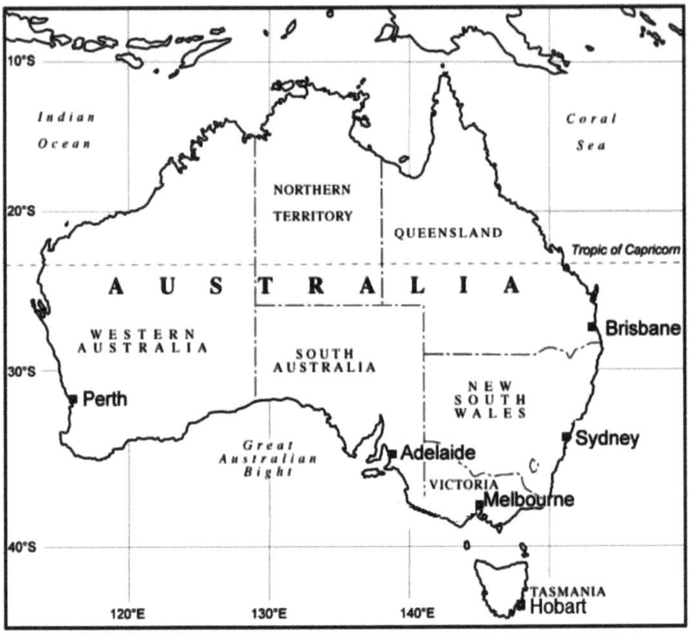

Fig. 7.1 Map of Australia

The main functions of Australian local governments are community needs such as waste collection, public recreation, local roads, and town planning. State governments define the powers of local governments and decide what geographical areas each local government is responsible for (Australian Government 2014). There are 560 local governments in Australia varying in geographic size from 1.1 to 371,000 km^2 and have populations ranging from 109 to 1,089,000 people. Furthermore, Australian local governments have population densities ranging from zero to 7,649 persons per square kilometer (Australian Bureau of Statistics 2013). The number of local governments covering the geographic area of capital cities varies from 6 in Hobart up to 42 in Sydney.

7.4 Methodology

To date, studies exploring e-government and social media usage by local government have employed web site content reviews, interviews, surveys, and workshops. More recently, Hofmann et al. (2013) and Sobaci and Karkin (2013) have used contemporary data collection methods and sentiment analysis to analyze social media data in an effort to understanding how social media is being used by local governments. This analysis builds on these approaches by undertaking, firstly, a desktop review of local government web sites in all six Australian capital cities, and, secondly, Twitter sentiment analysis using freely available sentiment analysis tools.

7.4.1 Web Site Review

The data collection involved a desktop review of social media service availability on 127 local government web sites that operate in Australia's six state capital cities—23 % of all local governments. Local governments located within capital cities were the focus of this study as they have higher social media adoption and usage rates compared to local governments in rural and regional areas. Comparative analysis of capital cities adoption rates is also considered more equitable than comparisons of regional areas that vary significantly in geographic size and population. The web site reviews were conducted between November and December 2013. The reviews used binary coding for services either being available (1) or not available (0). This method is based on McMillan's (2002) web communications model and previously used by Shackleton et al. (2006), Fan (2011), Bonsón et al. (2012), and Williamson and Parolin (2012, 2013).

7.4.2 Twitter Sentiment Analysis

Sobaci and Karkin (2013) advise that there is a lack of literature focusing on the use of social media tools and Twitter, in particular, has received little attention. Like Sobaci and Karkin (2013), this study seeks to investigate the use of Twitter by local governments and mayors to gain an understanding of how the tool is utilized. This analysis focused on the capital city local governments and a sample of six Sydney suburban local governments. The suburban local governments were selected because their social media use was significant enough to produce results from the analysis tools and were previously used in studies by Williamson and Parolin (2012, 2013); therefore, a longitudinal analysis could be undertaken. Capital city local governments are located at the center of Australian capital cities and typically have a high population density, a central business district, large transport interchanges, major public services, and tourist attractions. The size and function of these local governments is considerably larger than capital city suburban local governments which cover predominantly residential areas.[2]

[2] Brisbane is the exception to this description, as it is Australia's largest local government and covers the central business district and a large proportion of Brisbane's suburban areas.

In order to gain an understanding of how local government is using social media, an analysis of Twitter account data was undertaken. In particular, sentiment analysis was conducted using the online sentiment analysis tools of *sentiment140* (http://www.sentiment140.com) and Twitalyzer (http://www.twitalyzer.com).

Sentiment analysis is a form of data mining performed on social media data using a range of techniques to determine the sentiment expressed on particular topics. Sentiment analysis uses linguistic and textual assessment to analyze word use and word combinations, and to categorize a string of text as positive or negative (Kennedy 2012). Sentiment analysis returns a positive or negative result for each row of text analyzed. Difficulties with cleanliness of data can affect sentiment analysis accuracy (Kennedy 2012). Accuracy can also vary on highly topic-dependent data and cannot identify complex linguistic formulations, such as sarcasm or irony (Thelwall 2014).

Data was collected from *Twitter* for each of the local governments; including *followers, following,* and *number of tweets* to date. The *Sentiment140* tool was used to indicate the positive/negative sentiment of tweets in each Twitter account. This tool looks at the tweets from the past 7 days and determines if there are positive or negative sentiment contained within the tweets. The *Sentiment140* tool only takes a snapshot of activity for the previous 7 days and does not compile data for the full history of the account.

Twitalyzer was also used to investigate the Twitter accounts. The strength of this tool is that it produces a suite of statistics including; the style of Twitter user, *Impact* and *Klout* statistics, key topics, and major influences on the Twitter account. *Twitalyzer* generates an *Impact*[3] *score* by taking into account the following factors: number of followers, unique references and citations, frequency of being retweeted, frequency of retweeting, and frequency of tweeting (Twitalyzer 2012). *Klout*[4] scores are generated by analyzing Twitter activity including retweets, mentions in other people's tweets, list membership, number of followers, and replies (Klout 2013). The actual algorithms used to calculate a *Klout* score are not public; however, the *Klout* score is regarded as a good indicator of someone's influence in social media.

The primary limitation of this study is that the web content analysis is just a snapshot in time, and as such, the results will not be valid for an extended period of time. Secondly, the study only focuses on data collected from local governments in Australian capital cities. A more comprehensive study should involve collecting data from regional and rural local governments outside of the capital cities. Nevertheless, this chapter provides a snapshot of social media adoption by Australian local governments, which is currently lacking in the literature, and also suggests factors that may influence social media adoption by local governments.

---

[3] Twitalyzer defines impact as a measure one's activity in a network.

[4] Twitalyzer defines Klout as a number between 1–100 which represents your influence. Influence is the ability to drive action. When you share something on social media or in real life and people respond, that's influence. The more influential you are, the higher your Klout Score.

7.5 Results

This section addresses the central research questions.

RQ1: What is the level of social media adoption by local governments in Australian capital cities?

The breakdown of social media types for each capital city is shown in Table 7.1. Overall, 91 % of local governments sampled displayed links to Facebook, while 83 % displayed a link to Twitter. These two forms of social media far exceeded the use of other forms of social media. The third and fourth most common social media platforms were YouTube and the Flickr that were found on 73 % and 44 % of local government websites, respectively. Pinterest and LinkedIn were found on 38 and 28 %, respectively, of local government websites, while 12 % of local government web sites had a link to Google+.

It is noted that Google+was a relatively new entrant to social media, which would affect its current adoption rate. The adoption of LinkedIn was relatively low, potentially because it is an organization and employment-based platform, which is not typically used to communication with the wider community. There are good adoption rates for the visual-based platforms, such as YouTube, Pinterest, and Flickr, which could aid local governments to visually communicate events or proposed changes to a local government area and also deliver information in different languages. Social media platforms such as YouTube, Pinterest, and Instagram are also particularly useful for the community to share what they see and like or dislike in their local government area.

The three largest capital cities of Sydney, Melbourne, and Brisbane on Australia's east coast show higher adoption rates of Facebook, Twitter, Pinterest, YouTube, and Flickr than other three smaller capitals, while Melbourne and Brisbane demonstrate the highest adoption rates in Australia.

The smaller capital cities of Perth and Adelaide have good adoption rates and Australia's smallest capital city of Hobart ranks last with significantly less adoption of most social media platforms. The very small number of six followers of the City of Hobart's Twitter account (Table 7.2) suggests there is a lack of citizen demand for social media use by this local government. The data presented in Table 7.1 suggests that larger populations have an influence on the adoption of social media by local governments. Further analysis of the demand-side factors, such as a previous study by Gauld et al. (2010), needs to be conducted to gain an understanding of the drivers for online participation by Australian local governments.

RQ2: What is the level of activity and influence of the Twitter accounts of local governments in Australian capital cities?

Building upon the website review of local governments' web sites, this section focused on Twitter usage to provide a more detailed analysis of social media used by local governments (Table 7.2). Sentiment analysis was conducted in March 2014 for all capital city local governments. The functions of these local governments are

Table 7.1 Social media adoption by capital city local governments

	Sydney	Melbourne	Brisbane[a]	Perth	Adelaide	Hobart	Total
Population[b]	4,667,283	4,246,345	2,780,767	1,897,548	1,277,174	216,959	15,086,076
Local Government areas	42	28	10	23	18	6	127
Facebook (%)	93	100	100	87	83	83	91
Twitter (%)	81	93	100	74	83	67	83
Google+ (%)	31	7	30	0	6	0	12
YouTube (%)	79	93	80	65	72	50	73
Pinterest (%)	48	46	70	9	22	33	38
Flickr (%)	52	68	50	26	50	17	44
Instagram (%)	29	43	40	4	17	0	22
LinkedIn (%)	14	39	50	26	6	33	28

[a]Includes South East Queensland
[b]Australian Bureau of Statistics (2012)

Table 7.2 Sentiment analysis for capital city local governments

Local government name and handle	Population[a]	Followers	Following	Number of Tweets	Positive/ Negative ratio[b]	Impact[c]	Klout[c]
City of Brisbane@BrisbaneCityQld	1,041,839	32,800	511	10,800	26/19	7	77
City of Sydney@CityofSydney	182,226	38,200	619	5,057	49/2	9.4	64
City of Melbourne@CityofMelbourne	100,611	30,600	631	2,237	40/10	7.3	63
City of Hobart@CityofHobart	48,703	6	7	0	No Result	0	0
City of Adelaide@CityofAdelaide	19,639	15,100	799	4,809	45/4	3.6	60
City of Perth@CityofPerth	19,043	10,500	1,095	3,526	61/3	2.9	60

Data captured 6 April 2014

[a]Australian Bureau of Statistics (2012)

[b]Sentiment140

[c]Twitalyzer

considerably larger than capital city suburban local governments which cover predominantly residential areas.

The capital city local governments have significant numbers of Twitter followers, peaking at 38,000 for the City of Sydney and also post a significant number of tweets. The positive/negative sentiment ratio suggests approximately 30-40 tweets per week. With significant followers and tweets come healthy *Impact* and *Klout* scores. The City of Sydney tops the list with a high *Impact* score of 9.4, which suggests a high frequency of retweeting and the City of Sydney retweeting the tweets of others. Likewise, Brisbane, Melbourne, and Sydney also have relatively high *Klout* scores, which are measured by the number of mentions, replies generated, and their Twitter activity. All local governments were labelled as *Reporters*,[5] which reflects the volume of tweets and followers.

RQ3: What is the level of activity and influence of the Twitter accounts of local governments in Australian suburban cities?

Important differences are observed when comparing capital city local government and suburban local governments. In order to draw out these differences, the focus of this research question is on suburban local government in Sydney (Table 7.3). A sample of 6 local governments was selected, with sentiment analysis performed in December 2012 by Williamson and Parolin (2012, 2013) and March 2014. These data allow changes in the use of social media to be traced over this period. This sample of local governments is predominantly residential areas, many with large populations (e.g., Penrith and The Hills).

In 2012, most local governments had a positive sentiment ratio, with less than 3 or 4 negative tweets (Table 7.3)—although Penrith Council had a relatively high number of negative tweets associated with their account, which suggest the community is willing to engage with Penrith Council on local issues through social media channels.

In 2014, local governments again have a predominantly positive sentiment ratio. It is noted that some local governments had a lower number of tweets at the time of data collection. Most suburban local governments were given both very low *Impact* and *Klout* scores, which reflects the low number of followers for an organization, and in most cases, low Twitter activity. Pittwater Council registered the highest *Impact* and *Klout* scores in 2012 and again in 2014.

Between December 2012 and March 2014, the number of followers increased by between 40 % and 65 %, respectively, for most local governments, while North Sydney increased by 157 %. Furthermore, the number of Twitter accounts being followed has decreased for Manly and Waverley, but increased for all other local governments. It is unknown why these local governments reduced the number of Twitter accounts they follow. North Sydney and The Hills increased the Twitter accounts they are following by over 200 %, which suggest these local governments were relatively new to Twitter in 2012. The number of tweets posted increased for

[5] Twitalyzer describes 'reporters' as user who are likely to communicate outwardly but often don't generate a specific response from their network.

Table 7.3 Sentiment analysis for Sydney suburban local governments

		2012						2014					
Local government name	Population[a]	Followers	Following	Number of Tweets	Positive/negative ratio[b]	Impact[c]	Klout[c]	Followers	Following	Number of Tweets	Positive/Negative ratio[b]	Impact[c]	Klout[c]
Manly@Manly_Council	41,925	1,591	435	2,882	No result	0.3	42	2,455	424	3,001	No result	0.5	45
North Sydney @NthSydCouncil	64,795	367	25	95	2/0	0.1	36	946	76	299	2/1	0.3	42
Penrith @penrithcouncil	186,221	2,430	2,397	1,304	35/16	0.5	46	3,447	2,569	2,106	7/0	0.8	46
Pittwater@about Pittwater	59,847	2,321	2,078	9,345	5/1	0.6	49	3,319	2,176	12,400	6/1	0.8	50
The Hills@TheHills Council	197,716	1,701	572	1,748	4/1	0.4	45	2,839	1,821	2,496	1/1	0.6	45
Waverley@Waverley Council	69,420	1,517	1,846	436	4/0	0.3	44	2,443	1,598	841	No result	0.5	44

Data captured 16 December 2012 and 25 March 2014

[a]Australian Bureau of Statistics (2012)

[b]Sentiment140

[c]Twitalyzer

all the local governments, with Manly and North Sydney showing a moderate increase of between 150 and 200 tweets, while Penrith, Pittwater, and The Hills demonstrated significant activity by posting between 700 and 3,000 tweets during the period. The number of tweets in the 7-day analysis period has slightly increased for all local governments observed, but only marginally.

It is noted that while Pittwater is a high activity Twitter account, however, on both occasion that data was collected, the number of tweets used for the positive/negative ratio was relatively low. The *Impact* and *Klout* scores for all local governments have slightly increased or have remained unchanged. However, the scores remain very low due to the relatively low numbers of followers and the generally low activities of these Twitter accounts. All local governments observed were labelled *casual user*.[6]

RQ4: Does community functions and the geographic area impact the use of Twitter.

Sentiment analysis identified topics in the Twitter accounts of capital city local government were dominated by Australia, Australian government, and business. Moreover, the majority of local governments are also engaged in topics such as their state (e.g., South Australia, Western Australia), Arts festivals, sustainability, recycling, water, libraries, disaster recovery, community, social issues, and sport. These topics could be described as focusing on more region-wide topics, rather than the immediate day-to-day community functions. An example of this regional focus is the City of Sydney's Vivid Light Festival (http://www.vividsydney.com), which is heavily promoted through social media, and among other communication channels, attracts international participants and draws spectators from a much wider geographic area than the City of Sydney is responsible for. These findings are a contrast to the findings of Foth (2006) that citizen-initiated social networks are predominately placed-based planning efforts and are populated by people who live locally. This study suggests that capital city local governments are looking to engage with communities of a larger geographic area.

For suburban local governments, the social media topics listed for each local government included skateboarding, swimming, environment, community, dogs, art, media, entertainment, and small business, which are similar topics to those identified by Hofmann et al. (2013). These topics demonstrate that the Twitter accounts in this sample of local governments are being used for a wide range of local community facilities such as use of open space and recreation, entertainment, and local retail business. These findings suggest that suburban council uses social media for more local issues compared to their capital city counterparts. This is a potentially useful finding as it contrasts with the findings of the capital city local governments who seem to be seeking to employ social media to promote regional ambitions, rather than local issues.

RQ5: Does mayor presence on Twitter impact the use of Twitter by Australian local governments?

[6] Twitalyzer states that 'casual users' are individuals who drop in and out of Twitter on a whim, treating the network as a social channel when it suits their needs.

Table 7.4 Correlation between Local government and mayor Klout scores

	Local government Klout	Mayor Klout
Local Government Klout Pearson correlation	1	0.654[a]
Sig. (2-tailed)		0.021
N	12	12
Mayor Klout Pearson correlation	0.654[a]	1
Sig. (2-tailed)	.021	
N	12	12

[a]Correlation is significant at the 0.05 level (2-tailed)

In an attempt to understand if a local government mayor's presence on social media influences a local governments' use of social media, the *Klout* scores of the capital city and suburban local governments from Tables 7.2 and 7.3 are correlated against the *Klout* scores of mayors of these local governments. Our analysis has found a significant positive relationship between mayor social media use and the corresponding local government's use of social media. When the data is interrogated, Mayor Clover Moore of City Sydney, Mayor Robert Doyle of City of Melbourne, and Mayor Graham Quirk of City of Brisbane, have healthy *Klout* scores of 61, 60, and 49, respectively, which suggests that these elected officials are pursuing their own social media presence, in parallel with their local governments. However, mayors of suburban local governments either have no social media presence or significantly lower *Klout* scores. This suggests that elected officials in suburban local governments are less likely to pursue a social media presence as part of their political persona, which may also influence the organization's adoption of social media (Table 7.4).

7.6 Discussion

This chapter presented a snapshot of social media adoption and use by Australian local governments, which found the majority of local governments in Australian capital cities have embraced social media to some extent. In 2009, the use of social media such as Facebook and Twitter was observed on 21 % of Sydney local government web sites; by 2012, data collection revealed a 45 % increase. This was the largest increase of all communication channels observed, and also the only communication type to significantly increase across the entire state of New South Wales (Williamson and Parolin 2012, 2013). By 2014, social media is now observed on 93 % of Sydney local government web sites. This longitudinal data set demonstrates significant adoption rates for social media by local government in Sydney over the past 5 years. Furthermore, the capital cities of Brisbane and Melbourne are at a more advanced stage of social media adoption than Sydney. This study concurs with Norris and Reddick (2013) and Mossberger et al. (2013), whose studies also found significant local government adoption of social media, with Facebook being the most common platform.

The data analysis also demonstrates that local governments are using social media to engage with a wide variety of topics that cut across several sections of their local communities. Evidence of this is shown by suburban local governments using their Twitter accounts to share information on typical local government topics, while capital city local governments are trying to engage on more regional issues and events. It is clear that capital city councils are actively pursuing online community participation strategies, which seem to be producing notable results in the form of high *Impact* and *Klout* indicators, strong numbers of followers, and regular social media activity. This supports Bonsón et al.'s (2012) arguments that local governments are taking steps to adopt social media; however, they are lagging behind citizens with up to 50 % of local governments taking a more passive role. Bonsón et al. (2012) also argues that the adoption of social media and web 2.0 by local governments predictably corresponds to the previous adoption rates seen in e-government. In the Australian context, geographic location also plays a role in adopting e-government, as previously identified by Teicher and Dow (2002).

Local governments are tailoring their social media use in accordance with the role they play in their community and the geographic area they are responsible for. In particular, the sentiment analysis demonstrated that the inner city local governments have a much stronger usage pattern than the suburban local governments responsible for the predominantly residential suburban areas. While local governments in Australia were created to undertake specific functions, the day-to-day implementation of these functions relies heavily on their geographic area, the demographic makeup of the community, and other factors such as business clusters, community services, and tourism. It is a positive insight to be able to distinguish different applications of social media in different forms of local governments. Furthermore, this study identified a significant correlation between local government mayor use of Twitter and the corresponding use by their local government organization. This finding confirms Mossberger et al.'s (2013) observations that the primary social media activity was taking place in either the parks department or the mayor's office and concurs with Mergel's (2013b) observations that government reacts to observations of stakeholders changing preferences for using social media, as a significant driver in Australian capital city local governments seems to be the mayor's use of social media.

While it could be argued that local government adoption rates are less than non-government organizations and some sections of the community, the data presented in this chapter show adoption rates are now at significant levels and numerous local governments are pursuing an online presence using social media.

References

Australian Bureau of Statistics (2012). *2011 Census QuickStats*. Retrieved June 29, 2014, from http://www.abs.gov.au/websitedbs/censushome.nsf/home/quickstats.

Australian Bureau of Statistics (2013). *3218.0—Regional population growth, Australia, 2012–13*. Retrieved July 23, 2014, from http://www.abs.gov.au/ausstats/abs@.nsf/DetailsPage/3218.02012-13?OpenDocument.

Australian Government (2014). *The Australian Government*. Retrieved July 23, 2014, from http://australia.gov.au/about-australia/our-government/australian-government.

Bertot, J. C., Jaeger, P. T., & Grimes, J. M. (2010). Using ICTs to create a culture of transparency: E-government and social media as openness and anti-corruption tools for societies. *Government Information Quarterly, 27*(3), 264–271.

Brabham, D. (2009). Crowdsourcing the public participation process for planning projects. *Planning Theory, 8*(3), 242–262.

Bonsón, E., Torres, L., Royo, S., & Flores, F. (2012). Local e-government 2.0: Social media and corporate transparency in municipalities. *Government Information Quarterly, 29*(2), 123–132.

Boyd, D., & Ellison, N. (2008). Social network sites: Definition, history, and scholarship. *Journal of Computer-Mediated Communication, 13*(1), 210–230.

Fan, Q. (2011). An evaluation analysis of e-government development by local authorities in Australia. *International Journal of Public Administration, 34*(14), 926–934.

Foth, M. (2006). Analyzing the factors influencing the successful design and uptake of interactive system to support social networks in urban neighborhoods. *International Journal of Technology and Human Interaction, 2*(2), 65–79.

Gauld, R., Gray, A., & McComb, S. (2009). How responsive is e-government? Evidence from Australian and New Zealand. *Government Information Quarterly, 26*(1), 69–74.

Gauld, R., Goldfinch, S., & Horsburgh, S. (2010). Do they want it? Do they use it? The 'Demand-Side'of e-government in Australia and New Zealand. *Government Information Quarterly, 27*(2), 177–186.

Heeks, R., & Bailur, S. (2007). Analyzing e-government research: Perspectives, philosophies, theories, methods and practice. *Government Information Quarterly, 24*(2), 243–265.

Hofmann, S., Beverungen, D., Räckers, M., & Becker, J. (2013). What makes local governments' online communications successful? Insights from a multi-method analysis of Facebook. *Government Information Quarterly, 30*(4), 387–396.

Kavanaugh, A., Fox, E., Sheetz, S., Yang, S., Li, L., Shoemaker, D., Natsev, A., & Xie, L. (2012). Social media use by government: From the routine to the critical. *Government Information Quarterly, 29*(4), 480–491.

Kennedy, H. (2012). Perspectives on sentiment analysis. *Journal of Broadcasting and Electronic Media, 56*(4), 435–450.

Klout (2013) *How the Klout score is calculated*. Retrieved January 16, 2013, from http://www.klout.com/corp/klout_score.

McMillan, S. (2002). A four-part model of cyber-activity: Some cyber-places are more interactive than others. *New Media and Society, 4*(2), 271–291.

Mergel, I. (2013a). A three-stage adoption process for social media use in government. *Public Administration Review, 73*(3), 390–400.

Mergel, I. (2013b). Social media adoption and resulting tactics in the US federal government. *Government Information Quarterly, 30*(2), 123–130.

Mossberger, K., Wu, Y., & Crawford, J. (2013). Connecting citizens and local governments? Social media and interactivity in major US cities. *Government Information Quarterly, 30*(4), 351–358.

Norris, D. F., & Reddick, C. G. (2013). Local e-government in the United States: Transformation or incremental change? *Public Administration Review, 73*(1), 165–175.

O'Reilly, T. (2005). What is web 2.0? Design patterns and business models for the next generation of software. http://oreilly.com/web2/archive/whatis-web-20.html.

Picazo-Vela, S., Gutiérrez-Martínez, I., & Luna-Reyes, L. (2012). Understanding risks, benefits, and strategic alternatives of social media applications in the public sector. *Government Information Quarterly, 29*(4), 504–511.

Reddick, C. G., & Norris, D. F. (2013). E-Participation in local governments: An examination of political-managerial support and impacts. *Transforming Government People, Process and Policy, 7*(14), 453–476.

Robinson, D. G., Yu, H., & Felten, E. W. (2010). Enabling innovation for civic engagement. In D. Lathrop & L. Ruma (Eds.), *Open government: Collaboration, transparency and participation in practice* (pp. 83–89). Sebastopol, CA: O'Reilly Media.

Sandoval-Almazan, R., & Gil-Garcia, J. R. (2012). Are government internet portals evolving towards more interaction, participation, and collaboration? Revisiting the rhetoric of e-government among municipalities. *Government Information Quarterly, 29*(S1), 72–81.

Shackleton, P., Fisher, J., & Dawson, L. (2006). E-government services in the local government context: an Australian case study. *Business Process Management Journal, 12*(1), 88–100.

Shi, Y. (2006). E-Government web site accessibility in Australia and China a longitudinal study. *Social Science Computer Review, 24*(3), 378–385.

Smith, A. (2010). Government online. Pew Research Center. Retrieved May 31, 2010, from http://www.pewinternet.org/media//Files/Reports/2010/PIP_Government_Online_2010.pdf.

Sobaci, M. Z., & Karkin, N. (2013). The use of twitter by mayors in Turkey: Tweets for better public services? *Government Information Quarterly, 30*(4), 417–425.

Teicher, J., & Dow, N. (2002). E-government in Australia: Promise and progress. *Information Polity, 7*(4), 231–246.

Thelwall, M. (2014). Sentiment analysis and time series with Twitter. In K. Weller, A. Bruns, J. Burgess, M. Mahrt, & C. Puschmann (Eds.), *Twitter and society* (pp. 83–95). New York: Lang.

Twitalyzer (2012). Twitalyzer. Retrieved December 16, 2012, from http://www.twitalyzer.com/5/index.asp.

United Nations (2014). United Nations E-Government survey 2014: E-government for the future we want. Retrieved October 22, 2014, from http://unpan3.un.org/egovkb/Portals/egovkb/Documents/un/2014-Survey/E-Gov_Complete_Survey-2014.pdf.

Wellman, B., & Haythornthwaite, C. (2002). *The internet in everyday life*. Oxford, England: Blackwell.

Williamson, W., & Parolin, B. (2012). Review of web-based communications for town planning in local government. *Journal of Urban Technology, 19*(1), 43–63.

Williamson, W., & Parolin, B. (2013). Web 2.0 and social media growth in planning practice: A longitudinal study. *Planning Practice and Research, 28*(5), 544–562.

Yildiz, M. (2007). E-government research: Reviewing the literature, limitations and ways forward. *Government Information Quarterly, 24*(3), 646–665.

Part III
Adoption and Diffusion

Chapter 8
Adopting Social Media in the Local Level of Government: Towards a Public Administration 2.0?

J. Ignacio Criado and Francisco Rojas-Martín

Abstract This chapter analyses the dynamics of adoption of social media in Spanish local governments with over 50,000 inhabitants. Specifically, the study seeks to respond to the following questions: (1) What are the key factors that explain the use of social media in public administrations? (2) What is the perception of those who manage social media regarding the level of development in their institution? (3) What are the key inhibitors for the development of these technologies in local administrations? This chapter is based on a questionnaire aimed at those in charge of social media in all Spanish local governments with over 50,000 inhabitants (146), which obtained a response rate above 97 % and presents the results through descriptive statistics relating to the defined indicators. The most significant conclusions are, on the one hand, that despite there being a high level of diffusion of these technologies at the level of local administrations, initial actions and strategies for their promotion have either not been clearly defined, or have been inadequately implemented. Second, we are at an early stage of development of social media in the local government sphere. Nonetheless, this is a field of widespread academic interest, bearing in mind the potential for innovation in management and in improved public administration interaction with citizens.

8.1 Introduction

Interest in digital social networks (social media) in public administrations has grown substantially in recent years. This chapter seeks to contribute to this field of study by analysing the adoption and use of these technologies in Spanish municipalities with more than 50,000 inhabitants. Specifically this study has a descriptive

J.I. Criado, Ph.D. (✉) • F. Rojas-Martín
Department of Political Science and International Relations, Universidad Autónoma de Madrid, Building of Law, Politics and Economics, 1st floor, office 2, C/Marie Curie, 1, Ciudad Universitaria de Cantoblanco, Madrid 28049, Spain
e-mail: ignacio.criado@uam.es; francisco.rojas@inv.uam.es

M.Z. Sobaci (ed.), *Social Media and Local Governments*, Public Administration and Information Technology 15, DOI 10.1007/978-3-319-17722-9_8

character and aims *to provide a first approximation at* identifying the management departments that are leading the process, to establish whether documents exist that orientate and normalise the use of social media, to analyse the type of technologies that local governments are adopting, to specify the motivations behind their adoption and to identify the inhibitors that are slowing their introduction. Additionally, this chapter seeks to contribute to the debate about whether this generation of technologies is contributing towards bringing citizens closer to public administrations and making them more permeable and open organisations. The study concludes by suggesting steps that could be taken to promote their introduction.

The importance of social media is related to their recent and rapid diffusion across broad layers of society worldwide. In Spain, it is calculated that around 79 % of Internet users employ social media (Elogia 2014): predominantly *Facebook*, *Tuenti*, and *Twitter*, as well as a new generation of applications designed exclusively for use through mobile devices, like *WhatsApp*. By way of example, it is estimated that *Facebook* has 18 million users, in a Spanish population of around 47 million. At the same time, Spanish citizens show a preference for social media as a way to access public information (Urueña 2013). Therefore, a positive environment clearly exists for the adoption of social technologies, and it is for this reason that public administrations must not remain distant to this process of innovation.

This chapter assumes that social media are technologies that could significantly innovate the areas of transparency, participation, and collaboration in public administrations. Authors such as Mergel (2012) suggest that the application of social media in the public sector might even be considered as a 'fifth wave' of information and communication technologies (ICTs). These technologies are disruptive because of their capacity to create, organise, exchange, combine, and provide information through social networks by means of interconnected individuals with common interests and objectives (Bertot et al. 2010; Chun et al. 2010; Meijer and Thaens 2010).

The research aim of this study is to analyse the adoption and use of social media at municipal level in Spain. Previous studies in this field have shown us that public administrations are still in a phase of initial development in the use of these social technologies (Bonsón et al. 2012; Criado and Rojas-Martín 2013b; Sáez-Martín et al. 2014). At the same time, the level of diffusion of social media is very high and already there are outstanding examples worth analysing. This chapter seeks to respond to three research questions: (1) What are the key factors that explain the use of social media in public administrations? (2) What is the perception of those who manage social media regarding the level of development in their institution? (3) What are the key inhibitors for the development of these technologies in local administrations?

Methodologically, this study uses data collected from a questionnaire to the managers in charge of social media strategies of the 146 Spanish municipalities with more than 50,000 inhabitants. The instrument includes questions oriented towards identifying key aspects of the introduction strategy and the perception of those in charge of social media. This survey has been employed previously to analyse the same object of study at the level of Spanish regions (Criado and Rojas-Martín 2013b).

A bibliographic review in this recently emerging field highlights a lack of systematic empirical studies. Therefore, the results that are presented in this chapter have relevance at both a theoretical and an empirical level. Firstly, because they contribute to the development of studies of technologies in the public sector. In second place, because they offer primary data derived from research in progress that covers a gap in this field of study in Spain.

The remainder of the chapter is structured in the following way. The next two sections, respectively, define the theoretical and analytical framework of the research. The fourth section, which is of a descriptive character, provides the data and the results of the study. The fifth section is dedicated to a discussion of the results and considers the extent to which the research questions formulated at the start have been addressed. Finally, some conclusions are put forward and future lines of research are suggested.

8.2 Theoretical Framework: Social Technologies to Innovate Public Administrations

Social media are phenomena that, despite only being barely a decade old, have been diffused to the point that they have now reached hundreds of millions of people across the world. In this context of mature technologies and high social demand, the majority of public administrations are adopting social media as a way of getting closer to citizens and improving their profiles (Heidinger et al. 2010). It is not surprising, therefore, that a dynamic field of research is being generated around this phenomena that seeks to analyse the results of the use of these social technologies by public administrations (Criado et al. 2013).

This chapter presents three definitions that bring together key elements to understand what we refer to when we talk about social media. In first place, social networks can be defined as '*a group of Internet-based applications that build on the ideological and technological foundations of Web 2.0, and that allow the creation and exchange of user generated content*' (Kaplan and Haenlein 2010, p. 61). An alternative definition puts emphasis on the interaction between members of the community: '*We define social network sites as web-based services that allow individuals to (1) construct a public or semi-public profile within a bounded system, (2) articulate a list of other users with whom they share a connection, and (3) view and traverse their list of connections and those made by others within the system*' (Boyd and Ellison 2007, p. 211). Finally, Chun et al. (2010, p. 2) propose a definition that situates the individual as '*prosumer*': '*Web 2.0 Technologies' refer to a collection of social media through which individuals are active participants in creating, organizing, editing, combining, sharing, commenting, and rating Web content as well as forming a social network through interacting and linking to each other.*'

Social technologies are based on Web 2.0 and facilitate bidirectional communication—a characteristic that allows users to connect with other actors and to publish, exchange, and form opinions, share experiences and knowledge, as well as to collaboratively mark, evaluate, and filter information for sharing—that could give rise to a generation of virtual communities. In the sphere of public administrations, social media could represent a step forward in the evolution of electronic administration. This would transform the process of mediation between public institutions and society (Bailey and Singleton 2010; Dixon 2010; Bertot et al. 2012; Bonsón et al. 2012; Criado and Rojas-Martin 2012; Criado and Gil-Garcia 2013). Some authors go further and consider social media to be key tools that could promote *open government* (Bertot et al. 2012) or even create a *public administration 2.0* (Chun et al. 2010).

When we speak of social media, we refer to various Web 2.0 tools among which are included: microblogging (like Twitter), those that allow the sharing of multimedia (like YouTube, Instagram, Pinterest, Vimeo and Flickr), those that enable users to evaluate places or premises through geolocalisation (like Foursquare), the mashups and open data applications (like Datos.gob.es), crowdsourcing, (like Mechanichal Turk), social messaging tools through mobile devices (like WhatsApp and Line), collaborative sites (like WikiGovernment), generalist massive social networks (like Facebook and Tuenti), or professional networks (like NovaGob, Govloop and Linkedin), among other tools (Boyd and Ellison 2007; Kaplan and Haenlein 2010; Urueña 2011; Criado and Rojas-Martin 2013a). Appropriate selection of these tools is fundamental because each offers specific characteristics. However, recent studies show that the selection criteria used by public administrations is more related to the social media's size (Criado et al. 2013). Finally, these technologies offer the opportunity to evaluate their use by exploiting the *'big data'* generated by users, which is a key element to bear in mind for their appropriate management.

In sum, the existing literature highlights innovation of social media in the public sphere. In this context, there are those who believe that these technologies contribute to: generating public information collectively (Nam 2012; Bertot et al. 2012), increasing administrative transparency (Meijer and Thaens 2010; Bertot et al. 2012; Bonsón et al. 2013), improving efficiency in terms of costs (Andersen et al. 2012), boosting participation (Ellison and Hardey 2014; Linders 2012), facilitating the co-production of public services (Chun and Warner 2010), and generating administrations that are more innovative and more focused on the citizenry (Bonsón et al. 2012). In other words, applied to society, social media could help create more open and perceptive governments, while their use at an organisational level could shift bureaucratic public administrations towards more horizontal and collaborative models.

Public administrations are using social media, mainly Facebook and Twitter, as tools to boost their relationship with citizens. Specifically, public administrations trust these 2.0 tools to increase information, participation, transparency, and collaboration in their relationships with citizens (Criado and Rojas-Martín 2013b). However, recent studies show that we are at an initial stage of development and that sections of the Spanish public administration have not met some of these objectives (Criado and Rojas-Martín 2013b; Graells and Ramilo 2013). These conclusions coincide with recent analogous studies at international level (Bonsón et al. 2012; Agostino 2013; Mossberger et al. 2013; Ellison and Hardey 2014; Sharif et al. 2014; Mainka et al. 2014).

8.3 Analytic Strategy and Methodology

This section presents the analytical strategy that guides the study. This research aims to analyse the process of adoption and use of social media in Spanish municipalities with more than 50,000 inhabitants. In order to achieve this objective, the following research questions have been established: (1) What are the key factors that explain the use of social media in public administrations? (2) What is the perception of those who manage social media regarding the level of development in their institution? (3) What are the key inhibitors for the development of these technologies in local administrations?

There are over 8,000 local governments in Spain, although the overwhelming majority are small in size. These types of public administrations have a long historical trajectory in the Spanish politico-administrative map. The Spanish Constitution of 1978, article 140, guarantees the autonomy of the municipalities, which has led to them taking on significant responsibilities for public services (Vallés and Brugué 2001), despite recent legislative reforms. In this study we have selected municipalities with more than 50,000 inhabitants (146), given that they have a population size and a volume of activity that is conducive to technological innovations. Of those, we have specifically focused on local governments that have at least an active profile in the leading social media, through an institutional account; and therefore the universe is 124 cases (N).

The technique employed to collect data consists in a questionnaire developed by the authors from previous research in the same field of study (Criado and Rojas-Martín 2013b; Hrdinová et al. 2010) (the survey is openly available for those interested by demand to the authors). The work developed for the *National Survey of Social Media Use in State Government* by Bailey and Singleton (2010) has also been taken into account. The questionnaire comprised 21 questions directed at the people in charge, which has allowed us to collect primary data of great value. The data provides information about the state of adoption of these technologies, but they also focus on the personal perceptions that public managers have about their adoption and use. The data collection process took place between March and July 2014 and the rate of response was above 97 % (121 cases), which confirms the representativity and quality of the study's data, as well as the high level of commitment of those in charge of social media in the local governments under analysis.

The dimensions identified (that have served to develop the analysis of the questionnaire) are:

- *Presence of* social media. In this initial phase, studies are seeking to establish the level of presence of public administrations on social media through official accounts (Agostino 2013; Mossberger et al. 2013; Ellison and Hardey 2014; Sharif et al. 2014; Mainka et al. 2014). Generally, this dimension focuses on getting to know in an aggregate way the ratio of presence and the main tools employed.
- *Factors that explain the use of* social media. The purpose of this dimension consists in establishing the reasons that have driven those in charge of social media management in local governments to use these technologies. This is a dimension

that has been previously employed in similar studies about social media (Mergel 2013; Criado and Rojas-Martín 2013b; Gil-García 2012). The identification of these factors will help establish if they are fulfilling their original objectives.

- *Perception about the development of* social media. This dimension is used to analyse the perception of those responsible for social media projects. As has already been shown in previous studies, it is expected that we will find an optimistic outlook about the development and potential of these technologies (Bailey and Singleton 2010).
- *Inhibitors for the development of* social media. One of the aspects that receives least attention in this field of study is that related to inhibitors to the adoption of these technologies in public administrations. More than a few challenges have been identified in relation to these technologies in the public sphere (Han 2013).

In sum, this study is based on the analysis of the previously defined dimensions. The interpretation of the data collected through the questionnaire and of the observation of the official accounts of local governments provides some conclusions of interest in this incipient field of study. The following section presents data analysis on each of the dimensions of study.

8.4 Data and Results

In this section, we are going to present the data collected from the questionnaire about the adoption of social media. Of the 146 local governments with more than 50,000 inhabitants that exist in Spain, a total of 124 institutions have official accounts (84.9 %). Besides the information collected through the questionnaire, this data has been checked by observation and direct identification of the official accounts of the local governments. Of the 124 local governments with social media, 121 responded to the questionnaire, which represents 97.6 % of the total.

The analysis must be interpreted within the context of a recent diffusion of these technologies at this level of government, and therefore, they are at an early stage of development. Specifically, descriptive data will be shown to try to respond to each of the dimensions identified in the analytic strategy: (a) the departments responsible for their management, (b) user guides, (c) main social technologies employed, (d) motivations for their adoption, (e) perception about its development, and (f) inhibitors for its use.

8.4.1 Departments Responsible for the Management of Social Media

This organisational dimension aims to identify the department, unit, or area of the town hall where social media management is undertaken. The data shown in Fig. 8.1 can serve to help us understand the strategic direction that is being taken in the

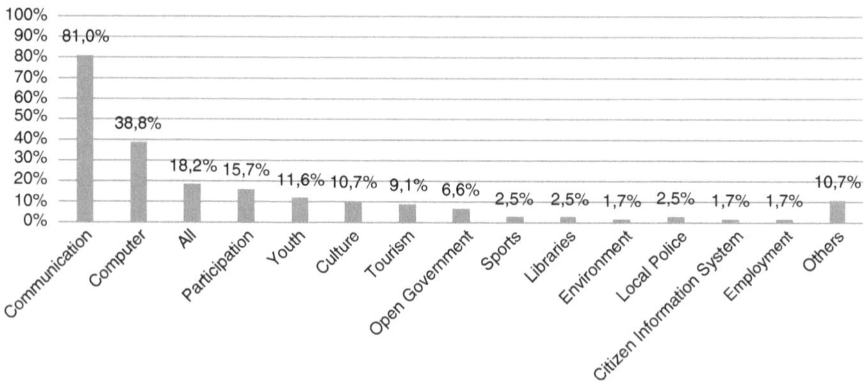

Fig. 8.1 Departments responsible for the management of social media. *Source:* own elaboration. Question 8. Could you indicate which unit/s or department/s are involved in the management of social networks in the town hall? ($N = 121$)

introduction of these technologies. Additionally, we are going to focus on whether the management of social media is centralised or decentralised, given that cases exist in which various, or all, departments of the town hall participate in their management (see Fig. 8.1). This aspect is significant because it will help us understand if the strategy is aligned with the 2.0 philosophy, which seeks to create more horizontal and inclusive organisations.

The data collected show that a preponderance of communication and computer departments are involved in the management of social media. Specifically, the department of communication managed social media in 81 % of local governments, while the computer department was identified in 38.8 % of cases. The department of communication's involvement in the management of social media could be due to the informational dimension of these tools. However, this leaves in the background other relevant elements such as participation and collaboration, which coincides with the conclusions of previous studies at the level of Spain's regions (Criado and Rojas-Martín 2013b). Furthermore, communication departments are commonly located in the area of the mayor's office, which indicates the important role that they are granted within the organisation. On the other hand, the significance of computer departments in the management of social media could be explained by the technological dimension of these tools.

Additionally, a significant number of local governments have other departments that also participate in social media management. As can be seen in Fig. 8.1, the survey predominantly identified the departments of citizen participation, youth, culture, and tourism. It seems significant that there are so many departments involved in social media management. This fact could be interpreted as a step towards the distribution of their management among various town hall departments. In fact, 18.2 % of local governments responded that *all* departments are involved in the management of social media. This percentage could indicate a tendency towards growth in the future, given that decentralised management is one of the characteristics that define these types of tools.

Finally, it is worth mentioning that the first departments specialising in *open government* are starting to appear. Specifically, eight local governments now manage social media through these types of specialised units (6.6 %), which is something entirely novel in the Spanish municipal sphere. In the years that follow, scholars will need to be alert to the spread of these departments, as their appearance will be accompanied predictably by the most distinct development of 'the most distinct aspect of the adoption of' social media as facilitating tools.

8.4.2 The Introduction of Policies or Guidance for the Use of Digital Social Media

User guides are formal documents that draw together the most relevant points for the appropriate management of social media in public administrations. These documents seek to formalise, organise, and orientate; taking into account the fact that social media have only been recently adopted by the public sector. Therefore, the identification of the existence of guides—or their non-existence—can serve as an indicator of a certain 'normalisation' of their use within an organisation. Their absence does not mean that municipalities are doing things incorrectly, but those institutions that have developed them demonstrate their commitment by the mere fact of having dedicated time and resources to reflect upon and formalise the use of social media.

In order to clarify what is being referred to when we speak of user guides, and without seeking to offer a definitive definition, the definition included in the 'Use and style guide of Catalonia's region' (Generalitat de Cataluña 2013) has been chosen, as it was pioneering in Spain: "*The use and style guide in social networks establishes some common guidelines for a homogeneous presence in social networks. The Guide contains the procedure recommended to open email accounts or create accounts and profiles in any department, service [...] in these spaces of relationship and participation. It also enumerates the different social networking tools, the diverse uses and objectives of each, recommendations for an appropriate and fruitful presence, and the style criteria that is most appropriate for each tool.*"

As can be seen in Fig. 8.2, in order to establish if local governments have user guides available, five possible alternatives were established, and those in charge of local governments were consulted. In first place, 26.4 % of local governments were found to have a document of this type. In second place, 43.8 % of municipalities confirmed that they do not have a user guide—and furthermore that they do not foresee them being developed. In third place are local governments that do not have a user guide, but state that they are planning to develop them in less than a year (21.5 %). In fourth place are local governments that do not have a user guide, but foresee them being developed in more than a year (7.4 %). Finally, other examples

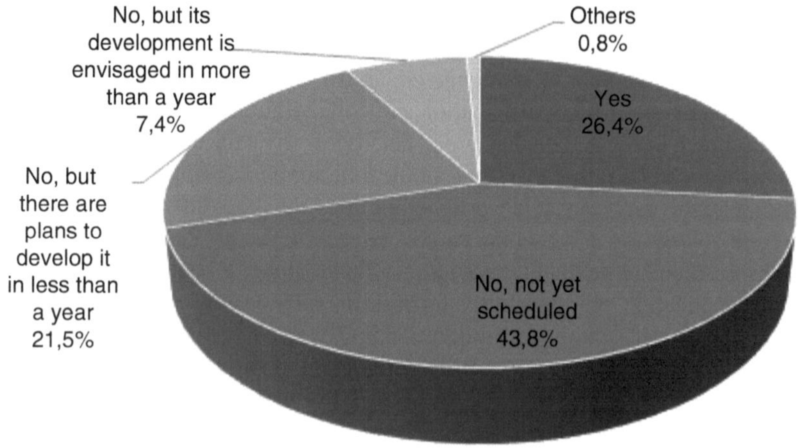

Fig. 8.2 Existence of user guides for social media. *Source:* own elaboration. Question 4. Please indicate if a user guide has been developed for use in digital social networks in your administration. ($N = 120$)

that do not feature among the above are not discussed here because they barely represent 1 % of the total cases.

The data show that only a quarter of the local governments state that they have a document with these characteristics. As we have just seen, this could be interpreted as a weakness in the process of adoption of these technologies by local governments. At the same time, there are reasons for pessimism because almost half the local governments stated that they are not planning to establish a document of this type. In sum, in the majority of cases studied, there exists an absence of formal documents that establish the criteria and minimum management procedures for the use of social media.

8.4.3 Principal Social Technologies Employed

As we have previously seen in this chapter, there exists a wide variety of social media available on the market. Each application offers specific characteristics, and so by identifying the tools most widely employed, we are able to establish the focus of local governments in their adoption of these technologies. That is the reason for our interest in establishing the main tools that the municipalities have chosen.

Local governments have almost unanimously opted for exogenous tools to the organisation (95 %). That means, they have selected a social media created and managed by private companies rather than establishing their own tools. This first feature could indicate a strategy by local governments that is oriented towards the tools which are most used by citizens. However, the presence of social media that are foreign to public institutions introduces unknown factors that are worth bearing in mind. In sum, this group of local governments has not implemented internal social platforms (in the vein of *challenge.gov* in the United States, or *irekia.net* in the Basque Country) to foster participation and collaboration with the citizenry.

The data shown in Fig. 8.3 display broad heterogeneity in the use of social media. Local governments opt, rather than for a single tool, for a *toolkit* of social technologies. Among all the networks, it is worth highlighting the preeminence of *Facebook* (99.2 %) and *Twitter* (96.7 %). In the case of *Facebook,* we are speaking about the most widespread social media in the world; in Spain alone, it has some 18 million users. This application predominantly focuses on relationships with friends and families, but companies, public institutions, and other social organisations also have a place. *Twitter*, on the other hand, is a *microblogging* application that has experienced high growth in recent years and that allows a high degree of interaction with other users through the exchange of information.

Besides *Facebook* and *Twitter*, we find, in third and fourth place, two tools oriented to multimedia exchange. On the one hand, *YouTube*—that allows videos contributed by users to be shared, commented upon, and evaluated—situates itself as the third most used tool by local governments (79.3 %). On the other, there is *Flickr*, oriented to sharing, commenting upon, and evaluating images uploaded by users (52.1 %). All these tools have some characteristics in common: they are free, anyone with a connection to the Internet can access them, and they are owned by companies that are external to local governments.

As has been mentioned, local governments choose tools that are: operated by companies outside their organisation and free and have the largest number of users like *Facebook*, *Twitter,* and *YouTube*. This could be explained by the budgetary restrictions that local governments have recently been experiencing. Additionally, it

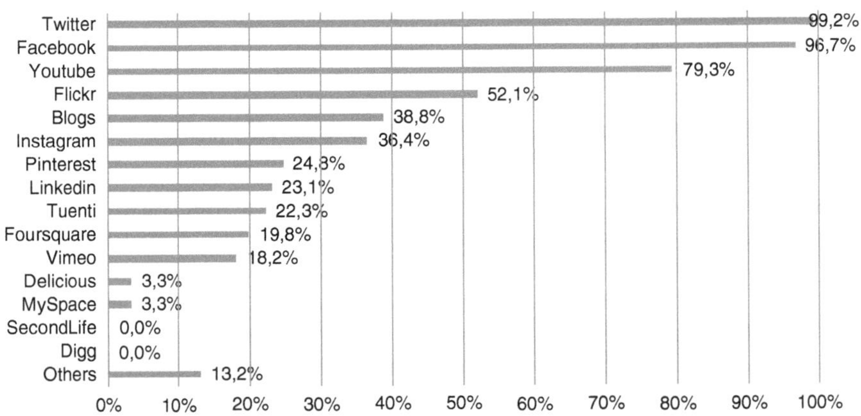

Fig. 8.3 Principal social media employed. *Source:* own elaboration. Question 7. Please indicate in which digital social networks your town hall has a presence and the number of active profiles ($N = 121$)

is congruent with similar studies presented in recent years (Urueña 2011; Criado and Rojas-Martin 2012). The use of applications that are managed by companies external to local governments opens up diverse unknown factors, such as the fact that data and legislation correspond to countries that are foreign to Spanish local governments.

8.4.4 *Motivations for the Use of Social Media*

The fourth aspect to be analysed are the motivations that have moved local governments to adopt social media. As said above, understanding the reasons for their use will indicate municipalities' current stage of development and establish whether their stated objectives have been achieved. For that reason, it is essential to know the motivations of those who are responsible for their management in Spanish local governments.

Generally, more attention is being paid to the use of social media as a tool that can improve relationships with citizens: specifically regarding information, transparency, and participation. However, internally they can serve to boost collaboration and efficiency (Andersen et al. 2012) within public organisations. In the analysis of motivations behind the use of social media, we are going to focus on whether they are more oriented towards the external or internal dimension (Fig. 8.4).

The three main reasons given by local governments are, in first place, to *offer information* (96.7 %), in second place, *increase participation* (80.2 %), and in the third place, *increase transparency* (76 %). The first point worth highlighting is that these three elements are directed towards *outside* the organisation, or in other words, towards society. Therefore, one can infer that the local governments are principally backing social media as a tool directed towards improving communications and

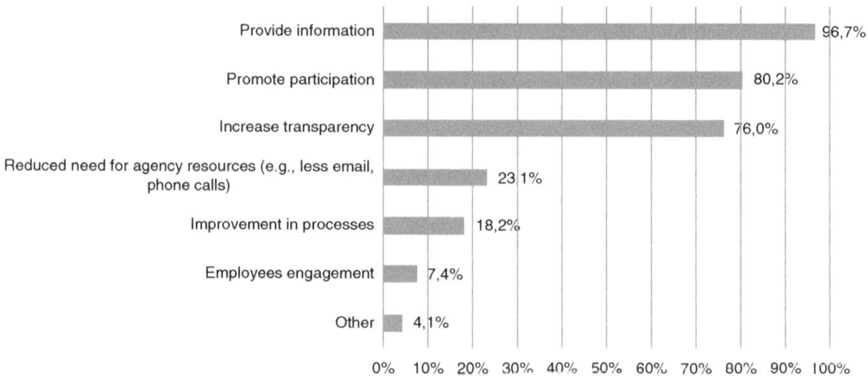

Fig. 8.4 Motivations for the use of social media. *Source:* own elaboration. Question 14. What are the main reasons that your town hall employs digital social networks? ($N=119$)

their relationships with citizens. This coincides with the results of previous studies at regional level (Criado and Rojas-Martin 2012). These results could also be related to the fact that it is the department of communication in the local governments that lead the process of adopting social media.

On the other hand, the questions related to the internal dimension remain in the background, including the possibility of: *reducing the resources necessary for the functioning of the administration* (23.1 %), *improving processes* (18.2 %), and *involving employees of the administration* (7.4 %). Therefore, it can be seen that there is considerable margin for improvement for the adoption of social media in this internal dimension, which could benefit efficiency in management (Andersen et al. 2012) by means of the improvement of channels of internal communication, intra and inter-administrative collaboration, modernisation of the processes of recruitment, and/or an increase in participation in the taking of decisions.

8.4.5 Perception About the Level of Development of Social Media

Leadership is a significant factor when starting up technological projects in public organisations, and therefore there is a need to understand the self-perception of those in charge about the level of development of social media in their institution. Their vision will allow us to better interpret the future evolution of social media in their organisation. It is reasonable to think that if their perception indicates a high level of development, then the evolution of social media in the following years will probably be more limited. On the other hand, if a low level of development is perceived, the margin for improvement will be greater. In order to try to measure this variable, we employed the questionnaire to ask managers about their institution's current level of development; asking them to position themselves on a scale from 1 to 5; 1 being the minimum development and 5 the maximum.

As can be seen in Fig. 8.5, the data show a perception of a *high development level* (46.4 %) or *maximum* (6.6 %) by those in charge of social media in local governments. That means, in 53 % of cases they think that their development is high. On the other hand, a small percentage of the total considers that their development is *low* (6.9 %) or *minimum* (1.3 %). Without doubt, these data offer an optimistic vision by those who manage social media in municipalities. This optimism contrasts with other results from this study that point to an incipient phase of development in local governments. It could be argued that local governments' strategy is more oriented towards communication, and that as a consequence the objective of providing information through social media has already been completed; therefore, managers indicate that they are satisfied with their current level of development. If that is the case, this perspective would confirm the need to increase understanding about the potential of social technologies in the activity of Spanish local governments.

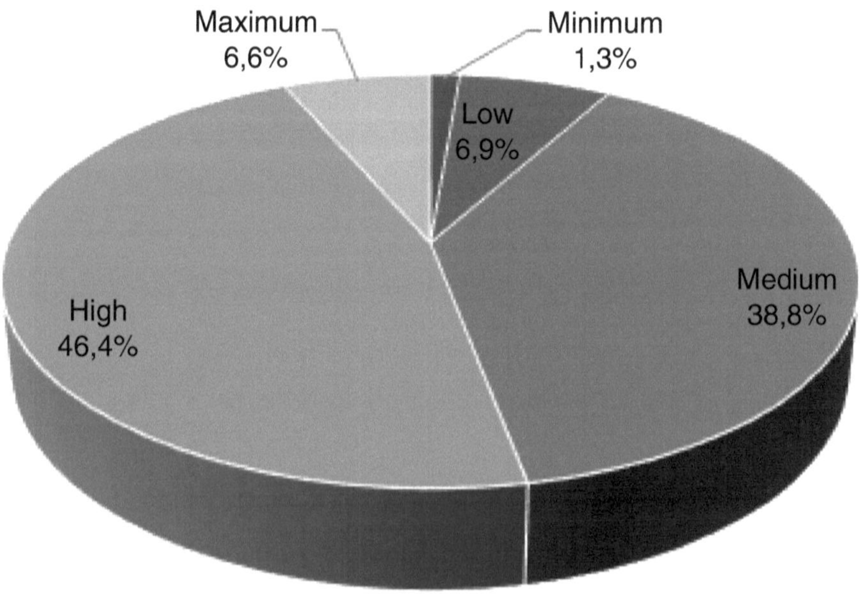

Fig. 8.5 Perception of the level of development of social media. *Source:* own elaboration. Question 16. Despite the concerns and aforementioned risks, how would you characterise the level of development of the digital social networks in your town hall? ($N=116$)

8.4.6 Inhibitors in the Use of Social Media

In this section, we are going to identify the main inhibitors for the use of social media in public administrations. For that reason, we have asked those in charge of these tools in local governments to choose between eight possible options that have been identified as barriers to the use of social technologies in public organisations (Bailey and Singleton 2010). Each of the possible responses must be marked on a scale where 1 is considered to be a very low inhibitor and 5 very high. This information will allow us to better understand the barriers that might slow, or even impede, the use of social media.

The data show the average of the responses of all the local governments. The greatest inhibitors to the use of social media in local governments are the: *organisational culture* (2.6/5) and *security* (2.6/5). These are followed closely by concerns about the absence of a governmental framework (2.4/5) and privacy (2.4/5). As can be seen, all of these inhibitors could be explained by the existing lack of experience in organisations in this sphere, as employees are dealing with technologies that have been introduced in recent years (Fig. 8.6).

It is notable that despite support for the use of social media, as we have seen above, the tools are external to local governments, and those in charge have to trust

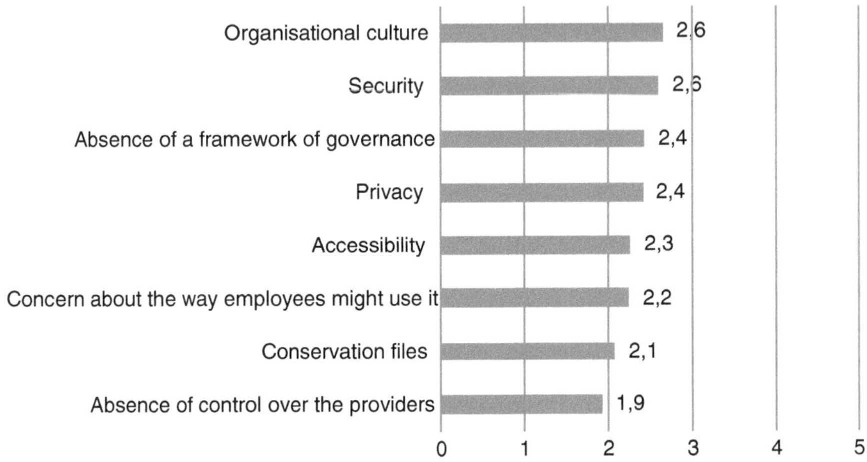

Fig. 8.6 Inhibitors for the use of social media. *Source:* own elaboration. Question 15. The following questions have been considered as inhibitors in the use of digital social networks in public administrations or as potential risks. (1 is very low and 5 very high). ($N=116$)

when faced with *a lack of control over the suppliers*. In fact, this inhibitor was selected as 'the least relevant' of the inhibitors (1.9/5). One possible explanation for this result would be that given that the use of social media is predominantly focused on improving information for citizens, there are no formal commitments for local governments. As has been shown by other available data, local governments are employing these tools as an additional channel of 'up-down' informal communication, more than as formal tools to increase *open government.* Given this conclusion, perhaps it is necessary to raise the question about what is the best strategy for leaders in the management of social media in public organisations.

8.5 Discussion and Conclusions

This section presents the main contributions of this research, as well as how it advances the study of social media in public administrations. This study responds to the research questions raised at the start: (1) What are the key factors that explain the use of social media in public administrations? (2) What is the perception of those who manage social media regarding the level of development in their institution? (3) What are the key inhibitors for the development of these technologies in local administrations? The data presented provide relevant information for the development of this field of study and help us better understand the strategies, uses, and level of development of social technologies in local governments.

The results obtained in this study show that the use of social media by local governments is both a reality and that *it has come to stay*. Spanish local governments with more than 50,000 inhabitants have adopted these technologies in a generalised way. The data obtained show a high diffusion of these technologies (84.9 %). Furthermore, the factors that have motivated the introduction of social media in local governments (*information, transparency, and participation*) coincide with the objectives described in the literature (Meijer and Thaens 2010; Nam 2012; Bertot et al. 2012; Bertot et al. 2012; Linders 2012; Criado and Rojas-Martin 2012; Bonsón et al. 2013; Ellison and Hardey 2014).

However, this high level of diffusion does not signify that they are achieving the objectives that inspired their adoption. The potential improvements that social media could bring to local governments have barely been achieved. It is possible that the adoption of social media has favoured an improvement in the dimension of information; however, data do not exist that demonstrate that local governments are achieving greater quotas of transparency and participation. The results obtained in this study show a still incipient development in the use of these social technologies, which besides are similar to the results of recent studies at international level (Agostino 2013; Bonsón et al. 2012; Ellison and Hardey 2014).

The adoption of social media by local governments clearly shows a double strategy on the basis of the tools adopted: (1) support for the use of external applications developed by private companies that are provided for free and (2) prioritisation for the use of the most popular applications among citizens. Local governments have rarely developed their own applications, but instead have chosen *Facebook, Twitter,* and *YouTube,* which already have broad diffusion. The reasons for this might be found in the context of restricted expenditure among local governments and the attempt to have an institutional presence where citizens can be found. In other words, local governments are employing social media as tools to get closer to citizens, as has been highlighted above, with the objective of improving information, transparency, and participation.

The perception of those responsible for the level of social media in their institutions in general terms is highly optimistic. Besides considering that their local governments have a high level of development, they rarely identify significant inhibitors to the use of social media. The two main elements identified as inhibitors are the *organisational culture* and *security*. However, as has been seen above, they have not been identified as critical elements. Similarly, those in charge have confidence in their use despite the fact that: (1) their management is not formalised in documents or formal user guides that orientate and assure their correct functioning and (2) the tools employed are outside the control of the local governments. This perception, that is considered *cyberoptimist*, could be due to the fact that local governments are employing these tools as means of communication, rather than as a new space to increase transparency, participation, and collaboration.

The results of this research show some weaknesses in the process of adoption of social media by local governments that could be resolved by putting in place specific strategies. Among the actions to develop, we would emphasise, in first place, the need to define a strategy to achieve the objectives that motivated their adoption. In second place, to formalise their uses, styles, and processes to achieve the said objectives. Additionally, to transform the organisational culture following the

2.0 philosophy, in a more inclusive and horizontal way, by adequately training public employees. Finally, local governments need to address the challenges of security, privacy, and ethics that the use of these technologies entails. These weaknesses, identified during the research, bring into question whether the management models that have been adopted, in their current forms, are the most appropriate to implement policies of transparency, participation, and collaboration in local governments.

This chapter has contributed to the field of study of social media in the public sector by presenting new data about the larger Spanish local governments, which additionally will be able to serve for future comparative studies at international level. Methodologically, this study sustains itself on the responses to the questionnaire sent to those in charge of social media in local governments and a review of the most current bibliography. Therefore, in this initial phase of introduction, this research will be of interest as much for professionals within the public sector as for researchers specialising in this field of study. At the same time, it is hoped to evolve the work with a statistical exploitation of the data in an even more sophisticated way.

The results obtained in this research deal exclusively with Spanish local governments with more than 50,000 inhabitants. Therefore, they must not be generalised to other sections of the public sector (or specific public policies areas), although many of the results coincide with studies previously undertaken in the Spanish regional sphere (Criado and Rojas-Martín 2013b). In order to go deeper in this field of study, new research of a systematic character and also comparative analysis between different countries are necessary to help contrast the data presented in this research, as well as other work already mentioned above. Additionally, it would be interesting to develop studies of a sectorial character focused on the analysis of social media for specific public policies.

Acknowledgement This research has been funded by the grant CSO2013-48641-C2-1-R, Spanish Ministry of Economy and Competitiveness, project: A new local architecture: efficiency, dimension, and democracy.

References

Agostino, D. (2013). Using social media to engage citizens: A study of Italian municipalities. *Public Relations Review, 39*(3), 232–234.

Andersen, K. N., Medaglia, R., & Henriksen, H. Z. (2012). Social media in public health care: Impact domain propositions. *Government Information Quarterly, 29*(4), 462–469.

Bailey, C., & Singleton, R. (2010). *National survey of social media use in state government.* Lexington, KY: NASCIO.

Bertot, J. C., Jaeger, P. T., & Grimes, J. M. (2010). Using ICTs to create a culture of transparency: E-government and social media as openness and anti-corruption tools for societies. *Government Information Quarterly, 27*(3), 264–271.

Bertot, J. C., Jaeger, P. T., & Hansen, D. (2012). The impact of polices on government social media usage: Issues, challenges, and recommendations. *Government Information Quarterly, 29*(1), 30–40.

Bonsón, E., Royo, S., & Ratkai, M. (2013). Analysis of European municipalities' Facebook channels activity and citizens' engagement. Retrieved August 16, 2014, from http://www.aeca.es/pub/on_line/comunicaciones_xviicongresoaeca/cd/84g.pdf.

Bonsón, E., Torres, L., Royo, S., & Flores, F. (2012). Local e-government 2.0: Social media and corporate transparency in municipalities. *Government Information Quarterly, 29*(2), 123–132.

Boyd, D. M., & Ellison, N. B. (2007). Social network sites: Definition, history, and scholarship. *Journal of Computer-Mediated Communication, 13*(1), 210–230.

Chun, S. A., Shulman, S., Sandoval, R., & Hovy, E. (2010). Government 2.0. Making connections between citizens, data and government. *Information Polity: The International Journal of Government & Democracy in the Information Age, 15*(1–2), 1–9.

Chun, S. A., & Warner, J. (2010). Finding information in an era of abundance: Towards a collaborative tagging environment in government. *Information Polity: The International Journal of Government & Democracy in the Information Age, 15*(1–2), 89–103.

Criado, J. I., & Gil-García, J. R. (2013). Gobierno Electrónico, Gestión y Políticas Públicas. *Gestión y Política Pública, 22*, 3–48.

Criado, J.I., & Rojas-Martin, F. (2012). *Strategies and realities of social media diffusion in the public sector: Evidence from the regional government in Spain.* Paper presented at the annual meeting of the European Group of Public Administration. Bergen, Norway.

Criado, J.I., & Rojas-Martin, F. (2013a). (Eds.). *Las redes sociales digitales en la gestión y las políticas públicas. Avances y desafíos para un gobierno abierto*. Barcelona: EAPC.

Criado, J. I., & Rojas-Martín, F. (2013b). Social media and public administration in Spain: A comparative analysis of the regional level of government. In J. Gil-Garcia (Ed.), *E-Government success around the world: Cases, empirical studies, and practical recommendations* (pp. 276–298). IGI Global: Hershey, PA.

Criado, J. I., Sandoval-Almazán, R., & Gil-García, R. (2013). Government innovation through social media. *Government Information Quarterly, 30*(4), 320–328.

Generalitat de Cataluña (2013). Guía de usos y estilo en las redes sociales de la Generalitat de Cataluña. Retrieved August 2014, from http://www.gencat.cat/web/meugencat/documents/guia_usos_xarxa_es.pdf.

Dixon, B. E. (2010). Towards e-government 2.0: An assessment of where e-government 2.0 is and where it is headed. *Public Administration & Management, 15*(2), 418–454.

Ellison, N., & Hardey, M. (2014). Social media and local government: Citizenship, consumption and democracy. *Local Government Studies, 40*(1), 21–40.

Elogia (2014). *V Estudio Anual sobre Redes Sociales IAB*. Madrid, Spain.

Gil-García, J. R. (2012). *Enacting electronic government success: An integrative study of government-wide websites, organizational capabilities, and institutions*. New York: Springer.

Graells i Costa, J., & Ramilo Araujo, M. (2013). *Ciudadanía y administraciones en red: la Administración Pública ante la nueva sociedad en red.* Oleiros: Netbiblo.

Han, B.-C. (2013). *La Sociedad de las transparencia*. Barcelona: Herder.

Heidinger, C., Buchmann, E., & Böhn, K. (2010). Impact assessment in public policy: Towards a web 2.0 application. *Information Polity: The International Journal of Government & Democracy in the Information Age, 15*(1–2), 33–50.

Hrdinová, J., Helbig, N., & Peters, C. S. (2010). Designing social media policy for government: Eight essential elements, Albany: The Research foundation of State University of New York. Retrieved August 16, 2014, from http://www.ctg.albany.edu/publications.

Kaplan, A. M., & Haenlein, M. (2010). Users of the world, unite! The challenges and opportunities of social media. *Business Horizons, 53*(1), 59–68.

Linders, D. (2012). From e-government to we-government: Defining a typology for citizen coproduction in the age of social media. *Government Information Quarterly, 29*(4), 446–454.

Mainka, A., Hartmann, S., Stock, W. G., & Peters, I. (2014). Government and social media: A case study of 31 informational world cities. In R. H. Sprague (Ed.), *Proceeding of the 47th Hawaii international conference on system sciences* (pp. 1715–1724). Waikoloa: CPS.

Meijer, A., & Thaens, M. (2010). Alignment 2.0: Strategic use of new internet technologies in government. *Government Information Quarterly, 27*(2), 113–121.

Mergel, I. (2012). The social media innovation challenge in the public sector. *Information Polity, 17*(3–4), 281–292.
Mergel, I. (2013). Social media adoption and resulting tactics in the U.S. federal government. *Government Information Quarterly, 30*(2), 123–130.
Mossberger, K., Wu, Y., & Crawford, J. (2013). Connecting citizens and local governments? Social media and interactivity in major U.S. cities. *Government Information Quarterly, 30*(4), 351–358.
Nam, T. (2012). Dual effects of the internet on political activism: Reinforcing and mobilizing. *Government Information Quarterly, 29*(1), 90–97.
Sáez-Martín, A., Haro-de-Rosario, A., & Caba-Perez, C. (2014). A vision of social media in the Spanish Smartest Cities. *Transforming Government: People, Process and Policy, 8*(4), 521–544.
Sharif, M. H. M., Troshani, I., & Davidson, R. (2014). Adoption of social media services: The case of local government organizations in Australia. In Z. Sun & J. Yearwood (Eds.), *Handbook of research on demand-driven web services: Theory, technologies, and applications* (pp. 207–308). Hershey, PA: IGI Global.
Urueña (2011). Las Redes Sociales en Internet. Madrid:ONTSI. Retrieved August 14, 2014, from http://www.ontsi.red.es/ontsi/es/estudios-informes.
Urueña, A. (2013). La Sociedad en Red. Informe Anual 2013. Madrid:ONTSI. Retrieved August 14, 2014, from http://www.ontsi.red.es/ontsi/es/estudios-informes.
Vallés, J. M., & Brugué, Q. (2001). El gobierno local. In M. Alcántara & A. Martínez (Eds.), *Política y Gobierno en España* (pp. 267–302). Valencia: Tirant lo blanch.

Chapter 9
Greek Local E-Government 2.0: Drivers and Outcomes of Social Media Adoption

Amalia Triantafillidou, Georgios Lappas, Prodromos Yannas, and Alexandros Kleftodimos

Abstract Are Greek local governments moving towards e-government 2.0 model? What are the factors that impact adoption of Web 2.0 tools? What is the effectiveness of these tools in terms of citizens' awareness, interest, and engagement? The present study addresses these questions by investigating the usage and effectiveness of Web 2.0 applications employed by the 325 Greek local governments. Results indicate that local authorities in Greece are moving towards an e-government 2.0 era, albeit slowly. Local governments originating from municipalities with a large number of educated inhabitants who have made use of e-government services are more likely to be adopters of Web 2.0 tools. In addition, findings suggest that Greek citizens are beginning to be more aware of the Facebook pages of their local governments while they seem more interested in their YouTube channels. Hopefully, local governments can increase their citizens' engagement by being active on Facebook. Officials of local governments should increase their presence on social media such as Facebook and YouTube but their strategies should be differentiated for each social medium in order to benefit from their potential.

9.1 Introduction

During the Web 1.0 era, ICTs technologies did not manage to transform the traditional bureaucratic government model into a more participatory, deliberative, and citizen-centric model (Tat-Kei Ho 2002). However, the e-government 1.0 paradigm failed to enhance public participation (Scott 2006) as it focused on the digitization

A. Triantafillidou (✉) • G. Lappas • A. Kleftodimos
Department of Digital Media and Communication, Technological Education Institute of Western Macedonia, P.O. Box 30, Fourka Area 52 100, Kastoria, Greece
e-mail: amtriantafil@aueb.gr; lappas@kastoria.teikoz.gr; kleftodimos@kastoria.teikoz.gr

P. Yannas
Department of Business Administration, Technological Education Institute of Piraeus, Petrou Ralli & Thivon 250, 122 44, Aigaleo, Greece
e-mail: prodyannas@teipir.gr

M.Z. Sobaci (ed.), *Social Media and Local Governments*, Public Administration and Information Technology 15, DOI 10.1007/978-3-319-17722-9_9

of administrative processes (Dixon 2010), information dissemination, service delivery, and cost reduction (Christensen 2013). Following a customer orientation approach, e-government 1.0 did not reach its maturity stage (i.e., e-participation and e-transformation) (Coursey and Norris 2008). However, expectations towards e-democracy models have risen again with the emergence of Web 2.0 applications. Interactive platforms such as social media have been described as "new innovative ways to deliver public value" (Linders 2012, p. 446) capable of reinforcing democracy and citizens' involvement in policy making (Larsson 2013).

The role of social media in spearheading political participation becomes even more vital for local governments since citizens feel more connected with their local authorities (Avery and Graham 2013). Despite the importance of social media in engaging citizenship in participatory democracy, their successful adoption by government agencies at the local level is relatively low. Moreover, empirical evidence suggests that a great amount of variability exists in the implementation of Web 2.0 platforms in municipalities around the globe. For example, studies in the United States have revealed high adoption rates of social media at the local level (Mossberger et al. 2013; Oliveira and Welch 2013). However, these interactive platforms have not been effectively employed by the US local governments which instead insist on using these interactive tools primarily as one-way communication vehicles (Norris and Reddick 2013; Reddick and Norris 2013). On the other hand, adoption of e-government 2.0 at the local level in Europe has not yet reached a stage of maturity. Bonsón et al. (2012) investigating 15 large European cities found that local governments are not utilizing to a great extent social media platforms. Low to moderate usage of social media platforms by local governments were also found in countries like Germany (Hofmann et al. 2013; Van Veenstra et al. 2011), Sweden (Larsson 2013), Finland (Christensen 2013), and Italy (Agostino 2013). In a similar vein, municipalities in Egypt have been exploiting social media in their web pages quite slowly (Abdelsalam et al. 2013) while poor levels of interactive communication were also found in the websites of several Mexican local government authorities (Sandoval-Almazan and Gil-Garcia 2012). Hence, few government agencies at the local level have fully exploited social media, and even fewer have yet actualized the potential offered by social media in engaging their citizens.

A number of prospective studies have been carried out in recent years about the use of social media by local governments. However, our knowledge about the way local governments are implementing social media strategies (Hofmann et al. 2013) and the derived benefits from such implementation (Guttormsen and Sæbø 2013) is limited. According to Larsson (2013), most of the studies on the use of social media by local governments have been conducted in the United States while more research is needed to explore the way local public administrations in other countries are utilizing social media. Greece presents an interesting case for the study of local government 2.0 even though evidence on the usage e-government 2.0 platforms in Greek municipalities remains scarce. The introduction of ICT in Greek public sector is dated back to the late nineties. Most of the Greek e-government initiatives at the municipality level have been focused around the (a) training of mayors and elected officials in ICT, (b) development of digital services, and (c) implementation of management information systems (e-Government in Greece 2010). In 2005, 53 % of Greek local governments made use of websites in order to communicate with their citizenry (Drogkaris et al. 2010). At that time, most of the e-government tools used by local authorities in Greece focused on information provision rather on the interaction with citizens and the implementation of online transactions (Yannas and Lappas 2007, 2010). After the 2010 "Kallikratis Reform Program," the number of Greek municipalities was reduced from 1,031 to 325 resulting in decentralization of power across local authorities by strengthening the size and organizational level of them. This reform along with the limited funding for e-government initiatives due to the economic crisis places additional burden on the successful adoption of social media by local government in Greece. Hence, the purpose of this study is threefold: (a) to examine the extent to which local government of Greek municipalities are utilizing Web 2.0 applications, (b) to identify the various drivers of social media adoption at the local government level, and (c) to investigate which of Web 2.0 tools is the most effective in terms of citizens' awareness, interest, and engagement.

The present study is organized around eight sections. In the first section, the theoretical background of the study is provided which describes the impact of social media usage on e-government and e-participation, as well as the various social media strategies implemented by governments. Next, the conceptual framework is developed by presenting the findings of other studies regarding the drivers of social media adoption by local governments and the measurement of the effectiveness of social media tactics. Then, the methodology and the results of the study are analyzed followed by a critical discussion of the study's findings and a short conclusion. In the final section, the main limitations of this study are pointed out and future research suggestions are proposed.

9.2 Literature Review

9.2.1 E-Government 2.0: An Emerging Paradigm Shift

The introduction of Web 2.0 technologies in the public sector has been regarded as a turning point in the traditional e-government model (Chun and Reyes 2012). A typical e-government model evolves from initial stages of simple web presence and information dissemination to more transformational stages whereby citizens interact with government agencies, perform transactions, and participate electronically to the activities initiated by the government (Hiller and Belanger 2001; Baum and Di Maio 2000; Wescott 2001). Social media can advance and improve almost every stage of e-government by providing more opportunities for information diffusion (i.e., RSS feed), two-way communication (i.e., Facebook and Twitter), as well as political participation (i.e., online voting, online attention of public hearings) (Dixon 2010). Following the framework proposed by Christensen (2013) for the study of e-democracy, it can be argued that Web 2.0 applications can contribute mainly to the two of the three democratic perspectives, that of participatory and deliberative democracy and not the representative perspective. Several researchers are optimistic of the potential social media have to move to more mature e-government models like Open Government or Government 2.0 (Chun et al. 2010); We-government (Linders 2012); and Social Government (Khan et al. 2010).

E-government 2.0 enthusiasts believe that social media can have positive effects not only for governments but for citizens as well (Chun and Reyes 2012). On the government side, interactive applications are a cost-effective and convenient way for information dissemination (Mossberger et al. 2013) and massive distribution of content to citizens (Bonsón et al. 2012). Social media can prove quite beneficial to local governments when they seek to inform citizens quickly for emergency matters (i.e., safety issues, natural disasters) (Kavanaugh et al. 2012). The increased penetration of social media such as Facebook helps local governments implement more egalitarian forms of governance, like reaching citizens who have never been involved in policy making before (Mergel 2012).

Local governments can also use social media to mine content generated from citizens about their attitudes and views on various issues (Abdelsalam et al. 2013). Crowd-sourcing opinions and ideas from citizens give local authorities the opportunity to effectively capture and manage citizens' critical knowledge which can serve as input in processes regarding public services design (Bonsón et al. 2012) and policy making (Mergel 2013). Besides mining citizens' generated content, local government can benefit from asking citizens for feedback about important community problems (Mergel 2012). This way, innovative solutions to important community problems can arise (Ferro et al. 2013) through citizens' engagement. In addition, interactive applications can help local governments find the most influential community members who are online and communicate with them more effectively (Kavanaugh et al. 2012). Increased transparency and accountability of local government initiatives are also other important benefits derived from the utilization of Web 2.0 technologies (Sandoval-Almazan and Gil-Garcia 2012). Moreover, relations between local governments can improve through the actualization of social media (Norris and Reddick 2013) resulting in a more networked (Mossberger et al. 2013) and integrated forms of governance.

On the demand side, all levels of e-participation (i.e., informing, consulting, advising, co-producing, and co-deciding) (Van Veenstra et al. 2011) could be enhanced through the exploitation of Web 2.0 applications at the local level. Specifically, citizens can become more informed (Chun and Reyes 2012) and interested (Mossberger et al. 2013) about local government activities and events. The interactive features of social media can advance the way citizens communicate with government officials as well as with other citizens (Kavanaugh et al. 2012; Bonsón et al. 2012), elaborating multi-party discussions (Mossberger et al. 2013), triggering the dialogue between citizens and local governments (Guttormsen and Sæbø 2013); thus, limiting the "distance" between citizens and local authorities (Hofmann et al. 2013) while cultivating stronger citizen-government relations (Avery and Graham

2013). Social media can enable more active forms of participation. For example, citizens can provide feedback to local authorities about new public services, thus becoming co-producers, co-designers, and co-developers of services (Ferro et al. 2013). As Linders (2012) notes citizens turn from passive consumers of public services to active participants in joint production of services. Moreover, citizens can be empowered to "participate in the public debate …and add issues to the political agenda" (Guttormsen and Sæbø 2013, p. 159). Co-deciding and collaborating with the local authorities about serious community problems is another important benefit derived from citizens' engagement with the social media used by local government (Mergel 2013). As a consequence, citizens feel that they have a say in local governance and become more involved with government activities. Increased involvement with local governments' social media heightens trust in local authorities resulting in greater public value (Tolbert and Mossberger 2006).

In Table 9.1, we summarize the possible benefits associated with the exploitation of Web 2.0 applications by local governments.

However, one should bear in mind that e-government 2.0 initiatives are not risk free. Several critics have cast doubt about the potential of social media in transforming government (Coursey and Norris 2008). Relying on opinions citizens upload on social media might endanger the outcomes of the policy-making process due to their low quality on substantive issues and lack of representativeness (Guttormsen and Sæbø 2013). Moreover, choosing policy requires knowledge and "attention to tradeoffs among values, to second-best possibilities, and to unexpected risks" (Weissberg 2001, p. 1) that citizens might not possess which in turn would lead to low quality policies. In addition the high penetration of social media along with the openness of their content runs the risk of issues slipping away out of the grid of local governments (Mergel 2013).

Table 9.1 Government 2.0 benefits

Supply side (Local government)	Demand side (Citizens)
• Effective information dissemination and massive distribution of content • Quick communication during emergency matters • Mining, crowd-sourcing of citizens' content • Efficient knowledge management • Influential marketing • Increased quality in local public services • Creative and innovative solutions of community issues • Transparency and accountability • Inter-government collaboration and integration	• Informed and interested citizens in local government activities • Increased involvement of nonelite individuals • Better interaction and dialogue between citizens and government • Stronger relations between citizens and government • Co-designing of local public services • Co-deciding about major community issues • Participation in public debates and agenda setting • Trust in local governance and greater public value

9.2.2 Social Media Implementation Strategies

According to Mergel (2013), local governments adopt social media for a number of reasons which are associated with the type of management and their organizational culture (Guttormsen and Sæbø 2013). Local governments which follow a citizen-centric approach might want to have the presence on social media in order to be where their citizens are, thus, satisfying their communication desires. On the other hand, several local governments decide to enter the social media arena simply because other local agencies have done so successfully. Last, there is the group of local governments termed late adopters that currently trail behind in social media adoption but through forced implementation induced by central government initiatives are expected to cover the distance in the future.

Most of the times implementation of social media by government agencies is a three-stage process (Mergel and Bretschneider 2013). During the first stage, few government employees set social media accounts for their departments or agencies unofficially. These social media innovators mainly use social media to disseminate information and interact with citizens in an informal manner. During the second stage, social media innovators begin to set informal guidelines for the use of social media which in the third stage are transformed into official protocols. Specifically, in the third stage the use of social media becomes more institutionalized and even new roles and departments might appear for the successful exploitation of social media.

Nowadays, as Ferro et al. (2013) note, government agencies are moving from simple social media practices such as creation of accounts and posting of updates manually, to more sophisticated ones like cross-posting of the same content to different social media platforms and data mining of citizen-generated content. Depending on their communication goals and the available resources local governments can pursue three basic social media strategies, namely: representation, engagement, and networking (Mergel 2013). By implementing a representation strategy local governments set accounts to popular social media (i.e., Facebook, Twitter, and YouTube) in order to provide top-down information to their citizens and massively distribute content about their initiatives and activities. This strategy does not enhance citizens' engagement and participation. Through the strategy of engagement local government try to interact with their citizens in order to co-produce and share with them critical content. The pursuit of this strategy requires the active role of the local government. Networking strategy aims at monitoring the opinions and views of citizens by facilitating interaction and dialogue between the various stakeholders of a local community. The active participation of local authorities in the online dialogue is not a necessity for the implementation of this kind of strategy. It should be noted that both engagement and networking strategies trigger citizens' participation.

9.3 Conceptual Framework

9.3.1 Drivers of Social Media Adoption

Several studies have tried to shed light on the factors that affect the adoption of Web 2.0 applications by government agencies at the local level. These factors are related to municipality (i.e., size, region), local government (i.e., structure), and citizens' characteristics (i.e., voters' turnout, internet usage, education). In the context of the United States, Norris and Reddick (2013) confirmed the effect of population size and region of the municipality on the adoption of social media by local authorities. Moreover, Oliveira and Welch (2013) reported a positive relation between the existence of an internal IT department and the implementation of social media practices by local government officials. Rather, the size of the municipality had no effect on social media usage. In a more recent study of Reddick and Norris (2013), the positive impact of citizens' education and year of website creation on adoption of e-government 2.0 initiatives was confirmed while a nonsignificant relationship was found between the existence of an IT department and the utilization of Web 2.0 technologies by local authorities. Citizens' education was also found to play an important role on the adoption of Facebook by municipalities in Sweden (Larsson 2013). Furthermore, the study of Larsson (2013) revealed a positive association between the size of the municipality and the usage of social media like Facebook, Twitter, and YouTube. Twitter adoption by Swedish local governments was also positively related with the level of citizens' Internet usage but negatively associated with voters' turnout. It seems that, in municipalities with high abstention levels local governments try to create bonds with citizens through extensive use of social networking sites (SNSs). Christensen (2013) investigating municipalities in Finland found that the size of municipality (i.e., population) affects the adoption of e-democracy applications (i.e., discussion forums, and commenting) by local governments. On the contrary, the study of Bonsón et al. (2012) regarding 15 European cities, found no evidence that factors such as citizens' access to Internet services and usage of e-government 1.0 services affect implementation of e-government 2.0 initiatives which are primarily influenced by local government's previous implementation of e-government 1.0 applications. Hence, research so far has produced contradictory results regarding which factors have a significant effect on the adoption of e-government 2.0 features. To shed more light on the drivers of e-government 2.0 adoption, the present study will address the following research question:

RQ1: What are the drivers of the adoption of e-government 2.0 applications by local governments in terms of (a) municipality characteristics such as size and tourism activity of the municipality, (b) local governments' characteristics such as operation of an internal IT department, and (c) citizens' characteristics in a given municipality such as the level of internet usage, the use of e-government services, the level of higher education and the voters' turnout.

9.3.2 Citizens' Participation Through Social Media: Myth or Measurable Reality

A number of studies claim that e-government 2.0 initiatives haven't triggered yet enough citizens' engagement and participation. Nevertheless, it should be noted that the majority of these studies measure engagement from the supply side by examining the presence of interactive applications in governmental websites and the existence of active social media accounts. Perhaps, citizens' apathy towards the interactive platforms of local governments is associated with improper use of social media platforms since government officials lack the skills and the knowledge for identifying the characteristics of their target audiences in order to interact with them in an effective manner (Kavanaugh et al. 2012). For example, Snead (2013) found that social media like blogs do not connect citizens with local authorities. Moreover, low engagement of citizens could also be related to the type of content posted on social media. As Hofmann et al. (2013) revealed citizens' interest and engagement increases when content such as photos and videos is posted on governmental social media.

So far, little is known about whether and which e-government 2.0 applications are successful in enhancing citizens' engagement and participation. Another critical issue that hasn't received enough attention by researchers is the way success (i.e., engagement, participation) is measured in social media tools used by local governments. Abdelsalam et al. (2013) measured success of a local government's Facebook profile in terms of page popularity and page effectiveness. Specifically, page popularity considered the number of page likes, posts, and "talking about" while page effectiveness was evaluated by dividing the number of people talking about the page with the number of people who have liked the page. In another study, Hofmann et al. (2013) measured success by counting the number and the polarity of comments posted by citizens on the Facebook pages of local governments. Agostino (2013) differentiated citizens' engagement with the social media of local governments from citizens' awareness. Awareness of social media platforms included items such as the number of Facebook page likes, Twitter followers, and YouTube subscribers per inhabitant. The metric of social media engagement was evaluated using three variables (a) number of Facebook "talking about" per friend, (b) number of tweets per follower, and (c) number of YouTube comment per subscriber. As Snead (2013) highlights, the count of tweets, Facebook posts, and uploaded videos on YouTube are not indicators of citizens' engagement with the social media of local governments since one cannot tell if connected citizens have read the posts and tweets or have viewed the videos. More appropriate measures of participation should evaluate the number of likes or comments per post on Facebook; the number of Re-tweets per tweet; and the number of views per uploaded video.

We herein posit that engagement of citizens with the social media of local governments is a three-stage process. During the first stage, a state of awareness about the presence of social media is created to citizens. This awareness level could be measured by evaluating the number of Facebook friends/page likes, Twitter

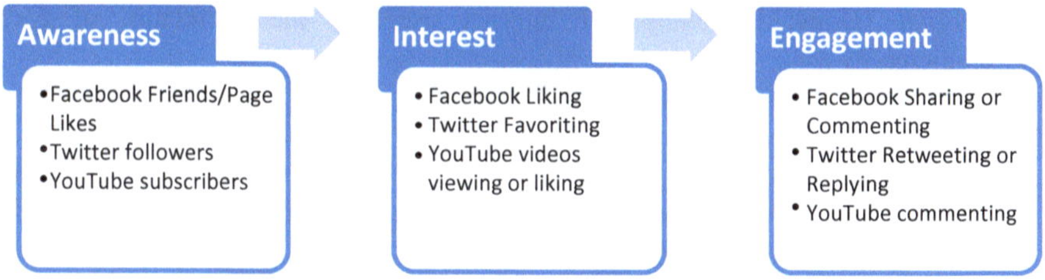

Fig. 9.1 Process of citizens' engagement with the social media of local governments

followers, and YouTube subscribers. As local governments exploit social media by posting, tweeting, and uploading videos citizens become more interested in the content and updates of their municipalities. Citizen interest could then be evaluated by considering the number of Facebook likes, Twitter favorites, YouTube video views or likes. At the final stage, citizens actively engage with the social media of local authorities. This engagement-participation is reflected on citizens' activities such as Facebook sharing or commenting, re-tweeting or replying on Twitter, and commenting on YouTube. Figure 9.1 illustrates the aforementioned engagement process.

With the aforementioned in mind, the present study will also try to answer the following research questions:

RQ2: Which social media platform (i.e., Facebook, Twitter, YouTube) is the most effective in terms of citizens' awareness, interest, and engagement?

RQ3: Is social media activity of local governments associated with citizens' awareness, interest, and engagement?

9.4 Methodology

The sample for this study consisted of the 325 Greek municipalities. Data collection took place from June to August 2014 and was conducted in two phases. During the first phase, data regarding general characteristics of each municipality (i.e., size, tourism industry, operation of IT department, internet usage, usage of e-government services, voters' turnout) were gathered from various sources such as the websites of the Ministry of the Interior (www.ypes.gr) the Hellenic Statistical Authority (www.statistics.gr), and the Observatory for the Greek Information Society (www.observatory.gr). The variables of the study were operationalized as follows:

- *Size*: Number of inhabitants as recorded in the 2011 Census of Population.
- *Higher Education*: Percentage of inhabitants with bachelor's or master's degree or doctoral diploma of each municipality.
- *Voters' Turnout*: Percentage of citizens who voted at the first round of the May 2014 Municipal Elections of each municipality.

- *Internet Usage*: Percentage of internet users in the prefecture of each municipality.
- *Usage of e-government services:* Percentage of individuals who have used e-government services in the prefecture of each municipality.
- *Tourism and Travel Industry Municipality*: Coded 1 if the municipality was characterized as a tourism and travel industry and 0 otherwise. Based on the Presidential Decrees of 899/76 and 664/77.
- *Operation of an Internal IT department*: Coded 1 if an Internal IT department exists in the organizational chart which appeared on the websites of the municipalities and 0 otherwise.

During the next phase, researchers examined whether each municipality had a Facebook profile or page, a Twitter account, and a YouTube channel. Nonofficial accounts were excluded from analysis. For each Facebook page, the total number of page likes, posts, likes on posts, and comments on posts were collected. We limited our analysis to the first 1,000 posts of each account. Moreover, we did not include the number of likes on users' comments. In a similar way, for municipalities with an official Twitter account the total number of followers, users who are followed, were tweets, favorites, and re-tweets were retrieved. It should be noted that we did not include tweets that were re-tweets from other accounts. Regarding YouTube channels, the total number of subscribers, videos uploaded, views, and comments were calculated.

Following a similar procedure with those reported in the studies of Bonsón et al. (2012), Mossberger et al. (2013), and Abdelsalam et al. (2013) a summative index was developed in order to measure the usage of social media by Greek local governments. The index was named Social Media and included three variables namely: Facebook page, Twitter account, and YouTube channel. This social media index could take values from 0 if the local government had no presence in any social medium to three if it exploited all three social media.

Citizens' awareness was measured by dividing the number of Facebook page likes, Twitter followers, and YouTube subscribers by the population of each municipality. Citizens' interest index calculated the number of Facebook likes on posts, Twitter favorites, and YouTube video views divided by the number of Facebook posts, tweets, and YouTube videos. Lastly, citizens' engagement was evaluated by dividing the number of Facebook comments on posts, Re-tweets, and YouTube comments by the number of Facebook posts, tweets, and YouTube videos.

9.5 Results

The majority of the Greek municipalities (75.1 %) were medium sized in regard to their population (between 10,000 and 249,000 inhabitants) and only two of them (Athens and Thessaloniki) were regarded as large municipalities. In addition, 33.3 % of the municipalities were classified as tourism and travel industries and 36.3 % had an internal IT department. As Table 9.2 shows, social media presence of

Table 9.2 Usage of social media by Greek municipalities

Social media usage	Frequency (Percentage)
Facebook profile	54 (16.6)
Facebook page	92 (28.3)
Twitter account	67 (20.6)
YouTube channel	71 (21.8)

Table 9.3 Social media index

Social media index	Frequency (Percentage)
0	144 (44.3)
1	107 (32.9)
2	45 (13.8)
3	29 (8.9)

Table 9.4 Regression analyses results

Variables	Social media index B
R^2 (%)	6.0
Size	0.160[a]
Tourism and travel industry	0.033
Higher education	0.132[a]
Voters' turnout	0.072
IT department	0.068
Use of Internet	−0.043
Use of e-government services	0.053

[a]Significant at $p<0.05$

municipalities was low. Of the 325 local governments 92 (28.3 %) of them had an official Facebook page while 54 of them had a Facebook profile (16.6 %). The use of Facebook profiles instead of Facebook pages is indicative of an informal and unofficial approach in the exploitation of this SNS. The second most frequently used social medium was YouTube (21.8 %) followed by Twitter (20.6 %).

Regarding social media presence, 44.3 % of the municipalities had no presence in any of the three SNSs (Table 9.3). In addition, 46.7 % of local governments were users of one or two SNSs and only 8.9 % of them had a presence on the three social media (i.e., Facebook, Twitter, and YouTube).

In order to answer the first research question a regression analyses were conducted. The dependent variable for the model was the social media index. Table 9.4 shows the results of the regression analysis. The R square value for the model was 6.0 % implying that other independent variables may exert influence upon the dependent variable which has not been included in the present model.

Regarding the regression model, results indicate that social media adoption index was significantly ($p<0.05$) and positively influenced by the size of the municipality ($\beta=0.160$, $p=0.006$) and the percentage of citizens with higher education ($\beta=0.132$, $p=0.017$). However, the value of the standardized beta coefficient was low. Nonsignificant effects ($p>0.05$) were found between tourism activity ($\beta=0.033$,

Table 9.5 Social media metrics

Facebook	Mean	Twitter	Mean	YouTube	Mean
Metrics		Metrics		Metrics	
Years since creation	2.20	Years since creation	2.03	Years since creation	2.24
Page likes	1,005.00	Followers	149.2	Subscribers	28.40
Talking about	79.88	Following	77.87	Views	352.0
Posts	321.72	Tweets	375.05	Videos	31
Links	143.29	Photos	12.58	Comments	0.15
Statuses	35.04	Favorites	4.71		
Photos	130.49	Re-tweets	8.70		
Videos	10.78	Replies	0.00		
Post likes	4,763.9				
Post comments	125.0				
Post shares	934.0				

$p=0.556$), voters' turnout ($\beta=0.072$, $p=0.194$), operation of an IT department ($\beta=0.068$, $p=0.234$), percentage of Internet users ($\beta=-0.043$, $p=0.457$), percentage of e-government services usage ($\beta=0.053$, $p=0.335$), and social media adoption index. Thus, addressing the first research questions it can be argued that important drivers of social media adoption by Greek local municipalities are the size of municipality as well as the percentage of citizens with higher education in a given municipality.

Of the 92 Facebook pages, 12 were inactive with no content posted by local governments. Similarly, 12 pages were highly active since they posted more than 1,000 posts from the date of their activation. Most of these 12 active accounts derive from medium-sized local governments (91.7 %). As Table 9.5 shows, on average local governments with a Facebook page posted 321 messages—during a 2-year period since the activation of the account—which were mainly links and photos. Moreover, Facebook pages were visible to 1,005 citizens and received 4,763 likes; 135 comments and 934 shares on average. Regarding Twitter activity of the 67 Twitter accounts only three were inactive while seven of them had more than 1,000 tweets. Intense twitter activity was found originating from local governments mainly in the regions of Attica and Crete (five out of seven). On average, local governments were visible to 149 followers, tweeted 375 times and received five favorites and nine re-tweets during a 2-year period since the activation of the account. As for YouTube activity, only one account was inactive and had no videos uploaded. On the other hand, 6 local governments were highly active on YouTube platforms since they posted more than 100 videos from the date of the account activation. On average, local government had 28 subscribers and posted 31 videos which were viewed 352 times during a 2-year period. Based on the analysis above, it seems that activity of local governments on Facebook outpaced the other two social media channels.

In order to answer the second research question, repeated measures analysis of variance was used to compare the citizens' awareness, interest, and engagement

Table 9.6 Repeated measures analysis of variance results for awareness, interest, and engagement

	Mean values		
Social media	Awareness	Interest	Engagement
Facebook	0.036	5.167	0.328
Twitter	0.008	0.087	0.099
YouTube	0.001	80.35	0.000
Geisser-Greenhouse	0.520	0.503	0.609
F—value	13.61[a]	14.95[a]	8.194[a]

[a]Significant at the $p=0.05$ level

across the three social media (Table 9.6). As Table 9.6 shows, low levels of awareness of and engagement with social media used by local government were found while citizens' interest to these SNSs was modest.

In regard to citizens' awareness, the Geisser-Greenhouse correction of the F distribution was used for the test of significance. Based on the results, there were significant differences at the $p<0.05$ level of significance, in the awareness of citizens across the three social media [$F(0.016, 1{,}039)=13{,}617$, $p=0.001$]. Bonferroni's post hoc tests were performed to test the differences in awareness level between each pair of social media. Citizens' awareness of the local governments' Facebook pages was significantly higher ($M=0.036$) than their awareness of Twitter accounts ($M=0.008$) and YouTube channels ($M=0.001$). Moreover, Twitter scored significantly higher on the citizens' awareness index compared to YouTube. Following, the same procedure as described above, significant differences at the $p<0.05$ level were found in the citizens' interest index across the three social media [$F(28{,}282, 1{,}007)=1{,}946$, $p=0.008$]. Based on the Bonferroni's post hoc tests, citizens' interest was significantly higher ($p<0.05$) for the YouTube channels of local governments ($M=80.35$) than for the Facebook pages ($M=5.167$) and the Twitter accounts ($M=0.087$). On the contrary, no significant differences were found in the citizens' interest scores ($p>0.05$) between Facebook and Twitter accounts. As above, the three social media differed significantly in regard to the level of citizens' engagement [$F(1{,}189, 1{,}218)=8.194$, $p=0.006$]. The Bonferroni's post hoc tests indicate that citizens tend to engage significantly more with the Facebook pages of local governments ($M=0.328$) than their YouTube channels ($M=0.001$). However, Twitter ($M=0.099$) did not differ significantly ($p<0.05$) in the level of citizens' engagement from Facebook and YouTube. Hence, it can be concluded that citizens are more aware of and engaged with the Facebook pages of local government while they seem more interested in their YouTube channels.

Next, a correlation analysis was performed using the Pearson's correlation coefficient to answer the third research question about whether social media activity as reflected by the number of Facebook posts, tweets, and YouTube videos is significantly related with the level of awareness, interest, and engagement of Facebook, Twitter, and YouTube, respectively. Results indicate that the number of Facebook posts is significantly correlated ($p<0.05$) with the awareness ($r=0.264$, $p=0.011$), interest ($r=0.446$, $p=0.000$), and engagement ($r=0.458$, $p=0.000$) of citizens with the Facebook page of local governments. It seems that when local government update frequently their Facebook accounts their connected citizens become more interested and engaged with their activities. On the contrary, no significant association ($p>0.05$) was found between Twitter activity and citizens' awareness ($r=0.222$, $p=0.071$), interest ($r=-0.183$, $p=0.162$) as well as engagement ($r=-0.227$, $p=0.081$) with the Twitter accounts of local governments. This non-effect could be attributed to the fact that Twitter is not a frequently used tool by Greek citizens in general. Regarding YouTube, the number of videos uploaded by local governments was significantly ($p<0.05$) correlated in a positive way with citizens' awareness ($r=0.323$, $p=0.007$). No significant correlation ($p>0.05$) was found between YouTube activity of local governments and citizens' interest ($r=-0.305$, $p=0.179$) and engagement ($r=-0.010$, $p=0.079$). The correlation between YouTube activity and citizens' awareness of the YouTube channel of local governments was modest. Thus, when local governments are uploading frequently videos about their activities more citizens are attracted to their YouTube accounts.

9.6 Discussion

The present study investigated the usage and effectiveness of social media exploited by Greek local governments. Evidence suggests that local authorities are moving towards e-government 2.0 era, albeit slowly. Results suggest that the exploitation of social media by local governments is still in its infancy and at their first stage of development (Mergel and Bretschneider 2013) since the majority of municipalities were not present on social media. For example, only 28 % of Greek local authorities own a Facebook page while almost 20 % of them are active on Twitter and YouTube. Hence, this small number of local governments which are active on social media could be characterized as innovators that probably might set the pace and other local governments might follow. Possible reasons for this low exploitation of Web 2.0 tools by Greek local governments could be attributed to their bureaucratic model of governance as well as the lack of resources and personnel. Note, that although Greek municipalities lag behind their counterparts in the United States where Facebook's penetration is over 90 % and Twitter's over 60 %, they go in hand with other European countries (Bonsón et al. 2012). Similar levels of social media presence with those found in the present study were reported for local municipalities in Italy (Agostino 2013) and Sweden (Larsson 2013).

The size of municipalities plays a significant role in the adoption of Web 2.0 applications. Specifically, municipalities with a large number of inhabitants tend to use more extensively Web 2.0 applications in order to distribute content and updates about their activities massively and quickly. Moreover, it seems that densely populated municipalities made use of Web 2.0 applications to reduce the spatial distance from their citizens by being where their citizens were and facilitating dialogue. The impact of population on local government's use of Web 2.0 tools was also reported in other studies (Norris and Reddick 2013; Christensen 2013). This study also revealed that municipalities with educated citizens are adopters of social media such as Facebook, Twitter, and YouTube. Hence, education impacts not only on the adoption of e-government 1.0 (Jaeger 2003) but of e-government 2.0 as well (Reddick and Norris 2013; Larsson 2013).

The present study also tried to shed light on the critical debate that exists on whether e-government 2.0 initiatives undertaken by local governments can enhance more participatory forms of democracy by actively engaging citizens. Based on the results of the present study, the social media tools used by Greek local governments performed poorly on citizens' engagement. Note, though, that there is evidence which suggest that by enhancing social media activity especially on Facebook, citizens' participation could be increased. Of special interest is the finding that a YouTube video, viewed 80 times on average, triggers the interest of Greek citizens more than a Facebook post, liked five times on average. Greek citizens are not aware of the social media activities of their local authorities with only 4 % of a municipality's inhabitants being aware about the local government's Facebook page. A closer look at the study's results reveals that although social media activities of government agencies at the municipal level are not well known to citizens, those who choose to connect with them are highly interested and supportive of such activities. This finding could be attributed to the low rates of Twitter (8 %) and YouTube (8.8 %) usage by Greek citizens (FocusBari 2014).

It is imperative for Greek local governments to move to the next stage of the e-government 2.0 model by increasing their exploitation of the new innovative and interactive tools. Local governments' social media presence should be enhanced. It should be noted, that for the exploitation of social media, government agencies should develop formal social media strategies that will be implemented under the supervision of personnel with high expertise on the area. Moreover, strategies should be differentiated for each social medium in order to benefit from their different characteristics. For example, Facebook should be preferred when local governments want to disseminate and inform massively Greek citizens since Facebook scored high in citizens' awareness compared to the other two SNSs. Furthermore, if local governments want to monitor the attitudes or pulse of their citizenry, relevant content should be disseminated in the form of YouTube videos as it was found that this video sharing application scored high in the level of citizens' awareness. In addition, uploading various versions of videos about a critical matter could further enhance citizens' awareness. When more active forms of participation from citizens' side are needed such as comments or dialogue, then efforts should focus on providing continuous updates about the relevant issues in the form of Facebook posts.

9.7 Conclusions

The present study explored the exploitation of social media by Greek local governments as well as their effectiveness in terms of citizens' awareness, interest, and engagement. Social media adoption by local governments in Greece was found to be low with almost 28 % of the municipalities maintaining a Facebook page.

YouTube and Twitter were adopted by almost 21 % of the investigated local authorities. Another indication of the low extent of social media usage was the limited social media sophistication of the Greek local governments since a minority of them (9 %) were present on the three social media platforms (i.e., Facebook, YouTube, and Twitter). The main drivers of social media adoption by local authorities in the Greek context were related to the size of the municipality as well as the education level of citizens in a given district. In general, social media used by Greek local governments were not highly visible to citizens. Moreover, it can be argued that the way these Web 2.0 platforms were used by municipalities did not attract the interest and involvement of the local community members. However, certain social media proved to be more effective in terms of citizens' engagement than others. For example, Facebook was found to be the most effective platform in reaching audiences in a massive way as well as in engaging citizens through sharing and commenting content. In addition, YouTube proved to be a successful medium for evoking the interest of citizens through viewing videos uploaded by local governments. Nonetheless, through frequent content updates municipalities can increase the level of citizens' awareness of and engagement with their Facebook pages. Citizens' interest could also be enhanced through frequent video uploads on the YouTube channels of local governments. Finally, contrary to our expectations Twitter scored pretty low on citizens' awareness, interest, and engagement.

9.8 Limitations and Future Research Suggestions

The main limitation of the present study is its non-exhaustive nature. Since this study focused only on several website applications and social media other Web 2.0 tools such as (e-polls, discussion forums, blogs) could be included in a future survey. In addition, this study focused on the supply side of e-government 2.0. More research from the demand size is needed to further determine the attitudes of Greek citizens towards e-government 2.0 initiatives and their intention to actively engage with them. Simply counting likes, favorites, and comments does not guarantee that attitudes and behavior of citizens are captured, since other stakeholders such as nongovernment agencies could also engage with the social media of local governments (Snead 2013). Comparing social media actualization of local governments across Europe could also provide a better view about the usage and effectiveness of e-government 2.0 adoption. Moreover, the proposed three-stage model for the measurement of citizens' engagement should also be validated or enhanced by implementing it across different countries.

Acknowledgements This research has been co-financed by the European Union (European Social Fund—ESF) and Greek national funds through the Operational Program "Education and Lifelong Learning" of the National Strategic Reference Framework (NSRF)—Research Funding Program: ARCHIMEDES III. Investing in knowledge society through the European Social Fund.

References

Abdelsalam, H., Reddick, C., Gamal, S., & Al-shaar, A. (2013). Social media in Egyptian government websites: Presence, usage, and effectiveness. *Government Information Quarterly, 30*(4), 406–416.

Agostino, D. (2013). Using social media to engage citizens: A study of Italian municipalities. *Public Relations Review, 39*(3), 232–234.

Avery, E., & Graham, M. (2013). Political public relations and the promotion of participatory, transparent government through social media. *International Journal of Strategic Communication, 7*(4), 274–291.

Baum, C., & Di Maio, A. (2000). *Gartner's four phases of e-government model*. Retrieved August 8, 2014, from http://www.gartner.com.

Bonsón, E., Torres, L., Royo, S., & Flores, F. (2012). Local e-government 2.0: Social media and corporate transparency in municipalities. *Government Information Quarterly, 29*(2), 123–132.

Christensen, H. (2013). Broadening democratic participation? An exploratory study of e-democracy in 188 Finnish municipalities. *Scandinavian Journal of Public Administration, 17*(3), 3–21.

Chun, S., & Reyes, L. (2012). Social media in government. *Government Information Quarterly, 29*(4), 441–445.

Chun, S., Shulman, S., Sandoval, R., & Hovy, E. (2010). Government 2.0: Making connections between citizens, data and government. *Information Polity, 15*(1), 1–9.

Coursey, D., & Norris, D. (2008). Models of e-government: Are they correct? An empirical assessment. *Public Administration Review, 68*(3), 523–536.

Dixon, B. (2010). Towards e-government 2.0: An assessment of where e-Government 2.0 is and where it is headed. *Public Administration and Management, 15*(2), 418–454.

Drogkaris, P., Gritzalis, S., & Lambrinoudakis, C. (2010). Transforming the Greek e-government environment towards the e-Gov 2.0 era. In K. Andersen, E. Francesconi, A. Grönlund, & T. van Engers (Eds.), *Electronic government and the information systems perspective* (pp. 142–149). Berlin: Springer.

Ferro, E., Loukis, E., Charalabidis, Y., & Osella, M. (2013). Policy making 2.0: From theory to practice. *Government Information Quarterly, 30*(4), 359–368.

FocusBari (2014). *WEBID survey*. Retrieved August 8, 2014, from www.focusbari.gr/media-research/internet-web-id.html.

Guttormsen, C., & Sæbø, Ø. (2013). Municipalities 'Like'Facebook: The use of social media in local municipalities. In P. Spagnoletti (Ed.), *Organizational change and information systems* (pp. 157–166). Berlin: Springer.

Hiller, J., & Belanger, F. (2001). Privacy strategies for electronic government. In M. A. Abramson & G. E. Means (Eds.), *E-government 2001* (pp. 162–198). Lanham, MD: Rowman & Littlefield.

Hofmann, S., Beverungen, D., Räckers, M., & Becker, J. (2013). What makes local governments' online communications successful? Insights from a multi-method analysis of Facebook. *Government Information Quarterly, 30*(4), 387–396.

Jaeger, P. (2003). The endless wire: E-government as global phenomenon. *Government Information Quarterly, 20*, 323–331.

Kavanaugh, A., Fox, E., Sheetz, S., Yang, S., Li, L., Shoemaker, D., Natsev, A., & Xie, L. (2012). Social media use by government: From the routine to the critical. *Government Information Quarterly, 29*(4), 480–491.

Khan, G., Moon, J., Rhee, C., & Rho, J. (2010). E-government skills identification and development: toward a staged-based user-centric approach for developing countries. *Asia Pacific Journal of Information Systems, 20*(1), 1–31.

Larsson, A. (2013). Bringing it all back home? Social media practices by Swedish municipalities. *European Journal of Communication*. doi: 10.1177/0267323113502277.

Linders, D. (2012). From e-government to we-government: Defining a typology for citizen coproduction in the age of social media. *Government Information Quarterly, 29*(4), 446–454.

Mergel, I. (2012). The social media innovation challenge in the public sector. *Information Polity, 17*(3), 281–292.

Mergel, I. (2013). Social media adoption and resulting tactics in the US federal government. *Government Information Quarterly, 30*(2), 123–130.

Mergel, I., & Bretschneider, S. (2013). A three-stage adoption process for social media use in government. *Public Administration Review, 73*(3), 390–400.

Mossberger, K., Wu, Y., & Crawford, J. (2013). Connecting citizens and local governments? Social media and interactivity in major US cities. *Government Information Quarterly, 30*(4), 351–358.

Norris, D., & Reddick, C. (2013). Local e-government in the United States: Transformation or incremental change? *Public Administration Review, 73*(1), 165–175.

Oliveira, G., & Welch, E. (2013). Social media use in local government: Linkage of technology, task, and organizational context. *Government Information Quarterly, 30*(4), 397–405.

Reddick, C., & Norris, D. (2013). Social media adoption at the American grass roots: Web 2.0 or 1.5? *Government Information Quarterly, 30*(4), 498–507.

Sandoval-Almazan, R., & Gil-Garcia, J. (2012). Are government internet portals evolving towards more interaction, participation, and collaboration? Revisiting the rhetoric of e-government among municipalities. *Government Information Quarterly, 29*(1), 572–581.

Scott, J. (2006). "E" the people: Do US municipal government web sites support public involvement? *Public Administration Review, 66*(3), 341–353.

Snead, J. (2013). Social media use in the US Executive branch. *Government Information Quarterly, 30*(1), 56–63.

Tat-Kei Ho, A. (2002). Reinventing local governments and the e-government initiative. *Public Administration Review, 62*(4), 434–444.

Tolbert, C., & Mossberger, K. (2006). The effects of e-government on trust and confidence in Government. *Public Administration Review, 66*(3), 354–369.

Van Veenstra, A., Janssen, M., & Boon, A. (2011). Measure to improve: a study of eParticipation in frontrunner Dutch municipalities. In E. Tambouris, A. MacIntosh, & H. de Bruijn (Eds.), *Electronic participation* (pp. 157–168). Berlin: Springer.

Weissberg, R. (2001). *Why policymakers should ignore public opinion polls*. Washington, DC: Cato Institute.

Wescott, C. (2001). E-government in the Asia-Pacific region. *Asian Journal of Political Science, 9*(2), 1–24.

Yannas, P., & Lappas, G. (2007). Evaluating local e-government: An analysis of Greek prefecture websites. In *Proceedings of second international conference on digital information management (ICDIM'07)*. Volume 1 (pp. 254–259) Lyon: IEEE.

Yannas, P., & Lappas, G. (2010). Evaluating local e-government: A comparative study of Greek prefecture websites. In S. Soomro (Ed.), *E-learning experiences and future* (pp. 441–452). Rijeka: InTech.

Chapter 10
The Diffusion of Microblogging in the Public Sector: Evidence from Chinese Provinces

Liang Ma

Abstract Microblogging has been increasingly used in the public sector across the world, and it is pivotal to understand the drivers of their diffusion. This chapter adapts innovation adoption and diffusion theories and uses panel data of China's 31 provinces (2010–2012) to empirically examine the diffusion of microblogging among government agencies and officials. The results suggest that the drivers of agency and individual microblogging are subtly distinct, implying their adoption may follow different routines. The findings also show that agencies and officials in jurisdictions with larger population, higher level of citizen demand, under advocating leadership, and bordering on pioneering peers are more likely to use microblogging.

10.1 Introduction

The past decade has witnessed the unprecedented use of social media applications (SMAs) by individuals and organizations. Facebook, Twitter, YouTube, Pinterest, and so forth have accumulated billions of users, accounting for one third of total netizens around the world (Nielsen 2012). Compared with its information technology (IT) predecessors like Web portal and email (Web 1.0 technologies), SMAs, or Web 2.0 technologies are revolutionary platforms characterized by much more freedom, interactivity, and immediacy (McAfee 2009).

SMAs have attracted numerous users across the world, and governments without an account in these platforms may find themselves increasingly isolated from the public debate (Rainie et al. 2012). As a response, more and more government agencies and officials have opened official accounts on these platforms to release information, respond to emergency, deliver online services, and cultivate public image (Eggers 2007; Bonsón et al. 2012; Thackeray et al. 2012; UN 2012; Katz and

L. Ma (✉)
Nanyang Centre for Public Administration, Nanyang Technological University, S3.2-B4-20, 50 Nanyang Avenue, Singapore 639798, Singapore
e-mail: liangma@ntu.edu.sg

M.Z. Sobaci (ed.), *Social Media and Local Governments*, Public Administration and Information Technology 15, DOI 10.1007/978-3-319-17722-9_10

Halpern 2013). However, public organizations and their members may not automatically and fully adopt SMAs (Picazo-Vela et al. 2012). Understanding what drives the adoption of SMAs among government officials and public managers can help us to better interpret the rationale of government innovation and the diffusion of new technologies.

The rapid and extensive use of SMAs among governments has given rise to the proliferation of research, but few studies have empirically investigated the antecedents of their adoption and diffusion (Mergel and Bretschneider 2013; Ma 2013, 2014; Katz and Halpern 2013). What drives the diffusion of SMAs? Are there any differences between government agencies and officials in SMA adoption? In this chapter, we report an empirical study examining the drivers of the diffusion of one specific SMA, microblogging, across governments, using multisource panel data from China's 31 provinces (2010–2012). In comparison with prior studies (Ma 2014; Katz and Halpern 2013), this study has several advantages and contributes to the literature.

First, we simultaneously investigate the adoption of both institutional and individual microblogging to detect their distinct patterns of diffusion and determinants. Prior studies either solely investigate the adoption of microblogging by governments or separately analyze the behaviors of politicians or public managers. Our results indeed identify the differences between agencies (institutions) and officials (individuals) in adopting microblogging.

Second, we examine the antecedents of microblogging diffusion from multiple perspectives, which enables us to depict a comprehensive landscape of government microblogging. Organizational innovation is driven by a battery of individual, organizational, and environmental factors (Kimberly and Evanisko 1981; Damanpour 1991; Walker 2006), and it is pivotal to simultaneously take them into account to identify the key antecedents and their relative effects. Our study develops a framework to accommodate theoretically important antecedents and finds institutional, managerial, and environmental characteristics matter significantly for microblogging adoption.

Furthermore, we longitudinally examine the temporal process of microblogging diffusion. Prior studies often draw on cross-sectional research design to elicit the notable drivers of microblogging owing to data constraints. We go a further step by employing longitudinal dataset to capture the temporal and spatial dynamics of microblogging diffusion.

Finally, different from prior studies solely using data from one platform (e.g., Sina Weibo), our dataset covers government microblogs in the four mainstream domestic platforms and depicts a more complete landscape of microblogging diffusion in China. The unique dataset we employ in the chapter enables us to simultaneously investigate the diffusion of microblogging in dominant platforms, to a great extent mitigating the potential estimate bias.

The remainder of the chapter is structured as follows. We first introduce the background and context of microblogging in China, followed by a summary of its spread in governments. We then briefly review the literature on innovation diffusion and propose hypotheses on the drivers of microblogging diffusion. The data and methods are then presented, followed by the empirical results. We finally discuss the implications of our findings, and conclude with research limitations and suggestions for future research.

10.2 The Use of Microblogging in Chinese Public Sectors

Mainstream SMAs such as Twitter and Facebook are censored or blocked from access by Chinese government, but domestic equivalent versions (e.g., Sina Weibo and Tencent QQ) have taken over the huge user market and are permitted to meet the online networking needs of the world's largest Internet user market (McDougall 2011). Although governments censor politically sensitive online information (e.g., Tibet and Xinjiang) (King et al. 2013), these domestic platforms are generally open and free. Many domestic Internet operators developed SMAs to meet the needs of the world's largest cohort of netizens, and governments also embrace the bandwagon to rebuild public legitimacy.

Sina Weibo, the Chinese version of Twitter, permits its users to post a post no more than 140 Chinese characters, with or without pictures or videos. Users can follow or comment on posts from others, following the same rule of word limit. 2009 is the landmark of microblogging in China, witnessing the blowout type growth of microblogs. By 2012 the total number of netizens in China has been 564 million, accounting for 42.1 % of total population. 309 million or 54.7 % of active netizens opened their microblog accounts, substantially increasing from 63.11 million or 13.8 % of total netizens by 2010 (CNNIC 2012). Microblogging has been one of the primary sources of news and other information for ordinary netizens, and its hot posts soon top line national news reports.

Many Internet operators invite governments to open official microblog accounts to attract individual users and expand value-added businesses. Governments also embrace the bandwagon to engage the public and rebuild public legitimacy (Noesselt 2014), making 2010 immediately becomes the milestone of government microblogging development (Zheng 2013; Schlæger and Jiang 2014).

The rapid growth of government microblogging makes its statistics soon outdated. A 2013 report reveals that there have been totally 70,605 public sector microblog accounts, with 41,377 and 29,228 accounts for government agencies and individual officials in Sina Weibo, respectively (Office of Internet Opinion at People's Daily Online 2013). Another report monitoring Tencent QQ shows that government agencies and officials have opened 82,591 and 37,529 accounts, respectively, totaling 122,820 accounts (Internet Research Center at Wuhan University 2013). The statistics covering four dominant platforms in China (Sina Weibo, Tencent QQ, *People's Daily* Online, and Xinhua) shows that 176,714 government users have registered at the end of 2012 (113,382 organs and 63,332 individuals), unbelievably increasing from 50,561 in 2011 (32,358 organs and 18,203 individuals) and 2,400 in 2010 (1,680 organs and 720 individuals) (E-Government Research Center 2012).

Governments and officials vary substantially in their attitudes towards microblogging, and we can find notable variations across agencies and policy areas. CCP Youth League committees, police departments, and CCP propaganda departments pioneer in social media use, whereas their peers in CCP organization departments, taxation bureaus, and tourism bureaus are relatively inactive. The use of SMAs in public sector also varies remarkably across geographic regions. For instance, Guangdong, Shandong, and Jiangsu consistently top in the list of government microblogging, while Qinghai, Guangxi, and Jiangxi always lag behind.

There are also notable variations across provinces in terms of microblogging adoption by government agencies and officials. Some provinces outperform their counterparts in both dimensions (e.g., Henan), while others are characterized by imbalance. In Shandong and Guangdong, agencies generally open accounts, but officials lag behind. In contrast, officials surpass agencies in using microblogging in Zhejiang and Beijing. Still others underperform in both dimensions, e.g., Tibet and Qinghai.

In a nutshell, we can see significant variations across provinces in their use of microblogging by agencies and officials. The varying landscape of microblogging adoption by agencies and officials imply they may be driven by different cohorts of factors, and we will investigate this possibility later. As there are no specific theories to distinguish their unique antecedents, we will propose the same hypotheses for the adoption of microblogging by government agencies and officials.

10.3 Theory and Hypotheses

Innovation is something new to its adopter, either ideas, practices, technologies, or policies, and diffusion refers to the spread of innovation among social actors (Rogers 2003). Microblogging is new to their potential adopters in public sector, and the adoption of microblogging in public sector can be viewed as a form of technological innovation. We can adapt the rich literature on innovation adoption and diffusion theories to investigate its antecedents and mechanisms (Mohr 1969; Walker 1969; Kimberly and Evanisko 1981; Damanpour 1991; Rogers 2003; Berry and Berry 2007; Lee and Xia 2006; Walker 2006; Hameed et al. 2012).

Mergel and Bretschneider (2013) proposed a theoretical framework to interpret the adoption process of SMAs in government (Mergel and Bretschneider 2013). Ma (2013, 2014) adapted organizational innovation and policy diffusion theories to empirically examine the drivers of government microblogging diffusion among Chinese cities (Ma 2013, 2014). Katz and Halpern (2013) use cross-country data and find the use of Web 2.0 applications by governments is driven by electronic participation features of web portals (Katz and Halpern 2013). By synthesizing the innovation adoption and diffusion theories, we expect that both internal and external factors contribute to the adoption of microblogging by governments.

In this chapter, we argue that the diffusion of microblogging across governments is primarily driven by four categories of factors. Internal factors include institutional, jurisdictional, and leadership attributes, while external factors mainly refer to inter-jurisdictional interaction.

10.3.1 Institutional Characteristics

The adoption of microblogging is primarily affected by governments' specific attributes (Walker 2006). Government size is beneficial to its investment in IT development. Political mandate, technological, and financial capacity are also key drivers of microblogging adoption.

Government Size: Prior studies have repeatedly confirmed the crucial role played by organizational size in fostering organizational innovativeness (Ho 2002; Moon and Norris 2005; Lee and Xia 2006; Pina et al. 2010; Rodríguez-Domíngueza et al. 2011; Hameed et al. 2012). Innovation involves risk and uncertainty, and it is usually unaffordable for small organizations. Larger organizations are rich in resources and expertise, and they are more ready to adopt new practices and technologies. We predict government size is positively associated with the adoption of microblogging. Either the number of government employees or total jurisdictional population can be used to gauge the size of government (Wu and Lin 2010).

- H1: Government size is positively related to the number of official microblogs adopted by government agencies and officials.

Financial Capacity: The adoption of microblogging by governments involves both technological and financial challenges. Although microblogging service is totally free of charge, governments and officials have to invest in substantial human resource and energy. Hot government and official microblog accounts can attract millions of followers, and they cannot respond promptly and effectively to surging online enquiries without the support of professional teams. For instance, Beijing Release (http://weibo.com/bjfbt), the official microblog account of Beijing Municipal Government Office of News in Sina Weibo, has sent out nearly 10,000 posts and accumulated 3.35 million followers since the late 2011. It relies on its team of ten full-time employees to operate the account 24/7. Without sufficient financial capacity, governments may not jump in the movement of microblogging. Jurisdictional wealth (often measured by GDP per capita) is commonly highly correlated with financial capacity, and we use fiscal health to gauge financial capacity of governments (Berry 1994).

- H2: Fiscal health is positively related to the number of official microblogs adopted by government agencies and officials.

E-Government Performance: As the next step of e-government development, SMAs are more likely to be successfully implemented in organizations with strong IT infrastructure and expertise. Management capacity is found to be crucial for organizational innovation (Kim and Lee 2009). A meta-analysis shows that organizational readiness is the most important antecedent of organizational adoption of IT innovation (Hameed et al. 2012). Jurisdictions pioneering in e-government development may be inclined to initiate microblogging, which are in line with their existing IT infrastructures and applications. We expect e-government performance is positively related to government microblogging.

- H3: E-government performance is positively related to the number of official microblogs adopted by government agencies and officials.

Government Transparency: Political mandate and legitimacy plays a key role in shaping the behaviors of governments and officials. Political mandatory is also a key antecedent of e-government innovation adoption. Political mandate can be investigated from diverse perspectives, e.g., transparency, democracy, accountability, integrity, and so forth (Lee et al. 2011). In the context of Chinese provinces, we focus on government transparency as one of the core political mandates shaping government behaviors. We focus on government transparency, and it is one of the key components of government microblogging (Bertot et al. 2010). We hypothesize that governments with higher level of transparency and openness are more likely to adopt microblogging. Government transparency is hypothesized to be positively related to the number of microblog accounts.

- H4: Government transparency is positively related to the number of official microblogs adopted by government agencies and officials.

10.3.2 Jurisdictional Attributes

Conventional jurisdictional characteristics are key determinants of government innovation diffusion. These characteristics are principally concerned about citizen demand of government actions, and they shape governments' propensity and behavior to adopt specific innovation (Berry and Berry 2007; Lee and Xia 2006). Jurisdictional characteristics driving the adoption of microblogging by governments are commonly related to demographics and resources and can be further split into three categories, including the education level of jurisdictional population, urbanization rate, and Internet penetration rate (IPR).

Governments and officials are prone to citizen demand of online services, information disclosure, and mutual interaction. Even in authoritarianism like China, citizen demand is also one of the key drivers of government change and innovation (Saich and Yang 2003). In empirical study, several variables have been developed to gauge the extent of public demand of specific government innovations. In the context of government microblogging, we consider the effects of jurisdictional demographics including IPR, education level, and urbanization rate.

Internet Penetration Rate: First, jurisdictions with higher percent of population with Internet access are more likely to apply microblogging in public administration and service delivery, as their applications may enjoy large user base (Lee et al. 2011). Although prior studies did not find significant correlation between IPR and e-government development (McNeal et al. 2003), we expect it may be a profound predictor of microblogging. Microblogging emphasize bidirectional communication between citizens and governments, and an online community engaged by mass active netizens will prompt its use (Katz and Halpern 2013).

- H5: IPR of provinces is positively related to the probability of government microblogging adoption.

Education Level: The digital divide suggests jurisdictions with a large cohort of populations with Internet access are more likely to respond with priority in e-government (Norris 2001). E-government and other IT applications in public sector are more acceptable to citizens with relatively higher level of formal education (Lee et al. 2011). Education level is found to be a significant predictor of e-government development (Tolbert et al. 2008). We expect jurisdictions having a population with a higher level of formal education are more likely to develop microblogging use in public sector, since citizens' active engagement will push governments to deliver online services to and initiate mutual communication with netizens (Wu and Bauer 2010; Katz and Halpern 2013).

- H6: Provinces having a population with a higher education level will adopt more government microblogs.

Urbanization: Internet use is more pervasive in urban area than in rural area and such digital divide also generate heterogeneous rural–urban development gap of e-government (Xia 2010). Urban residents are relatively more proficient than their rural counterparts in using Internet to search online information and communicate with government, which can form strong pressure to push government to develop e-government and relevant IT applications. Urbanization rate of jurisdictions is expected to be positively associated with their adoption of government microblogging.

- H7: Provinces having a population with a higher level of urbanization will adopt more government microblogs.

10.3.3 Leaders' Championship and Advocacy

Apart from the determinants mentioned above, the attitudes and behaviors of top leaders should also be investigated. Leadership matters. Organizations are to a great extent a reflection of its upper echelons, and characteristics of top managers can partially predict organizational strategies and performance (Hambrick and Mason 1984). The championship of top managers is crucial to the persistence and success of organizational innovation (Hsu et al. 2008). If microblogging is advocated and supported by top leaders, agencies, and officials are more likely to adopt it.

IT innovations usually incur uncertainty and risk, and the adoption of these innovations highly depends on top leadership support and advocacy (Moon and Norris 2005; Fernandez and Wise 2010). Innovative leadership is crucial for successful organizational innovation (Kim and Lee 2009). What is more important is political risk of managerial career, which may be augmented by technological failure or misuse (Mohr 1969; Christensen et al. 2004). The adoption of innovation by governments is heavily influenced by the attitudes and behaviors of political and organizational leaders (Borins 1998; Kelman and Myers 2011). Without strong support and policy mandate from upper-tier authorities, government officials may not have sufficient incentive to adopt microblogging (Kelman 2005; Sahni et al. 2013). Vertical pressures or leadership mandates are notable antecedents of government innovation adoption (Welch and Thompson 1980). Evidence from the US states shows that presidential speeches or congress debates on specific policy issues strongly encourage the adoption of these policies by state governments (Karch 2012).

Provincial leaders' advocacy is crucial for the use of microblogging. We focus on provincial Party secretaries and governors, as they are the most powerful officials in provinces. Their voices and behaviors are usually regarded as the strongest signals of provincial governments. Numerous studies reveal provincial leaders' characteristics (e.g., tenure in office and career background) significantly affect provincial fiscal expenditure, performance target setting, and economic growth (Wu et al. 2013). If provincial leaders publicly support or advocate the use of government microblogging, local organs, and officials are more likely to adopt microblogging.

- H8: Top leaders' advocacy is positively related to the number of official microblogs adopted by government agencies and officials.

10.3.4 Inter-Jurisdictional Diffusion Effects

Jurisdictions may be influenced by the adoption of microblogging by their counterparts, owing to either inter-jurisdictional competition or learning. The adoption of specific innovation is not solely the task of governments in isolation, and the attitudes and behaviors of their peers also play key roles (Walker 1969; Berry and Berry 1990). When their counterparts with similar socioeconomic and political attributes adopted microblogging, the focal government is under strong institutional legitimacy and peer pressure to go with the stream.

Inter-jurisdictional competition and emulation has been argued by scholars as one of the key drivers of policy diffusion (Berry and Berry 1990; Mooney 2001; Boehmke and Skinner 2012). Governments may refer to their neighbors or peers having similar socioeconomic characteristics to frame their innovation adoption strategies, which will help them to evaluate the effectiveness and popularity of specific innovations. Experiences from their peers also help governments to mitigate the risk of potential failures concerning the adoption of innovations (Dobbin et al. 2007). Jurisdictions may compete in the dimension of IT innovation, as it is a key element of public relations and marketing strategies for government. Provinces neighboring counterparts adopting more microblogging accounts may face stronger pressure from public accountability and competition effects to use microblogging. Prior studies on microblogging in government find robust evidences to support the significant influences of inter-jurisdictional competition (Ma 2013, 2014). We expect peer competition is an important antecedent of microblogging adoption.

- H9: The average number of government microblogs adopted by adjacent provinces is positively related to the number of official microblogs adopted by the focal provincial government agencies and officials.

10.4 Methods

10.4.1 Sample and Data Sources

The unit of analysis in the empirical study is provinces (subnational governments). Mainland China is administratively structured by five tiers, including the State Council, 31 provinces (including 4 municipalities, 22 general provinces, and 5 autonomous regions), nearly 290 prefecture-level cities, about 3,000 counties (districts or county-level cities), and over 40,000 towns (subdistricts or townships) (National Bureau of Statistics of China 2012). Due to different political regimes and statistics, Hong Kong, Macau, and Taiwan are usually excluded from empirical analysis. In some regression models reported later, the observations of Tibet are excluded due to data missing and the number of observations is 30 then.

The resilience of authoritarian China to a great extent roots in its institutional innovation, adaption, and learning (S. Wang 2009). The past three decades since the reform and opening-up policy in 1978 have witnessed unprecedented scope and extent of administrative and fiscal decentralization in China, with generous authorities granted from the center to local governments (Zheng 2007). Provinces have been increasingly autonomous in policy decision-making and resource redistribution, and they even bargain with central government on specific policies and issues (Huang 1996). The regime transition process has also generated substantive disparities among provinces in terms of economic growth and social development owing to heterogeneous natural endowment, regional heritages, and preferential policies (Tsui and Wang 2008). Provinces also vary remarkably in their orientation and capacity of innovation (Zhao 2012). The substantial autonomy of and considerable variation among provinces suggest they are appropriate units of analysis to examine the diffusion of microblogging in government.

The data used in this chapter cover 3 years from 2010 to 2012, and the number of observations is 93 (31×3). The data are derived from multiple sources. Data on the number of government microblogs are from the reports compiled by the Chinese Academy of Governance (CAG), which released the data on government microblogging in 2011–2012 (E-Government Research Center 2012). The 2010 data are from Zhang and Jia (2011), who released the first report on the national coverage of government microblogging in China (Zhang and Jia 2011).[1] We collect data on e-government performance from the Chinese government website performance

[1] Zhang and Jia (2011) only disclosed top 20 provinces in institutional and personal accounts of government microblogging, respectively. The data for other provinces are from the author's personal contact with Zhang (2013-06-14).

assessment reports prepared by the China Software Testing Center (CSTC 2012). Data on IPR are gleaned from the latest reports completed by the China Internet Network Information Center (CNNIC 2012). Government transparency is measured by data from the Center for Public Participation Studies and Supports (CPPSS) of Peking University (CPPSS 2012). We glean data on other provincial attributes from official statistics and authors' online search.

10.4.2 Dependent Variables

The adoption of government microblogging is measured by two indicators. As both agencies and officials can open official accounts to engage in microblogging, we separately measure their prevalence in provinces. The number of microblog accounts at year-end is used to gauge the adoption of microblogging. The data are provided by operators of four dominant platforms in China (Sina Weibo (http://www.weibo.com/), Tencent QQ (http://t.qq.com/), *People's Daily* Online (http://t.people.com.cn), and Xinhua (http://t.home.news.cn/), and replicated accounts opened by the same government agency or official on different platforms are counted as one account. Although agencies and officials may open accounts on other platforms (e.g., national platforms like Sohu (http://t.sohu.com) and local platforms like Xinmin (http://t.xinmin.cn) in Shanghai), the four dominant platforms are the most prevalent Internet operators, and we can account for the most majority of their activities. Compared with prior studies using sole platform as data sources, our coverage of the top three platforms makes the analysis be more comprehensive and representative.

One concern of the measures is the number of microblog accounts in specific provinces may be amplified by their amount of government agencies and officials, as large amount of potential users usually generate more adopters. It is not an easy task to accurately estimate the number of government agencies and officials, but generally speaking they are calibrated by upper-level authorities in line with jurisdictional population size (Ang 2012). We include provincial population size in our regression model, and the concern can then be eliminated to a great extent.

10.4.3 Independent Variables

Government size is gauged by population size, since public sector personnel are commonly determined by jurisdictional population (Wu and Lin 2010). Provincial population size is measured by the total number of residents at year-end. We use its logarithm term to normalize this measure.

Fiscal health is measured by provincial budgetary revenue minus budgetary expenditure and divided by budgetary expenditure (Berry 1994). The larger the measure, the healthier provincial fiscal conditions are.

E-government performance is measured by performance of provincial government web portals. The framework is composed of information disclosure, online service delivery, and interactivity. The data used to assess government website performance are derived from expert evaluation, daily monitoring, and user survey (CSTC 2012). The framework remains substantially stable across time and the relative scores can be compared across different provinces and years.

Government transparency is measured by an index of administrative transparency developed by researchers at Peking University (CPPSS 2012). The enactment of the *Regulations on Open Government Information* by the State Council in 2007 has substantially advanced the process of government transparency in China, but the discrepancies in their implementation are remarkable across sectors and regions. The index is composed of five dimensions to gauge the actual implementation of OGI Regulations in provinces, including institutional arrangements (e.g., specific offices and staffs), legal regulations (e.g., specific formal regulations), disclosure on own initiative (e.g., the coverage and accessibility of government information), disclosure on citizen request (e.g., timeliness of government response), supervision and remedy (e.g., litigation and accountability). The index is scored by policy experts in each province and higher values denote better implementation of OGI Regulations.

IPR is gauged by the percent of provincial population who has Internet access (CNNIC 2012). The measure is a proxy of citizens' demand of government use of microblogging. Human capital is measured by the percent of provincial population with high education certification. Urbanization rate is the percent of urban (or non-rural) residents in provinces. The aforementioned independent variables concerning citizen demand are highly correlated and simultaneously entering them will generate serious multicollinearity threats to the model estimates. To mitigate the problem, we use factor analysis with principal component analysis method to merge these variables into an index of citizen demand.[2] The resulting citizen demand factor is still highly correlated with fiscal health, and we categorize by its quartile to alleviate multicollinearity problem.[3]

Although provincial leaders may use many instruments and leverage diverse channels to promote the use of microblogging, their public advocacy will be one of the most profound signals to inform their subordinates to adopt microblogging. Due to high ranking and tight scheduling, provincial top leaders have no incentive to open an official microblog account. What provincial leaders can do is to highlight the importance of microblogging in their speeches and interviews, which are

[2] The Pearson's correlation coefficients among the three citizen demand measures are all higher than 0.90, suggesting they are substantially overlapped in measuring the same thing. One factor with Eigenvalue (=2.665) larger than 1.0 is retained, explaining 88.85 % of total variance ($\chi^2 = 162.67$, $p < 0.001$). The factor scores using regression scoring are employed to gauge citizen demand.

[3] The Pearson's correlation coefficient between citizen demand factor and fiscal health decreases substantially from 0.814 to 0.769, and the multicollinearity threat is then depressed.

commonly reported and circulated to the officialdom and then strongly influence government behaviors.

As a dummy variable, provincial leadership support is measured by whether provincial leaders endorse the adoption of microblogging in governments. We search by using the names of provincial Party secretaries and governors and "government microblog" as keywords in a mainstream search engines (Baidu and Google) and national newspaper dataset in Chinese to position the provinces with top leaders' advocacy. If provincial leaders opened microblog accounts or positively mentioned government microblog in public speeches, we code the corresponding provinces one; otherwise zero. Thus, our measure of leadership support can accurately capture the timing and behaviors of provincial leaders in advocating microblogging use in government.

To gauge inter-jurisdictional competition effects, we follow the literature to use the average number of official microblog accounts opened by adjacent provinces (Berry and Berry 1990; Lee and Xia 2006). We again use their logarithm terms to normalize the measures.

10.4.4 Analytic Methods

The dependent variables of our analysis are count data and ordinary least square (OLS) model is inappropriate due to the violation of its assumptions (e.g., normality of regression error terms). In this case, Poisson, overdispersed Poisson, or negative binomial models can be employed to estimate the model (Gardner et al. 1995). Zeros are allowed and the data are not zero-inflated, as government agencies and officials in most provinces have opened official microblog accounts. The variances of our two dependent variables are disproportionately larger than their means, and the Pearson's dispersion statistics are both greater than 1.0. The results suggest there is over dispersion problem and Poisson model is inappropriate to estimate the results (Hilbe 2011). We use negative binomial model to accommodate the over dispersion and test our hypotheses. The marginal effects at the mean (dy/dx) of regression coefficients are reported for better interpretation.

Our dataset is typical panel data structure, and the model can simultaneously estimate cross-sectional and temporal variances (Zhu 2013). Some of our independent variables are temporally invariant, and fixed effects model could not estimate their effects. We use random-effects negative binomial model to estimate our model. Our independent variables are measured 1 year lagged to alleviate autocorrelation. As such, we run the datasets with 2 years (2011–2012) due to data constraints of inter-jurisdictional competition effects.[4]

[4]We also control year dummies in the model to take account the accumulative effect of social media diffusion in government, but it is highly correlated with other independent variables (e.g., inter-jurisdictional competition effects) and we drop it from the final model. Municipalities (Beijing, Tianjin, Shanghai, and Chongqing) are commonly leaders in adopting new policies, prac-

Table 10.1 Descriptive statistics of key variables

Variable	Obs	Mean	Std. Dev.	Min	Max
Number of agencies' microblogs	62	2,272.548	2,635.571	21	16,071
Number of officials' microblogs	62	1,253.306	1,165.556	22	4,171
Government size[a]	62	4,313.355	2,744.436	301	10,505
Fiscal health	62	−0.504	0.214	−0.934	−0.074
E-government performance[a]	62	51.630	14.590	23.01	82.2
Government transparency	60	62.092	8.980	45.5	90
Citizen demand factor (by quartile)	62	2.484	1.127	1	4
Leaders' advocacy	62	0.516	0.504	0	1
Average number of agencies' microblogs of adjacent provinces[a]	62	2,446.511	1,933.986	292	8,393.5
Average number of officials' microblogs of adjacent provinces[a]	62	1,256.504	876.800	90.67	3,357.5

[a]The variables are reported in their original values to facilitate interpretation

10.5 Results

The descriptive statistics of key variables are reported in Table 10.1. Provinces vary substantially in these two dependent variables, and it is meaningful to identify the key drivers of government microblogging.

The correlation matrices of our variables are illuminated in Table 10.2. We find the number of microblog accounts in provinces is positively and significantly associated with most of the independent variables (except for government transparency), preliminarily supporting our hypotheses. The variance inflation factor (VIF) values of all independent variables are substantially smaller than 10, suggesting there is no serious multicollinearity threat.[5]

Table 10.3 reported the random-effects negative binomial regression results. We estimate the two dependent variables by all independent variables, and the estimation results are substantially consistent. Both models are statistically significant at the level of 0.01, and our group of independent variables generates notable explanatory

tices, and technologies, whereas autonomous regions (Xinjiang, Ningxia, Inner Mongolia, Tibet, and Guangxi) often lag behind in the adoption of government innovations. Geographical distribution may also matter for the adoption of new technologies by different provinces. Coastal provinces (e.g., Zhejiang and Jiangsu) are usually more open to new concepts and practices, and they are more likely to adopt social media. In contrast, inland provinces (Shaanxi and Yunnan) are generally conservative and reluctant to accept new technologies like microblogging. We can create provincial dummies to take provincial administrative attributes and geographical distribution in to account, but their variances are mostly absorbed in other jurisdictional attributes such as citizen demand and fiscal health. For instance, municipalities are much higher in urbanization education rate while autonomous regions are all located in western region. To sum up, we drop these variables in the final model to make it parsimonious.

[5]The average VIF values for agency and official microblogging models are 2.02 and 2.01, respectively.

Table 10.2 Correlation matrices of key variables

Variable	1	2	3	4	5	6	7	8	9
1. Number of agencies' microblogs	1								
2. Number of officials' microblogs	0.568	1							
3. Government size	0.428	0.361	1						
4. Fiscal health	0.365	0.298	0.398	1					
5. E-government performance	0.298	0.392	0.335	0.617	1				
6. Government transparency	0.040	0.184	0.155	0.463	0.313	1			
7. Citizen demand factor	0.263	0.233	0.050	0.769	0.477	0.351	1		
8. Leaders' advocacy	0.498	0.436	0.067	0.168	0.338	−0.133	0.217	1	
9. Average number of agencies' microblogs of adjacent provinces	0.511	0.492	0.055	0.204	0.328	−0.075	0.145	0.622	1
10. Average number of officials' microblogs of adjacent provinces	0.506	0.457	0.009	0.130	0.245	−0.130	0.100	0.660	0.914

Note: The absolute values of Pearson's correlation coefficients larger than 0.250 are statistically significant at the 0.05 level

Table 10.3 Results of random-effects negative binomial regression models

Variable	Model 1 Agencies' microblog	Model 2 Officials' microblog
Government size	0.699*** (0.123)	0.535*** (0.145)
Fiscal health	−0.443 (0.659)	0.0293 (0.885)
E-government performance	−0.00746 (0.264)	0.420 (0.312)
Government transparency	−0.488 (0.563)	0.0678 (0.713)
Citizen demand factor	0.205* (0.110)	0.0728 (0.138)
Leaders' advocacy	0.510*** (0.177)	0.360* (0.194)
Average number of agencies' microblogs of adjacent provinces	0.304*** (0.0475)	
Average number of officials' microblogs of adjacent provinces		0.277*** (0.0501)
Constant	−4.325 (2.705)	−5.996 (3.674)
Ln R	2.038*** (0.447)	1.493*** (0.333)
Ln S	7.347*** (0.665)	6.351*** (0.505)
Observations	60	60
−2 Log likelihood	963.600	909.222
Wald χ^2	204.48***	166.46***

Note: Standard errors in parentheses. ***$p<0.01$, **$p<0.05$, *$p<0.1$

power. We can find that the number of microblog accounts opened by government agencies and individual officials are driven by subtly different cohorts of antecedents, suggesting individual and organizational adoption of microblogging should be treated as distinct phenomena. The model fit statistics (Wald χ^2) suggest that macro-level factors (e.g., jurisdictional and institutional characteristics) can reasonably explain the variance of microblogging adoption by government agencies, but they matter relatively weaker for government officials' probability to adopt microblogging.

Among our four variables of institutional characteristics, only government size is significantly and positively correlated with the number of government microblog accounts. As shown in Model 1 for agency microblogging, the regression coefficient of fiscal health, e-government performance, and government transparency are all negative and insignificant. Model 2 reveals that the effects of the three institutional variables on individual microblogging are positive albeit insignificant. In sum, H1 is fully supported whereas H2, H3, and H4 are not supported.

Citizen demand has positive effect on both dependent variables, but only statistically significant at the level of 0.10 for agency microblogging. The effect of citizen demand on individual microblogging does not pass the significance level of 0.10, suggesting it is institutions rather than individual officials responding to citizen pressures on online services and communication. The results suggest that H5, H6, and H7 are partially supported.

Leadership championship and advocacy is a key antecedent of government microblogging adoption, and our results confirm this hypothesis. Leadership championship has encouraged agencies and officials to embrace microblogging.

Interestingly, the effect of leadership on the number of microblog accounts is larger for agencies ($dy/dx = 0.510$, $p < 0.01$) than officials ($dy/dx = 0.360$, $p < 0.10$), both in the values of regression coefficient and significance level. In a nutshell, H8 is supported.

Inter-jurisdictional competition effects are both significant and positive for two models, suggesting provinces surrounded by peers opening more government microblog accounts are more likely to embrace microblogging. The marginal effects of neighboring competition and emulation on the adoption of microblogging by agencies (0.304) and officials (0.277) are almost similar. The results imply governments compete in the adoption of new technologies in both institutional and individual levels. Thus, H9 is fully supported.

10.6 Discussions

In the chapter, we examine the diffusion of microblogging across government agencies and officials through the perspective of innovation adoption and diffusion theories. We propose the adoption of microblogging is driven by institutional characteristics, citizen demand, top leaders' support and advocacy, and inter-jurisdictional competition effects. We draw on longitudinal data from Chinese provinces to empirically test the hypotheses, and most of them are supported by the evidence.

We find that government size (H1) is the only institutional characteristics that matter for microblogging diffusion, whereas fiscal health, e-government performance, and government transparency have insignificant effects. In line with prior studies on e-government development (Ho 2002; Moon and Norris 2005; Lee and Xia 2006), our findings suggest that government size is one of the profound antecedents of IT innovation in public sector.

We do not find robust support of fiscal health hypotheses (H2), suggesting it is relatively unimportant for government microblogging. The initial stage of government microblogging may not require large-scale IT infrastructure investment and fiscal resources are not essentials for its adoption.

Although microblogging are the natural development of traditional e-government features like web portals, the predicted positive effect of e-government performance on government microblogging is not supported by the results (H3). A study of federal agency blogs in the USA also finds that IT sophistication of web portals has no clear link with government blogging (Mahler and Regan 2011).

The political mandate hypothesis on government transparency is also not supported by the findings (H4). The imperative of government microblogging lies in mutual communication and immediate feedback, and we expect other norms like democracy and electronic participation plays more important roles in eliciting government adoption of microblogging.

Our results confirm the profound impact of citizen demand on the development of Government 2.0, but government officials are found to be insusceptible to public pressure (H5, H6, and H7). The results imply the distinct logics leveraged by institutions and individuals in adopting microblogging. Government officials are busy in administrative affairs and they have little time and energy to operate their official microblogs usually attracting millions of followers and thousands of inquiries. They are more likely to respond to citizen demand through formal institutional channels, which may be more effective in coordinating resource allocation and personnel arrangement. In such case, citizen demand and public pressures of opening microblog accounts may be tunneled to government agencies instead of public officials. Local officials are also reluctant to be personally involved in the politically sensitive and tough tasks like the maintenance of grassroots social stability (Lee and Zhang 2013), as microblogging has emerged as one of the key channels for public petition.

The findings demonstrate the importance of top leaders' endorsement for government microblogging (H8). Although our measure of leaders' championship is far from fine-grain, the analysis shows it does work for the diffusion of government microblogging. If provincial leaders publicly encourage and support the use of microblogging, government agencies and officials in these provinces are more likely to embrace microblogging. Interestingly, the effect of leadership on microblogging is relatively stronger for government agencies than public officials, again suggesting individual public managers may respond to external pressures by formal institutional means. To our knowledge, there are no studies empirically examining the effects of managerial characteristics and behaviors in shaping government microblogging and our results contribute to the literature with preliminary evidence on the significant effects of leaders' advocacy.

Inter-jurisdictional competition effects are revealed to be pervasive for government microblogging (H9). We provide further evidence to support the crucial role played by inter-jurisdictional competition in fostering innovation diffusion among jurisdictions (Lee et al. 2011; Ma 2013). The literature on technological and organizational innovations usually does not take interorganizational forces into account, while political scientists only consider the diffusion of policies and programs. Our findings suggest the adoption of microblogging is not solely the isolated behaviors of each government and official, rather it is heavily shaped by the actions taken by their peers.

10.7 Conclusion

This chapter empirically examines the diffusion of government microblogging among provinces in China. We hypothesize that microblogging diffusion is driven by four categories of antecedents, namely government resources and capacity, citizen demand, leaders' advocacy, and inter-jurisdictional competition effects. The empirical analysis shows that all four groups of factors matter for microblogging diffusion. Notably, the model explains much better of the variances of agency microblogging than individual microblogging, and citizen demand only has significant effect on agency microblogging. The findings suggest that microblogging diffusion can be partially explained by the innovation adoption and diffusion theories, although some adaptions should be taken into account.

Our studies suggest that the diffusion of microblogging across public sectors is driven by both internal and external variables. Governments can leverage these controllable factors to promote microblogging use. Our results reiterate the pivotal role played by top leaders in advancing innovation adoption in bureaucracy, in which creativity and risk-taking are usually depressed. The experiences from China imply that bottom-up emerging of technological innovation such as microblogging in the nascent stage requires top-down mandates and support to sustain the momentum of innovation (Mergel 2012). The findings also suggest that inter-jurisdictional competition is significant driver of government microblogging adoption. The democratic laboratories in federalism in the USA and other Western countries can also be found in authoritarian regimes like China, where government can simulate quasi-market competition circumstance to foster healthy creativity and innovation climate (Florini et al. 2012).

One of the limitations of the study lies in that the unique context in local China impedes us to over generalize the findings reported in this chapter. We welcome future studies to replicate and extend our study. The short episode of microblogging use in China also disables us to cover a longer period of its diffusion to detect the changing effects of the antecedents as suggested by previous studies (Ma 2013). As for future research on the adoption and diffusion of microblogging, we suggest the following directions.

Some government agencies and officials opened their official accounts but seldom update and respond to their followers, and such microblogs are commonly called as "zombie microblogs." Institutional theory expects organizations may adopt some popular practices accepted by the community to retain their legitimacy in the industry but would not actually utilize them in organizational operations (Abrahamson 1991). Microblogging have been widely adopted by public sectors, but they vary remarkably in the frequency and resilience of updating. Some accounts update frequently and respond to public inquires actively, whereas others opened but rapidly disappeared from the public sphere. The illusory diffusion of IT fashion may harm organizational performance due to its intensive investment and inefficient utilization (Fichman and Kemerer 1999; P. Wang 2009). The adoption-implementation gap or post-adoption behaviors have been extensively investigated in private sector (Jon et al. 2005), and further studies could examine their extent of prevalence and antecedents in microblogging in public sector.

Government agencies and officials vary substantially in their policy functions and stakeholder orientations, and future studies could analyze their influences on the adoption and use of microblogging. A study shows that state agencies working close with private sectors are more likely to adopt strategic planning (Berry 1994). Another study suggests federal agency mission matters for the forms and audience types of agency blogs, and distributive agencies are active and outreach in blogging than regulatory, redistributive, and constituent agencies (Mahler and Regan 2011). Agencies and officials with intensive connections with ordinary citizens may have stronger motivation to open their official accounts. In contrast to agencies mainly concerning market regulation or office work, government agencies having strong public service orientation are more likely to adopt microblogging. Individual-level factors may be valuable to be included to examine the drivers of officials' adoption of microblogging. The findings imply further research need to dig deep into government officials' individual attributes and their influences on the adoption of microblogging (Golbeck et al. 2010). We hope future researchers to elicit testable hypotheses to examine this phenomenon, which will enrich our understanding of heterogeneous innovation adoption behaviors among government agencies and officials.

The diffusion of microblogging will go through several stages, and its derivers and processes will be distinct then (Mergel and Bretschneider 2013). The nascent stage of microblogging adoption is characterized by informal experiment and bottom-up spread, and formal government regulation usually lags (Bertot et al. 2012). The free institutional space facilitates the adoption of microblogging by governments, but the lack of formal regulation also hinders further their diffusion. In response to this situation, several local governments (e.g., Beijing, Sichuan, and Xinjiang) promulgate formal rules on microblogging and its use in public sector to advance its institutionalization. As a double-edged sword, the effects of formal regulatory framework on the adoption and use of microblogging by governments deserve further exploration. Such research may also help the regulators to identify effective policy interventions to boom and harness microblogging.

References

Abrahamson, E. (1991). Managerial fads and fashions: The diffusion and rejection of innovations. *The Academy of Management Review, 16*(3), 586–612.

Ang, Y. Y. (2012). Counting cadres: A comparative view of the size of China's public employment. *The China Quarterly, 211*, 676–696.

Berry, F. S. (1994). Innovation in public management: The adoption of strategic planning. *Public Administration Review, 54*(4), 322–330.

Berry, F. S., & Berry, W. D. (1990). State lottery adoptions as policy innovations: An event history analysis. *The American Political Science Review, 84*(2), 395–415.

Berry, F. S., & Berry, W. D. (2007). Innovation and diffusion models in policy research. In P. A. Sabatier (Ed.), *Theories of the policy process* (2nd ed., pp. 223–260). Boulder, CO: Westview Press.

Bertot, J. C., Jaeger, P. T., & Grimes, J. M. (2010). Using ICTs to create a culture of transparency: E-government and social media as openness and anti-corruption tools for societies. *Government Information Quarterly, 27*(3), 264–271.

Bertot, J. C., Jaeger, P. T., & Hansen, D. (2012). The impact of polices on government social media usage: Issues, challenges, and recommendations. *Government Information Quarterly, 29*(1), 30–40.

Boehmke, F. J., & Skinner, P. (2012). State policy innovativeness revisited. *State Politics & Policy Quarterly, 12*(3), 303–329.

Bonsón, E., Torres, L., Royo, S., & Flores, F. (2012). Local e-government 2.0: Social media and corporate transparency in municipalities. *Government Information Quarterly, 29*(2), 123–132.

Borins, S. (1998). *Innovating with integrity: How local heroes are transforming American government*. Washington, DC: Georgetown University Press.

Christensen, C. M., Anthony, S. D., & Roth, E. A. (2004). *Seeing what's next: Using the theories of innovation to predict industry change*. Cambridge, MA: Harvard Business School Press.
CNNIC. (2012). *The 30th statistical report on internet development in China*. Beijing: China Internet Network Information Center.
CPPSS. (2012). *China administrative transpareny annual watch 2010–2011*. Beijing: Law Press.
CSTC. (2012). *Performance assessment of government websites in China 2012*. Beijing: China Software Testing Center.
Damanpour, F. (1991). Organizational innovation: A meta-analysis of effects of determinants and moderators. *Academy of Management Journal, 34*(3), 555–590.
Dobbin, F., Simmons, B., & Garrett, G. (2007). The global diffusion of public policies: Social construction, coercion, competition, or learning? *Annual Review of Sociology, 33*(1), 449–472.
E-Government Research Center. (2012). *2012 China government microblogging assessment report*. Beijing: Chinese Academy of Governance Publisher.
Eggers, W. D. (2007). *Government 2.0: Using technology to improve education, cut red Tape, reduce gridlock, and enhance democracy*. Lanham, MD: Rowman & Littlefield.
Fernandez, S., & Wise, L. R. (2010). An exploration of why public organizations "Ingest" innovations. *Public Administration, 88*(4), 979–998.
Fichman, R. G., & Kemerer, C. F. (1999). The illusory diffusion of innovation: An examination of assimilation gaps. *Information Systems Research, 10*(3), 255–275.
Florini, A., Lai, H., & Tan, Y. (2012). *China experiments: From local innovations to national reform*. Washington, DC: Brookings Institution Press.
Gardner, W., Mulvey, E. P., & Shaw, E. C. (1995). Regression analyses of counts and rates: Poisson, overdispersed Poisson, and negative binomial models. *Psychological Bulletin, 118*(3), 392–404.
Golbeck, J., Grimes, J. M., & Rogers, A. (2010). Twitter use by the US Congress. *Journal of the American Society for Information Science and Technology, 61*(8), 1612–1621.
Hambrick, D. C., & Mason, P. A. (1984). Upper echelons: The organization as a reflection of its top managers. *The Academy of Management Review, 9*(2), 193–206.
Hameed, M. A., Counsell, S., & Swift, S. (2012). A meta-analysis of relationships between organizational characteristics and IT innovation adoption in organizations. *Information & Management, 49*(5), 218–232.
Hilbe, J. M. (2011). *Negative binomial regression* (2nd ed.). Cambridge, England: Cambridge University Press.
Ho, A. T.-K. (2002). Reinventing local governments and the e-government initiative. *Public Administration Review, 62*(4), 434–444.
Hsu, M. L. A., Chen, M. H.-F., & Lin, B. (2008). Top management and organisational innovation: Review and future directions. *International Journal of Innovation and Learning, 5*(5), 533–556.
Huang, Y. (1996). *Inflation and investment controls in China: The political economy of central-local relations during reform era*. New York: Cambridge University Press.
Internet Research Center at Wuhan University. (2013). *Report on Tencent government microblogging by the first half year of 2013*. Wuhan: Wuhan University.
Jon, J., Carter, P. E., & Zmud, R. W. (2005). A comprehensive conceptualization of post-adoptive behaviors associated with information technology enabled work systems. *MIS Quarterly, 29*(3), 525–557.
Karch, A. (2012). Vertical diffusion and the policy-making process: The politics of embryonic stem cell research. *Political Research Quarterly, 65*(1), 48–61.
Katz, J., & Halpern, D. (2013). Political and developmental correlates of social media participation in government: A global survey of national leadership websites. *International Journal of Public Administration, 36*(1), 1–15.
Kelman, S. (2005). *Unleashing change: A study of organizational renewal in government*. Washington, DC: Brookings Institution Press.

Kelman, S., & Myers, J. (2011). Successfully achieving ambitious goals in government: An empirical analysis. *The American Review of Public Administration, 41*(3), 235–262.
Kim, S. E., & Lee, J. W. (2009). The impact of management capacity on government innovation in Korea: An empirical study. *International Public Management Journal, 12*(3), 345–369.
Kimberly, J. R., & Evanisko, M. J. (1981). Organizational innovation: The influence of individual, organizational, and contextual factors on hospital adoption of technological and administrative innovations. *The Academy of Management Journal, 24*(4), 689–713.
King, G., Pan, J., & Roberts, M. E. (2013). How censorship in China allows government criticism but silences collective expression. *American Political Science Review, 107*(2), 326–343.
Lee, C., Chang, K., & Berry, F. S. (2011). Testing the development and diffusion of e-government and e-democracy: A global perspective. *Public Administration Review, 71*(3), 444–454.
Lee, C. K., & Zhang, Y. (2013). The power of instability: Unraveling the microfoundations of bargained authoritarianism in China. *American Journal of Sociology, 118*(6), 1475–1508.
Lee, G., & Xia, W. (2006). Organizational size and IT innovation adoption: A meta-analysis. *Information & Management, 43*(8), 975–985.
Ma, L. (2013). The diffusion of government microblogging: Evidence from Chinese Municipal Police Bureaus. *Public Management Review, 15*(2), 288–309.
Ma, L. (2014). Diffusion and assimilation of government microblogging: Evidence from Chinese cities. *Public Management Review, 16*(2), 274–295.
Mahler, J., & Regan, P. M. (2011). Federal Agency blogs: Agency mission, audience, and blog forms. *Journal of Information Technology & Politics, 8*(2), 163–176.
McAfee, A. (2009). *Enterprise 2.0: New collaborative tools for your organization's toughest challenges*. Boston: Harvard Business School Press.
McDougall, M. (2011). *The Chinese social media universe*. Sydney: Bullara Press.
McNeal, R. S., Tolbert, C. J., Mossberger, K., & Dotterweich, L. J. (2003). Innovating in digital government in the American states. *Social Science Quarterly, 84*(1), 52–70.
Mergel, I. (2012). *Social media in the public sector: A guide to participation, collaboration and transparency in the networked world*. San Francisco, CA: Jossey-Bass.
Mergel, I., & Bretschneider, S. I. (2013). A three-stage adoption process for social media use in government. *Public Administration Review, 73*(3), 390–400.
Mohr, L. B. (1969). Determinants of innovation in organizations. *American Political Science Review, 63*(1), 111–126.
Moon, M. J., & Norris, D. F. (2005). Does managerial orientation matter? The adoption of reinventing government and e-government at the municipal level. *Information Systems Journal, 15*(1), 43–60.
Mooney, C. Z. (2001). Modeling regional effects on state policy diffusion. *Political Research Quarterly, 54*(1), 103–124.
National Bureau of Statistics of China. (2012). *China county statistical yearbook 2011*. Beijing: China Statistics Press.
Nielsen. (2012). *State of the media: The social media report 2012*. New York: Nielsen.
Noesselt, N. (2014). Microblogs and the adaptation of the Chinese Party-State's governance strategy. *Governance, 27*(3), 449–468.
Norris, P. (2001). *Digital divide?: Civic engagement, information poverty, and the internet worldwide*. New York: Cambridge University Press.
Office of Internet Opinion at People's Daily Online. (2013). *Report of Sina Government microblogging by the first quarter of 2013*. Beijing: People's Daily Online.
Picazo-Vela, S., Gutiérrez-Martínez, I., & Luna-Reyes, L. F. (2012). Understanding risks, benefits, and strategic alternatives of social media applications in the public sector. *Government Information Quarterly, 29*(4), 504–511.
Pina, V., Torres, L., & Royo, S. (2010). Is e-government promoting convergence towards more accountable local governments? *International Public Management Journal, 13*(4), 350–380.
Rainie, L., Smith, A., Schlozman, K. L., Brady, H., & Verba, S. (2012). *Social media and political engagement*. Washington, D.C.: Pew Research Center.

Rodríguez-Domíngueza, L., García-Sáncheza, I. M., & Álvareza, I. G. (2011). Determining factors of e-government development: A worldwide national approach. *International Public Management Journal, 14*(2), 218–248.
Rogers, E. M. (2003). *Diffusion of innovations* (5th ed.). New York: Free Press.
Sahni, N. R., Wessel, M., & Christensen, C. M. (2013). Unleashing breakthrough innovation in government. *Stanford Social Innovation Review, 11*(3), 26–31.
Saich, T., & Yang, X. (2003). Township elections in China: Extending democracy or institutional innovation. *China Report, 39*(4), 477–497.
Schlæger, J., & Jiang, M. (2014). Official microblogging and social management by local governments in China. *China Information, 28*(2), 189–213.
Thackeray, R., Neiger, B. L., Smith, A. K., & Van Wagenen, S. B. (2012). Adoption and use of social media among public health. *BMC Public Health, 12*(1), 242–247.
Tolbert, C. J., Mossberger, K., & McNeal, R. (2008). Institutions, policy innovation, and e-government in the American States. *Public Administration Review, 68*(3), 549–563.
Tsui, K.-Y., & Wang, Y. (2008). Decentralization with political trump: Vertical control, local accountability and regional disparities in China. *China Economic Review, 19*(1), 18–31.
UN. (2012). *United Nations E-Government Survey 2012: E-Government for the people*. New York: United Nations.
Walker, J. L. (1969). The diffusion of innovations among the American States. *The American Political Science Review, 63*(3), 880–899.
Walker, R. M. (2006). Innovation type and diffusion: An empirical analysis of local government. *Public Administration, 84*(2), 311–335.
Wang, P. (2009). Chasing the hottest IT: Effects of information technology fashion on organizations. *MIS Quarterly, 34*(1), 63–85.
Wang, S. (2009). Adapting by learning: The evolution of China's rural health care financing. *Modern China, 35*(4), 370–404.
Welch, S., & Thompson, K. (1980). The impact of federal incentives on state policy innovation. *American Journal of Political Science, 24*(4), 715–729.
Wu, A. M., & Lin, M. (2010). Determinants of government size: Evidence from China. *Public Choice, 151*(1–2), 255–270.
Wu, J., Deng, Y., Huang, J., Morck, R., & Yeung, B. (2013). Incentives and outcomes: China's environmental policy. *National Bureau of Economic Research Working Paper Series.*
Wu, Y., & Bauer, J. M. (2010). E-Government in China: Deployment and driving forces of provincial government portals. *Chinese Journal of Communication, 3*(3), 290–310.
Xia, J. (2010). Linking ICTs to rural development: China's rural information policy. *Government Information Quarterly, 27*(2), 187–195.
Zhang, Z.-a., & Jia, J. (2011). Chinese government microblogging study. *Journalism Review, 6*, 34–39.
Zhao, Q. (2012). The regional disparities in Chinese provincial government innovation. *Innovation: Management, Policy & Practice, 14*(4), 595–604.
Zheng, L. (2013). Social media in Chinese government: Drivers, challenges and capabilities. *Government Information Quarterly, 30*(4), 369–376.
Zheng, Y. (2007). *De facto federalism in China: Reforms and dynamics of central-local relations*. Singapore: World Scientific.
Zhu, L. (2013). Panel data analysis in public administration: Substantive and statistical considerations. *Journal of Public Administration Research and Theory, 23*(2), 395–428.

Part IV
Communication and Citizen Engagement

Chapter 11
Digital Civic Participation in Australian Local Governments: Everyday Practices and Opportunities for Engagement

Julie Freeman

Abstract Digital technologies and social media platforms are changing civic expectations surrounding interaction with government. Local governments hold key positions in the development of digital spaces for civic participation in the issues that directly impact citizens' everyday lives. However, local practices largely prioritise information and services over reciprocal dialogue with citizens. This chapter explores digital civic engagement in Australian local governments. It draws from a nation-wide survey of councils' digital practices to highlight that opportunities for civic participation are increasing, particularly through social media. However, substantial discrepancies exist between the digital practices of rural and urban local governments. This discrepancy is further examined through comments from seven rural councils that participated in a workshop on digital engagement, and the views of urban citizens (through focus groups) whose local government offers advanced digital practices. For the rural authorities, key challenges to digital development include limited connectivity, capacity, and financial resources, as well as the different expectations that citizens have in relation to social media use. For the (urban) citizens, participation in online spaces has gone unanswered by their government, which is creating a sense of disenfranchisement. While there is evidence of innovation in Australian digital local government, civic demand and government use largely fail to align. Councils need to reconceptualise current approaches to digital engagement by considering the purpose of participatory spaces and integrating their use into everyday operations. Moreover, greater government receptivity and responsiveness is required to enable civic participation to inform local decision-making. Such involvement allows citizens to develop a sense of connection with local government and facilitates increased civic engagement.

J. Freeman (✉)
News & Media Research Centre, University of Canberra, ACT, Australia
e-mail: Julie.Freeman@canberra.edu.au

M.Z. Sobaci (ed.), *Social Media and Local Governments*, Public Administration and Information Technology 15, DOI 10.1007/978-3-319-17722-9_11

11.1 Introduction

In an era when user-generated content, viral marketing, and googling are normalised, government communication needs to be redefined to suit the digital environment. Digital government applications are encouraged and endorsed as promoting open and accessible governments that facilitate direct citizen connection with representatives, increase transparency, and enable more deliberative and participatory democratic systems (see, for example, Coleman and Blumler 2009; Bertot et al. 2012). The reality, however, often demonstrates government reluctance to cede control of online communication, resulting in the implementation of digital government strategies that privilege one-way communication between governments and citizens over opportunities for two-way civic engagement (Jimenez et al. 2012; Bekkers and Homburg 2007).

The rapid proliferation of digital media into individuals' everyday lives has changed civic expectations surrounding digital interaction with government and created increasing demand for new forms of political participation (Jaeger and Bertot 2010; Holland 2014). Governments have the opportunity to respond to changing civic expectations by incorporating social media and other platforms for two-way consultation into their communicative practices. When used as everyday mechanisms for civic engagement, digital technologies can provide avenues for improved connections between governments and citizens (Mossberger et al. 2013). This chapter argues that local government use of social media and other participatory spaces must extend beyond improved access to information and services to enable citizens to actively engage in the communication flows and decision-making processes that directly relate to their lives and locales. In order to achieve this, receptivity and responsiveness need to be incorporated into ongoing government avenues for digital civic participation (Macnamara 2013).

This chapter draws from findings from a nation-wide survey of 559 Australian local governments' digital practices. It highlights that avenues for online citizen participation are increasing, particularly through social media. However, there are considerable discrepancies between the digital practices employed by smaller rural local governments and those implemented by larger urban authorities that have improved connectivity and more substantial resources. As such, this chapter draws from the views of rural local governments that govern small and geographically dispersed communities to demonstrate the disadvantages they face in relation to connectivity and capacity in the digital media environment. It furthermore outlines insights from citizens from a metropolitan municipality that has employed advanced digital practices. Their comments suggest that current digital engagement opportunities are largely tokenistic gestures that do little to aid civic connection with government.

11.2 Social Media and Civic Engagement in Digital Local Government

The prevalence of digital technologies in citizens' everyday lives is redefining understandings and practices associated with democratic participation. Digital initiatives allow governments to address increasing demand for political involvement through new methods of civic engagement. In particular, as social media have become embedded within society (Meikle and Young 2012), platforms such as Twitter and Facebook offer opportunities to supplement existing interactions between citizens and governments with additional spaces for reciprocal conversations (Ellison and Hardey 2013; Mossberger et al. 2013; Hofmann et al. 2013). Such government-led spaces through social media commonly follow typologies of maturity with stages including: one-way information dissemination and increased data transparency; improved service delivery; and soliciting public input into decision-making to enable more open government through collaboration with citizens and other stakeholders to co-create solutions for complex problems (Lee and Kwak 2012; Bonsón et al. 2012; Chun et al. 2010).

Similar to early models of e-government development (Moon 2002; Thomas 2004), progression through these stages of social media use is often viewed as a linear process with governments initially providing increased access to information before offering new avenues for services and then slowly enabling increased interaction and civic participation. However, when considering that e-government developments to-date have largely failed to achieve enhanced civic engagement (Bekkers and Homburg 2007; Norris 2010), such gradual and linear development of social media use may not meet changing civic demand resulting from the ubiquitous nature of interactive technologies in citizens' everyday lives. Bonsón et al. (2012) found that European local governments are lagging behind their citizens in the use of social media for political engagement. They suggest that this situation presents missed opportunities for governments as their citizens discuss local policy options online, and argue that it is unlikely that social media tools will revolutionise government–citizen interactions when following predictable paths of e-government development (Bonsón et al. 2012; see also Norris and Reddick 2012). Mergel (2012) suggests that, rather than treating social media as broadcasting mechanisms, governments should refocus on emerging trends in public expectations and civic behaviours (see also Reddick and Norris 2013a). Governments should consider civic demand so that technological developments can be undertaken in a more citizen-centric and holistic manner. Such an approach would address the need for greater access to digital information and services as well as enable direct participation through everyday opportunities for civic engagement.

This chapter explores social media use at the local level in order to highlight some of the challenges that arise when civic demand and government use do not align (see Bonsón et al. 2012). Spaces for social media-enabled engagement hold promise at the local government level as the proximity of place retains importance in both digital and political practices (Farman 2012; Wilken and Goggin 2012;

Margolis and Moreno-Riaño 2009; Malina 1999). Moreover, connectivity and the broader social, economic, and political contexts of locales influence digital experiences (Martin 2014; Farman 2012). The communicative practices of local governments are therefore important spaces for democratic participation. Local government-run avenues for civic participation can capitalise on the fact that citizens perceive democratic involvement to primarily take place at the local level (Couldry and Langer 2005). The majority of everyday civic contact with government occurs locally, and citizens' increased sense of immediacy and familiarity with local issues drives political participation (Ellison and Hardey 2013; Shackleton 2010; Malina 1999). Furthermore, local digital spaces for civic participation often face fewer challenges than other levels of political involvement, particularly in relation to issues surrounding the scale and manageability of large volumes of data that often require filtering in order to increase usefulness (Kavanaugh et al. 2012; Jimenez et al. 2012; Mossberger et al. 2013). Councils can also draw upon their community knowledge in order to target digital initiatives to more effectively suit the needs of their citizens and locales (Bradford 2008).

Social media platforms offer governments at all levels opportunities to engage citizens, but they are particularly useful for councils that do not have the financial, technological, or staffing resources necessary to develop other mechanisms for digital participation. Mossberger et al. (2013) highlight that use of social media has been the fundamental change in local e-government practices in recent years. Other forms of digital interaction at the local level are also developing, although to a lesser extent (Mossberger et al. 2013). However, previous research has also demonstrated that local online mechanisms have been largely used for information dissemination and service delivery, rather than focused on new avenues for citizens' political participation (O'Toole 2009; Jensen 2009). The capacity of social media to enhance digital civic engagement therefore remains largely underutilised (Jimenez et al. 2012). For example, disseminating the headlines of media releases or allowing users to like, follow, or share posts does little in terms of enabling active citizen involvement (Macnamara 2012).

Macnamara (2012) suggests "there is a fundamental dichotomy between old politics and new media at multiple levels, which has not been adequately recognised by governments and political organisations jumping on the bandwagon of social media" (p. 81). He argues that receptivity and responsiveness need to be designed into the frameworks of digital communicative practices so that public involvement is afforded consideration in decision-making (Macnamara 2013; Jensen 2009). The capacity to impact decision-making, leading to action and change, makes participation more meaningful and enables citizens to develop a genuine sense of connection with government. It is this sense of connection that in turn facilitates greater civic engagement (Coleman and Blumler 2009). However, without an ongoing digital presence through which citizens can connect with governments, citizens may utilise these technologies to create their own volatile sites of resistance (Thompson 2005; Lester and Hutchins 2012). Government-led initiatives are therefore necessary to address an increasing demand for political participation and to help prevent instances of digital civic dissent.

Often research into local authorities' social media use centres on acute events, such as times of crises and elections (see, for example, Bruns 2012; Bird et al. 2012; Margo 2012; Kavanaugh et al. 2012). These and other studies broadly highlight the benefits and limitations of government social media use, such as addressing citizens as partners rather than consumers, the value obtained through crowd sourcing voluntary public input, improved transparency of government operations, and the complexities and challenges surrounding responsibility and accountability for shared decision-making (Linders 2012; Hilgers and Ihl 2010; Henman 2010). However, exploring social media use around specific events limits insight into the ways that these technologies are redefining longer-term understandings and experiences of democratic participation. A distinction should therefore be made between government social media use in response to triggering events (such as natural disasters or elections) and civic use of social media to trigger government responses.

In his examination of social media use by five local governments in the Australian state of New South Wales, Holland (2014) argues that civic participation through councils' social networking sites makes visible behaviours that require government action (see also Thompson 2005). However, a dichotomy exists between civic and government expectations surrounding the purpose of social media use, with citizens' seeking participation and engagement and local governments often focusing on information provision (Holland 2014; see also Bonsón et al. 2012). This chapter seeks to further explore social media use in the everyday practices of Australian local governments, removed from triggering events, in order to determine whether these tools facilitate effective and ongoing government-to-citizen communication.

The Australian Centre of Excellence for Local Government has undertaken research into councils' social media use. For example, Purser (2012) draws from a survey of approximately 40 % of Australian local authorities which found that 69 % of the participating councils were using some form of social media; although she notes that councils without a social media presence were less likely to participate in the survey. Howard (2012) utilises a survey of the homepages of all Australian local government websites as well as a series of interviews with local government officials. She highlights that 11.4 % of Australian local governments use Facebook, 10.9 % use Twitter, and 4.1 % use YouTube (as indicated on their homepages in mid-2011). While these statistics differ, correlating findings between the studies include that many councils are yet to adapt to interactive possibilities, instead continuing to follow one-way communicative designs in their digital practices. The most significant barriers to social media use were found to be lack of resources and knowledge, with loss of control of messages and negative feedback from the community viewed as significant risks. While local governments do recognise that social media can help increase public engagement, both studies highlight insufficient levels of social media training and education offered to council staff (Purser 2012; Howard 2012). Interestingly, the two studies diverge in relation to community expectations. Purser's (2012) report suggests increased expectations are not seen as a significant risk. However, Howard's (2012) report indicates concern that local government social media use will raise expectations (such as response times) to a level beyond councils' capacity.

Despite increasing focus on digital civic engagement at the local level, participatory practices are often not accepted as fundamental or formal spaces for communities to interact with governments (Aulich 2009). Local spaces for civic engagement are frequently considered to be tokenistic attempts to placate the community as there are few opportunities for citizens to directly influence the decision-making processes that shape their everyday lives (Scott et al. 2007; Jensen 2009). While many authorities are failing to exploit the conversational possibilities enabled by digital technologies, social media and other platforms for civic engagement do hold potential to provide "local citizens increased political voice in what is inevitably becoming an increasingly complex communications environment" (Ellison and Hardey 2013, p. 894). As such, it is necessary to explore current barriers to local digital civic engagement so that future practices may overcome existing limitations.

11.3 The Australian Context

Australia has three-tiers of representative government. According to the Australian Bureau of Statistics (ABS 2012), there are 559 local governments in Australia. The diversity of Australian local authorities provides a challenging context for equitable digital government development, with municipal populations ranging from just over a hundred citizens (such as the Shires of Murchison, Sandstone, and Westonia in Western Australia) to well over a million (the City of Brisbane in Queensland), and some local government areas that are larger than many countries (the Shire of East Pilbara in Western Australia covers more than 370,000 km^2). Local governments have limited authority but are responsible for most day-to-day services and facilities such as waste collection, libraries and community centres, town planning, and local transport.

The importance of digital government at the local level is recognised in Australian federal policy including the *National Digital Economy Strategy*, which stresses that digitally aware local governments will drive greater engagement by communities (Department of Broadband and Communications and the Digital Economy (DBCDE) 2011a). The emphasis on improving Australia's position in the digital economy—through e-government and other areas—directly links to broadband internet infrastructure developments under the National Broadband Network (NBN). The Federal Government is investing significant resources into the provision of ubiquitous high-speed broadband through fibre optic, fixed wireless, and satellite technologies (see Bowles and Wilson 2012). While internet access is increasing under the NBN, infrastructure developments to-date have been uneven, particularly between urban and remote areas (Dobson et al. 2013). But the increased attention on access to the internet has also contributed to greater emphasis on developing digital government practices, particularly in relation to service delivery. The Federal Government has subsequently set a goal to transition government services into "digital first" format by the end of 2017 (DBCDE 2013).

The Australian Federal Government provides assistance to a limited number of local governments and their communities through the "digital local government" and "digital communities" programmes. Under these schemes, public training hubs have been provided in 40 areas with NBN access and their local governments are eligible to apply for funding to develop their digital services (DBCDE 2011a, b). However, there is little assistance offered directly to the remaining councils, and this has resulted in the autonomous development of ad hoc local digital practices. Most local digital practices continue to focus on information dissemination and service delivery as these offer financial savings through increased efficiency (O'Toole 2009). The capacity of information and communication technologies as platforms for increased political participation and to facilitate direct connections between citizens and local representatives remains largely overlooked. The increased costs and time involved in more participatory two-way opportunities for civic engagement are deterrents for many local governments, particularly smaller authorities with limited resources such as those governing small or geographically dispersed rural communities.

11.4 Methodology

This chapter draws from a range of research projects into local e-government, digital civic participation, and connectivity issues in Australia. The quantitative data is taken from a nation-wide survey of the digital activities of 559 Australian local governments. The purpose of the survey was to document the extensive range of current e-government mechanisms at the local level, particularly through councils' websites. The survey included both quantitative and qualitative measures to explore a variety of functions including the usability of websites, the types of content available, forms of information dissemination, the availability of e-commerce transactions, and different types of interaction between governments and citizens. Due to the substantial number of Australian local governments, the survey was undertaken during 2012 and 2013 by the researcher and two assistants. In order to help ensure consistency, a detailed coding sheet was used to guide data collection, which was particularly necessary for areas that required individual judgements—for example, when determining perceived usability of websites as opposed to more straightforward assessments relating to the availability of certain information or functions. For the purpose of this chapter's focus on civic engagement, results related to the use of commonplace social media platforms and other types of direct government-to-citizen interaction are primarily discussed here. The results of the survey were also used to identify individual local governments that offer innovative digital practices.

There are some limitations of the survey that should be recognised, which largely relate to the challenges of studying a field in which frequent technological and political changes take place. The time frame of data collection meant that digital practices were likely to change during the collection period. For example, local governments assessed early may have updated their digital practices before the research was finalised, and those assessed later on had additional time in which digital developments may have taken place. The time frame was also drawn out due to the fact that local government elections were held during the collection period. This meant that local governments shifted into caretaker mode; while their administrative roles continued, any significant decisions or new developments could not be made until election results were finalised and returning or new representatives were in office. In terms of e-government, councils' digital activities, particularly those that involved interactive features such as social media use, were temporarily suspended and could not be assessed during this time. For these reasons, the quantitative data presented in this chapter are intended only to provide a snapshot into digital local government in Australia.

Further qualitative contextual information about local e-government development is also offered to compliment the survey results and highlight the challenges involved in digital civic participation practices for both governments and citizens. Such an approach is necessary in order to demonstrate the complexities of local digital civic engagement that may be masked within larger statistical datasets (see Wolff and Andrews 2010). The comments from local government officials offered in this chapter are drawn from a full-day workshop on digital engagement held in May 2014 with seven rural local governments from the state of New South Wales. Participants included mayors, councillors, general managers, economic development officers, and information officers. The comments from citizens are drawn from focus groups conducted with residents of a large and well-resourced urban municipality in the state of Victoria during mid-2013. Their local government offers advanced avenues for digital engagement including use of social media and online discussion forums. Further details of the methodologies for the workshop and focus groups are available in Park et al. (2015) and Freeman and McCallum (2013), respectively. While these projects were not specifically designed to interconnect, their findings provide an opportunity to highlight contrasting experiences of the value and usefulness of digital participation opportunities at the local level, and compliment conclusions drawn from the survey data. Their integration therefore enables a more detailed understanding of the nuances surrounding both limited and advanced digital local government practices, and offers insight into the overall state of everyday contexts for local digital civic engagement in Australia.

11.5 Digital Civic Engagement with Australian Local Governments

Social media and other spaces for civic participation are gaining prominence in the digital practices of Australian local governments. This section presents indicative findings in relation to local e-government development from the survey outlined above, and suggests implications in terms of civic engagement. It begins by briefly highlighting the results for a selection of information dissemination and service delivery practices through local government websites before exploring current levels of digital government-to-citizen interaction through participatory spaces.

The data is separated to provide: the overall percentage across all 559 Australian local governments; the results for local government authorities that govern municipal populations of less than 15,000 (based on 2012 population figures from the ABS); and the results for capital city local governments. The reason for this breakdown is to offer insight into the digital practices offered in various regions in Australia. Reddick and Norris (2013b) note that population size and geographic location are key variables that influence the adoption of e-government practices. Approximately 55 % of Australian local governments have municipal populations of less than 15,000 (ABS 2012). These smaller local governments from rural or remote regions face different issues in comparison to urban city local governments, particularly in terms of digital connectivity, resources, and capacity to implement digital participatory practices. Capital city local governments were selected only to offer indicative figures for urban digital government development. Percentages have been rounded to the nearest whole number.

11.5.1 Information Dissemination and Service Delivery

Like elsewhere in the world (Ellison and Hardey 2013; Sobaci and Karkin 2013; Norris and Reddick 2012), digital information and services dominate Australian local e-government. These types of practices are important aspects of e-government as they facilitate the development of informed citizenries and can help build civic confidence in government (Linders 2012; Bonsón et al. 2012). Tables 11.1 and 11.2 highlight that Australian authorities are actively using their websites to increase the dissemination of local information and to offer digital services. Two noticeable characteristics emerge from the below data. The first is that across all categories of evaluation, urban city governments consistently perform better in terms of the

Table 11.1 Australian local government internet use—information dissemination

	Australian local government average (%)	Local governments, populations <15,000 (%)	Capital city local governments (%)
Local service information	95	92	100
Council news	88	82	100
Media releases	60	40	100
Minutes/agendas of council meetings	96	93	100
Policy documentation	82	70	100
Budget information	86	79	100
E-newsletters	33	20	43

Table 11.2 Australian local government internet use—service delivery

	Australian local government average (%)	Local governments, populations <15,000 (%)	Capital city local governments (%)
Downloadable forms	84	72	100
Online submission of forms	12	–	43
E-service requests	58	39	100
Digital payments for rates	70	47	100

digital information and services offered than their rural counterparts. The second is that as digital practices become more complex, they are significantly less likely to be used.

It is worth noting that these figures are offered only to provide an indication of Australian local e-government development and in some cases the quantitative measures do not necessarily reflect the quality of the information or services provided. For example, while 88 % of Australian local governments provide council news through their websites, more than half of these were classified as offering only minimal information where there were fewer than 15 items in total and content was updating irregularly. Cases like these suggest that many Australian local governments still have a substantial task ahead of them in order to capitalise on the internet to increase the transparency of detailed information.

Local governments have a responsibility to keep their communities informed and the internet offers a cost-efficient tool through which they can distribute local news and information (O'Toole 2009). Australian local governments, particularly those that are urban based, have recognised this and provide detailed information online. However, the vast majority of these developments rely upon citizens actively seeking information through government websites. Significantly fewer councils (a third overall) take the initiative to actively send out newsletters via email to their citizens. As can be expected in rural Australian areas with limited infrastructure access and lower digital literacy levels (Morris 2012), the figures for rural local governments indicate they are less likely to provide digital information. However, accessible local community news is becoming particularly important in rural areas where traditional sources (such as regional newspapers) are rapidly disappearing in the networked environment (Kavanaugh et al. 2014). This suggests that, as digital access and capacities increase, there may be a future opportunity for rural councils to provide greater online information for their communities.

Straightforward service delivery practices, such as downloadable forms that must be submitted by post (e.g. planning permit applications), were very common amongst Australian local governments. Additionally, more than half of Australian authorities enable simple service requests (such as ordering replacement rubbish bins) to be completed entirely online. However, more complex applications—such as allowing planning permits to be both completed and submitted online—are less common. This signals that Australian authorities have a significant challenge ahead in developing digital first services. Rural councils again lag behind with this inconsistency likely stemming from limited levels of connectivity and less capacity to develop digital services (Morris 2012). Interestingly, however, rural Australian councils provide more community services than urban authorities in order to help ensure social inclusion (Broadband for the Bush Alliance 2013). This suggests that connectivity and capacity issues in rural areas will require greater consideration as government services transition into digital first format.

Given the financial benefits that digital information and services offer governments (Bekkers and Homburg 2007), the results presented in this section are unsurprising. However, as digital first information and services become more pervasive with the widespread acceptance of technologies, citizens are likely to expect and demand the use of digital technologies for other forms of interaction with government.

11.5.2 Civic Participation

This section explores opportunities for ongoing deliberation through two-way dialogue between citizens and local governments. Table 11.3 highlights that digital participation through social media is still largely in its formative stages in Australian local governments, although there are promising signs of development and innovation in urban areas.

The use of discussion forums provides evidence that a small number of local governments are trying new methods to connect with the community and gain more detailed feedback. Across Australia, approximately 7 % of councils enable online discussions with citizens through forums. The majority of these are metropolitan and urban fringe governments, with only rare rural and remote cases (0.3 %). The forums are often framed around topical issues predetermined by the governments as

Table 11.3 Australian local government internet use—civic participation

	Australian local government average (%)	Local governments, populations <15,000 (%)	Capital city local governments (%)
Discussion forums	7	0.3	29
Twitter	26	6	86
YouTube	13	4	43
Facebook	39	26	86
• *Person instead of organisation*	1	3	
• *Restricted*	10	5	–
• *Unrestricted*	28	18	86

opposed to allowing citizens to have a general space to connect with representatives and raise their own queries (Freeman 2013). More than half of the discussion forums available are outsourced to commercial companies, suggesting there are issues surrounding local government capacity to develop and manage their own discussion forums, such as having sufficient technical knowledge and the staff time required for moderation (Mossberger et al. 2013). Outsourcing also indicates that there may be a broad reluctance to directly incorporate this type of space for civic engagement into the everyday and official operations of councils, which is particularly evident when many of the forums do not use the government internet domain. Unfortunately, while these types of forums often enable increased citizen-to-citizen interaction, they currently provide little evidence of direct interactions between governments and citizens (Freeman 2013). This suggests these spaces are largely tokenistic gestures for community engagement, with little capacity for community members to actively engage in deliberative discussions with representatives.

Social media, such as Twitter and Facebook, offer useful alternatives for local governments that wish to connect with citizens but are unable to afford to outsource discussion forums. While dialogue through social media can be limited in comparison to discussion forums (e.g. due to character restraints), these platforms require little digital training, are free to implement (excluding costs of staff time), and can capitalise on an already existing pool of users. Table 11.3 indicates that social media use by Australian local governments is more prominent than discussion forums; however, there are substantial differences between urban and rural local governments. For example, while 26 % of councils across Australia use Twitter, when considering the different levels of its use in rural (6 %) and urban (86 %) areas, Twitter is significantly more dominant in metropolitan municipalities. Also worth noting is that the number of councils using Twitter does not necessarily reflect the quality of its use, with many further disseminating headlines of media releases or promoting local events, rather than using it to facilitate two-way civic participation (Holland 2014; Purser 2012).

Similarly, YouTube has a higher proportion of use amongst urban areas, with these governments often uploading media coverage for promotion or using YouTube to host videos that encourage tourism or relocation to the municipality. Use of YouTube was more common than direct webcasting through council websites; less than 2 % of all Australian local governments webcast, and slightly fewer offer podcasts (there was no overlap between the councils that webcast and those that podcast). No local governments with populations of less than 15,000 offer either type of application even though these councils often cover larger geographical areas, which makes it harder for citizens to, for example, physically attend council meetings. Overall, Facebook (39 %) is the most common form of social media used by Australian local governments (Purser 2012; Howard 2012). Table 11.3 also highlights, however, that there appears to be some ambiguity around the type of account that local governments should employ (person, restricted, unrestricted), which suggests there is uncertainty amongst councils about the best way to use social media platforms, such as their level of openness and how they should be managed (see Oliveira and Welch 2013; Hofmann et al. 2013).

There are limited instances of local governments using other interactive tools such as Flickr, Pinterest, and Instagram to address the growing relationship between mobile devices and place (Wilken and Goggin 2012). For example, approximately 4 % of Australian local governments use the mobile application Snap Send Solve, including just under 3 % of smaller authorities (note, this figure is based on the number of councils that indicate they use Snap Send Solve on their websites). This (purchasable) tool enables citizens to take photos of issues such as potholes or graffiti on their smart phone or tablet device, tag the location with their GPS coordinates, and submit a report to the corresponding local authority. There are also a handful of urban councils that have developed their own innovative applications. For example, Parramatta City Council (near Sydney) has a smart parking application that allows users to view nearby available car parking spaces through interactive maps. These types of developments predominantly focus on information dissemination and service delivery practices, rather than capitalising on the increasing use of mobile devices in everyday life to establish new forms of two-way communication with citizens.

A notable exception is Randwick City Council, which is a large metropolitan municipality in the suburbs of Sydney with a population of approximately 134,000 citizens. Randwick has implemented its own myRandwick mobile application that allows citizens to, amongst other things, monitor development proposals in their area, look up local service information or latest news and events, complete surveys, and join discussions forums on topical issues. This example demonstrates innovation in Australian digital local government; however, it is worth noting that the two-way features enabled by this mobile application face similar challenges to mechanisms run directly through websites. An example is a consultation that ran between 2011 and 2013 on the development of a light rail system. In this instance and in addition to traditional forms of information dissemination and formal submissions, the government provided extensive digital documentation to help inform the community (including videos), ran a survey, and provided online discussion spaces (operated by an outsourced company). There were eight topic areas in the light rail forum, all set by the government, which asked for feedback on issues including funding, potential impacts and benefits, routes, and citizens' current travel arrangements, and it enabled people to agree or disagree with other posts. In all, there were 767 comments posted across the eight topic areas, with 42,383 views of the discussions (as of August 2014).

The council recognised the significance and direct impact of the proposed development on the local community, and this is reflected by the level of community engagement that took place including the number of civic comments on the site, the fact that citizens were interacting with each other, and as many of the posts provided extensive well-considered suggestions. Following the approval of the light rail development, the council acknowledged that they "have listened to the community" (Berejiklian 2014) particularly in relation to managing the development in order to minimise the impacts of construction (such as noise) on the surrounding community. Moreover, the government is continuing to keep the community informed of progress through both traditional (letterbox drops, community forums, newspaper advertisements) and digital (website) means. The consultation and opportunities for civic engagement offered by Randwick City Council are commendable. However, there was one element that was clearly missing from the digital consultation, which was government involvement in the forum's discussions. Of the 767 comments, only two posts were directly identified as being by someone affiliated with the local government (Randwick Administrator), with one containing only a picture of the proposed light rail route and the other containing only the words "test comment". There was also evidence that the administrator had removed two civic posts (one due to duplication). Amid otherwise admirable efforts, overlooking the importance of joining in dialogue with citizens means the local government missed a key opportunity to enable citizens to develop a genuine sense of connection with government that would help to further strengthen local democracy.

11.6 Challenges for Local Digital Engagement

As the figures in the above section suggest, despite significant investments in broadband connectivity in recent years there are ongoing discrepancies between urban and rural local governments' digital media use. Rural local governments face additional challenges when implementing digital civic engagement practices. Morris (2012) indicates that digital access and literacy are the biggest challenges to social media use in rural, remote, and Indigenous local government areas in Australia, followed by the financial and human resource limitations that urban municipalities also experience (Purser 2012; Howard 2012). This section seeks to provide greater insight into the challenges that rural local governments face in terms of advancing digital engagement practices and draws from the views of seven rural New South Wales councils. It then offers insights into local digital engagement from the views of citizens from a metropolitan municipality within the state of Victoria, where the local government has already employed the use of social media and discussion forums for increased citizen engagement.

11.6.1 Barriers to Rural Digital Practices

The seven participating rural local governments understood the benefits and opportunities that improved access to the internet would offer their communities, such as facilitating social and economic development for their regions (see Hogan and Young 2013; Wolff and Andrews 2010). However, the governments were reluctant to implement more interactive digital practices when they could not be done well. At the time of the survey, three of the seven councils were active on social media (each with a Facebook account and one also used Twitter). Four councils had no social media presence. Since this time and as evidence of the rapid proliferation of social media in both society and government processes (see Mossberger et al. 2013), another council has created both a Facebook and Twitter profile, one has begun using Facebook and another has begun using Twitter. Currently then, six of the seven councils are using social media (including five on Facebook and three on Twitter). Only one council remains to have no social media presence, and none offer online discussion forums.

The rural local governments highlighted key issues surrounding their connectivity, capacity, and resources to use social media and other digital forms of civic engagement. In terms of connectivity, current plans for broadband development under the NBN have done little to aid rural access to the internet in these regions (Park et al. 2015). Fibre optic connections remain rare and those citizens connected to NBN broadband through fixed wireless and satellite connections continue to be inundated with issues surrounding latency, intermittent signals, dropped connections during peak use times, and higher costs of connection than urban citizens. As Prieger (2013) notes, "Even when broadband is available to rural communities, its quality—whether measured by speed of other characteristics like mobility—often lags that found in the nearest urban centre" (pp. 489–490). Such a situation presents significant challenges for rural local governments when using digital practices to communicate with citizens.

In addition to connectivity, one of the main barriers that these governments face for digital practices relates to sufficient resources, particularly in terms of staffing costs:

> With Twitter we've gone from zero users a year ago to nearly 400 now... We don't promote it very heavily because we don't have the staff to really sustain an interaction but we do interact on the two sites [Twitter and Facebook]. If you were going to do it the way the platforms really are being driven elsewhere, you'd have several staff doing it and doing it much more aggressively. (Chief Information Officer)

The councils recognised that social media offer new means for communicating with citizens, but these smaller rural local governments are significantly less likely to possess the necessary resources needed to manage interactive communication through social networking sites. As such, the councils using social media predominantly focus on information dissemination to further distribute media releases and promote local events, and recognised the value added by this practice (see also Purser 2012; Howard 2012). For example, one official highlighted that their Twitter account was followed by a radio station in a nearby city, which has frequent holiday makers travel to the municipality. The radio station re-tweets information to their larger base of followers, which provides useful notifications of highway closures and delays. There was also evidence, however, that the current levels of information dissemination through social media were not sufficient for citizens. In particular, citizens sought out information from councils in response to emergency situations where they viewed local governments as a source of authority, but did not realise that the councils were not necessarily in the right position to coordinate emergency information:

> We got into a difficult situation with the bushfires out here recently where users of social media didn't understand that council wasn't necessarily the source of information about the bushfires... unless you've got massive resource levels to man Twitter and Facebook, any sort of response is just totally unrealistic. (Mayor)

The above quotation provides evidence that civic and local government uses of social media do not always align (Bonsón et al. 2012). The governments using social media limited their current interactions through the sites due to insufficient resources as well as different civic and government expectations:

> It's important to think at the start of going into any of this [digital government] what the potential consequences are and what the community expectations at play may be... [citizens are] using social media as an alternative to the more standard means of communication that we've had in the past within local government... people in the community think if they're going to give the council some information or raise an issue it should be addressed. The whole window of what social media is now means that what's considered reasonable by someone in the public is very different for social media compared to when they send something through the mail in writing. (General Manager)

The prominence of digital technologies in everyday life has contributed to changing civic understandings of communicating with government (Jaeger and Bertot 2010). While these governments view social media largely as non-official communication channels, they thought citizens viewed posting to the governments' Twitter or Facebook sites as just as official as lodging formal requests (see also Howard 2012). Moreover, citizens' expected immediate responses to comments posted on social media: "There's this expectation of immediate response" (Mayor). While social media offer local governments opportunities to respond to misinformation through mainstream media and distribute important information rapidly (Howard 2012), this does not mean they are able to manage responses to civic comments in such a timely manner. The need to further educate the community on the governance processes that shape action surrounding civic concerns was subsequently suggested. However, the reverse is also applicable. As digital media are becoming embedded in all aspects of society and as governments continue to push citizens to use digital first services, then it is likely that governments at all levels will need to reconsider and adapt their processes to new conceptions surrounding digital civic participation. At the moment, these governments are failing to engage the community within the spaces in which the community wants to engage the government, instead redirecting their involvement to other channels, which can present a frustrating situation for citizens.

To some degree, however, recognition of changing forms of political dialogue is taking place within the local governments. One general manager, for example, highlighted that governments' social media accounts can provide platforms for increased citizen-to-citizen interaction:

> I would never enter into an arrangement where people from the public thought that they were going to get a response on every issue that they raise through social media. I'd make it clear up front that council is doing this as an information sharing idea, but there should not be an expectation that everything will be responded to. (General Manager)

Repurposing social media as information sharing platforms between citizens may potentially partially alleviate government workloads by enabling citizens to help each other in resolving issues. These governments are not currently in a position to be able to offer their communities more receptive and responsive government-to-citizen interaction through social media and currently have to prevent such forms of digital civic engagement due to their limited resources (see also Purser 2012): "From a policy point of view, I'd say there'd be no guarantee of any response to social media. The expectations are just ludicrous" (Mayor).

Use of mobile applications for service delivery was also discussed. However, there was strong reluctance to spend limited resources purchasing products when they are not necessarily compatible with all brands of devices. Moreover, for these councils, use of more innovative service applications was not necessary when they are already aware of local issues, they just do not have the resources required to address them:

> In the end people by and large can just email things into our records email address and do it that way. There was actually push back inside the council from staff in the sense of saying we don't need Snap Send Solve; we know where the pot holes are, we just don't have the staff to get out there and do it. So someone sending us another 12 pictures of it isn't going to help. (Chief Information Officer)

There are currently inequitable opportunities for digital civic engagement in rural and urban Australian areas. As the comments in this section suggest, rural local governments are at a significant disadvantage when it comes to enabling civic engagement through social media and other digital platforms, particularly due to their limited connectivity and resources. While urban governments are further ahead in terms of the interactive opportunities they offer citizens, provision of these spaces does not necessary ensure their effective use.

11.6.2 Limitations of Urban Digital Practices

While larger urban local governments often possess greater resources and the advanced connectivity needed to develop digital practices, governing sizeable populations is also likely to impact on their capacity to manage ongoing dialogue with citizens. The citizens from the urban municipality conveyed a strong desire to engage with their local government, but they were largely disenfranchised with the government's disinterest and unwillingness to engage with the community through consultative processes (Freeman and McCallum 2013). While the government offers an extensive website, social media interaction (including Twitter, Facebook, and YouTube), and an online discussion portal, opportunities for civic engagement were viewed as "just a token" (Citizen). The citizens unanimously thought they were "never going to have an impact" (Citizen) on local decision-making. Overall, methods for public participation were understood to be hollow gestures, and citizens' perceived that the local government "don't really want us to have a say or an opinion" (Citizen).

In terms of digital interactions, the citizens' comments indicated that while they were reaching out to connect with their local government online, their attempts were left unanswered: "As far as I can tell, they [the local government] never respond. But there's a lot of citizens commenting to other citizens" (Citizen). This individual has highlighted what was recognised by the rural local government official above, in that government-run spaces do enable new forms of citizen-to-citizen political dialogue. However, civic political discussions do not equate to engagement with government. Without government-to-citizen interaction, civic comments through social networking sites are unlikely to influence the decision-making processes that shape the community: "I'd like to know that the council look at them [online comments] and base some decisions around the feedback they get from people, because, after all, it's our rates that are supporting the city" (Citizen).

The citizens also demonstrated a broad range of concerns surrounding the council's implementation of its online discussion forum. These concerns included that, like other platforms, the government fails to respond to matters citizens raise through the site and there was no evidence to suggest that civic comments were informing local decision-making: "It is a bit like Facebook in a way, that you can say something, but it's not going to go anywhere" (Citizen). Citizens are unable to create their own topics for discussion, meaning they were limited to topics predetermined by the government: "the way they set it up is that it's essentially a website with lots of different discussion areas, but *they* get to *set* the discussion areas" (Citizen, emphasis added). Moreover, there was also concern about the fact that, like most Australian councils' discussion forums, the site is developed and managed by an external company:

> My biggest beef is that that particular website is managed by an outsourced [company]… you have to agree to all these conditions to be on this website, and I'm thinking, I don't want all these third party people to have my information. If it was a council operated one, they have your details already, we don't have to give them to somebody else. (Citizen)

Mergel (2014) highlights that governments may be reluctant to use social media sites due to the fact that they cannot control changes in sites run by third parties. The above comment suggests that citizens too dislike using third party providers. While outsourcing discussion forums may relieve pressure on local governments, it suggests to citizens that these spaces are not official channels and raises questions surrounding the privacy and security of data. As such, it may be better—for both governments and citizens—to incorporate discussion forums directly into government websites and everyday operations. Such an approach would be in line with Macnamara's (2013) suggestion that receptive and responsive practices need to be built into the architecture of communicative processes in order to facilitate digital civic engagement. At the moment, the fact that this local government is failing to provide any feedback to citizens about how their online views are received and considered in decision-making (if at all) is leading citizens to withdraw from this digital space and disengage with local political matters:

> They have an online thing [discussion forum] where you can comment on certain things, for example transport issues, but you only get to have your say; you don't get any feedback from it. It's all one way. You might get a reply, 'We've received your reply', but… you don't get any feedback about how it's going or not. So I don't bother with that anymore because I thought this is a good thing to do, but it just isn't followed through. (Citizen)

There is no indication that any forum posts are from local representatives or officials; there is only evidence of a moderator from the third party provider who infrequently posts standardised responses on behalf of the local government. Having moderators post generic responses offers little capacity for improved government-to-citizen interaction. Notably, civic comments on the forum also question the council's sporadic and generic responses that fail to provide feedback, and they even suggest that the site has been set up as a "front" to stop citizens from bothering the council (Freeman 2013).

There is little point in developing opportunities for digital civic engagement if they are not used effectively by local governments. The citizens who participated in these focus groups were eager to be involved in local political matters: "I should have the right to have my say, I should have the right to be heard, and I should have the right not to be dismissed" (Citizen). However, ineffective spaces for digital engagement lead to a sense of disconnection from government and create a reluctance to further engage on local political matters: "the perceptions of a lot of the residents is there's no point because they're not going to listen to you in any case" (Citizen). Such withdrawal is the result of an unmet civic desire for political engagement and should not be confused with political apathy. In this instance, the limitations of government-run digital practices are impacting upon civic engagement and inhibiting citizens' willingness to be involved in local political matters. Left un-remedied, such digital spaces threaten to exacerbate civic dissatisfaction with, and disconnection from, local government.

11.7 Conclusion

Social media and other interactive platforms are often viewed by governments as disruptive technologies, with reluctance to enable two-way civic participatory spaces where information cannot be controlled (Chun et al. 2010; Margo 2012). As a result, governments have continued to prioritise the development of digital information and service delivery practices over new avenues for civic engagement. However, as interactive technologies become part of the everyday and citizens appropriate digital platforms for their own purposes, civic expectations surrounding digital participation with governments are changing (Mergel 2012; Jaeger and Bertot 2010; Holland 2014). Increasing civic demand for participation and direct connection with representatives requires governments move beyond the provision of information and services to take a more holistic and citizen-centric approach to digital government development. Digital communicative practices must offer receptivity and responsiveness so that involvement can inform decision-making, in turn enabling a sense of connection with government and greater civic engagement (Macnamara 2013; Coleman and Blumler 2009). Gradual and linear progression through stages of digital government maturity (Lee and Kwak 2012; Chun et al. 2010) may be insufficient to take account of and address rapidly changing civic demand in the current era of communicative abundance.

This chapter illustrates a precarious and inequitable state of local digital civic engagement in Australia, with everyday practices remaining heavily focused on disseminating information and new avenues for service delivery (see also Purser 2012; Howard 2012; Holland 2014). Australian local governments have begun to recognise changing civic expectations surrounding digital interaction with government and are adapting to new communicative possibilities, particularly through social media platforms commonly used by citizens. However, current government uses of these and other spaces for digital civic participation do not yet align with civic demand (Bonsón et al. 2012). Employing interactive tools for predominantly one-way communication fails to capitalise on the possibilities enabled by the technologies, which is leading citizens to view opportunities for digital discourse as tokenistic and is causing civic dissatisfaction with government. In order to avoid such situations, governments must reconceptualise how they approach digital participation.

The findings of this research suggest two key initial steps that can be taken. The first is for governments to fully consider the purpose of digital participation spaces and recognise that a shift in government use—away from the current culture of controlling information (Margo 2012; Howard 2012)—is necessary. Government officials' current reluctance to interact with citizens online and the perception that digital participation is not a genuine form of civic involvement will need to be overcome. The second point relates to the hesitation to incorporate spaces for digital citizen participation directly into the ongoing, everyday and official channels of government communication, as evidenced by local governments' outsourcing the development and management of discussion forums. Outsourcing is a considerably costly use of limited resources (particularly given citizens distrust third party providers) if civic input through forums is not considered by governments. Including discussion spaces within official government websites and mobile applications—and allowing citizens to propose discussion topics—will help increase citizens' perceived legitimacy of these engagement initiatives and will offer governments a better sense of the issues important to their communities.

There are, however, substantial barriers to the development and use of participatory practices at the local government level in Australia. In particular, the diversity of local governments means there are unequal levels of financial and staffing resources as well as technological capacity (Purser 2012; Howard 2012), with additional constraints deriving from variable levels of connectivity (Morris 2012). Rural local governments are considerably disadvantaged in relation to the development and implementation of digital spaces for civic participation. While the Federal Government is investing in improved broadband infrastructure (DBCDE 2011a), divides in access, skills and capacity are unlikely to be swiftly remedied. In order to help ensure equitable opportunities for digital participation, the Federal Government could provide greater assistance specifically to rural councils. Additional resources and support may include, for example, training and education programmes for council staff or the provision of digital archetypes to help save development costs (Broadband for the Bush Alliance 2013; Wolff and Andrews 2010). Moreover, local governments that already receive assistance as part of the limited federal programmes available could be encouraged to share the digital resources and knowledge obtained with other councils. Alternatively, capacity may be enhanced if councils develop digital programmes in partnership with local government associations at state or federal level (Howard 2012).

While urban local government digital practices are more advanced—and there are promising signs of innovation, such as the myRandwick mobile application—there is still a need for greater government interaction through ongoing and reciprocal conversational spaces (see Ellison and Hardey 2013). Opportunities for digital civic participation are being implemented without local governments fully considering their purpose (Howard 2012). Reddick and Norris (2013a) highlight that in order for governments to take digital participation seriously, they must find out what citizens want and act on their preferences. It is not sufficient to simply provide digital spaces or jump on the bandwagon of social media (Macnamara 2012). Ironically, this point was recognised by the participating rural councils that indicated the need to think ahead in terms of potential consequences and community expectations; of course this also shaped their hesitation to implement digital practices if they could not be done properly.

While spaces for digital civic participation are unlikely to radically transform representative government (Bonsón et al. 2012), they do offer opportunities to enhance government-to-citizen interaction, provide greater voice to citizens, and help foster local democracy. This, of course, relies on governments being prepared to take part in ongoing reciprocal conversations with citizens and consider public input in decision-making (Ellison and Hardey 2013; Macnamara 2013). Bonsón et al. (2012) argue that, "For local governments, not engaging now involves a greater risk than engaging: citizens will use these networks to talk about them, whether local governments add their voices to the conversation or not" (p. 131). Not engaging with citizens online certainly presents risks for local governments, as adept citizens can easily use networked tools for civic dissent. But, if used ineffectively, government spaces for digital civic engagement are also problematic. Governments that fail to partake in two-way ongoing and everyday dialogue risk disenfranchising citizens, causing civic reluctance to engage on political matters, and creating a sense of disconnection from government.

References

Aulich, C. (2009). From citizen participation to participatory governance in Australian local government. *Commonwealth Journal of Local Governance, 2*, 44–60.

Australian Bureau of Statistics (ABS). (2012). Population estimates by local government area, 2011–2012. *3218.0 Regional Population Growth, Australia, 2011–2012*. Available: http://www.abs.gov.au/AUSSTATS/abs@.nsf/DetailsPage/3218.02011-12?OpenDocument.

Bekkers, V., & Homburg, V. (2007). The myths of e-government: Looking beyond the assumption of a new and better government. *The Information Society, 23*(5), 373–382.

Berejiklian, G. (2014). *Transforming Sydney: Planning approval granted for $1.6B CBD and South East light rail* [media release]. Randwick City Council. http://yoursayrandwick.com.au/lightrail/news_feed/media-release-transforming-sydney-planning-approval-granted-for-16b-cbd-and-south-east-light-rail.

Bertot, J. C., Jaeger, P. T., & Grimes, J. M. (2012). Promoting transparency and accountability through ICTs, social media, and collaborative e-government. *Transforming Government: People, Process and Policy, 6*(1), 78–91.

Bird, D., Ling, M., & Haynes, K. (2012). Flooding Facebook—The use of social media during the Queensland and Victorian floods. *The Australian Journal of Emergency Management, 27*(1), 27–33.

Bonsón, E., Torres, L., Royo, S., & Flores, F. (2012). Local e-government 2.0: Social media and corporate transparency in municipalities. *Government Information Quarterly, 29*(2), 123–132.

Bowles, M., & Wilson, P. (2012). Appraising the importance of the National Broadband Network in Australia's race to compete in the digital economy. *Australian Quarterly, 83*(1), 11–19.

Bradford, N. (2008). *Canadian social policy in the 2000s: Bringing place in*. Ottawa, Ontario: Canadian Policy Research Networks.

Broadband for the Bush Alliance. (2013). *Better telecommunications for rural and remote Australians: A Broadband for the Bush Alliance policy paper*. Desert Knowledge Australia. http://broadbandforthebush.com.au/wp-content/uploads/2013/05/Broadband-for-the-Bush-Alliance-Policy-June-2013.pdf.

Bruns, A. (2012). Towards distributed citizen participation: Lessons from WikiLeaks and the Queensland Floods. *eJournal of eDemocracy and Open Government, 4*(2), 142–159.

Chun, S. A., Shulman, S., Sandoval, R., & Hovy, E. (2010). Government 2.0: Making connections between citizens, data and government. *Information Polity, 15*(1–2), 1–9.

Coleman, S., & Blumler, J. G. (2009). *The internet and democratic citizenship: Theory, practice and policy*. New York: Cambridge University Press.

Couldry, N., & Langer, A. I. (2005). Media consumption and public connection: Towards a typology of the dispersed citizen. *The Communication Review, 8*(2), 237–257.

Department of Broadband, Communications and the Digital Economy (DBCDE). (2013). *Advancing Australia as a digital economy: An update to the National Digital Economy Strategy*. Canberra, ACT: DBCDE.

Department of Broadband, Communications and the Digital Economy (DBCDE) (2011a). *#au20 National Digital Economy Strategy: Leveraging the National Broadband Network to drive Australia's digital productivity*. Canberra, ACT: DBCDE.

Department of Broadband, Communications and the Digital Economy (DBCDE). (2011b). *Digital local government program guidelines*. http://www.communications.gov.au/__data/assets/pdf_file/0015/140307/Digital-Local-Government-Program-Guidelines.pdf.

Dobson, P., Jackson, P., & Gengatharen, D. (2013). Explaining broadband adoption in rural Australia: Modes of reflexivity and the morphogenetic approach. *MIS Quarterly, 37*(3), 965–991.

Ellison, N., & Hardey, M. (2013). Developing political conversations? Social media and English local authorities. *Information, Communication & Society, 16*(6), 878–898.

Farman, J. (2012). *Mobile interface theory: Embodied space and locative media*. New York: Routledge.

Freeman, J. (2013). Local e-government and citizen participation: Case studies from Australia and Italy. In J. R. Gil-Garcia (Ed.), *E-Government success around the world: Cases, empirical studies, and practical recommendations* (pp. 235–258). Hershey, PA: IGI Global.

Freeman, J., & McCallum, K. (2013). Public connection with local government: Desires and frustrations of articulating local issues. In J. Freeman (Ed.), *Proceedings of the emerging issues in communication research and policy conference, 2013—Refereed papers* (pp. 137–148). Canberra: News & Media Research Centre, University of Canberra.

Henman, P. (2010). *Governing electronically: E-government and the reconfiguration of public administration, policy and power*. Basingstoke, Hampshire: Palgrave Macmillan.

Hilgers, D., & Ihl, C. (2010). Citizensourcing: Applying the concept of open innovation to the public sector. *The International Journal of Public Participation, 4*(1), 67–88.

Hofmann, S., Beverungen, D., Räckers, M., & Becker, J. (2013). What makes local governments' online communication successful? Insights from a multi-method analysis of Facebook. *Government Information Quarterly, 30*(4), 387–396.

Hogan, A., & Young, M. (2013). Visioning a future for rural and regional Australia. *Cambridge Journal of Regions, Economy and Society, 6*(2), 319–330.
Holland, T. (2014). Social networks as sites of eparticipation in local government. In D. Bossio (Ed.), *The Digital and the social: Communication for inclusion and exchange—Proceedings of the 2014 Australian and New Zealand Communication Association Conference*. http://www.anzca.net/conferences/past-conferences.html
Howard, A. E. (2012). *Connecting with communities: How local government is using social media to engage with citizens*. Canberra: ANZSOG Institute for Governance at the University of Canberra and Australian Centre of Excellence for Local Government.
Jaeger, P. T., & Bertot, J. C. (2010). Designing, implementing and evaluating user-centred and citizen-centred e-government. In C. G. Reddick (Ed.), *Citizens and e-government: Evaluating policy and management* (pp. 1–19). Hershey, PA: IGI Global.
Jensen, M. J. (2009). Electronic democracy and citizen influence in government. In C. G. Reddick (Ed.), *Handbook of research on strategies for local e-government adoption and implementation: Comparative studies* (pp. 288–305). Hershey, PA: IGI Global.
Jimenez, B. S., Mossberger, K., & Wu, Y. (2012). Municipal government and the interactive web: Trends and issues for civic engagement. In A. Manoharan & M. Holzer (Eds.), *E-governance and civic engagement: Factors and determinants of e-democracy* (pp. 251–271). Hershey, PA: IGI Global.
Kavanaugh, A. L., Fox, E. A., Sheetz, S. D., Yang, S., Li, L. T., Shoemaker, D. J., Natsev, A., & Xie, L. (2012). Social media use by government: From the routine to the critical. *Government Information Quarterly, 29*(4), 480–491.
Kavanaugh, A., Krishnan, S., Pérez-Quiñones, M., Tedesco, J., Madondo, K., & Ahuja, A. (2014). Encouraging civic participation through local news aggregation. *Information Polity, 19*(1–2), 35–56.
Lee, G., & Kwak, Y. H. (2012). An open government maturity model for social media-based public engagement. *Government Information Quarterly, 29*(4), 492–503.
Lester, L., & Hutchins, B. (2012). The power of the unseen: Environmental conflict, the media and invisibility. *Media, Culture & Society, 34*(7), 847–863.
Linders, D. (2012). From e-government to we-government: Defining a typology of citizen coproduction in the age of social media. *Government Information Quarterly, 29*(4), 446–454.
Macnamara, J. (2013). Beyond voice: Audience-making and the work and architecture of listening as new media literacies. *Continuum: Journal of Media & Cultural Studies, 27*(1), 160–175.
Macnamara, J. (2012). Democracy 2.0: Can social media engage youth and disengaged citizens in the public sphere? *Australian Journal of Communication, 39*(3), 65–86.
Malina, A. (1999). Perspectives on citizen democratisation and alienation in the virtual public sphere. In B. N. Hague & B. D. Loader (Eds.), *Digital democracy: Discourse and decision making in the information age* (pp. 23–38). London: Routledge.
Margo, M. J. (2012). A review of social media use in e-government. *Administrative Sciences, 2*(2), 148–161.
Margolis, M., & Moreno-Riaño, G. (2009). *The prospect of internet democracy*. Farnham, Surrey: Ashgate.
Martin, J. A. (2014). Mobile media and political participation: Defining and developing an emerging field. *Mobile Media & Communication, 2*(2), 173–195.
Meikle, G., & Young, S. (2012). *Media convergence: Networked digital media in everyday life*. Basingstoke, Hampshire: Palgrave Macmillan.
Mergel, I. (2014). Social media adoption: Toward a representative, responsive or interactive government? In J. Zhang & J. R. Gil-Garcia (Eds.), *Proceedings of the 15th annual international conference on digital government research (d.go'14)* (pp. 163–170). New York: ACM.
Mergel, I. (2012). The social media innovation challenge in the public sector. *Information Polity, 17*(3–4), 281–292.
Moon, M. J. (2002). The evolution of e-government among municipalities: Rhetoric or reality? *Public Administration Review, 62*(4), 424–433.

Morris, R. (2012). *Community engagement in rural-remote and Indigenous local government in Australia*. Sydney: Australian Centre for Excellence in Local Government, University of Technology Sydney.

Mossberger, K., Wu, Y., & Crawford, J. (2013). Connecting citizens and local governments? Social media and interactivity in major U.S. cities. *Government Information Quarterly, 30*(4), 351–358.

Norris, D. F. (2010). E-government… not e-governance… not e-democracy: Not now! Not ever? In J. Davies & T. Janowski (Eds.), *Proceedings of the 4th international conference on theory and practice of electronic governance (ICEGov'10)* (pp. 339–346). New York: ACM.

Norris, D. F., & Reddick, C. G. (2012). Local e-government in the United States: Transformation or incremental change? *Public Administration Review, 73*(1), 165–175.

Oliveira, G. H. M., & Welch, E. W. (2013). Social media use in local government: Linkage of technology, task, and organizational context. *Government Information Quarterly, 30*(4), 397–405.

O'Toole, K. (2009). Australian local government and e-governance: From administration to citizen participation? In M. Khosrow-Pour (Ed.), *E-government diffusion, policy and impact: Advanced issues and practices* (pp. 171–184). Hershey, PA: IGI Global.

Park, S., Freeman, J., Middleton, C., Allen, M., Eckermann, R., & Everson, R. (2015). The multi-layers of digital exclusion in rural Australia. In *Proceedings of the 48th Annual Hawaii International Conference on System Sciences*. Washington, DC: Computer Society Press.

Prieger, J. E. (2013). The broadband digital divide and the economic benefits of mobile broadband for rural areas. *Telecommunications Policy, 37*(6–7), 483–502.

Purser, K. (2012). *Using social media in local government: 2011 survey report*. Sydney: Australian Centre for Excellence in Local Government, University of Technology Sydney.

Reddick, C., & Norris, D. F. (2013a). E-participation in local governments: An examination of political-managerial support and impacts. *Transforming Government: People, Process and Policy, 7*(4), 453–476.

Reddick, C. G., & Norris, D. F. (2013b). Social media adoption at the American grass roots: Web 2.0 or 1.5? *Government Information Quarterly, 30*(4), 498–507.

Scott, M., Russell, P., & Redmond, D. (2007). Active citizenship, civil society and managing spatial change in the rural-urban fringe. *Policy & Politics, 35*(1), 163–190.

Shackleton, P. (2010). Engaging citizens through local e-government: An Australian experience. In C. G. Reddick (Ed.), *Citizens and e-government: Evaluating policy and management* (pp. 418–434). Hershey, PA: IGI Global.

Sobaci, M. Z., & Karkin, N. (2013). The use of twitter by mayors in Turkey: Tweets for better public services? *Government Information Quarterly, 30*(4), 417–425.

Thomas, J. (2004). Horizons of expectation: Imaginary trajectories of electronic government. In G. Goggin (Ed.), *Virtual nation: The internet in Australia* (pp. 258–272). Sydney: University of New South Wales Press.

Thompson, J. B. (2005). The new visibility. *Theory, Culture & Society, 22*(6), 31–51.

Wilken, R., & Goggin, G. (2012). Mobilizing place: Conceptual currents and controversies. In R. Wilken & G. Goggin (Eds.), *Mobile technology and place* (pp. 3–25). New York: Routledge.

Wolff, R. S., & Andrews, E. (2010). Broadband access, citizen enfranchisement, and telecommunications services in rural and remote areas: A report from the American frontier. *IEEE Communications Magazine, 48*(5), 128–135.

Chapter 12
The Use of Facebook to Promote Engagement with Local Governments in Spain

Arturo Haro De Rosario, Alejandro Sáez Martín, and María Del Carmen Caba Pérez

Abstract Social media have changed how governments communicate with society, encouraging participation and the interaction of citizens in public affairs. The main aim of this study is to analyse the online practices of Spanish local governments, through Facebook, to examine the factors that influence these practices and to determine citizens' mood in this respect. The results obtained show that the popularity and virality of municipal Facebook pages are greater than their followers' degree of commitment. Users take a positive view of the pages, and the type of information most commonly shared on Facebook by Spanish local governments is of a social nature. Factors that influence local government's Facebook practices include the level of internet use among the population, the level of municipal debt, the number of inhabitants and the economic capacity of the population.

12.1 Introduction

Social networks have the potential to change the relationship between citizens and government (Sandoval and Gil 2012) and are increasingly used by different levels of government to interact with the population (Grimmelikhuijsen 2010). In a context in which the role of local government is undergoing constant change, it is useful to consider how social networks might facilitate new forms of dialogue and participation (Ellison and Hardey 2014).

Furthermore, local governments can make use of social networks to perceive and respond to the needs and interests of society, strengthen the legitimacy of their actions and enhance the democratic process. In short, social networks have the potential to increase citizen–government interactions and communication, which represent the essence of democracy (Hong 2013).

Therefore, public administrations (at all levels of government) should develop strategies to encourage the population to make use of the public sector's social

A.H. De Rosario • A.S. Martín • M.D.C.C. Pérez (✉)
Department of Economics and Business, University of Almería,
Carretera de Sacromonte s/n, 04120, Almería, Spain
e-mail: arturo.haro@ual.es; sma945@ual.es; ccaba@ual.es

M.Z. Sobaci (ed.), *Social Media and Local Governments*, Public Administration and Information Technology 15, DOI 10.1007/978-3-319-17722-9_12

network presence (Sæbø et al. 2009) and to regulate the public-sector presence in social networks. In 2012, Spain adopted its Action Plan—Open Government Partnership, which among other aims urged social networks to facilitate citizens' participation. Subsequently, in 2013, the Spanish government approved the Digital Agenda for Spain to develop the digital economy and society during the period 2013–2015.

In 2013, too, Spain adopted its Digital Communication Guide for the State Administration, which included recommendations on the government's presence in social networks. Similar guides to style and use of the social networks have been published by the regional governments of Catalonia in 2010, the Basque Country in 2012, the Canary Islands in 2013 and La Rioja in 2014. This has also been the case at the local level, albeit to a lesser extent, with guides for the municipal use of social networks being presented by the towns of San Sebastian de los Reyes in 2012, Lorca in 2014 and the city of Madrid in 2012.

One of the social networks most commonly used by local governments is Facebook (Akadwani 2014). This social network provides the opportunity for them to efficiently interact with citizens and is a valuable tool for engaging with society (Strecker 2011; U.S. Census Bureau 2011). At 31 December 2013, Facebook had 1.23 billion monthly active users worldwide (Facebook 2013a). In Spain, some 12 million users access the Internet every day, and 58 % of them are on Facebook (Facebook 2013b).

For governments to make best use of social networks, they need accurate, targeted performance to improve service delivery and to interact and engage with citizens, and for this purpose an appropriate metric is required. Although there is debate about how Facebook can be successfully integrated into communication strategies, little research has appeared regarding the construction of a set of metrics in order to assess reactivity, dialogic communication and stakeholder commitment (Bonsón and Ratkai 2013) and less still with respect to the metrics of governmental use of Facebook. To explain and assess the use of Facebook by local governments, diverse theories can be considered, including dialogic communication theory (Kent and Taylor 1998, 2002; Kent et al. 2003), legitimacy theory (Dowling and Pfeffer 1975; Deegan 2006) and stakeholder theory (Freeman 1984; Takagi et al. 2011).

The objective of this chapter is threefold. First, to analyse the dialogic communication, interactivity and social legitimacy of Spanish local governments, by examination of their official Facebook pages. Second, to determine citizens' mood and participation in this respect, through Facebook pages. And finally, to determine the extent to which a particular set of factors influence dialogic communication, people's responses to it and the type of information disclosed in local government Facebook pages.

The remaining sections of this chapter are structured as follows. The second section presents the theoretical framework and a review of the literature. The next section describes the research methodology applied and explains how the study sample was selected. Section 4 presents the empirical study, and discusses the results obtained. We then present the discussion section, and the final section summarises the main conclusions drawn.

12.2 Theoretical Framework and Literature Review

Numerous studies have analysed the use of social networks by governments, according to the type most commonly used, the number of followers, the number of messages sent or their content, among other parameters (Bortree and Seltzer 2009; Chi and Yang 2010; Rybalko and Seltzer 2010; Linders 2011; Rodríguez et al. 2011; Bonsón et al. 2012; Purser 2012; Towner and Dulio, 2012; Snead, 2013). However, few have examined the use of social networks by stakeholders and the benefits that accrue to society and public organisations, although such studies have been conducted with respect to the private sector (Hoffman and Fodor 2010; Bonsón and Ratkai 2013; Moreno 2013; Peters et al. 2013). Nevertheless, both the public and the private sectors suffer from a lack of standardised indicators to measure their use of social networks.

The strategies and actions implemented by local governments through social networks, to legitimise and increase democracy, are based on a framework constructed from various theories, including dialogic communication, legitimacy and stakeholder theory.

The theory of dialogic communication (Kent and Taylor 1998) provides a useful framework for understanding how organisations build and maintain their online social relationships. It explains how enhancing the interactivity of social media builds up social relationships, increases the frequency of communication, improves user satisfaction through greater transparency and participation and strengthens trust between organisations and their stakeholders (Bortree and Seltzer 2009; Bonsón et al. 2013, 2014). Over the last 15 years, the Dialogic Communication Theory has been validated, and it is now a primary theoretical framework on how online social relations are established (Waters et al. 2009; Bortree and Seltzer 2009; Wright and Hinson 2009; Waters et al. 2010; Rybalko and Seltzer 2010; McAllister 2012; Bonsón et al. 2013, 2014).

The theory of legitimacy suggests there is a social contract between the firm and society (Deegan 2006; Deegan and Samkin 2009). In this sense, society constitutes a broader category than 'stakeholders'. In the field of public administration, it is based on the idea that local governments must act within the limits of what society identifies as socially acceptable behaviour (Dowling and Pfeffer 1975). This pressure is stronger on local governments than in the private sector because the former are politically visible and attract more attention from external stakeholders; therefore, they must provide a higher degree of response in order to legitimise themselves before society (Frost and Semaer 2002).

According to stakeholder theory, companies should seek to achieve different goals, depending on their stakeholders (Freeman 1984). In this regard, Guthrie et al. (2006) argued that organisations should inform stakeholders of their activities, as this information provided added value, exceeding that of the mere provision of economic or financial information. Furthermore, authors such as Deegan and Samkin (2009) have shown that loyalty to stakeholders can be the basis for a good social relationship. Accordingly, one of the key elements that local governments can use

Table 12.1 Classification of information to be posted on Facebook, according to EC Directive 2003/98/EC

Economic information (I_1) including data from the Chamber of Commerce, business records, patent and trademark information, public tendering databases and all relevant municipal economic and financial information
Geographic information (I_2) including addresses, aerial photographs, buildings, cadastral information, geodetic networks and geologic, hydrographic data and topographic data
Legal information (I_3) including plenary decisions, bylaws, the rulings of national, foreign and international courts, national and regional legislation and treaties
Meteorological information (I_4) including climate data and models and the weather forecast
Social information (I_5) including information relating to employment, health, population, public administration and council activities
Transport information (I_6), including information about traffic congestion, road works, public transport and vehicle registration

in managing relationships with their stakeholders is to establish more direct and fluid channels of communication. In this respect, social networks represent an essential instrument to enable the participation of citizens in public administration, thus helping local governments comply with their public responsibilities. Moreover, social networks can reveal the opinions of citizens regarding local government actions and thus contribute to making accountability effective (Bonsón and Ratkai 2013; Bonsón et al. 2014). Taking into account the above theories, this chapter addresses the following research questions (see Table 12.1):

Q1. What level of interactivity and dialogic communication is achieved by local governments through Facebook?
Q2. What level of citizens' participation is achieved through local governments' Facebook presence?
Q3. How do citizens feel about local governments' Facebook presence?
Q4. What type of information is disclosed by local governments through their Facebook pages in order to legitimise their policies and actions?

Previous studies have analysed the impact of various factors on the development of online relationships between organisations and their stakeholders through social networks and websites. These factors include the level of internet use among the population (Bonsón et al. 2012), experience in social networks (Huang 2010), network activity (Bortree and Seltzer 2009; Rybalko and Seltzer 2010; Nah and Saxton 2012), network extensiveness (Bortree and Seltzer 2009; Nah and Saxton 2012; Sun and Wu 2012), political competition (Gandía and Archidona 2008; Rodríguez et al. 2011), political ideology (Tolbert et al. 2008; Rodríguez et al. 2011), the level of communication and public participation (Agostino 2013), the population size (Serrano et al. 2009; Norris and Reddick 2013) and economic capacity (Styles and Tennyson 2007; Rodríguez et al. 2011).

Following this review of the literature, the following determinants were selected in order to analyse their effects on dialogic communication and on the public mood, and the type of information published in local governments' Facebook pages.

12.2.1 Local Population Size

The size of the local population influences the implementation of e-government initiatives (Norris and Reddick 2013): the larger the population, the greater the pressure on the government to disclose information, especially via the Internet (Serrano et al. 2009). Therefore, given that social networks are one of the main tools for implementing e-government (Bonsón et al. 2012; Bretschneider and Mergel 2010; Snead 2013), we expect governments to make use of this possibility. Accordingly, the following hypothesis is proposed:

H1. The size of the municipal population positively influences dialogic communication, citizens' disposition toward government and the type of information disclosed in local governments' Facebook pages.

12.2.2 Economic Capacity

Studies have highlighted the existence of a strong relationship between the economic level of the population and its access to internet and new technologies (Serrano et al. 2009). In consequence, municipalities with lower levels of income per capita are less likely to adopt a sophisticated design for their website, due to the lower demand for their online services (Ho 2002; Styles and Tennyson 2007). On the other hand, local governments where per capita incomes are higher will be more likely to develop and implement e-government (Rodríguez et al. 2011). In view of these findings, the following hypothesis is proposed:

H2. The economic capacity of the local population positively influences dialogic communication, citizens' disposition toward government and the type of information disclosed in local governments' Facebook pages.

12.2.3 Political Ideology

The political ideology of the governing party is a key factor in decision-taking on matters related to innovation and the implementation of e-government initiatives (Alcaide et al. 2013). Thus, authors such as Tolbert et al. (2008) and Rodríguez et al. (2011) have referred to the impact of the governing party's ideology on the development of municipal e-government. Therefore, under the assumption that governments with a right-wing ideology tend to implement programmes or activities of a financial nature, while left-wing and other ideologies are more likely to focus on social policies and citizens' participation (Ni and Bretschneider 2007), the following hypothesis is proposed:

H3. The fact that a municipality is governed by a left-wing political party positively influences dialogic communication, citizens' disposition toward government and the type of information disclosed in local governments' Facebook pages.

12.2.4 Political Competition

Municipalities in which the governing party does not have an absolute majority have an additional incentive to improve their communication strategies through the better use of municipal web pages (Gandía and Archidona 2008; Rodríguez et al. 2011). In this respect, studies have shown that a high degree of political competition can create a favourable environment for technological reforms (Tolbert et al. 2008). Taking into account these considerations, the following hypothesis is proposed:

H4. Political competition positively influences dialogic communication, citizens' disposition toward government and the type of information disclosed in local governments' Facebook pages.

12.2.5 Internet Use Among the Population

In municipalities where citizens make greater use of information technology, this environment encourages governments to offer more services and information via the Internet (Bonsón et al. 2012). Thus, the higher the proportion of internet users, the larger the population that is potentially receptive to receiving public information through the Internet and participating via this medium. Therefore, the level of internet use among the population is a determinant of the degree of online information disclosure (Serrano et al. 2009), and so we postulate the following hypothesis:

H5. Internet use by the population positively influences dialogic communication, citizens' disposition toward government and the type of information disclosed in local governments' Facebook pages.

12.2.6 Municipal Debt

The level of municipal debt is another factor that has been widely analysed as a determinant of online information disclosure (Gallego et al. 2009). In this respect, Alt and Dreyer (2006) and Gallego et al. (2009) reported a negative relationship. Taking into account these precedents, we examine whether there is a relationship between municipal borrowing and local governments' use of Facebook pages. In consequence, the following hypothesis is proposed.

H6: The level of municipal debt is inversely associated with dialogic communication, citizens' disposition toward government and the type of information disclosed in local governments' Facebook pages.

12.3 Methodology

To achieve our study goals, and to address the above hypotheses, the research method was divided into two phases. First, a descriptive analysis was conducted to determine, on the one hand, the levels of communication, interaction and legitimacy acquired by local governments through their Facebook pages, and on the other hand, citizens' level of participation and type of disposition toward government, in response to its Facebook page. In the second phase, an explanatory analysis was performed to examine the impact of various factors on dialogic communication, citizens' disposition toward the government and the type of information disclosed on municipal Facebook pages.

12.3.1 Descriptive Analysis

In line with Bonsón and Ratkai (2013) and Bonsón et al. (2013, 2014), our descriptive analysis is divided into three parts. In the first, we analyse the reactivity and dialogic communication capacity of the local governments and citizens' participation, by examining municipal Facebook pages. In the second part, we consider the citizens' disposition toward their local government, and in the third part, we analyse the social legitimacy and information disclosure of local governments, by reference to their Facebook pages (see Table 12.2).

In the first part of this descriptive analysis, reactivity, dialogic communication and stakeholder commitment are analysed in terms of the popularity, commitment and virality of the local government's Facebook page. Virality is defined as the diffusion and extension achieved by the government's messages posted on its Facebook page. Facebook popularity is measured as the number of 'likes' received, commitment by the number of comments made, and virality by the number of users who share the post (see Table 12.2). The following quantitative parameters are used to apply this measure: numbers of fans of Facebook pages, numbers of local governments' posts, and the likes, comments and items shared by users on local governments' Facebook pages.

In the second part of our analysis, on citizens' mood regarding their government, a quantitative and qualitative analysis was made of the comments made in response to local government Facebook pages. These comments were classified into three categories, reflecting the citizens' reaction, as positive, negative or neutral (see Table 12.2).

The third analysis, of social legitimacy and information disclosure via Facebook, was conducted by examining the content of local government posts to Facebook (see Table 12.1). In this analysis, posts were classified in accordance with the provisions of EC Directive 2003/98/EC on the provision and reuse of public sector information for all Member States (see Table 12.1).

Table 12.2 Questions, theories and metrics for the study analysis

Reactivity, dialogic communication and stakeholder engagement					
Questions	Theory	Concept	Formula	Measure	
Q1 and *Q2*	Dialogic theory	Popularity	P1	Posts 'liked'/Total posts	Proportion of posts with 'likes'
			P2	Total 'likes'/Total posts	Average 'likes' per post
			P3	(P2/No. of followers) × 1,000	Popularity of posts among followers
		Commitment	C1	Posts with comments/Total posts	Proportion of posts with comments
			C2	Total comments/ Total posts	Average comments per post
			C3	(C2/No. of followers) × 1,000	Followers' engagement
		Virality	V1	Posts shared/Total posts	Proportion of shared posts
			V2	Total shared/Total posts	Average number of posts shared
			V3	(V2/No. of followers) × 1,000	Virality of posts among followers
Citizens' mood					
Question	Theory	Metric	Formula	Measure	
Q3	Stakeholders theory	Citizens' mood according to comments	+	Positive comments/Total comments	Proportion of comments reflecting a positive reaction
			–	Negative comments/Total comments	Proportion of comments reflecting a negative reaction
			=	Neutral comments/ Total comments	Proportion of comments reflecting a neutral reaction

(continued)

Table 12.2 (continued)

Social legitimacy and voluntary disclosure					
Question	Theory	Metric	Formula	Measure	
Q4	Legitimacy theory	Type of information disclosed online	I_1	Posts of an economic nature/ Total posts	Proportion of posts with economic information
			I_2	Posts of a geographic nature/ Total posts	Proportion of posts with geographic information
			I_3	Posts of a legal nature/Total posts	Proportion of posts with legal information
			I_4	Posts with meteorological information/Total posts	Proportion of posts with meteorological information
			I_5	Posts with social information/Total posts	Proportion of posts with social information
			I_6	Posts with transport information/Total posts	Proportion of posts with transport information

12.3.2 Explanatory Analysis

In line with our review of the literature on factors that influence local governments' online relationships through social networks, the factors described in Sect. 12.3 were selected for analysis of their effects on dialogic communication, citizens' disposition toward government and the type of information disclosed on local government Facebook pages (see Table 12.3).

Having identified and defined these determinant factors, we determined the correlation between them and the following dependent variables: the index of popularity, commitment and virality (IPCV), the index of citizens' mood (ICM), the index of social legitimacy and voluntary disclosure (ISLVD) and five sub-indices, by type of information: $ISLVD_{I1}$, $ISLVDI_{I2}$, $ISLVDI_{I3}$, $ISLVDI_{I4}$, $ISLVDI_{I5}$ and $ISLVDI_{I6}$. Then, taking into account that the dependent variables are censored, taking values between 0 and 1, we conducted a Tobit regression analysis (statistical calculations were performed using STATA 11.1).

The structural equation in the Tobit model is:

$$y_i^* = X_i\beta + \varepsilon_i$$

Table 12.3 Explanatory variables, measurement and expected sign in the use of dialogic principles

Explanatory variables	Unit of measurement	Source	Expected sign
Population	Natural logarithm of number of inhabitants in the municipality (Norris and Reddick 2013)	National Institute of Statistics (2013)	H1. Population has a positive influence
Economic capacity	GDP per capita in the municipality (Alcaide et al. 2013)	National Institute of Statistics (2012) L.R. Klein Institute	H2. Economic capacity has a positive influence
Political ideology	Political ideology of the governing party: 1 = Right wing; 0 = Left wing	Interior Ministry	H3. Left-wing government has a positive influence
Political competition	Number of councillors belonging to the governing party/Total councillors elected at Total councillors elected at the most recent elections (Alcaide et al. 2013)	Interior Ministry	H4. Political competition has a positive influence
Internet use	Band width used in the province (2012)	National Markets and Competition Commission (CNMC)	H5. Internet use has a positive influence
Debt	Natural logarithm of municipal debt (thousands of €)	Ministry of Finance and Public Administration	H6. The level of debt has a negative influence

where $\varepsilon_i \sim N(0, \sigma^2)$. y^* is the dependent variable and X_i are the independent variables.

12.3.3 Sample

Taking into account the 2012 Open Government Partnership Action Plan and the Digital Agenda for 2013–2015 to promote the use of social networks by the public, we decided our Facebook analysis should be focused on Spanish municipalities, because this level of government, due to its proximity, is well placed to be aware of citizens' information needs (Watt 2004).

Local governments were selected for this analysis because citizens are more directly involved in local affairs and are more likely to participate at the local level (Oakerson 1999). Moreover, it is at the local level where the concerns of citizens coincide most directly with those of government (Gaventa and Valderrama 1999), and where the current process of strengthening participatory democracy is most evident (Licha 2002). Moreover, given the distribution of powers between central government, the regions and local administrations, and in accordance with Article 3 of the European Charter of Local Self-Government (15 October 1985), ratified by Spain on 20 January 1988, and Article 25 of Local Government Act 7/1985 of 2 April, local administrations, in order to address their interests and within the scope of their powers, can promote activities and provide public services that contribute to meeting local needs. Among these activities and services, the use of social networks is discretionary for each local government, in the absence of national or regional regulations in this respect in Spain.

In assessing the social network activities of local governments, numerous studies have used for their sample the largest city by population (Holzer and Kim 2005), or the largest cities and the national capital of each country (Pina et al. 2010). Accordingly, to evaluate the use of social media in local government, we selected the largest cities in Spain (in line with Sáez-Martín et al. 2014), under the assumption that the largest cities have traditionally been at the forefront in the adoption of e-government innovations and new technologies, that they enjoy lower relative costs of implementation and that they have greater information-disclosure needs (Moon 2002; Ho 2002; Bonsón et al. 2012). Therefore, our study sample is composed of the Facebook pages of the 80 largest municipalities in Spain (in terms of population).

Of the 80 local governments analysed, only 49 have an official Facebook page. These latter municipalities represent 24 % of the total Spanish population and constitute our final study sample. The content analysis, and that of the posts and comments for each Facebook page in the sample, was carried out with respect to the whole month of June 2014.

12.4 Results

The results obtained for reactivity, dialogic communication and stakeholder engagement through local government Facebook pages (see Table 12.4) show that the popularity of Facebook pages, as reflected by the 'likes' received, obtains the highest scores, followed by virality (the number of times a post is shared) and finally by commitment (comments received). However, we must acknowledge, in accordance with Bonsón and Ratkai (2013) and Bonsón et al. (2013, 2014), that it is faster and easier to send a 'like' or to share a post than to comment on it. Thus, as shown in

Table 12.4 Reactivity, dialogic communication and stakeholder engagement

	P1 (%)	P2	P3	C1 (%)	C2	C3	V1 (%)	V2	V3
Median	76	18.29	3.80	25	1.06	0.47	44	4.97	0.91
Std. Dev.	0.26	57.92	4.68	25	2.18	1.35	30	14.52	0.92
Maximum	100	403.44	28.99	100	13.00	8.04	100	101.44	3.74
Minimum	11	0.11	0.22	0	0.00	0.00	0	0.00	0.00

Table 12.5 Analysis of quantitative parameters used for Facebook pages

Facebook pages	Total posts	Number of fans	Number of posts liked	Total likes	Number of post commented	Total comments	Number of posts shared	Total shares
Median	61	5,637	41	587	13	52	28	219
Std. Dev	66	12,916	40	1,061	17	80	42	362

Table 12.5, of the 61 comments posted on average by local governments during the month analysed, 41 received ‘likes’, while only 28 were shared and 13 received comments. However, high levels of deviation were observed in each of these parameters, which reflects the heterogeneity of the Facebook profiles analysed.

Our analysis of the levels of popularity of local governments’ Facebook pages shows that the average acceptance of posts (P1) is 76 % and the mean number of ‘likes’ per post (P2) is 18.29. However, the number of ‘likes’ per comment taking into account the number of followers of the page (P3) is very low, and so, following Bonsón and Ratkai (2013), these figures were multiplied by one thousand. Fifteen of the cities surveyed received at least one ‘like’ for every one of their posts. The local governments that received most ‘likes’ per post were Barcelona (average: 403), followed by Cartagena and Elche (80 and 40, respectively). However, when we examined this question in terms exclusively of the economically active population following the local government page, the municipalities with the highest popularity by number of followers were Granada and Santiago de Compostela (see Table 12.10 in Appendix).

The levels of engagement with local governments’ Facebook pages were low (Table 12.4); only 25 % of posts received at least one comment (C1) and on average only one comment per post (C2) was received. When the number of followers (C3) is taken into consideration, this reveals the generally low level of participation by the followers of local governments’ Facebook pages. Only Bilbao received at least one comment in response to all its posts, while the municipalities that received the highest average number of comments per post were Badajoz (13) and Barcelona (7). The city council that obtained the highest level of engagement, by the number of active followers of its Facebook page, was Murcia, followed by Badajoz (see Table 12.10 in Appendix).

The results for virality (Table 12.4) show that less than half of the local governments’ Facebook posts are shared at least once by their followers (P1) and that an average of almost five posts are shared by users. As with the previous cases, the results for the analysis by the number of followers are low; we conclude, therefore, that the information disclosed by Facebook is very limited in its impact. Of the local governments analysed, only four have all of their posts shared by users. Most ‘shares’ were obtained by Barcelona (101), well ahead of the other cities, while in terms of followers among the economically active population, the posts of Badajoz and Valladolid presented greatest virality (see Table 12.10 in Appendix).

The results for the citizens’ mood, with respect to these local governments’ Facebook pages (see Table 12.6), show that half of the comments made are positive. The cities achieving the best results in this respect were Burgos, Girona, Las Rozas

Table 12.6 Citizens' mood

Comments	Positive	Negative	Neutral
Total	1,264	1,022	244
Median	0.49	0.40	0.11
Std. Dev.	0.30	0.27	0.15
Maximum	1.00	1.00	0.70
Minimum	0.00	0.00	0.00

Table 12.7 Social legitimacy and voluntary disclosure

	Economic	Geographic	Legal	Meteorological	Social	Transport
Median	2.15 %	0.92 %	0.45 %	3.13 %	86.58 %	4.72 %
Std. Dev.	0.08	0.03	0.02	0.09	0.18	0.06
Maximum	55.6 %	12.5 %	11.1 %	50.0 %	100.0 %	28.6 %
Minimum	0.0 %	0.0 %	0.0 %	0.0 %	0.0 %	0.0 %

and Santiago de Compostela, each with 100 % positive feedback. By contrast, the local governments of Granada and Bilbao received the highest number of negative comments, and Logroño and Jerez de la Frontera received the highest number of neutral comments (70 % and 60 %, respectively) (see Table 12.10 in Appendix).

Regarding social legitimacy and voluntary disclosure, the results set out in Table 12.7 clearly show that the information most often provided through the Facebook pages of local governments is related to the social aspects of government. Thus, for 30 local governments, over 90 % of the information they provide is of a social nature. On the contrary, very little use is made of Facebook as a channel for the provision of legal information; only two local governments, Terrassa and Lorca, disclose this type of information; in each case, 11 % of the information provided is of a legal nature (see Table 12.10 in Appendix). After social information, the next type most commonly provided on local government Facebook pages concerns transport (Table 12.7), with Málaga and Logroño providing the highest proportions of this information in their posts (28 % and 25 %, respectively) (see Table 12.10 in Appendix). The third information type most often provided is economic, with Sabadell at the head, where 55 % of all posts concern this area.

Our explanatory analysis focused on the relationships among factors influencing the popularity, engagement, virality and social legitimacy of Spanish local governments as regards their Facebook pages, together with the citizens' mood in this respect. To illustrate this, Table 12.8 shows the two Pearson correlation matrices constructed. Only two moderately strong significant correlations were found, between population and debt and between ideology and political competition. However, we detected no problems of multicollinearity that might compromise the model.

The results of the Tobit regression are shown in Table 12.9. Two of the three models initially proposed are statistically significant (evidenced by the LR chi2 statistic in Table 12.9), but no conclusions can be drawn about which factors determine the greater or lesser degree of social legitimacy presented by the Facebook pages analysed. However, the variable social legitimacy and voluntary disclosure is made up of six categories of information and, as noted in the descriptive section of

Table 12.8 Pearson correlation matrix

Correlation between explanatory variables						
	Population	Economic capacity	Political ideology	Political competition	Internet use	Debt
Population	1					
Economic capacity	0.1218	1				
Political ideology	0.1113	−0.1320	1			
Political competition	0.0238	−0.2081	0.5360***	1		
Internet use	−0.1740	−0.0364	−0.0992	−0.0715	1	
Debt	0.6686***	−0.1019	0.0843	−0.0520	−0.0998	1

*Correlation is significant at the 0.10 level (2-tailed)
**Correlation is significant at the 0.05 level (2-tailed)
***Correlation is significant at the 0.01 level (2-tailed)

this study, most local government posts to Facebook (86.58 %) contain social information. Therefore, we decided to perform a regression analysis only for this category, which was found to be statistically significant.

Regarding the significance of the explanatory variables, the Tobit regression analysis produced the following results: internet use and debt were significant in three models (IPCV, ICM and $ISLVDI_{15}$), economic capacity in two (ICM and $ISLVDI_{15}$) and population size in only one (IPCV).

With respect to the level of internet use among the population, there was found to be a positive relationship in every case. Thus, and in accordance with the expected relationship, the results obtained suggest that in municipalities with a greater degree of internet use, the local government achieves higher levels of popularity, engagement and virality in its Facebook page, and makes a higher number of social posts to Facebook. Furthermore, in these municipalities the citizens' mood is more positive than elsewhere.

This analysis also shows that debt has a negative impact in all three models, and so the relationship posed a priori is confirmed. Thus, the Facebook pages of local governments with lower levels of borrowing are more popular, committed and viral, and make more posts of a social nature. These results indicate, moreover, that a low level of debt is positively associated with the citizens' mood.

In terms of economic capacity, the results obtained are also as expected, showing that it is in the municipalities where GDP per capita is highest that local governments make most Facebook posts of a social nature. Here, too, citizens make most comments of a positive nature and fewest of a negative one on the local governments' Facebook pages.

As concerns the population variable, the only positive relationship observed was with IPCV; thus, the Facebook pages of the most populous local governments enjoy higher levels of popularity, engagement and virality. This result is in accordance with our hypothesis in this respect, and reflects the greater efforts made by the governments of large cities to attract a larger number of citizens and to interact with them through social networks.

Table 12.9 Tobit regression analysis

	IPCV		ICM		ISLVDI		$ISLVDI_{15}$	
LR chi2 (6)	12.85**		18.18***		7.23		15.99***	
	Coef.	*T*	Coef.	*t*	Coef.	*t*	Coef.	*t*
Population	0.08916	2.38**	−0.09074	−1.26	−0.02526	−0.61	0.09865	1.47
Economic capacity	1.58e-06	0.53	0.00001	3.25***	−5.20e-06	−1.61	8.19e-06	1.73*
Political ideology	0.04808	1.10	0.10992	1.31	−0.05784	−1.23	0.02661	0.38
Political competition	−0.08200	−0.49	0.23268	0.74	0.13974	0.78	−0.17154	−0.66
Internet use	0.40473	1.98**	1.11455	2.84***	0.13993	0.63	0.70212	2.14**
Debt	−0.04285	−1.93*	−0.08507	−1.97**	0.03156	1.26	−0.10903	−2.60***

*Significant at the 0.10 level (2-tailed)
**Significant at the 0.05 level (2-tailed)
***Significant at the 0.01 level (2-tailed)

12.5 Discussion

The results obtained show that the levels of popularity and virality of local governments' Facebook pages are higher than those of their engagement with citizens. However, the design of Facebook itself offers a possible explanation for this situation, since it facilitates the posting of 'likes' and shared posts more than that of comments.

Despite the potential offered by this social network, our results reflect little active participation by citizens with their local governments' Facebook pages. Nevertheless, the local governments analysed receive more positive comments than negative ones, and so, in general, citizens appear to be satisfied with their local government's presence in Facebook.

Most of the content of municipal Facebook posts concerns social issues, and the social network is underutilised as a tool to communicate, in real time, other interesting information for citizens, such as information about transport or weather conditions. It could also be used to communicate important decisions of a legal nature, or economic data, in order to increase the government's social legitimacy.

In view of the study data obtained and presented here, local governments need to improve some of their strategies for social networks. For example, they could promote more activities open to public participation, such as consultations, surveys, forums and open debates. They should also strengthen the relationship between their social network presence and the municipal website. Such actions would call for the professionalisation of online relationships, and so a Community Manager should be employed to administer the content of the social network and to facilitate and strengthen interactions and communication between the local government and the population.

According to the explanatory variables analysed, the Spanish cities with high levels of internet use and little public debt are those in which local government Facebook pages enjoy the highest levels of popularity, engagement, virality and social legitimacy. Furthermore, in these cities, the stakeholders' mood toward the municipal Facebook presence is most favourable.

12.6 Conclusions

Dialogic communication theory, legitimacy theory and stakeholder theory jointly provide an appropriate framework to examine the establishment of online social relationships and to measure and analyse the use of social networks. The use of these theories can produce significant benefits, since social networks in themselves favour relations between the government and the population. In recent years, guidelines and recommendations have been developed in the public sector to regulate the presence of national, regional and local governments in the social networks. The results of the present study enable us to better understand the strategies and actions employed by local governments in Spain to enhance the popularity, engagement, virality and social legitimacy of their Facebook pages, and to determine the mood of stakeholders in this respect.

However, the existence of a large number of followers on Facebook does not automatically ensure an engaged audience. Thus, although citizens' involvement in this respect, in general, is low, the action of registering a 'like' obtains a higher degree of participation in the local government Facebook pages observed. However, less interest is shown in sharing information about the local government with friends or in participating in a dialogue via the 'comments' facility. Therefore, although previous studies have highlighted the potential of social networks, and of Facebook in particular, to achieve citizens' participation in relations with local government, in practice these networks do not seem to constitute an effective platform in this respect, or at least, they are not being exploited as such.

According to the findings of our analysis, local governments need to improve some of their communication strategies in Facebook. For example, it would be useful to apply policies to promote interaction between government and society, by means such as surveys, consultations and debates. Moreover, improving the speed and availability of responses to users (or simply providing them, if this is not already done) by means of the Facebook page will encourage citizens to seek answers to their questions and to present the issues that concern them. In addition, the administrators of Facebook pages should focus the content of their messages toward citizens' interests and examine best practices in this field, in order to facilitate participation and to obtain more feedback, through likes, comments and sharing. What is needed, thus, is a greater professionalisation of the government's profile, making more use of the community manager, who should be responsible for promoting online relationships between local government and society.

For future research, it would be interesting to conduct a longer-term analysis, to measure the evolution of Facebook pages over a period of several months, thus revealing changes and trends in the pattern of social network use. It would also be useful to conduct a comparative study, incorporating other social networks, and to expand the sample of local governments. In this line of action, it would be interesting to extend the sample to determine whether there are differences in the use of Facebook by local governments and by the regions (Autonomous Communities), from a descriptive and explanatory standpoint, and to analyse the impact of cultural, social and economic differences among the regions of Spain. Finally, work should be done to standardise the metrics used to evaluate, improve and manage online communication by organisations, especially public ones, with their stakeholders.

Acknowledgement This research was carried out with financial support from the Regional Government of Andalusia (Spain), Department of Innovation, Science and Enterprise (Research Projects P10-SEJ-06628 and P11-SEJ-7700) and FPU/2013 grant from the Spanish Ministry of Science and Innovation (MCINN).

Appendix

Table 12.10 Popularity, engagement, virality, citizens' mood and voluntary disclosure

Local government	Population	P1 (%)	P2	P3	C1 (%)	C2	C3	V1 (%)	V2	V3	Positive (%)	Negative	Neutral	Economic (%)	Geographic	Legal	Meteorological	Social	Transport
Barcelona	1,620,943	100	403.4	4.5	87.5	7.3	0.1	100	101.4	1.1	75	20.7	4.3	0	12.5	0	0	87.5	0
Sevilla	702,355	61.8	14.7	1	26.5	1.1	0.1	38.2	12.5	0.9	35.1	59.5	5.4	0	0	0	0	100	0
Zaragoza	679,624	86.7	9.3	1.5	15.8	0.2	0	45	1.6	0.3	73.1	19.2	7.7	0	0	0	0	97.5	2.5
Lorca	567,433	100	27.3	8.9	44.4	0.8	0.3	72.2	4.8	1.6	60	40	0	0	11.1	11.1	5.6	66.7	5.6
Mostoles	441,354	72	3.3	2.6	10.8	0.2	0.1	21.5	0.7	0.5	50	33.3	16.7	0	0	0	0	92.5	7.5
Oviedo	407,648	90.1	36.7	6	28.6	1.2	0.2	64.8	2.8	0.5	78.2	14.5	7.3	0	0	0	0	98.9	1.1
Bilbao	351,629	100	8	7.5	100	1	0.9	100	1.5	1.4	0	100	0	0	0	0	0	100	0
Cordoba	328,841	47.6	2.4	2.9	14.3	0.2	0.2	4.8	0	0.1	75	25	0	0	0	0	23.8	76.2	0
Valladolid	311,501	93.2	13.8	5.9	25.6	1.2	0.5	46.2	7.8	3.3	70.6	23.5	5.9	0	0	0	0	99.1	0.9
Vitoria	242,223	93.8	10.4	4.2	24.7	0.5	0.2	65.4	3.3	1.3	53.8	10.3	35.9	0	0	0	0	90.1	9.9
Granada	239,017	100	6	29	14.3	0.4	1.7	7.1	0.1	0.3	0	100	0	0	0	0	0	85.7	14.3
Elche	230,587	100	40	10.4	66.7	3	0.8	79.2	9.8	2.5	32.4	49.3	18.3	4.2	0	0	0	79.2	16.7
Orihuela	225,973	73.7	4.2	0.7	15.8	0.2	0	10.5	0.3	0.1	70	30	0	0	0	0	0	94.7	5.3
Cartagena	216,655	100	80.9	4.1	72.7	1.4	0.1	63.6	16.2	0.8	80	6.7	13.3	0	0	0	0	100	0
Tarrasa	215,678	76.7	4	0.6	10	0.1	0	28.9	1.2	0.2	50	33.3	16.7	0	0	11.1	4.4	81.1	3.3
Jerez de la Frontera	211,900	71.4	2.9	2.1	2.6	0	0	22.1	0.3	0.2	33.3	0	66.7	0	0	0	0	0	0
Salamanca	207,938	54.5	1.7	1.4	13.6	0.2	0.2	0	0	0	20	60	20	0	0	0	50	45.5	4.5
Mataro	206,031	50	1.3	1.9	0	0	0	12.5	0.3	0.5	0	0	0	0	6.3	0	0	93.8	0
Fuenlabrada	198,132	74.8	2.9	0.8	22.4	0.7	0.2	78.5	4.1	1.1	53.9	34.5	11.5	0	0	0	11.8	79.3	8.9
Las Rozas	187,125	100	3.7	5.4	6.7	0.1	0.1	0	0	0	100	0	0	0	6.7	0	0	93.3	0
Sant Cugat del Vallès	186,409	56	1.2	0.4	16	0.4	0.1	0	0	0	55.6	44.4	0	0	0	0	4	96	0

Castellon	180,204	69.3	4.5	0.3	32.3	0.9	0.1	85.8	8.3	0.6	56	34.5	9.5	0	0	0	0	93.7	6.3
Burgos	179,906	16.7	0.2	0.6	3.3	0	0.1	6.7	0.1	0.3	100	0	0	0	0	0	0	100	0
Girona	171,280	100	17.1	6.6	9.1	0.2	0.1	81.8	4.8	1.9	100	0	0	0	0	0	0	90.9	9.1
Alcorcon	169,308	50	5.1	2.4	20.5	0.6	0.3	18.2	0.6	0.3	65.4	30.8	3.8	4.5	0	0	0	90.9	4.5
Lleida	153,402	90.6	10.2	3.8	15.6	0.4	0.1	59.4	1.8	0.7	50	33.3	16.7	0	0	0	0	100	0
Roquetas de Mar	153,224	53.7	2.2	0.5	24.6	0.4	0.1	59.7	2.8	0.6	42.9	50	7.1	0	0	0	9	84.3	6.7
Badajoz	152,270	95.2	12.1	4.8	90.5	13	5.2	71.4	9.4	3.7	51.3	37.4	11.4	0	0	0	0	95.2	4.8
San Fernando	152,048	97.5	15.5	1.6	22.3	1.6	0.2	26.4	1.4	0.1	20.6	71.1	8.2	0	0	0	28.1	69.4	2.5
Malaga	140,473	95	37.6	4.6	35	1.8	0.2	75	8.7	1	57.1	8.6	34.3	0	0	0	0	75	25
Leganés	139,834	98.5	4.9	2.9	21.5	0.6	0.3	36.9	2.8	1.7	47.2	36.1	16.7	0	0	0	0	96.9	3.1
Tarragona	133,954	49.2	3.8	1.3	23.5	0.6	0.2	36.4	1.5	05	64	24	12	2.3	0	0	0	92.4	5.3
Marbella	124,084	38.4	0.7	0.9	3.5	0.1	0.1	26.7	0.8	1	57.1	28.6	14.3	2.3	0	0	0	93	4.7
Alcobendas	111,040	100	1.8	0.7	0	0	0	100	2	0.7	0	0	0	0	0	0	0	100	0
Palma de Mallorca	107,211	100	3.4	1.1	0	0	0	33.3	0.4	0.1	0	0	0	11.1	0	0	0	77.8	11.1
Telde	101,300	100	1.8	2.3	0	0	0	100	2	2.7	0	0	0	0	0	0	0	100	0
Barakaldo	100,369	25	0.5	1.4	3.1	0	0.1	9.4	0.1	0.4	40	40	20	1.6	0	0	0	96.9	1.6
Getafe	97,198	100	9.3	2.5	30.8	0.5	0.1	23.1	0.3	0.1	83.3	16.7	0	0	0	0	7.7	92.3	0
San Sebastian	96,772	31.3	4.3	0.9	21.9	0.6	0.1	43.5	2.8	0.6	67.5	24.5	8	1.2	0	0	1.5	95.7	1.5
Sabadell	95,671	11.1	0.1	0.3	0	0	0	0	0	0	0	0	0	55.6	0	0	0	44.4	0
Caceres	95,668	100	14.7	2.3	33.3	0.4	0.1	60	4	0.6	83.3	0	16.7	13.3	6.7	0	0	80	0
Logrono	92,865	100	22.1	6.7	85.7	1.4	0.4	57.1	2.4	0.7	20	10	70	0	0	0	0	71.4	28.6
Coslada	91,832	75	8.9	9.9	25	0.9	1	37.5	2.3	2.5	14.3	85.7	0	0	0	0	0	100	0

(continued)

Table 12.10 (continued)

Local government	Population	P1 (%)	P2	P3	C1 (%)	C2	C3	V1 (%)	V2	V3	Positive (%)	Negative	Neutral	Economic (%)	Geographic	Legal	Meteorological	Social	Transport
La Laguna	90,390	46.2	17.8	3.4	18.3	0.5	0.1	34.4	6	1.2	52.2	39.1	8.7	3.2	0	0	0	94.6	2.2
Reus	90,358	88.9	5	4.3	8.3	0.3	0.2	52.8	1.4	1.2	66.7	33.3	0	0	0	0	0	83.3	16.7
Murcia	90,087	100	2.9	4.4	30	5.4	8	26	0.3	0.4	4.1	91	4.9	6	2	0	0	86	6
Talavera de la Reina	88,755	46.8	0.9	1.3	4.3	0	0.1	23.4	0.3	0.5	50	50	0	0	0	0	0	100	0
Santiago de Compostela	84,946	93.3	6.6	12.3	6.7	0.1	0.1	40	1.7	3.1	100	0	0	0	0	0	0	93.3	6.7
Guadalajara	84,803	69	3.7	0.2	41.3	1.7	0.1	83.7	5.8	0.3	59.7	34	6.3	0	0	0	7.6	87.5	4.9

References

Agostino, D. (2013). Using social media to engage citizens: A study of Italian municipalities. *Public Relations Review, 39*, 232–234.

Akadwani, A. M. (2014). Gravitating towards Facebook (GoToFB): What it is? and how can it be measured? *Computers in Human Behavior, 33*, 270–278.

Alcaide, L., Caba, C., & López, A. (2013). *Public managers' perceptions of e-government efficiency: A Case study of Andalusian municipalities*. EGPA Annual Conference, 11–13 September 2013, Edinburgh, Scotland.

Alt, J., & Dreyer, D. (2006). Fiscal transparency, political parties, and debt in OECD countries. *European Economic Review, 50*(6), 1403–1439.

Bonsón, E., Torres, L., Royo, S., & Flores, F. (2012). Local e-government 2.0: Social media and corporate transparency in municipalities. *Government Information Quarterly, 29*, 123–132.

Bonsón, E., & Ratkai, M. (2013). A set of metrics to assess stakeholder engagement and social legitimacy on a corporate Facebook page. *Online Information Review, 37*(5), 787–803.

Bonsón, E., Royo, S., & Ratkai, M. (2013). *Analysis of European municipalities' Facebook channels activity and citizens' engagement*. XVII Congreso AECA "Ética y emprendimiento: valores para un nuevo desarrollo", Pamplona (Spain).

Bonsón, E., Royo, S., & Ratkai, M. (2014). Facebook practices in Western European Municipalities: An empirical analysis of activity and citizens' engagement. *Administration & Society*, http://aas.sagepub.com/content/early/2014/09/04/0095399714544945.abstract

Bortree, D., & Seltzer, T. (2009). Dialogic strategies and outcomes: An analysis of environmental advocacy groups' Facebook profiles. *Public Relations Review, 35*(3), 317–319.

Bretschneider, S. I., & Mergel, I. (2010). Technology and public management information systems: Where have we been and where are we going. In D. C. Menzel & H. J. White (Eds.), *The state of public administration: Issues, problems and challenges* (pp. 187–203). New York: M.E. Sharpe.

Chi, F., & Yang, N. (2010). *Twitter in Congress: Outreach vs. transparency*. Social Sciences, 1–20.

Deegan, C. (2006). Legitimacy theory. In Z. Hogue (Ed.), *Methodological issues in accounting research: Theories and methods* (pp. 161–182). London: Spiramus Press.

Deegan, C., & Samkin, G. (2009). *New Zealand financial accounting*. Sydney: McGraw-Hill.

Dowling, J., & Pfeffer, J. (1975). Organizational legitimacy: Social values and organizational behavior. *The Pacific Sociological Review, 18*, 122–136.

EC (2003). *Directive 2003/98/EC of the European Parliament and of the Council of 17 November 2003 on the Re-use of Public Sector Information*. http://ec.europa.eu/information_society/policy/psi/docs/pdfs/directive/psi_directive_en.pdf.

Ellison, N. R., & Hardey, M. (2014). Social media and local government: Citizenship, consumption and democracy. *Local Government Studies, 40*(1), 21–40.

Facebook, (2013a). *Key facts*. Facebook. http://newsroom.fb.com/key-facts.

Facebook, (2013b). *The annual Facebook emagazine*. http://techcrunch.com/2013/12/29/facebook-international-user-growth/.

Freeman, R. E. (1984). *Strategic management: A stakeholder approach*. Boston: Pitman Press.

Frost, G., & Semaer, M. (2002). Adoption of environmental reporting and management practices: An analysis of New South Wales public sector entities. *Financial Accountability and Management, 18*, 103–127.

Gallego, I., García, I. M., & Rodríguez, L. (2009). Universities' websites: Disclosure practices and the revelation of financial information. *The International Journal of Digital Accounting Research, 9*, 153–192.

Gandía, J. L., & Archidona, M. C. (2008). Determinants of web site information by Spanish city councils. *Online Information Review, 32*(1), 35–57.

Gaventa, J., & Valderrama, C. (1999). *Participation, citizenship and local governance*. Workshop Report. Paper presented at the workshop on strengthening participation in local governance. Institute of Development Studies, June 21–24, 1999, Brighton.

Grimmelikhuijsen, S. G. (2010). Transparency of public decision-making: Towards trust in local government? *Policy and Internet, 2*(1), 5–35.
Guthrie, J., Petty, R., & Ricceri, F. (2006). The voluntary reporting of intellectual capital: comparing evidence from Hong Kong and Australia. *Journal of Intellectual Capital, 7*(2), 254–271.
Ho, A. T. K. (2002). Reinventing local governments and the e-government initiative. *Public Administration Review, 62*(4), 434–444.
Hoffman, D. L., & Fodor, M. (2010). Can you measure the ROI of your social media marketing? *MIT Sloan Management Review, 52*(1), 40–49.
Hong, H. (2013). Government websites and social media's influence on government-public relationships. *Public Relations Review, 39*, 346–356.
Holzer, M, & Kim, S.T. (2005). Digital Governance in Municipalities Worldwide, A Longitudinal Assessment of Municipal Web Sites Throughout the World. The E-Governance Institute, Rutgers University, Newark and the Global e-policy e-government Institute, Sungkyunkwan, University.
Huang, C. (2010). Board, ownership and performance of banks with a dual board system: Evidence from Taiwan. *Journal of Management and Organization, 16*(2), 219–234.
Kent, M., & Taylor, M. (1998). Building dialogic relationships through World Wide Web. *Public Relations Review, 24*, 321–334.
Kent, M. L., & Taylor, M. (2002). Toward a dialogic theory of public relations. *Public Relations Review, 28*, 21–37.
Kent, M., Taylor, M., & White, W. J. (2003). The relationship between web site design and organizational responsiveness to stakeholders. *Public Relations Review, 29*, 63–77.
Licha, I. (2002). *Citizen participation and local government in Latin America: Advances, challenges and best practices*. Washington, DC: Inter American Development Bank.
Linders, D. (2011). *We-government: An anatomy of citizen coproduction in the information age*. Paper presented at the 12th Annual International Digital Government Research Conference: Digital Government Innovation in Challenging Times, June 12–15, 2011, College Park, MD.
McAllister, S. M. (2012). How the world's top universities provide dialogic forums for marginalized voices. *Public Relations Review, 38*(2), 319–327.
Moon, M. J. (2002). The evolution of e-government among municipalities: Rhetoric or reality? *Public Administration Review, 62*(4), 424–433.
Moreno, M. (2013). 5 métricas en social media para evaluar tu gestión de comunicación. http://augure.es/default.aspx?ID=58&TITLE=M%C3%A9tricas+en+Social+Media.
Nah, S., & Saxton, G. D. (2012). Modeling the adoption and use of social media by nonprofit organizations. *New Media & Society, 15*(2), 294–313.
National Institute of Statistics (2012). Spanish National Accounts. National Institute of Statistics. http://www.ine.es/jaxi/menu.do?type=pcaxis&path=%2Ft35%2Fp008&file=inebase&L=1.
National Institute of Statistics (2013). Population figures and Demographic Censuses. National Institute of Statistics. http://www.ine.es/en/inebmenu/mnu_cifraspob_en.htm.
Ni, A. Y., & Bretschneider, S. (2007). The decision to contract out: A study of contracting for e-Government services in state governments. *Public Administration Review, 67*(3), 531–544.
Norris, D. F., & Reddick, C. G. (2013). Local e-government in the United States: Transformation or incremental change? *Public Administration Review, 73*(1), 165–175.
Oakerson, R. J. (1999). *Governing local public economies: Creating the civic metropolis*. Richmond, VA: ICS Press.
Peters, K., Chen, Y., Kaplan, A. M., Ognibeni, B., & Pauwels, K. (2013). Social media metrics—A framework and guidelines for managing social media. *Journal of Interactive Marketing, 27*, 281–298.
Pina, V., Torres, L., & Royo, S. (2010). Is e-government promoting convergence towards more accountable local governments? *International Public Management Journal, 13*(4), 350–380.
Purser, K. (2012). *Using social media in local government: 2011 survey report*. Sydney: Australian Centre of Excellence for Local Government, University of Technology.

Rodríguez, L., Garcia, I. S., & Gallego, I. (2011). Determining factors of e-Government development: A worldwide national approach. *International Public Management Journal, 14*(2), 218–248.

Rybalko, S., & Seltzer, T. (2010). Dialogic communication in 140 characters or less: How Fortune 500 companies engage stakeholders using Twitter. *Public Relations Review, 36*(4), 336–341.

Sæbø, Ø., Rose, J., & Nyvang, T. (2009). The role of social networking services in eParticipation. In A. Macintosh & E. Tambouris (Eds.), *Electronic participation: Lecture notes in computer science* (pp. 46–55). Linz: Springer.

Sáez-Martín, A., Haro-de-Rosario, A., & Caba-Perez, C. (2014). A vision of social media in the Spanish smartest cities. *Transforming Government: People, Process and Policy, 8*(4), 521–544.

Sandoval, R., & Gil, J. R. (2012). Government-citizen interactions using web 2.0 tools: The case of Twitter in Mexico. In C. G. Reddick & S. K. Aikins (Eds.), *Web 2.0 technologies and democratic governance: Political, policy and management implications* (pp. 233–248). New York: Springer.

Serrano, C., Rueda, M., & Portillo, P. (2009). Factors influencing e-disclosure in local public administrations. *Environment and Planning C, 27*(2), 355–378.

Snead, J. T. (2013). Social media use in the U.S. Executive branch. *Government Information Quarterly, 30*, 56–63.

Styles, A. K., & Tennyson, M. (2007). The accessibility of financial reporting of U.S. municipalities on the Internet. *Journal of Public Budgeting, Accounting and Financial Management, 19*(1), 56–92.

Strecker, A. (2011). *Flocking to Facebook: How local governments can build citizen engagement.* Paper presented at the annual Capstone Conference for the University of North Carolina at Chapel Hill Public Administration Program, Chapel Hill, NC.

Sun, T., & Wu, G. (2012). Traits, predictors, and consequences of Facebook self-presentation. *Social Science Computer Review, 30*(4), 419–433.

Takagi, K., Rzepka, R., & Araki, K. (2011). *Just keep tweeting, dear: web-mining methods for helping a social robot understand user needs*. AAAI Spring Symposium—Technical Report, SS-11-05, 60–65. www.aaai.org/ocs/index.php/SSS/SSS11/paper/view/2379/2884

Tolbert, C. J., Mossberger, K., & McNeal, R. (2008). Institutions, policy and e-government in the American states. *Public Administration Review, 68*, 549–563.

Towner, T. L., & Dulio, D. A. (2012). New media and political marketing in the United States: 2012 and beyond. *Journal of Political Marketing, 11*(1/2), 95–119.

U.S. Census Bureau (2011). U.S. & World Population Clocks. http://www.census.gov/main/www/popclock.html.

Waters, R. D., Burnett, E., Lamm, A., & Lucas, J. (2009). Engaging stakeholders through social networking: How non-profit organisations are using Facebook. *Public Relations Review, 35*(2), 102–106.

Waters, R. D., Tindall, T. J., & Morton, T. S. (2010). Media catching and the journalist—Public relations practitioners relationship: How social media are changing the practice of media relations. *Journal of Public Relations Research, 22*(3), 241–264.

Watt, P. (2004). Financing local government. *Local Government Studies, 30*(4), 609–623.

Wright, D. K., & Hinson, M. D. (2009). Examining how public relations practitioners actually are using social media. *Public Relations Journal, 3*(3), 1–33.

Chapter 13
Social Media and the City: Analyzing Conversations in Municipal Facebook Pages

Azi Lev-On and Nili Steinfeld

Abstract What characterizes the discourse that takes place on social media platforms involving municipal pages and their fans? Does the character of the activities on these social media platforms differ in periods preceding or following municipal elections, compared to non-election periods? The article examines the scope and character of Facebook activities on Israeli municipality pages before and after municipal elections, in comparison to non-election periods. For this purpose, the article surveys municipalities' Facebook presence and analyzes its correlations with socio-demographic and geographic indicators. The distributions of various engagement indices of municipal pages (number of fans, and average number of likes, comments, and shares of posts) are presented, and the contents uploaded by the page managers and fans are compared. We conclude by reviewing municipalities' Facebook activity and engagement over time, with the aim of identifying changes in Facebook pages in pre-election and post-election periods.

13.1 Introduction

What characterizes the discourse that takes place on social media platforms between municipal governments and their fans? Do the functions and character of activities on social media platforms differ in periods preceding or following municipal elections, compared to non-election periods?

Use of the Internet in general, and of municipal Facebook pages in particular, may have unique significance in periods preceding municipal elections. In pre-election periods, incumbents and candidates have strong incentives to share their positions on a variety of issues with the public, respond to questions, and comment on current events. Such conversations may develop in diverse settings including parlor and town hall meetings and employ various means such as billboard and street

A. Lev-On (✉) • N. Steinfeld
Institute for the Study of New Media, Politics and Society, School of Communication, Ariel University, Ariel, Israel
e-mail: azilevon@gmail.com; nilisteinfeld@gmail.com

M.Z. Sobaci (ed.), *Social Media and Local Governments*, Public Administration and Information Technology 15, DOI 10.1007/978-3-319-17722-9_13

advertising (Nadeau et al. 2008). Gradually, Facebook has become a leading arena for such public debates and discussions during election campaigns (Lev-On 2015).

A local perspective on the Facebook interactions of governments and citizens is important for several reasons (Bertot et al. 2012; Deakin 2010; Shkabatur 2010). First, studies indicate that municipality webpage usage is correlated with both public trust in local governments (Tolbert and Mossberger 2006) and with municipality interactions with the public (Feeney et al. 2011; Garrett and Jensen 2011).

Second, decisions at the local level have a direct impact on the everyday lives of citizens, especially in areas where decisions are made at the local rather than the national level, such as education and social welfare. Municipality Facebook pages, whose contents are easily accessible, may function as attractive arenas in which residents participate in multi-stakeholder conversations about such issues (Shkabatur 2010).

Third, the number of voters in local elections is significantly smaller compared to the national level, and municipal election results are occasionally determined by a small number of votes. As a result, the significance of individual voter decisions may be proportionately greater at the municipal level. Consequently, when a municipality Facebook post captures public attention, it holds considerable potential to generate significant change (especially before elections). A local Facebook page offers significant incentives and opportunities for residents to create conservations and mobilize activities, especially before elections (Shkabatur 2010).

Few studies have analyzed Internet usage at the municipal level, and even fewer have analyzed the relatively recent appearance of municipality Facebook pages. Nonetheless, several key insights emerge from these studies:

Scope of adoption and activity: Studies show incremental yet consistent increases in the scope and sophistication of municipality Facebook use (Deakin 2010; Mossberger 2013; Oliveira and Welch 2013), as Facebook becomes a major channel for municipalities for communicating with their local public in Europe and the US (Bonsón et al. 2012; Norris and Reddick 2013).

Correlates with e-government adoption of Facebook: Adoption of e-government platforms by municipalities, and specifically social media platforms, has not been uniform. Studies have found that the important factor affecting municipal-level adoption and use of new media channels in general, and Facebook in particular, is *municipality size*. Municipality size not only influences the initial decision to adopt e-government tools, but also affects the ongoing management of a municipality's online presence: Large municipalities have been found to maintain more extensive activities on their sites and Facebook pages than small municipalities (Ahn 2011; Borge et al. 2009; Garrett and Jensen 2011; Haug 2008; Holden et al. 2003; Moon 2002; Norris and Reddick 2013; Wohlers 2009).

Studies also show that the variables that predict usage, in addition to municipality size, are peripherality (central/peripheral municipalities; Norris and Reddick 2013; Wohlers 2009; Haug 2008), structural attributes such as the functions in charge of maintaining the municipality's online presence (Wohlers 2009; Carrizales 2008; Reddick and Norris 2013; Norris and Reddick 2013), and population income and education levels (Reddick and Norris 2013).

Character of activities: A recurrent finding in e-government studies is that municipality *websites* place greater weight on static contents such as tenders and information on municipal activities, with much less emphasis on interactive contents (Haug 2008; Mossberger 2013; Musso et al. 2000; Norris and Reddick 2013; Scott 2006; Torres et al. 2006). The static character of municipality websites is apparently reproduced in municipalities' *Facebook pages*, despite the inherently interactive character of Facebook. Municipalities tend to disregard the transactional potential of social media, choosing instead to post informational materials that also appear on other, more traditional, media (Lovari and Parisi 2012; Perlman 2012; Graham and Avery 2013; Oliveira and Welch 2013).

Several studies illustrate that municipalities rather than residents are the dominant actors in uploading content to municipal websites (Graham and Avery 2013; Hofmann et al. 2013; Magnusson et al. 2012). Moreover, municipality webpages may create an impression of municipality indifference since many of the questions posted by residents on the municipality page wall remain without a response as municipalities tend to contact residents privately rather than respond in public (Hand and Ching 2011; Strecker 2011).

The aim of the current study is to update the research on municipal-level e-government. This is the first study in Israel to focus on municipal-level Facebook usage and practices. The few studies exploring Internet adoption by municipalities in Israel (Purian-Lukach 2011; Ravitsch 2005; Rotem 2007) have focused on municipality *websites*. These studies show that Internet use by local governments in Israel is growing constantly, but large and small municipalities differ in adoption scope and practices in several respects. Israel-based studies suggest that some local governments "lag behind" in Internet adoption due to the profile of their residents (for example, Ultra-Orthodox or Arab populations). One study on the use of websites in municipal campaigns found a correlation between municipality website use and municipality size, location (center/periphery), and population age, education, and income, in line with other studies conducted elsewhere (Lev-On 2014).

The current study focuses on Facebook, which has emerged as the main site of communications involving municipalities and residents (Gulati and Williams 2013; Lev-On 2015; Williams and Gulati 2013). Israel, with one of the highest Facebook penetration and usage rates in the world (ComScore 2011), is an appropriate site for the study of residents' Facebook use for communications with local governments. Facebook use may be conceivably more appealing to Internet users as a means of communicating with local governments than dedicated websites: While specific effort must be made to locate a municipality website, a municipality Facebook page is easily accessible through contents uploaded in one's own or one's friends' personal feeds. Facebook also allows users to upload contents with greater ease and immediacy than a municipal websites and allows users to receive messages and alerts in real time, including push messages routed to smartphones.

Although all municipalities in Israel are required by law to maintain an official website, no such requirement exists with regard to presence on social media. Municipalities are similarly not required by law to transmit specific information to residents through the Facebook. This fact adds another dimension to the current analysis, as it allows us to compare municipalities that maintain Facebook pages with those that do not and characterize the "haves" and "have nots" in terms of demographics and socio-economic indicators.

13.2 Research Questions and Hypotheses

The present study examines the scope and character of Facebook activity at the municipality level in Israel. In view of the paucity of previous research in this field, we present some of the research questions without proposing specific hypotheses.

RQ1: What is the adoption rate of official Facebook pages by municipalities? Due to Israel's high Facebook usage statistics, we assume that a significant share of Israeli municipalities have adopted this platform.

H1: Adoption will be more limited in municipalities with majority Ultra-Orthodox or Arab populations. This hypothesis is in line with previous studies in Israel (Purian-Lukach 2011; Ravitsch 2005; Rotem 2007) that found significant differences in the prevalence of official websites in such municipalities.

H2: In line with previous studies, we also expect to discover correlations between municipality Facebook adoption and municipality features, including size, location (center/periphery), and population age, income, and education.

RQ2: What is the level of engagement with the municipal Facebook pages? To develop an understanding of the practices on municipality Facebook pages, we collected data on several engagement measures (number of fans, Likes, Comments, Shares, and Comment-likes).

RQ3: What is the primary source of the contents uploaded to municipality Facebook pages—the municipalities themselves or their fans?

RQ4: Does municipality Facebook usage differ during election campaigns, compared to post-election periods and non-election periods?

13.3 Methodology

To analyze municipalities' activities on Facebook, we used a list of all 75 cities (in general, municipalities with over 20,000 residents) in Israel, based on information available on the Central Bureau of Statistics web site. To locate the Facebook page of each municipality, we used the Google search engine, and in each case, entered the city's name in Hebrew, Arabic, and English (Israel's three official languages). No relevant Facebook pages were found in the searches in Arabic. The search identified three municipality Facebook pages in English, and the remainder of the pages were in Hebrew. We also scanned the municipalities' own web sites for links to their Facebook pages.

One municipality used a personal profile instead of a Facebook page and was consequently excluded from the analysis; such usage violates Facebook policy that prohibits the use of personal profiles by official organizations.

Also excluded from our analyses were several pages, which bore the names of cities and whose contents concerned city affairs, had been created by residents and were not maintained by, or had no formal connection to, the relevant municipality, as we concluded from a search of the page's authors by reading the pages' "about" section, searching the municipality's web site for a hyperlink to the Facebook page, or reading through posts by the page managers. One such example is the Facebook page for Kiryat Gat, described as "the official Kiryat Gat page," which features the city emblem and contains contents that are relevant to residents' lives, including information originating in the municipality. The page is, however, managed by city residents and is not an official municipality page.

A total of 43 official municipality Facebook pages were found, and all were included in our sample. Socio-economic, demographic, and geographic data pertaining to these cities were collected from the CBS website. These data include the city's socio-economic cluster, population's median age, percentage of 12th graders who earned a Matriculation Certificate in the 2011–2012 school year (the most recent year for which statistics are available for this measure, which is an indicator of the mean education level in the city), and location in Israel measured by the peripherality index developed by the CBS. These measures were selected for the significance they were found to have in predicting Internet usage, in previous studies.[1]

After collecting the above data on the municipality Facebook pages in our sample, we applied Netvizz, a Facebook application developed by the Digital Methods Initiative[2] for downloading Facebook data. The application runs from within Facebook and uses the Facebook API to mine the contents of posts and comments on official pages, including information on the posts and comments, such as the post author (page/user), time of publication, post format (photo, video, status, etc.), and all engagement measures (number of Likes, Comments, Shares, and Comment-likes the post received). The results are in tab-separated format and can be uploaded to Excel and to SPSS for statistical analysis. We used this application to mine all the messages posted on the official municipality Facebook pages by the page itself and by fans, as well as all the engagement measures for each post. An Engagement Index was calculated as an aggregation of the Likes, Comments, Comment-likes, and Shares for each post on the page. We also mined the contents of the comments to the posts on each page.

We used Netvizz to mine all posts and comments published on each municipality page for the 6-month period between October 22, 2012 and April 22, 2013. Several of the pages were created in the course of this period. For these pages, we analyzed

[1] Local government data were taken from the website of the Central Bureau of Statistics at http://www.cbs.gov.il/reader/cw_usr_view_SHTML?ID=357. Peripherality data were also taken from the CBS. See www.cbs.gov.il/hodaot2008n/24_08_160b.pdf.

[2] We thank Digital Methods Initiatives and Bernhard Rider for permission to use their tool.

all the posts from the date the account was set up until April 22, 2013. Municipal elections took place in Israel on October 22, 2013, 6 months after the conclusion of the data collection period. In total, 23,768 posts and 71,338 comments appeared on 43 municipality Facebook pages in this non-election period. These posts and comments constitute the study population.

We also tracked and documented the changes in the number of fans (i.e., number of "likes" to the page) for each municipality Facebook page at monthly intervals, beginning from June 2013.

Furthermore, to compare patterns of activity during election campaigns and other periods, we used Netvizz to mine activity data on municipality Facebook pages between August 23, 2013 and December 22, 2013, a period beginning 2 months before and ending 2 months after the municipal elections, which were held in October 22.

To study whether municipal Facebook pages are used by municipalities differently before elections, after elections, and in non-election periods, we compared between three periods: the 2 months immediately preceding municipal elections in Israel (August 23 to October 22, 2013, the date of the nation-wide local elections in Israel); the 2 months immediately following the elections (October 23 to December 22, 2013); and the corresponding period of the previous year (October 23, 2012 to December 22, 2012) as a control group.

For each of the three periods, we mined all posts published during that period on all of the cities' pages. We then compared the number of posts and measurements of engagement with the posts (Likes, Comments, Shares, Comment-likes, and engagement) in the three periods. We furthermore compared these measures for cities where the incumbent mayor lost the elections and cities where the incumbent won the elections.

Posts related to 42 municipalities were included in the analysis. One municipality (Nazareth Elith) was excluded from the sample as no posts were published on the municipality's Facebook page during this period. In the 2-month period preceding the elections, from August 23 to October 22, 2013, a total of 7,127 posts were uploaded to municipality Facebook pages, while in the 2 months following the elections, from October 23 to December 22, 2013, a total of 7,895 posts were uploaded. In the control period, October 23 to December 22, 2012, a total of 7,522 posts were uploaded to municipality Facebook pages.

13.4 Findings

13.4.1 Facebook Presence

Of the 75 cities in Israel, 43 (58.1 %) maintained an official Facebook page during the data collection period, suggesting an impressive rate of Facebook adoption by Israeli municipalities. The mean number of posts per page over the 6 months from

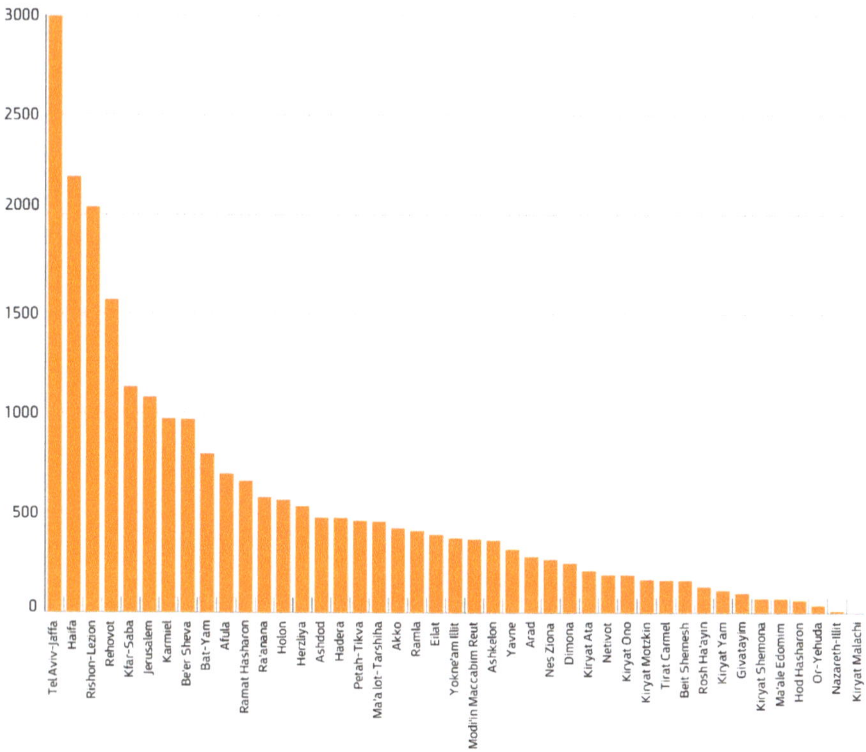

Fig. 13.1 Posts per page

October 22, 2012 to April 22, 2013 was 553, and the mean number of Comments was 1,659. Likes are the most common mode of engagement with posts: The mean number of Likes per post was 23.69, the mean number of Comments per post was 3.09, and the mean number of Shares per post was 2.1. The mean number of Comment-likes (i.e., likes to comments published with regard to a post) per post was 2.66, and the mean engagement score per post (summarizing all engagement measures) was 31.55. Figures 13.1 and 13.2 present the distribution of the total number of posts and Comments *per page* during the entire period (October 22, 2012 to April 22, 2013). Figure 13.3 presents the distribution of the total number of Likes per page.

Municipalities are much more active in uploading content to their pages than users: Of the total 23,768 posts in our sample, 9,930 posts were uploaded by the municipalities (on average, municipalities uploaded 240 posts on their page) and 13,838 posts were uploaded by all other users (419 posts on average per page). The content uploaded to the pages varies in format and often includes more than text: The most prevalent post type was an image: 43 % or 10,117 posts contained an image. The second most prevalent post type (38 % or 9,071 posts) was a status post,

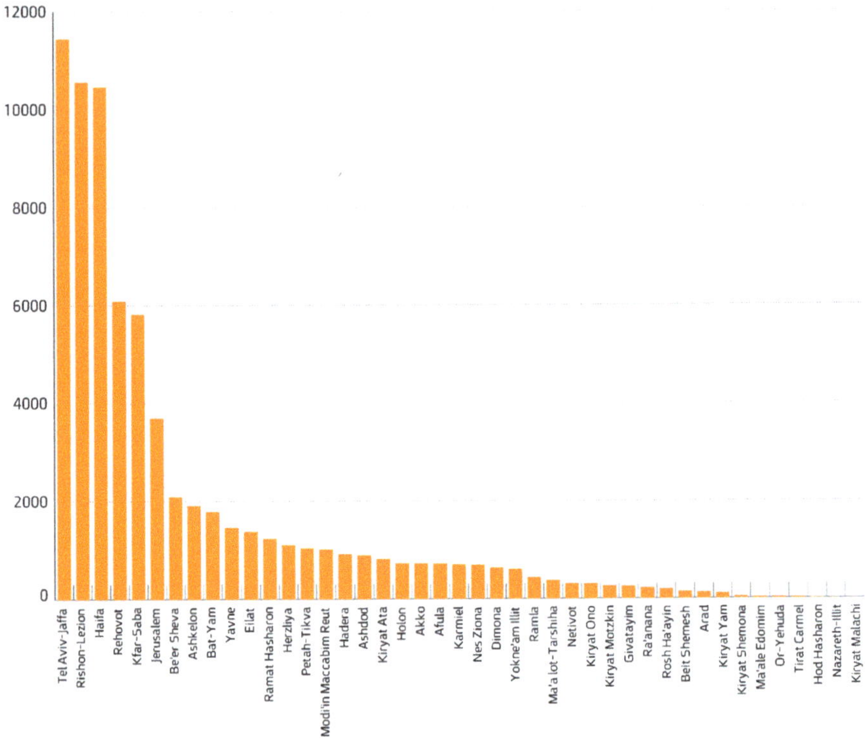

Fig. 13.2 Comments per page

which contained only text. A significantly smaller proportion of the posts (14 % or 3,341) were link posts, which contained a URL address (either in or outside Facebook). Videos were included in 5 % of all posts (or 1,216).

In June 2013, we counted the number of fans per page (users who “like” the page). Fans are not necessarily residents of the city, but they do express a relation to it and a desire to remain abreast of the city’s activities. The mean number of municipality page fans was 7,654. Leading this category was Haifa, with 67,403 fans on June 22, 2013. Or Yehuda, with 45 fans on June 22, 2013, was in last place.

A study of the distribution of fans relative to municipality size indicates that the number of fans per page does not necessarily correspond to municipality size, as several small and medium-sized cities lead in the number of their Facebook fans relative to size. Figures 13.4 and 13.5 present the distribution of municipality Facebook page fans in absolute terms and relative to municipality size.

The initial mapping of municipality Facebook usage indicates that cities vary significantly in the scope of their Facebook activity. In addition, the distribution of Facebook adoption by municipalities is not random, and it is defined by the population: No municipality with a majority of Arab or Ultra-Orthodox population main-

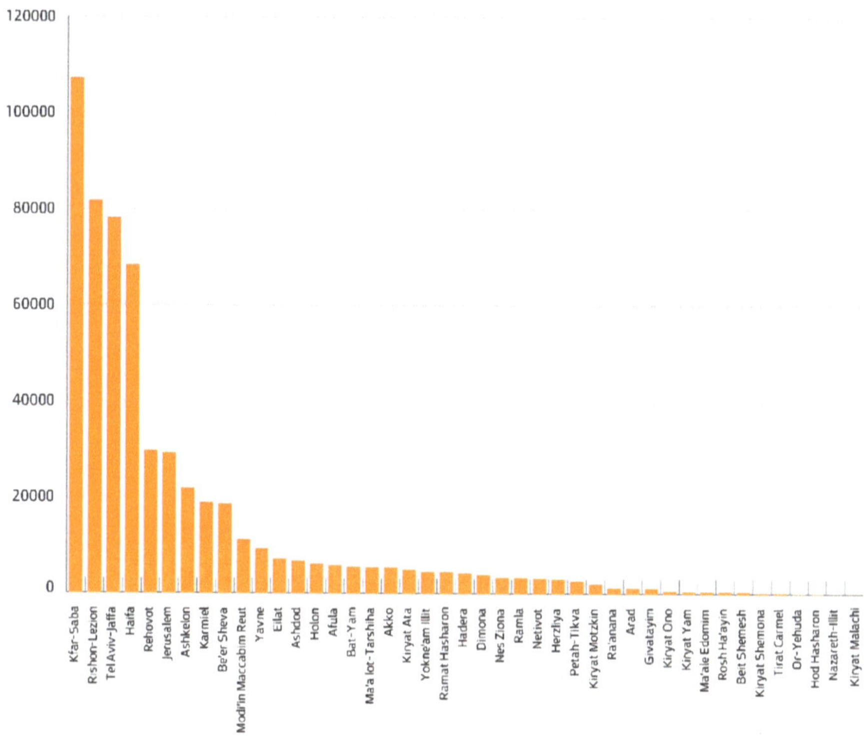

Fig. 13.3 Likes for posts on municipal Facebook pages in Israel

tains an official Facebook page. These figures, and specifically the absence of a single Facebook page for an Arab or Ultra-Orthodox municipalities, confirm H1.

To test H2, we used X^2 tests to measure Facebook presence with reference to municipality size. We found that the larger the municipality, the greater the probability that the municipality maintained an official Facebook page (*Cramer's* $V=.36$; $p<.05$). Comparing municipalities with and without Facebook presence, results of X^2 tests revealed significant differences for the following socio-economic indicators:

- A city's socio-economic status was found to be significantly correlated with the municipality's Facebook presence or absence. The higher the city's socio-economic cluster, the greater the probability that the municipality maintained an official Facebook page (*Cramer's* $V=.51$; $p<.001$).
- The age of the population was also significantly correlated with a municipality's Facebook presence or absence. The higher the median age of the population, the greater the probability that the municipality maintained an official Facebook page (*Cramer's* $V=.49$, $p<.001$).

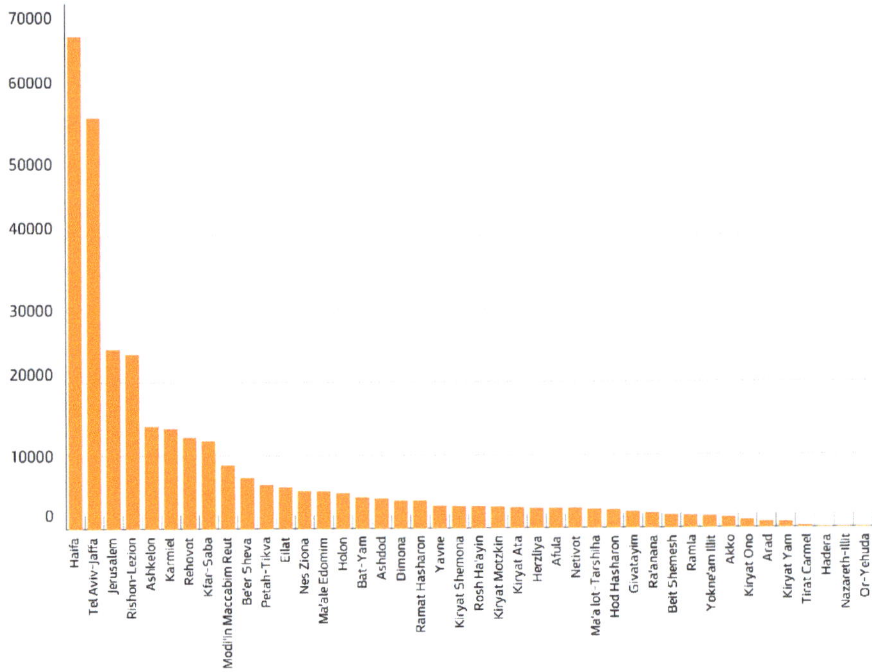

Fig. 13.4 Distribution of fans by municipality

- Finally, population education levels, measured as the proportion of all 12th graders in the city who earned a Matriculation Certificate in the 2011–2012 school year, are also significantly related to municipality Facebook presence. Cities with a higher percentage of Matriculation Certificate earners have a greater probability of maintaining a Facebook presence (*Cramer's* $V = .36$, $p < .05$).

The above results suggest that cities characterized by more well-off, educated populations are more likely to utilize Facebook as a communication channel with residents. No statistically significant correlation was found between peripherality and municipality Facebook presence. During the study period, several peripheral municipalities even demonstrated quite vivid Facebook activity and engagement compared to central municipalities.

13.4.2 Engagement Measures of Municipal Facebook Pages

The engagement score was a summary of all engagement measures: the number of likes, comments, shares, and comment-likes. The engagement score was influenced primarily by the number of likes, as liking was the most frequent type of

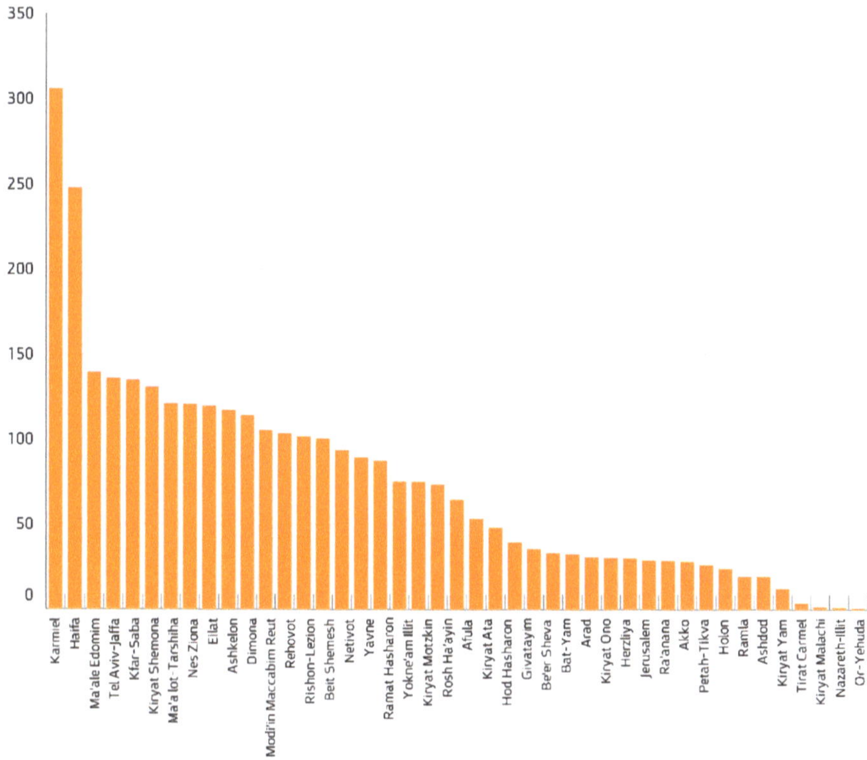

Fig. 13.5 Distribution of fans by municipality. The *Y* axis represents the number of fans per 1,000 residents

engagement associated with municipality Facebook pages. Kfar Saba has the highest engagement score of 105.16 (the median, however, is only 4, suggesting that one or several unusual posts received an unusually large number of likes, and affected the average), followed by Ashkelon ($M = 72.38$; Mdn = 40) and Rishon Lezion ($M = 55.99$; Mdn = 3). Figure 13.6 presents the distribution of municipality Facebook page engagement scores.

13.4.3 Post Origin and Engagement

Facebook pages were much more active than fans in uploading contents: Of the 23,768 posts collected during the study period, 9,930 posts were uploaded by the pages and 13,838 were uploaded by fans. Posts uploaded by the page attracted statistically significantly higher engagement rates than posts by users. Results of

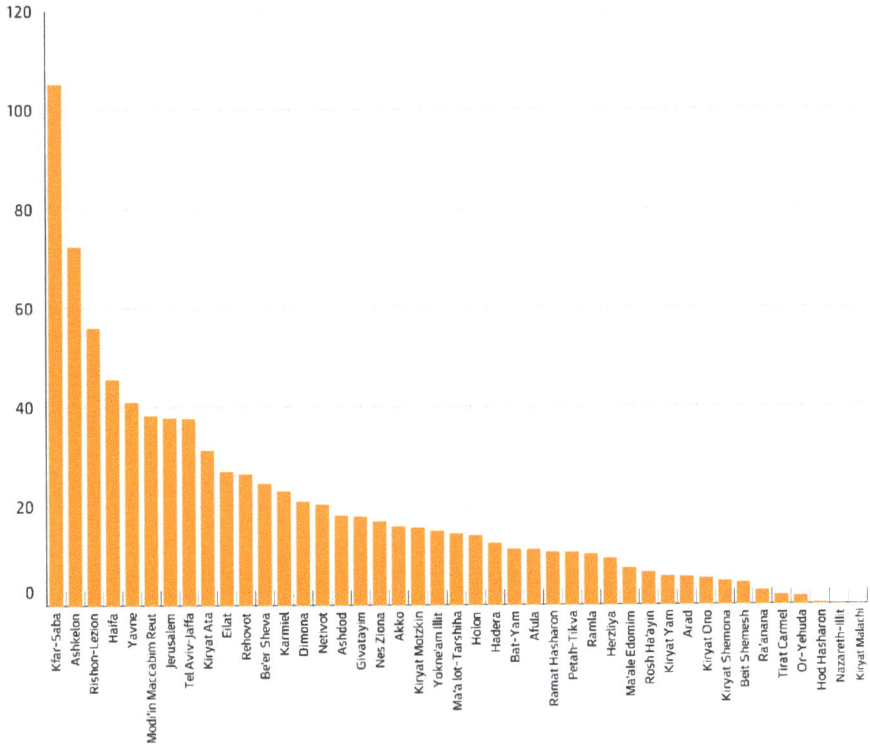

Fig. 13.6 Average engagement per post by municipalities

t-tests for independent samples indicate differences in engagement levels with posts originating in Facebook page owners and citizens. In general, posts by the pages generated a mean engagement score of 56.89, while posts by users received a mean engagement score of a mere 13.37. This finding is not surprising, as posts made by pages appear in the timelines of page fans, who are exposed to the page's posts without having to visit the page itself. In contrast, posts made to municipality pages by other fans do not appear in the timelines of other fans unless these fans are friends of the post author.

13.4.4 Comparing Activity and Engagement in Election and Non-election Periods

Few differences emerged in activity patterns and engagement levels in election and non-election periods. As noted above, in the 2-month period preceding the elections, from August 23 to October 22, 2013, a total of 7,127 posts were uploaded to municipality Facebook pages, while in the 2 months following the elections, from October 23 to December 22, 2013, a total of 7,895 posts were uploaded. In the control period, October 23 to December 22, 2012, a total of 7,522 posts were uploaded to the municipality Facebook pages in our sample.

An ANOVA test to compare *engagement* in these periods shows several significant differences in engagement with the municipality Facebook page posts, which reflect varying activity levels: First, a significant difference emerged in the mean *engagement scores* in these three periods ($F(_{2,22,541})=3.63$, $p<.05$). Using the LSD post hoc test, the control period (from October to December, 2012) was the period with the highest mean engagement levels. The mean engagement score in this period ($M=36.72$, SD=508.52) was significantly higher than in the pre-election period ($M=23.04$, SD=177.35). While engagement increased after the elections, the increase was not statistically significant compared to the post-election period ($M=27.28$, SD=101.87).

Second, a significant difference in the mean number of *Comments* per post was found when comparing periods ($F(_{2,22,541})=8.05$, $p<.001$). Results of a LSD post hoc test show that the most active period, measured by the mean Comments per post, was the control period (October to December 2012), and in this period, the number of Comments per post ($M=3.51$, SD=25.56) was significantly greater than the number of Comments in either the pre-election period ($M=2.49$, SD=8.06) or the post-election period ($M=2.71$, SD=9.33). While the number of Comments per post increased after the elections, the increase was not statistically significant compared to the pre-election period.

The three periods differed in the number of Likes per post in each period: These differences approached, but did not reach statistical significance ($F(_{2,22,541})=2.66$, $p=.07$) and indicate a similar trend: The mean number of *likes* per post was highest in the control period (M=26.66, SD=389.4), lowest in the pre-election period ($M=17.46$, SD=155.69), and the number rose again in the post-election period ($M=20.65$, SD=78.71). Although the model is not statistically significant, the difference between the control and pre-election periods was significant on the LSD test.

Other significant differences between periods emerged in cities where the incumbent mayor was re-elected. Of the 42 municipalities, the incumbent lost the elections in 10 municipalities. In the remaining 32 municipalities, the incumbent mayor was re-elected (In no municipality was it the case that the incumbent mayor did not run in the elections). In total, 18,997 posts were uploaded to Facebook pages of municipalities in which the incumbent mayor continued to another term, and 3,547 posts on Facebook pages of municipalities in which the incumbent lost the elections.

The municipality Facebook pages for municipalities whose incumbent mayors were re-elected showed similar patterns as those found in the total sample of pages: Significant differences in engagement scores between periods ($F(_{2,18,994})=3.10$, $p<.05$), and specifically between the control period ($M=39.46$, SD=545.45) and the pre-election period ($M=24.6$, SD=194.29), and a slight and non-significant increase in engagement in the post-election period ($M=29.06$, SD=109.51).

It is interesting to note that, with the exception of comments per post, no other significant differences emerged between periods in the Facebook pages of the 10 municipalities in which the incumbent lost the elections. In these cases, the sole significant difference ($F_{(2,3,544)}=4.18$, $p<.05$) was the difference in the number of Comments per post in the control period ($M=2$, SD=5.1) and the pre-election period ($M=1.48$, SD=3.9) and the difference between the control period and the post-election period ($M=1.6$, SD=4). Thus, the same pattern obtained: the most active period was the control period, and the period of lowest activity was the pre-election period.

13.4.5 *Distribution of Fans by Municipality and Period*

The number of Facebook page fans was recorded for each municipality and each month from June 2013. These data indicate that in the great majority of these cases, the number of fans of all municipality Facebook pages increased steadily over time, and this trend was not affected by pre-election and post-election periods.

Figure 13.7 summarizes the distribution of fans by municipality, for June and August 2013 (in the pre-election period), October 2013 (the election month), and

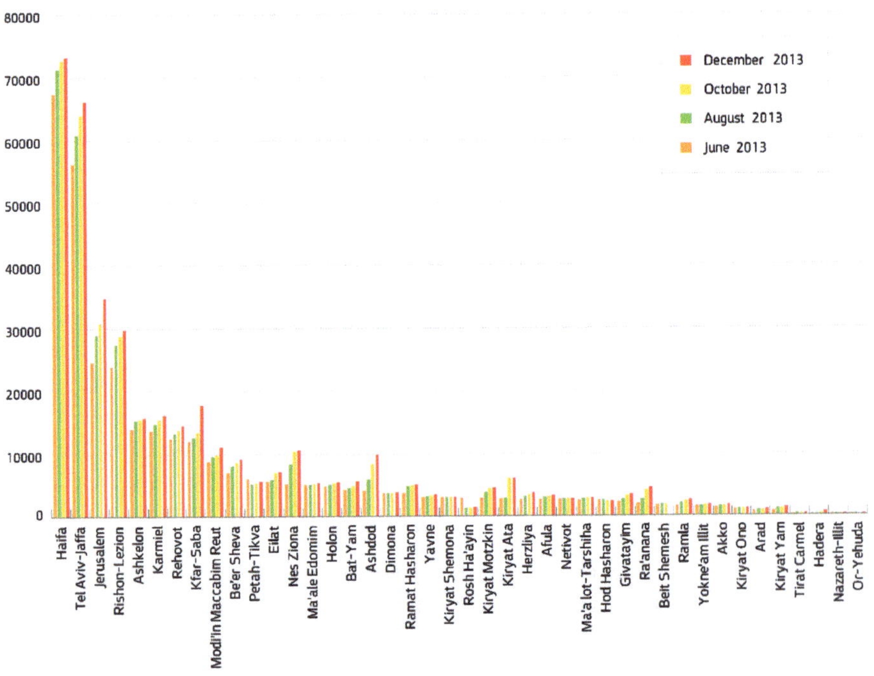

Fig. 13.7 Distribution of Facebook page fans by municipality in the pre-election, election, and post-election periods

December 2013 (in the post-election period). Figure 13.7 underscores that the steady increase in fans continued after the elections, with no significant differences between the pre-election and post-election periods.

13.5 Discussion

The findings of this study show that municipalities' adoption of Facebook pages in Israel is significant. More than one half (58.1 %) of the municipalities maintained an official Facebook page when the data for this study were collected (between October 2012 and April 2013), with a mean of 7,565 fans per municipality page. Facebook adoption is, however, not evenly distributed among cities and populations: The group of municipalities with no Facebook presence contains a large share of cities with Arab and Ultra-Orthodox populations, whose cultural norms arguably impede adoption of social networks by the municipal government. Furthermore, the low rate at which these municipalities adopt and use social media for communicating with residents may further increase the gaps between their already weakened populations and other strong populations that have the means to communicate directly with their municipalities with greater ease. Needless to say, in the municipalities where penetration of social media is low, social media does not constitute an arena of discourse between the municipality and the public.

Municipalities also showed significant variance in the extent of the activity and engagement generated by their Facebook pages. In line with findings of many other studies, the main factor affecting municipality Facebook presence is municipality size. The larger the population of a municipality, the greater the probability that the municipality will maintain an official Facebook page. This finding makes sense, since social networks are based on user activity and on networks generated between users. Therefore, larger populations are naturally more suitable for this type of activity. The finding is also in line with other studies on e-government adoption, including studies that have found that larger municipalities maintain a larger volume of activity on their Facebook page (Ahn 2011; Borge et al. 2009; Garrett and Jensen 2011; Haug 2008; Holden et al. 2003; Moon 2002; Norris and Reddick 2013; Wohlers 2009). Furthermore, we found that variables related to population characteristics (socio-economic status, education, and median age) are also significantly related to municipality Facebook presence: The higher a population's socio-economic status and education level, the greater the probability that the city will maintain a Facebook page. Also, the higher the age median of the population, which normally suggests a more modern and urbanized population, where the birth rate is lower—the greater the probability of a municipal Facebook page. In contrast to other studies, we found that a municipality's location (center/periphery) has no significant effect on municipality Facebook page presence, with a number of peripheral cities maintaining a lively and busy page.

When studying the ratio of fans to municipality size, findings of the present study show that the ratio is greater in intermediate-size municipalities and not necessarily in large municipalities (although obviously the absolute number of fans in large municipalities is greater). Large cities do not necessarily attract more attention to their Facebook page. Fans are also more significantly engaged in the municipal Facebook page in intermediate-size municipalities. To understand why specific municipality Facebook pages attract higher levels of engagement, a more complex content analysis is needed, which is beyond the scope of this study.

Based on a comparison of municipality Facebook pages in pre-election and post-election periods, and a control period 1 year prior to elections, the pre-election period appears to be characterized as having the lowest levels of activity and engagement, contrary to our hypotheses. The growth rate of fans of municipality Facebook pages over the entire study period remained stable through the data collection period, and the impact of elections on fan growth was insignificant. These trends emerged in Facebook municipality pages, independent of whether the incumbent mayor won or lost the elections, which further indicates that Facebook pages were not used as a major local public sphere during or immediately after elections. Public debates apparently were conducted in other spheres, including parlor meetings with candidates, candidates' web sites or Facebook pages, local newspapers, and other local sites. Also interesting to note is that the most active period in terms of average engagement, comments and likes per post, was the control period in late 2012. When comparing this period to the period before the election, or to the corresponding period 1 year later, it seems that user activity on municipality pages generally declined. When taking into account that the number of fans for the pages increased over time, this finding may suggest a diminution in the use of municipal Facebook pages by users, or even a more general downward trend in user engagement on Facebook, but this cannot be concluded based on the current research's data.

We also found that a large share of the posts uploaded to municipal pages are uploaded by the municipality, and that the contents uploaded by municipalities pages generated higher levels of engagement than contents uploaded by citizens. These findings indicate that the municipality Facebook page remains a public sphere that is controlled by municipalities. It will be interesting to see, in future studies, which types of contents generate the most engagement; such information could be used as the basis of a municipal strategy to transform its Facebook page into a more active public sphere, during elections or in non-election periods.

13.6 Summary and Conclusions

This paper explored the scope and character of Facebook page usage by municipalities in Israel. Previous studies point to a rise in government agencies' use of the Internet in general, and Facebook in particular, in order to connect with citizens and promote citizen engagement (Deakin 2010; Mossberger 2013; Oliveira and Welch 2013). Previous studies in Israel that examined local governments' web-based communications with citizens predated the significant rise in social networks and focused on the websites of these government agencies (Purian-Lukach 2011;

Ravitsch 2005; Rotem 2007). The present study, which focuses on Facebook pages of municipalities in Israel, attempts to fill the research lacuna in this respect and offers a description of the municipalities' Facebook presence, activity, and engagement, with a comparison of pre-election and post-election periods. The findings show that Facebook is widely used by municipalities in Israel as a platform for engaging citizens with city activities and issues. A steady increase in the number of fans for all pages suggests that these spaces increasingly attract users and citizens who find them relevant, and possibly effective.

Municipal Facebook pages are arenas of direct engagement between citizens and their cities. They allow citizens to raise issues concerning the city, become involved in and remain abreast of events and messages, influence other by attracting attention and engaging other citizens, and take part in local politics. Understanding the ways they are used by municipalities and by citizens can shed light on this new, increasing phenomenon of citizen e-participation.

Acknowledgment The study was conducted with the support of the Institute for the Study of New Media, Politics and Society at Ariel University. We thank Bar Ram, Hadas Schlussel, Valery Aronov, Veronika Makogon, and Avital Mandel for their assistance in data collection and processing and in the preparation of this manuscript.

References

Ahn, M. J. (2011). Adoption of e-communication applications in US municipalities: The role of political environment, bureaucratic structure, and the nature of applications. *The American Review of Public Administration, 41*(4), 428–452.

Bertot, J. C., Jaeger, P. T., & Grimes, J. M. (2012). Promoting transparency and accountability through ICTs, social media, and collaborative e-government. *Transforming Government: People, Process and Policy, 6*(1), 78–91.

Bonsón, E., Torres, L., Royo, S., & Flores, F. (2012). Local e-government 2.0: Social media and corporate transparency in municipalities. *Government Information Quarterly, 29*(2), 123–132.

Borge, R., Colombo, C., & Welp, Y. (2009). Online and offline participation at the local level: A quantitative analysis of the Catalan municipalities. *Information, Communication & Society, 12*(6), 899–928.

Carrizales, T. (2008). Functions of e-government: A study of municipal practices. *State and Local Government Review, 40*(1), 12–26.

ComScore. (2011). *It's a social world: Top 10 need-to-knows about social networking and where it's headed.* Retrieved from www.comscore.com/it_is_a_social_world

Deakin, M. (2010). A review of city portals: The transformation of service provision under the democratization of the fourth phase. In C. Reddick (Ed.), *Politics, democracy and e-government: Participation and service delivery* (pp. 215–224). Hershey, PA: Information Science Reference.

Feeney, M., Welch, E.W., & Haller, M. (2011). *Transparency, civic engagement, and technology use in local government agencies: Findings from a national survey.* Institute for Policy and Civic Engagement, University of Illinois at Chicago.

Garrett, R. K., & Jensen, M. J. (2011). E-democracy writ small: The impact of the Internet on citizen access to local elected officials. *Information, Communication & Society, 14*(2), 177–197.

Graham, M., & Avery, E. (2013). Government public relations and social media: An analysis of the perceptions and trends of social media use at the local government level. *Public Relations Journal, 7*(4), 1–21.

Gulati, G. J., & Williams, C. B. (2013). Social media and campaign 2012: Developments and trends for Facebook adoption. *Social Science Computer Review, 31*(5), 577–588.
Hand, L. C., & Ching, B. D. (2011). You have one friend request. *Administrative Theory & Praxis, 33*(3), 362–382.
Haug, A. V. (2008). Local democracy online: driven by crisis, legitimacy, resources, or communication gaps? *Journal of Information Technology & Politics, 4*(2), 79–99.
Hofmann, S., Beverungen, D., Räckers, M., & Becker, J. (2013). What makes local governments' online communications successful? Insights from a multi-method analysis of Facebook. *Government Information Quarterly, 30*(4), 387–396.
Holden, S. H., Norris, D. F., & Fletcher, P. D. (2003). Electronic government at the local level: Progress to date and future issues. *Public Productivity and Management Review, 26*(3), 1–20.
Lev-On, A. (2014). Campaigning online, locally. *International Journal of E-Politics, 5*(3), 14–28.
Lev-On, A. (2015). Online campaigning move to Facebook: Contenders' perspectives (in press).
Lovari, A., & Parisi, L. (2012). Public administrations and citizens 2.0: Exploring digital public communication strategies and civic interaction within Italian municipality pages on Facebook. In F. Comunello (Ed.), *Networked sociability and individualism: Technology for personal and professional relationships* (pp. 238–263). Hershey, PA: Information Science Reference.
Magnusson, M., Bellström, P., & Magnusson, M. (2012). *Facebook usage in government—A case study of information content*. Proceedings of AMCIS 2012.
Moon, M. J. (2002). The evolution of e-government among municipalities: Rhetoric or reality? *Public Administration Review, 62*(4), 424–433.
Mossberger, K. (2013). Connecting citizens and local governments? Social media and interactivity in major US cities. *Government Information Quarterly, 30*(4), 351–358.
Musso, J., Weare, C., & Hale, M. (2000). Designing web technologies for local governance reform: Good management or good democracy? *Political Communication, 17*(1), 1–19.
Nadeau, R., Nevitte, N., Gidengil, E., & Blais, A. (2008). Election campaigns as information campaigns: Who learns what and does it matter? *Political Communication, 25*(3), 229–248.
Norris, D. F., & Reddick, C. G. (2013). Local e-government in the United States: Transformation or incremental change? *Public Administration Review, 73*(1), 165–175.
Oliveira, G. H. M., & Welch, E. W. (2013). Social media use in local government: Linkage of technology, task, and organizational context. *Government Information Quarterly, 30*(4), 397–405.
Perlman, B. J. (2012). Social media sites at the state and local levels operational success and governance failure. *State and Local Government Review, 44*(1), 67–75.
Purian-Lukach, R. (2011). Municipal e-government: Comparative index, success factors and models for management and evaluation. In E. Cohen & A. Lev-On (Eds.), *Connected: Politics, technology and society in Israel*. Tel-Aviv, Israel: Israeli Political Science Association Press (Hebrew).
Ravitsch, P. (2005). *Difference between Israeli municipal websites, 2005: To what extent the inventory of online services fulfills the potentials of the medium and meets public expectations?* MA thesis, Bar-Ilan University, Department of political science (Hebrew).
Reddick, C. G., & Norris, D. F. (2013). Social media adoption at the American grass roots: Web 2.0 or 1.5? *Government Information Quarterly, 30*(4), 498–507.
Rotem, E. (2007). *Municipal e-government in Israel: A comparative perspective*. Tel-Aviv, Israel: Hartog School for Governance and Policy (Hebrew).
Scott, J. K. (2006). "E" the people: Do US municipal government web sites support public involvement? *Public Administration Review, 66*(3), 341–353.
Shkabatur, J. (2010). Cities at crossroads: Digital technology and local democracy in America. *Brooklyn Law Review, 76*, 1413–1485.
Strecker, A. (2011). *Flocking to Facebook: How local governments can build citizen engagement*. Doctoral dissertation, University of North Carolina, Chapel Hill, NC.
Tolbert, C. J., & Mossberger, K. (2006). The effects of e-government on trust and confidence in government. *Public Administration Review, 66*(3), 354–369.

Torres, L., Pina, V., & Acerete, B. (2006). E-governance developments in EU cities: Reshaping government's relationship with citizens. *Governance, 12*(9), 277–302.
Williams, C. B., & Gulati, G. J. (2013). Social networks in political campaigns: Facebook and the congressional elections of 2006 and 2008. *New Media & Society, 15*(1), 52–71.
Wohlers, T. E. (2009). The digital world of local government: A comparative analysis of the United States and Germany. *Journal of Information Technology & Politics, 6*(2), 111–126.

Part V
Local Campaigns and Elections

Chapter 14
The Net Effect of Social Media on Election Results: The Case of Twitter in 2014 Turkish Local Elections

Mehmet Zahid Sobaci, Kadir Yasin Eryiğit, and İbrahim Hatipoğlu

Abstract Today, social media offer political actors (i.e., politicians, political parties, NGOs, activists) opportunities for political communication, particularly during election periods. Political parties and candidates use social media tools such as Facebook, Twitter, and YouTube comprehensively to convey their messages to large audiences, persuade their voters, and mobilize their supporters. The use of social media causes changes in the nature of election campaigns and paves the way for a "co-generated campaign." However, studies focusing on the experiences of political actors' use of social media in the campaigns at the subnational level (regional or local) are rare in the relevant literature. In this context, this chapter aims to analyze the net effect of Twitter on the election success of the candidates in the 2014 local elections in Turkey. Findings of our analysis show that when other variables are fixed, candidates with a Twitter account have 4.5 times greater chance of winning the election than those without an account.

14.1 Introduction

Social media have a deep impact on politics today. Social media had an important role to play as a tool for political mobilization in political unrests and social protests in some Middle Eastern countries, such as Tunisia and Egypt. Protests in those countries were called "Facebook Revolution" or "Twitter Revolution" under the title "Arab Spring." Activists used social media extensively during the Occupy Wall Street movement, and social media are an integrative part of the campaigns of

M.Z. Sobaci (✉) • İ. Hatipoğlu
Faculty of Economics and Administrative Sciences, Department of Public Administration, Uludağ University, Gorukle Campus, Nilufer, Bursa, Turkey
e-mail: zsobaci@uludag.edu.tr; ihatipoglu@uludag.edu.tr

K.Y. Eryiğit
Faculty of Economics and Administrative Sciences, Department of Econometrics, Uludağ University, Gorukle Campus, Nilufer, Bursa, Turkey
e-mail: kyeryigit@uludag.edu.tr

M.Z. Sobaci (ed.), *Social Media and Local Governments*, Public Administration and Information Technology 15, DOI 10.1007/978-3-319-17722-9_14

political actors in national and local elections. All of these observations reflect the impact of these new technologies on politics. In other words, as the second-generation Internet, social media have become a crucial part of political processes and changed how politics functions.

Social media tools offer political actors (i.e., politicians, political parties, NGOs, activists) opportunities to organize, mobilize, and connect. Political parties and candidates are now well aware of the opportunities social media create for political communication, particularly during election periods. Political parties and candidates make use of social media tools such as Facebook, Twitter, and YouTube comprehensively to convey their messages to large audiences, persuade their voters, and mobilize their supporters. Moreover, the use of social media causes changes in the nature of election campaigns. Social media help involve the supporters or citizens in the organization, shaping the content of election campaigns and cracking the door open for a "co-generated campaign" instead of candidate-controlled one. In addition, social media tools allow the voters to feel closer to the candidates and have a closer connection with them. In fact, Sweetser and Lariscy (2008), who focused on the 2006 midterm elections in the USA, found that individuals who wrote something on the Facebook wall of a candidate perceived themselves as his or her "friend" and wrote supportive and positive messages.

As the use of social media become in election campaigns more prevalent, scholars from various academic disciplines have focused on this particular subject. Although the literature regarding the impact of social media on election campaigns is expanding, most studies have focused on American presidential and congressional elections. Therefore, studies focusing on the experiences of political actors' use of social media outside the USA have been rare. Furthermore, there is a need for studies focusing on the use of social media in the campaigns of those running for political posts at the subnational level (regional or local) in the relevant literature.

In this context, this chapter aims to analyze the impact of Twitter on the election success of the candidates in the 2014 local elections in Turkey. Within this framework, this chapter contributes to knowledge about the impact of social media on elections. This study is structured in five sections. After the introduction, the second section addresses the relationship between social media and election campaigns and reviews the literature on the use of the Internet and social media tools by politicians in election campaigns. The third section reveals the method, data, and model of the empirical study and presents the findings of the empirical study. The fourth section discusses the findings of the empirical study by comparing the findings of other studies in the relevant literature. The study concludes with suggestions for future studies.

14.2 Background

14.2.1 Social Media and Election Campaigns

Technological developments have been decisive in the evolution of political campaigns. The changes that technological developments have generated in election campaigns are generally grouped into three periods (Norris 2000; Farrell and Webb

2000). In the first phase or during the premodern campaign period, the election campaign is based on face-to-face communication between the candidates and citizens at the local level. Campaign preparation is short-term and sporadic. Mass rallies, doorstep canvassing, posters, and party presses became prominent tools of communication. In the second phase of political campaigns or during the modern period, the campaigns are coordinated at a centralized level by the political leaders. Long-term preparation and tapping into external professional advisors and expert campaign committees characterize modern campaigns. Television as an impersonal channel of communication is the basic political campaign tool in this period. In the postmodern period or in the third phrase, election campaigns have become integrated with information and communication technologies (ICTs), particularly the Internet. There are "permanent campaigns" in the postmodern period. This campaign format emphasizes direct modes of communication (Norris 2000; Farrell and Webb 2000). In this period, election campaigns are considered to take a more business-like approach (Gibson and Römmele 2001). In postmodern campaigns, voters are handled in a more personalized and professional manner. Voters are viewed as consumers and policies as products (Ward and Gibson 2003). Technical experts, media professionals, and campaign departments come to the fore. This particular phase has also been considered as the Americanization of political communication (Negrine and Papathanassopoulos 1996).

The Internet has played an important role in the transition to the third phase of election campaigns. Two theories describe how the Internet has affected the activities of political actors: equalization theory and normalization theory. Equalization theory "perceives campaigning on the Internet to lead to a situation in which electoral competition between different political actors is more equal than when they solely campaign off-line" (Strandberg 2006, p. 11). This theory is based on the fact that although the Internet offers opportunities for all political actors, small and fringe parties that receive either little or no coverage in the traditional media benefit more than others from the opportunities offered by the Internet (Margolis et al. 2003; Ward et al. 2003; Strandberg 2006). Conversely, normalization theory argues that the Internet causes no change in the rivalry among the political actors, and the established political patterns in the real world are replicated on the Web as well (Ward et al. 2003; Strandberg 2006; Margolis et al. 1999).

The Internet has great advantages in comparison to traditional media and can make various types of contributions to the election campaigns of political actors. The Internet offers political actors advantages, including the following (Demertzis et al. 2005; Ward and Gibson 2003; Benoit and Benoit 2000):

1. *Direct contact with voters*: The Internet enables political actors to convey their messages without any mediator or filtering. Therefore, political actors are not concerned about the distortion of their messages.
2. *Creating an ongoing dialogue with voters*: The Internet is more interactive than the traditional media. Internet-based tools allow political actors to seek for the opinions of voters and supporters about services and policies, create online public opinion polls, and obtain instantaneous feedback.

3. *Reaching different voter groups*: The Internet enables the personalization of campaign messages and individual appeals, and it allows the political actors to reach voter groups such as young voters.
4. *Informing and mobilizing voters more effectively*: The Internet-based campaigns are less expensive than other media. Although electronic campaigns have certain costs, the new tools provided by the Internet help the costs of campaign activities for political actors.
5. *Enhanced visibility*: The Internet encourages "self-presentation" and offers political actors the possibility of presenting aspects of themselves. Internet-based tools provide quick and easy management of the images of political actors.
6. *Decentralizing campaigning*: The use of ICTs can counter the trend of centralization of party campaigning evident in the television era.

Although the Internet has been used in election campaigns since the 1990s, the popularity of social media tools has given the election campaigns a new lease on life. In fact, Williams and Gulati (2009a) stated that together with the institutionalization of campaign websites and the standardization of their content, most political campaigns gravitate towards social networking sites in an attempt to differentiate themselves from the others in a manner to encourage participatory democracy and re-energize grassroots political organizing. Today, social media have become the vital medium of election campaigns.

In fact, the purposes of social media tools and the ultimate objective of political campaigns are similar. The ultimate objective of political campaigns is to reach more voters and enable voters to mobilize for a candidate (Slotnick 2009). For instance, the objective of social networking sites is to generate a sense of community among its members (Williams and Gulati 2009a). This similarity has the capacity to explicate the intensive use of social media in election campaigns in recent times.

Social media is based on the Web 2.0 philosophy. User-generated content, interaction, collaboration, and collective intelligence are the basic characteristics of Web 2.0. In this context, instead of Web 1.0-based political campaigns, which depend on the establishing websites by the candidates and publishing the content, the use of social media tools in campaigns brings into question a campaign style in which voters or supporters are more active in terms of shaping and setting the agenda of the campaign. Therefore, this development helps the voters and supporters to perceive themselves as parts of the campaigns. As a matter of fact, Gibson (2010) asserts that social media tools allow for a bottom-up campaign (citizen-campaigning) instead of a top-down one. In these types of campaigns, ordinary or nonofficial member carries out core campaign activities on behalf of the candidate.

In addition to helping the voters and supporters to become involved in the campaigns, the use of social media tools in political campaigns provides several benefits for the candidates. Compared with the traditional media or Web 1.0-based campaigns, the benefits of social media for candidates include more affordable campaigns (Strandberg 2013), more effective volunteer recruitment and fundraising (Karlsen 2013; Gasser and Gerlach 2012; Gueorguieva 2008), interactivity and bypassing intermediaries (Vergeer 2012; Towner and Dulio 2011; Larsson and Moe 2011; Marcinkowski and Metag 2014; Trammell et al. 2006), political mobilization (Towner and Dulio 2011; Westling 2007; Cogburn and Espinoza-Vasquez 2011; Gasser and Gerlach 2012; Ifukor 2010; Davis et al. 2009; Hurme 2009), tailored campaign messages to specific voter groups (Sweetser Trammell 2007; Kushin and Yamamoto 2010; Greyes 2011), bypassing the requirement of active user choices and exposing voters to campaign messages (Strandberg 2013), and viral marketing (Hurme 2009).

In addition to the opportunities offered by social media tools in election campaigns, the tools also raise several challenges for the candidates or campaign staff. The most important of these challenges is the weakening of candidates' and campaign staff's control over the campaign in an attempt to build an image for the candidate and convey the candidates' basic messages to the voters (Gueorguieva 2008; Johnson and Perlmutter 2010). In the age of social media, by posting a gaffe of the candidates or introducing their conflicting opinions about an issue, voters may enable millions of people to talk about this gaffe or a controversial attitude within a few days (Davis et al. 2009). Despite these challenges, political actors are receiving more support from social media for core campaign activities.

14.2.2 Literature Review: Identifying the Gap

Political actors have always been sensitive to the developments caused by ICTs. Political actors' use of ICTs in general and Internet-based tools in specific is not a new phenomenon. ICTs have always introduced some changes to political processes. In fact, Gibson et al. (2008) argued that technology was regarded as a stimulus for change in elections. The close relationship between politicians and the Internet has also attracted the attention of scholars.

Early studies regarding the use of Internet by politicians have focused on the impact of tools such as e-mail and websites on the communication between politicians and citizens (Campbell et al. 1999; Carter 1999; Taylor and Kent 2004). Since the mid-1990s in particular, websites have become the key strategic tool of political campaigns. Therefore, many previous studies have investigated online campaigns and websites as political communication tools during election periods, mainly in the USA and some European countries (*for USA see* Klotz 1997; Dulio et al. 1999; D'Alessio 2000; Williams et al. 2002; Myers 1993; Whillock 1997; Schneider and Foot 2002—*for European countries see* Ward and Gibson 2003; Ward et al. 2006; Lilleker and Malagón 2010; Vaccari 2008a; Newell 2001; Vaccari 2008b; Yannas and Lappas 2004; Demertzis et al. 2005; Lappas et al. 2008; Marcella et al. 2004; Carlson and Djupsund 2001; Gibson and McAllister 2003). These studies have mostly analyzed presidential and congressional elections in the USA or the general elections in some European countries.

With the impact of social media tools in the election victory of Barack Obama in the USA, recent studies have focused on the use of social media in election campaigns (*for USA see* Sweetser Trammell 2007; Williams et al. 2005; Robertson et al. 2010; Williams and Gulati 2009b, c; Sweetser and Lariscy 2008; Gulati and Williams 2011; Williams and Gulati 2012; Gulati and Williams 2013; Gueorguieva 2008; Church 2010; Klotz 2010; Steger et al. 2010; Towner and Dulio 2011; Bimber

2014—*for other countries see* Gibson 2010; Gibson and McAllister 2011; Vesnic-Alujevic 2011; Andersen and Medaglia 2009; Carlson and Strandberg 2008; Larsson and Moe 2011; Larsson 2014; Gilmore 2011; Chen and Smith 2011; Strandberg 2013; Hansen and Kosiara-Pedersen 2014). Similarly, studies related to the use of social media in election campaigns mostly investigate American experiences. Similar to the previous studies, these studies analyzed presidential elections, congressional elections, and the national general elections. Furthermore, these studies have mostly tried to analyze the impact of Facebook, YouTube, and Twitter.

Studies focusing on political actors' use of social media in local election campaigns have been rare. For instance, Criado et al. (2012) focused on the use of Twitter by candidates in the 2011 Spanish local elections. Criado and Martinez-Fuentes (2010) focused on the politicians' practices of blog in the 2007 local elections in Spain and found that few candidates attempted to be ambitious in the use of the innovative relational capacities of blogs. Yannas et al. (2011) argued that the use of Web and Web 2.0 tools had no statistically significant discernible impact on election results in the 2010 Greek local elections. Raynauld and Greenberg (2014) analyzed how and to what extent social networking platforms help shape the dynamics of local electioneering in the 2010 municipal elections in Ottawa, Ontario, Canada. Ozdesim Ikiz et al. (2014) focused on the use of twitter by metropolitan mayor candidates in 2014 local elections in Turkey. Lev-On (2012) analyzed the YouTube presence of candidates in municipal election campaigns in Israel. Segaard and Nielsen (2013) explore the role of the election blogs in the 2011 Norwegian local election campaigns. They found that election blogs are primarily used by those who are politically active in other arenas as well and that most communication consists of one-way information dissemination. In Norway, Skogerbø and Krumsvik (2014) seek to map and understand the intermedial agenda setting between social media and traditional news media by analyzing data from both local journalism and the social media activity of local politicians during the 2011 Norwegian local election campaigns.

Given the rarity of studies focusing on the use of social media in local elections, the need is great for studies focusing on the use of social media by political actors, particularly in local elections. Thus, this study aims to analyze whether the use of Twitter affected the election win of mayor candidates in the 2014 local elections in Turkey.

14.3 An Empirical Study: Net Effect?

14.3.1 Method

This study aims to analyze whether the fact that provincial municipality mayor candidates of the ruling party and main opposition party in the 2014 local elections were Twitter users affected the election outcomes. For this purpose, Logit model estimation was conducted, including other factors that potentially influenced election outcomes. The Logit model is an approach frequently used in the estimation of situations with binary results, such as present or absent or winning or losing, as in the topic of our study. This model requires the validity of logistic distribution instead of the hypothesis that the errors have a normal distribution for the estimator of ordinary least squares (OLS). However, in the logistic distribution, there occurs a need for an algebraic transformation over the usual linear regression model of

$$y = X\beta. \tag{14.1}$$

Here y represents the dependent variable vector, X the explanatory variables matrix, and β a vector of regression coefficients.

Principally, in this study, in the cases of y_i:

$$y_i = \begin{cases} 1 \text{ if the candidate } i \text{ has won the election} \\ 0 \text{ otherwise.} \end{cases} \tag{14.2}$$

where a dependent variable with two values is presumed. In other words, y_i is the realizations of the dependent variable y that takes the values of "1" and "0" for the probability of winning the election π_i and the probability of losing the election $(1 - \pi_i)$. Based on the hypothesis that π_i as the probability of winning the election depends on the observable common change of x_i, the following basic definition of

$$\pi_i = x_i'\beta \tag{14.3}$$

can be made. Equation (14.3) is known as the *linear possibility model*. Based on this, for the Logit model, the definition of

$$\begin{aligned} &\pi_i = \exp\{x_i'\beta\} / 1 + \exp\{x_i'\beta\} \\ &\Rightarrow \pi_i / 1 - \pi_i = \exp\{x_i'\beta\} \\ &\Rightarrow \ln(\pi_i / 1 - \pi_i) = x_i'\beta \end{aligned} \tag{14.4}$$

can be made. Here, $\pi_i / (1 - \pi_i)$ is the odds ratio representing the candidate's probability of winning the election over the probability of losing the election.

Generally speaking, because the error term in the Logit model has a heteroskedastic nature, the weighted least squares (WLS) estimation of (14.4) is a more correct approach. In this case, the estimator variance is calculated in the form of

$$\text{var}\left(\beta\right) = (X'WX)^{-1} \tag{14.5}$$

as heteroskedasticity robust. Here W is the weights matrix.

Due to this complicated algebraic statement, the Logit model cannot easily interpret the estimations. Therefore, the estimated coefficients should be converted into a more easily estimated *odds ratio* by using an exponential function. The *odds ratios* are equal to $\exp\left(\breve{\beta}\right)$. For instance, if the regression slope parameter has been estimated to be 0.7, the odds ratio is calculated as approximately 2.01. Thus, the probability of the dependent variable "1" increasing one unit against the value of explanatory variable has increased two times. In addition, for the goodness-of-fit of the Logit model to be implemented, the Hosmer and Lemeshov (HL) (1989) test is used.

14.3.2 Data and Model

Consistent with this study's purpose, the provincial municipality mayor candidates of the ruling party (Justice and Development Party—JDP) and main opposition party (Republican People's Party—RPP) for the 2014 local elections in Turkey were identified. Then, personal characteristics of the candidates were collected, such as age, gender, education level, and whether they had Twitter accounts. Moreover, the previous ruling party and winning party in 2014 elections were specified for each municipality. Political party and candidates' personal websites were analyzed to collect the personal information of mayoral candidates. The Google search engine was also used. Because the political parties introduced their candidates on their own websites during the election period, most of the personal information collected about the candidates was obtained from political party websites.

The following variables were used to determine the probability that JDP and RPP mayor candidates of provincial municipalities would win the 2014 elections in Turkey:

y_i: The dependent variable taking the value of "1" if the *i*th candidate won the election and the value of "0" if not.

x_i^{twt}: The explanatory variable taking the value of "1" if the *i*th candidate has a Twitter account and the value of "0" if not.

x_i^{age}: The age of the *i*th candidate.

x_i^{gen}: The explanatory variable taking the value of "1" if the *i*th candidate is male and the value of "0" if not.

x_i^{edu}: The explanatory variable taking the value of "1" if the education level of the *i*th candidate is secondary school, "2" if it is higher education, and "3" if it is post-graduate.

x_i^{spp}: The explanatory variable taking the value of "1" if the previous mayor is from the same political party as the *i*th mayor candidate and the value of "0" if not.

Based on these variables, the Logit model to be estimated together with the expectations is represented as:

$$y_i = \beta_0 + \overset{(+)}{\beta_1} x_i^{\text{twt}} + \overset{(+)}{\beta_2} x_i^{\text{age}} + \overset{(+)}{\beta_3} x_i^{\text{gen}} + \overset{(+)}{\beta_4} x_i^{\text{edu}} + \overset{(+)}{\beta_5} x_i^{\text{spp}} + u_i. \tag{14.6}$$

Table 14.1 Logit model estimation results

Dependent variable: election result	Coefficients	z	$p>\|z\|$	95 % Confidence intervals		Odds ratios
Constant	−5.03	−3.85	0.00	−7.59	−2.47	–
x_i^{twt}	1.51	2.86	0.00	0.47	2.55	4.53
x_i^{edu}	0.88	2.02	0.04	0.03	1.74	2.42
x_i^{spp}	1.63	7.08	0.00	1.18	2.08	5.11
N	162					
Likelihood ratio test	88.47 (0.00)					
Pseudo R^2	0.43					
HL test	11.49 (0.18)					

Notes:
1. The figures within the parentheses are *the p-values* representing the levels of marginal significance. Moreover, heteroskedasticity robust standard errors were used for the model estimation
2. Since they were estimated as statistically insignificant age and gender were excluded from the analysis

Here, β_i symbolizes the coefficient vector $(i = 0,1,2,3,4,5)$ and u_i symbolizes the error term.

14.3.3 Findings

The results of Logit model estimations specified in (14.6) are presented and evaluated in this part of the study. Table 14.1 illustrates the results of Logit model estimation for (14.6).

Table 14.1 indicates that the parameter estimation (1.51) of the variable illustrating whether the candidate has a Twitter account is individually significant ($p \leq 0.05$) and positive, in consistent with expectations. The *odds ratio* (4.53) for the same variable signifies that the probability of a candidate with a Twitter account to win the election is approximately 4.5 times higher than for candidates without Twitter accounts. In the model, the parameter estimation (0.88) related to the level of education of the candidate is individually significant ($p \leq 0.05$) and has a positive value compatible with expectations. Similarly, the *odds ratio* (2.42) for the education level variable means that the probability of a candidate winning the election increases 2.5 times if the candidate's education level increases one unit. Finally, the parameter estimation (1.63) of the variable illustrating whether the previous mayor is from the same political party as the current candidate is individually significant ($p \leq 0.05$) and has a positive sign compatible with expectations. The *odds ratio* (5.11) of this variable implies that candidates from the same political party as the prior mayor were approximately 5 times more likely to be elected.

In addition to the individual significance of parameter estimations of variables, the model is generally significant, given the likelihood ratio test. On the other hand, the Pseudo R^2 value indicates that the explanatory power of the model is 43 %. The HL goodness-of-fit test for estimation of the Logit model does not reject the null hypothesis that the goodness-of-fit of the model is high. Therefore, there is not any problem in terms of goodness-of-fit.

14.4 Discussion

Few previous studies have revealed findings regarding the direct impact of social media on election results. Previous research focuses on the impact of social media on basic campaign activities and the nature of election campaigns; how and to what extent the candidates use social media in election campaigns and how they adopt them, the analysis of content generated by social media tools (such as tweets, posts, hashtags, videos, and speeches of leaders) and network analysis, determining different types of users, analyzing the topics and themes circulating in the social media during the election campaigns and predicting the election results via the social media tools. Therefore, comparing our results with the findings of other studies is difficult.

Due to the dynamism social media provide election campaigns and their potential benefits to core campaign activities, by taking Barack Obama's election campaign as an example, it is indirectly demonstrated that social media have an important impact on election success or winning the election. However, few studies have analyzed the net effect of social media on the election results. The few existing studies demonstrate that the net effect of social media on election results is contentious. For instance, Gibson and McAllister (2011), who analyzed the net effect of web campaigning on the votes candidates received, found that web campaigning had a significant influence on vote totals. In particular, campaigning via personal websites was most clearly associated with increased electoral success. Moreover, although they had a positive effect on the vote, Web 2.0 campaigns did not generate significantly higher rates of support. Hansen and Kosiara-Pedersen (2014), who focused on the cyber-campaigning of candidates in 2011 Danish general elections, determined an online score for each candidate and argued that the online scores of candidates have an effect on the interparty competition for personal votes but have no significant effect when controlling for other relevant variables. Yannas et al. (2011) found that online presence did not significantly affect local elections in Greece in 2010, although the winning candidates used Web 1.0 and 2.0 tools. Gilmore (2011) found that social networking sites can directly affect election results in the case of the 2010 Brazilian elections. Koc-Michalska et al. (2014, p. 197) found that "having an online presence is consistently a strong predictor of gaining a greater share of votes."

Previous studies indicate that the use of social media tools in election campaigns generally has a positive impact on election victories. The study of Yannas et al.

(2011) alone argues that the use of social media tools by the candidates does not have an important impact on election results. When other variables are fixed, the findings of our study (i.e., that candidates with a Twitter account have 4.5 times greater chance of winning the election than those without an account) are consistent with the findings of other studies.

Conclusion

Social media deeply influence the understanding of political communication and the nature of election campaigns. Despite the intrinsic risks, these media bring benefits to candidates in terms of core election campaign activities. In the literature about social media in politics, many studies have focused on the impact of social media on election campaigns. However, few studies have focused on the direct impact of the candidates' use of social media in election campaigns on election results. In this context, this chapter contributes to knowledge about local elections and social media by focusing on the direct effect of social media use on local election outcomes in Turkey in 2014.

This study also has some limitations. Ultimately, when the other variables were constant, this study only analyzed whether the candidates' ownership of a Twitter account had any impact on the election results. How actively the candidates used their Twitter accounts was not analyzed. Within the framework of Web 2.0 campaigns, this study only focused on Twitter as a social media tool and other online campaign tools were not taken into consideration. This study also excluded the traditional (off-line) campaign activities that affect election results.

Therefore, more studies are needed focusing on how social media affect election results. Future studies may analyze the effect of candidates' use of social media on election results in countries with different national election systems from a comparative perspective. Moreover, scholars in the future may focus on the impact of both off-line and social media-based online campaigns on election results.

References

Andersen, K. N., & Medaglia, R. (2009). The use of Facebook in national election campaigns: Politics as usual? In A. Macintosh & E. Tambouris (Eds.), *Electronic participation (Lecture Notes in Computer Science 5694)* (pp. 101–111). Berlin, Germany: Springer.

Benoit, W. L., & Benoit, P. J. (2000). *The virtual campaign: Presidential primary websites in campaign 2000*. Retrieved from http://www.roguecom.com/roguescholar/benoit.html

Bimber, B. (2014). Digital media in the Obama campaigns of 2008 and 2012: Adaptation to the personalized political communication environment. *Journal of Information Technology & Politics, 11*(2), 130–150.

Campbell, A., Harrop, A., & Thompson, B. (1999). Towards to virtual parliaments—What computers can do for MPs. *Parliamentary Affairs, 52*, 387–403.
Carlson, T., & Djupsund, G. (2001). Old wine in new bottles? The 1999 Finnish election campaign on the internet. *Harvard International Journal of Press/Politics, 6*(1), 68–87.
Carlson, T., & Strandberg, K. (2008). Riding the Web 2.0 wave: Candidates on YouTube in the 2007 Finnish national elections. *Journal of Information Technology & Politics, 5*(2), 159–174.
Carter, M. (1999). Speaking up in the internet age: Use and value of constituent e-mail and congressional web-sites. *Parliamentary Affairs, 52*(3), 464–479.
Chen, P. J., & Smith, P. J. (2011). Digital media in the 2008 Canadian election. *Journal of Information Technology & Politics, 8*(4), 399–417.
Church, S. H. (2010). YouTube politics: You choose and leadership rhetoric during the 2008 election. *Journal of Information Technology & Politics, 7*(2), 124–142.
Cogburn, D., & Espinoza-Vasquez, F. (2011). From networked nominee to networked nation: Examining the impact of Web 2.0 and social media on political participation and civic engagement in the 2008 Obama campaign. *Journal of Political Marketing, 10*, 189–213.
Criado, J. I., & Martinez-Fuentes, G. (2010). Mayors' usage of blogs in local election campaign: The Spanish case study. *International Journal of Electronic Governance, 3*(4), 395–413.
Criado, I. J., Martinez-Fuentes, G., & Silvan, A. (2012). Social media for political campaigning: The use of twitter by Spanish mayors in 2011 local elections. In C. G. Reddick & S. K. Aikins (Eds.), *Web 2.0 technologies and democratic governance* (pp. 219–232). New York: Springer.
D'Alessio, D. (2000). Adoption of the World Wide Web by American political candidates 1996–1998. *Journal of Broadcasting & Electronic Media, 44*(4), 556–568.
Davis, R., Baumgartner, J. C., Francia, P. L., & Morris, J. S. (2009). The internet in U.S. election campaigns. In A. Chadwick & P. N. Howard (Eds.), *Routledge handbook of internet politics* (pp. 13–24). New York: Routledge.
Demertzis, N., Diamantaki, K., Gazi, A., & Sartzetakis, N. (2005). Greek political marketing online: An analysis of parliament members' web sites. *Journal of Political Marketing, 4*(1), 51–74.
Dulio, D. A., Goff, D. L., & Thurber, J. A. (1999). Untangled web: Internet use during the 1998 election. *Political Science and Politics, 32*(1), 53–59.
Farrell, D. M., & Webb, P. (2000). Political parties as campaign organizations. In R. J. Dalton & M. P. Wattenberg (Eds.), *Parties without partisans: Political change in advanced industrial democracies* (pp. 102–128). Oxford, England: Oxford University Press.
Gasser, U., & Gerlach, J. (2012). E-campaigns in old Europe: Observations from Germany, Austria, and Switzerland. In R. L. Fox & J. M. Ramos (Eds.), *iPolitics: Citizens, elections, and governing in the new media era* (pp. 125–150). Cambridge, England: Cambridge University Press.
Gibson, R. (2010). *Open source campaigning? UK party organisations and the use of the new media in the 2010 general election*. Paper prepared for the Annual Meeting of the American Political Science Association, Washington, DC.
Gibson, R., Lusoli, W., & Ward, S. (2008). Nationalizing and normalizing the local? A comparative analysis of online candidate campaigning in Australia and Britain. *Journal of Information Technology & Politics, 4*(4), 15–30.
Gibson, R., & McAllister, I. (2003). *Cyber campaigning and the vote: Online communication in the 2001 Australian election*. Paper prepared for the Annual Conference of the 2003 American Political Science Association, Philadelphia, PA.
Gibson, R., & McAllister, I. (2011). *A net again? Web 2.0 in the Australian 2010 election*. Paper presented at the Annual Conference of the American Political Science Association, 1–4 September 2011, Seattle, WA.
Gibson, R., & Römmele, A. (2001). Changing campaign communications: A party-centered theory of professionalized campaigning. *Harvard International Journal of Press/Politics, 6*(4), 31–43.
Gilmore, J. (2011). Ditching the pack: Digital media in the 2010 Brazilian congressional campaigns. *New Media & Society, 14*(4), 617–633.

Greyes, N. (2011). The untapped potential of social media: A primer for savvy campaigners. *Campaigns and Elections, 300*, 45–47.

Gueorguieva, V. (2008). Voters, MySpace, and YouTube: The impact of alternative communication channels on the 2006 election cycle and beyond. *Social Science Computer Review, 26*, 288–300.

Gulati, G. J., & Williams, C. B. (2011). *Social media in the 2010 congressional elections*. Paper presented at the Annual Meetings of the Midwest Political Science Association, Chicago, IL.

Gulati, G. J., & Williams, C. B. (2013). Social media and campaign 2012: Developments and trends for Facebook adoption. *Social Science Computer Review, 31*(5), 577–588.

Hansen, K. M., & Kosiara-Pedersen, K. (2014). Cyber-campaigning in Denmark: Application and effects of candidate campaigning. *Journal of Information Technology & Politics, 11*(2), 206–219.

Hurme, T. (2009). Online campaign strategy, Web 2.0 tools, and voter preference in the 2008 U.S. presidential election. *CEU Political Science Journal, 4*(4), 566–606.

Ifukor, P. (2010). Elections or selections? Blogging and Twittering the Nigerian 2007 general elections. *Bulletin of Science, Technology & Society, 30*(6), 398–414.

Johnson, T., & Perlmutter, D. (2010). Introduction: The Facebook election. *Mass Communications & Society, 13*, 554–559.

Karlsen, R. (2013). Obama's online success and European party organizations: Adoption and adaptation of U.S. online practices in the Norwegian Labor Party. *Journal of Information Technology & Politics, 10*(2), 158–170.

Klotz, R. (1997). Positive spin: Senate campaigning on the web. *Political Science and Politics, 30*(3), 482–486.

Klotz, R. J. (2010). The sidetracked 2008 YouTube Senate campaign. *Journal of Information Technology & Politics, 7*(2), 110–123.

Koc-Michalska, K., Lilleker, D. G., Surowiec, P., & Baranowski, P. (2014). Poland's 2011 online election campaign: New tools, new professionalism, new ways to win votes. *Journal of Information Technology & Politics, 11*(2), 186–205.

Kushin, M., & Yamamoto, M. (2010). Did social media really matter? College students' use of online media and political decision making in the 2008 election. *Mass Communication & Society, 13*, 608–630.

Lappas, G., Chatzopoulos, S., & Yannas, P. (2008). Parliamentary candidates running on the web for the 2004 Greek national elections. *Journal of Political Marketing, 7*(3–4), 256–277.

Larsson, A. O. (2014). Online, all the time? A quantitative assessment of the permanent campaign on Facebook. *New Media & Society*, 1–19. DOI: 10.1177/1461444814538798

Larsson, A. O., & Moe, H. (2011). Studying political microblogging: Twitter users in the 2010 Swedish election campaign. *New Media & Society, 14*(5), 729–747.

Lev-On, A. (2012). YouTube usage in low-visibility political campaigns. *Journal of Information Technology and Politics, 9*(2), 205–216.

Lilleker, D. G., & Malagón, C. (2010). Levels of interactivity in the 2007 French presidential candidates' websites. *European Journal of Communication, 25*(1), 25–42.

Marcella, R., Baxter, G., & Smith, S. (2004). The use of the internet by candidates as part of their campaign for election to the Scottish Parliament in 2003. *Journal of Systemics, Cybernetics and Informatics, 2*(2), 54–59.

Marcinkowski, F., & Metag, J. (2014). Why do candidates use online media in constituency campaigning? An application of the theory of planned behavior. *Journal of Information Technology & Politics, 11*(2), 151–168.

Margolis, M., Resnick, D., & Levy, J. (2003). Major parties dominate, minor parties struggle: US elections and the Internet. In R. Gibson, P. Dixon, & S. Ward (Eds.), *Political parties and internet: Net gain?* (pp. 53–69). New York: Routledge.

Margolis, M., Resnick, D., & Wolfe, J. D. (1999). Party competition on the internet in the United States and Britain. *Harvard International Journal of Press/Politics, 4*, 24–47.

Myers, D. (1993). New technology and the 1992 Clinton presidential campaign. *American Behavioral Scientist, 37*(2), 181–187.

Negrine, R., & Papathanassopoulos, S. (1996). The Americanization of political communication: A critique. *International Journal of Press/Politics, 1*(2), 45–62.
Newell, J. L. (2001). Italian political parties on the web. *Harvard International Journal of Press/Politics, 6*(4), 60–87.
Norris, P. (2000). *A virtuous circle: Political communications in postindustrial societies*. Cambridge, England: Cambridge University Press.
Ozdesim Ikiz, O., Sobaci, M. Z., Yavuz, N., & Karkin, N. (2014). *Political use of Twitter: The case of metropolitan mayor candidates in 2014 local elections in Turkey*. ICEGOV 2014, 27–30 October, Guimaraes, Portugal.
Raynauld, V., & Greenberg, J. (2014). Tweet, click, vote: Twitter and the 2010 Ottawa municipal election. *Journal of Information Technology & Politics, 11*(4), 412–434.
Robertson, S. P., Vatrapu, R. K., & Medina, R. (2010). Off the wall political discourse: Facebook use in the 2008 U.S. presidential election. *Information Polity, 15*(1), 11–31.
Schneider, S. M., & Foot, K. A. (2002). Online structure for political action: Exploring presidential campaign web sites from the 2000 American election. *Javnost—The Public, 9*(2), 43–60.
Segaard, S. B., & Nielsen, J. A. (2013). Local election blogs: Networking among the political elite. *Information Polity, 18*(4), 299–313.
Skogerbø, E., & Krumsvik, A. H. (2014). Newspapers, Facebook and Twitter: Intermedial agenda setting in local election campaigns. *Journalism Practice*, 1–17.
Slotnick, A. (2009). "Friend" the president: Facebook and the 2008 presidential election. In C. Panogopoulos (Ed.), *Politicking online: The transformation of election campaign communications* (pp. 249–271). New Brunswick, NJ: Rutgers University Press.
Steger, W., Williams, C., & Andolina, M. (2010). *Political use of social networks in 2008*. Paper prepared for the Annual Meeting of the American Political Science Association. 2–5 September, 2010, Washington DC.
Strandberg, K. (2006). *Parties, candidates and citizens on-line: Studies of politics on the internet*. Abo, Finland: Abo Akademi University Press.
Strandberg, K. (2013). A social media revolution or just a case of history repeating itself? The use of social media in the 2011 Finnish parliamentary elections. *New Media & Society, 15*(8), 1329–1347.
Sweetser Trammell, K. D. (2007). Candidate campaign blogs: Directly reaching out to the youth vote. *American Behavioral Scientist, 50*(9), 1255–1263.
Sweetser, K. D., & Lariscy, R. W. (2008). Candidates make good friends: An analysis of candidates' uses of Facebook. *International Journal of Strategic Communication, 2*(3), 175–198.
Taylor, M., & Kent, M. L. (2004). Congressional web sites and their potential for public dialogue. *Atlantic Journal of Communication, 12*, 59–76.
Towner, T. L., & Dulio, D. A. (2011). An experiment of campaign effects during the YouTube election. *New Media & Society, 13*(4), 626–644.
Trammell, K. D., Williams, A. P., Postelnicu, M., & Landreville, K. D. (2006). Evolution of online campaigning: Increasing interactivity in candidate web sites and blogs through text and technical features. *Mass Communication & Society, 9*(1), 21–44.
Vaccari, C. (2008a). Surfing to the Elysee: The internet in the 2007 French elections. *French Politics, 6*(1), 1–22.
Vaccari, C. (2008b). Research note: Italian parties' websites in the 2006 elections. *European Journal of Communication, 23*(1), 69–77.
Vergeer, M. (2012). Politics, elections and online campaigning: Past, present…and a peek into the future. *New Media & Society, 15*(1), 9–17.
Vesnic-Alujevic, L. (2011). Communicating with voters by blogs? Campaigning for the 2009 European Parliament elections. *Discourse & Communication, 5*(4), 413–428.
Ward, S., & Gibson, R. (2003). On-line and on message? Candidate websites in the 2001 general election. *British Journal of Politics and International Relations, 5*(2), 188–205.
Ward, S., Gibson, R., & Lusoli, W. (2006). *The same the world over? Candidate campaigning online in the UK and Australia*. Paper presented at the Elections, Parties and Opinion Polls Conference, 7–9 September 2012, Nottingham.

Ward, S., Gibson, R., & Nixon, P. (2003). Parties and the internet: An overview. In R. Gibson, P. Dixon, & S. Ward (Eds.), *Political parties and Internet: Net gain?* (pp. 11–38). New York: Routledge.

Westling, M. (2007). *Expanding the public sphere: The impact of Facebook on political communication.* Retrieved from http://guylifshitznotes.googlecode.com/svn/trunk/%20guylifshitznotes/2010%20Winter/Poli/Term%20Paper/References/Random/Facebook%20politics.pdf

Whillock, R. K. (1997). Cyber-politics: The online strategies of "96". *American Behavioral Scientist, 40*(8), 1208–1225.

Williams, C. B., Aylesworth, A., & Chapman, K. J. (2002). The 2000 e-campaign for U.S. Senate. *Journal of Political Marketing, 1*(4), 39–63.

Williams, C. B., & Gulati, G. J. J. (2009a). The political impact of Facebook: Evidence from the 2006 elections and the 2008 nomination contest. In C. Panogopoulos (Ed.), *Politicking online: The transformation of election campaign communications* (pp. 272–291). New Brunswick, NJ: Rutgers University Press.

Williams, C. B., & Gulati, G. J. J. (2009b). *Facebook and YouTube grow up: An empirical assessment of its role in the 2008 congressional elections.* Paper presented at the 2009 Annual Meeting of the Midwest Political Science Association, April 2–5, 2009, Chicago, IL.

Williams, C. B., & Gulati, G. J. J. (2009c). *Social networks in political campaigns: Facebook and congressional elections 2006, 2008.* Paper presented at the 2009 Annual Meeting of the American Political Association, September 3–6, 2009, Toronto.

Williams, C. B., & Gulati, G. J. J. (2012). Social networks in political campaigns: Facebook and the congressional elections of 2006 and 2008. *New Media & Society, 15*(1), 52–71.

Williams, A. P., Trammell, K. D., Postelnicu, M., Landreville, K. D., & Martin, J. D. (2005). Blogging and hyperlinking: Use of the web to enhance viability during the 2004 US campaign. *Journalism Studies, 6*, 177–186.

Yannas, P., Kleftodimos, A., & Lappas, G. (2011). Online political marketing in 2010 Greek local elections: The shift from web to web 2.0 campaigns. In G. Panigyrakis, P. Theodoridis, & A. Panopoulos (Eds.), *Proceeding of the 16th International Conference on Corporate and Marketing Communications* (pp. 38–50), Athens.

Yannas, P., & Lappas, G. (2004). E-Campaign in Greek elections: 2000–2004. *WSEAS Transactions in Information Science and Applications, 5*(1), 1332–1337.

Chapter 15
Social Media Indicator and Local Elections in the Netherlands: Towards a Framework for Evaluating the Influence of Twitter, YouTube, and Facebook

Robin Effing, Jos van Hillegersberg, and Theo Huibers

Abstract Social media has become a popular tool in the political landscape. As a result, it is of increased importance to evaluate social media campaigns of politicians. However, there is currently little knowledge how to measure and evaluate the influence of social media in political campaigns, especially at the local scale. This chapter is a step further towards the development of a theoretical framework and an algorithm that contributes to more reliable impact measurement of social media campaigns by politicians. The Social Media Indicator-2 framework and a related scoring algorithm are introduced to evaluate the influence of individual political candidates via social media on their social environment. The framework is tested by applying it in an empirical pilot study based on the local 2014 municipal elections in the Netherlands. We collected data for the political candidates and their parties in a pre-defined period and were able to relate scores to voting outcome. Positive correlations were revealed between social media contribution scores of politicians and their preference votes within the province of Overijssel in the Netherlands.

15.1 Introduction

In recent years, social media has become a key part of the web landscape. In 2014, Facebook has more than one billion active users. The group of active users on the micro-blogging service Twitter has increased to more than 250 million people. More than three-quarters of those who had access to the internet were using social media

R. Effing (✉)
Saxion University of Applied Sciences, P.O. Box 70000, 7500 KB, Enschede, The Netherlands
e-mail: r.effing@saxion.nl

J. van Hillegersberg • T. Huibers
University of Twente, P.O. Box 217, 7500, Enschede, The Netherlands
e-mail: j.vanhillegersberg@utwente.nl; t.w.c.huibers@utwente.nl

M.Z. Sobaci (ed.), *Social Media and Local Governments*, Public Administration and Information Technology 15, DOI 10.1007/978-3-319-17722-9_15

(Nielsen 2012; Van der Veer and Boekkee 2014). In most areas of the world, we have seen people adopting social media (Goode 2013). Social media channels such as Facebook, YouTube, Blogs, Instagram, LinkedIn and Twitter are, at the time of writing, dominating the web landscape (Lipsman et al. 2014). The use of social media is now predominantly taking place via mobile platforms such as smartphones and tablets according to Comscore (Lipsman et al. 2014). People and politicians can use these social media channels to produce and share their own so-called User Generated Content (Kaplan and Haenlein 2010). This underpins the idea that the web has continued to grow and evolve over the years towards a platform that fulfils the need of people to be socially connected with each other. This provides politicians with a unique public sphere to reach out to citizens. While there is a plethora of social media channels available, there is currently little knowledge how to measure the influence of social media within political campaign and elections, especially at the local scale. The role and impact of social media channels such as Facebook, Twitter, and YouTube at the local government are not well understood. In cases of Barack Obama and Ségolène Royal, it seemed that social media was a key success factor for electoral success (Montero 2009; Ren and Meister 2010), while in other political cases the electoral value was questioned (Jungherr 2012; Ren and Meister 2010). Furthermore, politicians easily lose interest in using social media after the Election Day. For example in Italy, there was a drastic decrease in social media use by politicians after the elections. Mario Monti, the ex prime minister, tweeted 273 times in campaign time and only three times in the following period (Di Fraia and Missaglia 2014). Others even completely disappeared from social media after the day of elections.

Yet online campaigning is not a complete replacement for the offline activities: "Linking the online community from myobama.com with offline actions such as making phone calls and organizing events, the campaign harnessed the full potential and user initiative of the online community. It made volunteer participation in the campaign easy—people could participate from their homes; they could participate with nothing but their mobile phones." (Ren and Meister 2010:18). Some argue that social media does not lead to a revolution of political systems (D'heer and Verdegem 2014; Deželan et al. 2014). Not all political social media examples as described in literature are equally successful. For example, the YouTube attempt by Prime Minister Gordon Brown in the United Kingdom in April 2009 to address the expenses controversy was disastrous. It resulted in negative sentiments and it "served as a warning to other leaders that these tools must be handled with care" (Ren and Meister 2010:13). In Turkish elections, for example, it became clear that "social media practices of Turkish political parties and leaders are unilateral and do not support interaction." (Bayraktutan et al. 2014:198). Consequently, local politicians have to be careful spending too much time on social media because generally they have little time for their political tasks and traditionally rely on personal forms of communication (Effing et al. 2013; Rustad and Sæbø 2013). In the end it seems that "the road from the 'likes' on Facebook to the ballot boxes appears to be more complicated and a way less predictable than what online activists or marketing enthusiasts might assume" (Štětka et al. 2014:242).

To our knowledge, effective frameworks and standards for measuring and comparing the influence of politicians via social media are currently lacking. In addition, more attention should be paid to the effects of social media at a local scale. This chapter is a step towards the development of a theoretical framework and an algorithm that contributes to more reliable impact measurement of social media campaigns by politicians. In order to maximize the impact of time and effort spent on social media, members of political parties could benefit from understanding the effects of these tools on their work and political campaigns. This research focuses on the most local form of the political system, the municipal level. Municipalities and their councils are relatively close to their citizens in comparison to national parliaments. Yet politicians within such local political communities know little about the effects of their social media campaigns in this local setting. Local social media campaigns are very much different from national campaigns and less media-driven. Local concerns should be an explicit part of the social media strategy in order for it to be effective (Berthon et al. 2012; Bottles and Sherlock 2011).

Studies have shown that there is a potential relationship between social media use of national political candidates on the one hand and the voting outcome on the other hand (Effing et al. 2011; Spierings and Jacobs 2012). However, most research carried out so far used very simple metrics to measure the extent to which politicians use social media. As a result, there is still a lack of understanding of the exact impact of social media, especially in the local political context. To address this, the main question of this study is:

How to best measure and compare social media influence levels of local political candidates during elections?

The aim of this chapter is to test a theoretical framework and a related scoring algorithm for evaluating the influence of individual candidates via social media on their social environment. A theoretical framework could help to develop a more comprehensive view on the use of social media by politicians and to make use levels comparable to each other. A scoring algorithm is necessary to obtain a feasible method for indicating the impact of someone on social media. Both a theoretical framework and a scoring algorithm are developed and tested by applying these in an empirical pilot study based on the local 2014 municipal elections in the Netherlands.

The remainder of this chapter is structured as follows. First, the method section will follow. It includes the proposed framework, its theoretical backgrounds, and the scoring algorithm. Second, the results of an empirical pilot study of the 2014 local elections in the Netherlands will be presented as a test case to validate the framework and its scoring algorithm. Third, the conclusion is presented. The final section presents the discussion and observed limitations.

15.2 Method and Introducing the Theoretical Framework

To address the research question, it is necessary to develop a theoretical framework for measuring and comparing social media influence levels of politicians. When developing such a framework, it is of importance to obtain a theoretical background.

After this theoretical background, the framework will be presented including its scoring instructions.

One of the key characteristics of social media channels is personal participation (Bonsón et al. 2012; Kaplan and Haenlein 2010). Since political campaigns nowadays tend to shift towards more personal campaigns, it is important to have instruments to assess personal influence levels via social media. The theoretical background partly draws upon theories from the field of e-participation. While existing frameworks (e.g. Participation Ladders in Grönlund 2009; Medaglia 2007; Sommer and Cullen 2009) to evaluate social media influence and participation are too high level, they need to be further developed for specific evaluation of social media practices (Dylko and McCluskey 2012; Sponder 2012; Stieglitz and Dang-Xuan 2012). Others who have investigated use and impact levels of social media have focused on single social media channels, like Twitter, or have used abstract indicators (e.g. Jungherr 2012). Social media is primarily about developing and maintaining personal relationships through computer-mediated communication. Therefore, we argue that the influence of a politician depends on the size his or her network of online relationships. Online followers and friends are indicators for influence (e.g. The theory of Three Degrees of Influence of Christakis and Fowler 2009). Anyone who follows someone is in some way acknowledging, if not directly influenced, the willingness to be reached and thereby the possibility of being influenced (Sponder 2012).

This section develops the revised Social Media Indicator 2 (SMI2) as an instrument used to address the construct of Social Media Use. The SMI2 is a revised version of and evolution of the first version of the SMI, as presented and employed in earlier studies (Effing et al. 2011, 2013; Withaar et al. 2013). Limitations were recognized and addressed in the new version. The SMI2 aims to contribute to the measurement and comparison of the use of social media by politicians.

The SMI2 draws upon the theoretical backgrounds of the Macintosh participation ladder (Grönlund 2009; Macintosh and Smith 2002; Medaglia 2007; Sommer and Cullen 2009) and the ROI model described by Hoffman and Fodor (2010). The theory of Macintosh consists of a hierarchy in electronic participation levels. These steps on the e-participation ladder are e-Enabling, e-Engaging, and e-Empowering (Grönlund 2009; Medaglia 2007; Sommer and Cullen 2009). Ann Macintosh created a three-step participation ladder, which is useful in describing the participation levels of the social media phenomenon at a high-level. The model from Macintosh was considered to be most suitable for social media. The participatory forms of communication related to social media fit well with the steps given in the ladder. Furthermore, the ladder's boundaries are better defined than in other theories. The first step on this ladder is e-Enabling. In this step, party members provide access and information to citizens. The second step is e-Engaging. During this stage, party members give opportunities to citizens to interact with them and start a dialogue. Citizens are frequently consulted on certain projects, decisions or activities, for instance through discussion forums and polls. The third step is e-Empowering. This step is about members working together with citizens, empowering the citizens with responsibilities, tasks, and opportunities to collaborate with the party's community. This theory is not specifically designed for social media, but it is a general theory helpful in understanding the various levels within electronic participation. The first two steps of the ladder are integrated in the SMI2 framework. The Contribution aspect is linked to the stage of e-Enabling. The Engagement aspect is linked to the step of e-Enabling. The highest step on the ladder of e-Empowering, however, cannot easily be captured by these quantitative metrics, but require additional content analysis.

In recent years, influence measurement of the individual users of social media has gained importance. Yet most of the available tools are based on the principle of monitoring keywords instead of monitoring individual influence levels. While keyword-based tools are highly relevant for understanding the impact of names of brands or organizations, they cannot help to understand the specific use levels of individual politicians. Stieglitz and Dang-Xuan (2012) have created a framework for social media analytics for political purposes, and among other categories, they distinguish between keyword-based tools and actor-based tools. An example of an existing actor-based tool is Klout.com. Klout, however, has been subject to criticism, since their method of calculation lacks transparency and is arguably biased (Edwards et al. 2013; Peters et al. 2013; Sponder 2012).

The SMI2 is an instrument that contributes to the actor-based category of social media analytics. The manual collection and analysis of social media parameters (such as number of messages, likes, and shares) can be time-consuming. The reliability of the observations can be questioned because, if conducted manually, errors are easily made. This problem of inaccuracy can be solved by developing a software tool that is capable of automatically analysing the social media profiles of all selected politicians. Another advantage of developing a software tool is the capability of monitoring all the participants' social media profiles in a more dynamic way, with multiple measurement points in time.

In order to find a software tool that could reliably measure the influence-levels of individual social media users, existing applications were compared. Well-known examples, at the time of writing, were social media analytics services such as Radian6, Teezir, Coosto, SocialMediaCheck, and Klout. We are not striving to provide a complete list of examples here, but many solutions were investigated to understand their approaches. In the following Table 15.1, some examples are shown of existing measurement tools for social media analytics, but we do not strive for completeness.

Table 15.1 List of examples of existing social media analytics tools

Tool	Approach
Radian6	Keyword based monitoring
Teezir	Keyword based monitoring
Hootsuite	Keyword based monitoring
Social Mention	Keyword based monitoring
Coosto	Keyword based monitoring
SocialMediaCheck	Keyword based monitoring
Klout	Individual network influence score

The main problem in using the available tools for our needs is that most of them are designed from the perspective of running search queries with keywords. The keyword approach has apparent disadvantages in measuring influence in networks and is useless for the comparison of the use and influence levels of political candidates. The keyword approach is problematic for at least three reasons:

1. These keyword-based tools scan the number of times the name of a person was mentioned on social media channels. The risk of this approach is that the results can be irrelevant and unreliable. This is because a higher number of retrieved results does not necessarily relate to a higher level of use or influence by that person.
2. There can be spam messages among the retrieved data. Since a vast amount of online posts can be categorized as spam, these posts can easily bias the outcomes (Sponder 2012).
3. There are semantic problems. The keyword approach can easily cause validity issues as keywords can have various meanings in language. Words can have multiple meanings (e.g. Ajax in mythology, as a football club or a programming framework) and can have different meanings in different languages. Also, it is difficult to reliably identify politicians who have the same or similar names as others. While there are sophisticated algorithms deployed in some of the solutions to cope with these problems, they cannot solve these issues completely.

While keyword-based tools primarily provide information about the larger collective mass in discussing a topic, the alternative approach, as proposed in this study, focuses on the influence from groups (e.g. political parties) and their people (e.g. political candidates).

To measure the levels of use and influence, it is necessary to have a framework of metrics. According to Peters et al. (2013:283), "Social media metrics require theoretical grounding, completeness, and a diagnostic nature; they also need to be credible to management and reliable over time." To meet these criteria, the revised SMI2 instrument is presented in Table 15.2. It comprises of the parameters (metrics) to measure personal influence in the social media channels of Facebook, Twitter, LinkedIn, YouTube, and Google+, while taking into account current technological limitations for each of them. Additionally, theoretical backgrounds are presented to sustain the matrix in the face of future changes in the application programming interfaces of social media channels.

Drawing upon theories such as Macintosh (Grönlund 2009; Medaglia 2007; Sommer and Cullen 2009), Sponder (2012), Hoffman and Fodor (2010), and others, the theoretical framework is presented in Table 15.2. Based on this framework, a scoring algorithm is designed that takes into account specific social network characteristics.

The SMI2 framework, as presented in Table 15.2, offers a distinction between two levels of participation. The SMI2 scores consist of both scores for Contribution and for Participation. Based on the metrics of important social media channels (Table 15.2), we can calculate scores. Basically, there is a score for contribution (C), which is based on the number of posts (X) related to the number of personal

Table 15.2 The Social Media Indicator-2 framework

Social media channel	Contribution (e-enabling) (*C*)		Engagement (e-engagement) (*P*)	
	Posts (*X*)	Network size (*N*)	Interaction (*I*)	Word of mouth (*W*)
Facebook page	# of posts	□ # of likes on page	□ # of talking about[a] • # of comments on post • # of likes on post	• # of shares of all posts
Facebook profile	• List of posts[b]	• # of friends • # of subscribers	• # of comments on post[b]	
Twitter	■ # of tweets	■ # of followers	■ # of reply's ■ # of favourites • List of mentions[c]	■ # of retweeted
YouTube	□ # of video's	□ # of subscribers	□ # of rates[b] □ Rating average[b] □ # of likes[b] □ # of dislikes[b]	□ # of favourite[b] □ # of views[b]
LinkedIn	■ # of updates[d]	■ # of first degree connections[d] ■ # of all connections[d]		■ # of recommenders[d]
Google+	□ List of activity's[e]	□ List of activity's[e]	□ # of comments per activity	□ # of +1 per activity □ # of re-shares per activity

[a] Number based on activity of the last 7 days
[b] Limited to retrieve 25 posts per request
[c] Limited to retrieve 20 tweets per request with a maximum of 800 tweets in total
[d] Limited to a maximum of 500 kb per request
[e] There are undefined limits for gathering activity per request
□ Data publicly available to developers
■ Data available to developers depending on privacy settings of the users and in certain cases user authentication is required
• Data only available with authentication of the user

connections—the network (*N*)—reached through these channels. The size of the network (*N*), at the individual participant level, is mostly used as the corresponding social media metric (Peters et al. 2013). Hoffman and Fodor (2010) address this as the level of exposure. For each separate channel, the score is calculated and then the sum of all channels is being calculated. For example, the contribution score for Twitter is calculated based on the number of tweets in relationship to the number of followers (Table 15.2). The participation score (*P*) is a sum of metrics that indicate the extent to which someone is sparking interaction (*I*) and the word-of-mouth (*W*) via social media. For example, Twitter's interaction score is the sum of replies, favourites, and mentions. The word-of-mouth score is based on the number of retweets.

The aim is to address every social media channel from the same perspective and to deliver an equivalent value for each channel, regardless of the number of available parameters. For each of these aspects of Posts (*X*), Network Size (*N*), Interaction (*I*), and Word of Mouth (*W*), metrics can be selected for specific social media channels. "As individuals may participate in several social media like Facebook and Twitter, any social network may not be fully understood in isolation" (Peters et al. 2013:289). Every social media channel has its own type of posts and ways of replying and sharing. The aim was to address every social media channel at the same level and return a number that was independent and comparable to all social media. The API's[1] provide us with the opportunity to directly connect to the databases of various social media channels. After that a list was made with all the parameters that were relevant and potentially measurable. They were included in the matrix to provide an overview based upon the types of parameters.

Software developers can register as official developers on various social media channels such as Facebook, Twitter, YouTube, LinkedIn, and Google. As a result access is provided to some of the database functions of these social media channels. There are no additional costs in obtaining the status of a developer on these included social media channels. Table 15.3 provides a list of developer links to the API of included social media channels.

The availability of each parameter in the matrix (Table 15.2) is marked by a symbol. However, even the parameters that seem available for developers, by default, may require user authentication depending on the user's privacy settings (Vitak 2012). Since most users decide themselves which posts they share publicly, the privacy control remains in the user's hands (Boyd and Ellison 2008). The user decides what is shared publicly and what is accessible to the public. Since publicly available data is the primary source for retrieving statistics, it is argued that the privacy consequences of these measurements are at an acceptable level. Nevertheless,

Table 15.3 List of API and links to developer documentation

Social media channel	Hyperlink to documentation for developers
[API-1] Facebook	https://developers.facebook.com/docs/reference/apis/
[API-2] Twitter	https://dev.twitter.com/docs/api/1.1
[API-3] YouTube	https://developers.google.com/YouTube/
[API-4] LinkedIn	https://developer.linkedin.com/apis
[API-5] Google+	https://developers.google.com/+/api/

[1]Application Programming Interfaces, open, public or semi-open interfaces to access functions with a programming language for accessing social data from the social media databases.

researchers should always be aware that there could be potential privacy risks and violations that are the result of combination of user data.

In addition to the theoretical framework, we are proposing a scoring algorithm to transform the metrics to comparative scores. The social media scores are proposed to be not merely the total sum of each metric of the SMI2. We propose a more refined scoring formula here to take into account the Network Size (*N*) of Posts (*X*).

We calculate the Contribution Score *C* as follows:

$$C = \log\left(\sum_{d=1}^{D} X_d\right) \cdot N_D^{\left(1+\frac{1}{N_D}\right)}$$

with

$d \in \{1,,,2,,,\ldots,D\}$ as an indicator for a day in the time horizon
D as the final day
X_d as the number of Posts on day d
N_D as the Network Size on day D

To calculate scores that reflect the influence of a post on its audience, the network has to be included as a leverage of the post. Therefore, it was decided to include the Network Size (*N*) as a weighting factor in the scoring approach. It is assumed that, for measuring influence, the size of the network is more important than the number of posts.

Table 15.4 displays a series of examples for the outcomes of such a scoring approach for the Contribution Score.

For the Engagement (Participation score—*P*) part of the SMI2, we have to count the sum of all the interactions (*I*) and also add the sum of the Word of Mouth (*W*) count for a selected period of time. The Word of Mouth count is proposed to have higher weight in the total participation score. This is because of the viral effect of sharing contents of someone.

Table 15.4 Example of contribution score for various network sizes

Posts (*X*)	Network size (*N*)	Contribution score (*C*)
5	150	108
10	150	155
50	150	264
100	150	310
5	500	354
10	500	506
50	500	860
100	500	1,013
5	2,000	1,403
10	2,000	2,008
50	2,000	3,411
100	2,000	4,015

The participation score P can be written as follows

$$P = W + I$$

With the word-to-mouth score W given by the following equation:

$$W = \sum_{d=1}^{D} W_d^2$$

The interaction score I is given by the following equation:

$$I = \sum_{d=1}^{D} I_d$$

However, the empirical test as elaborated upon in the next section of results is necessary to test the soundness of these proposed formulas.

In the end, the total SMI2 scores have to be calculated in the following way.

$$\text{SMI2} = C + P$$

Yet the formulas have to be tested with more empirical data before deciding on their exact calculation. An initial exploratory test was carried out during the Municipal elections of March 19, 2014 in The Netherlands as elaborated upon in the Results section of this chapter. The aim was to retrieve and compare social media indicator scores of the electoral candidates of the seven largest municipalities in the province of Overijssel, The Netherlands. We started with developing software to collect the necessary data from the databases of Facebook, Twitter, and YouTube. The software development was a joint initiative of a new consortium called Social Indicator. The following three parties have collaborated in developing such a software tool: Saxion University of Applied Sciences, The University of Twente, and eLabbs. eLabbs is a Research and Development software company that is closely attached to these universities and is located on the campus area. As a result of this initial test, and of the theoretical background (as discussed above), we propose the SMI2 score to be a useful indicator in measuring the use and influence of individual politicians and their parties.

The revised SMI2, as presented above, is expected to contribute to having more feasible measures to understand the social media influence of politicians. The SMI2 can easily be adapted to future social media channels that gain in popularity. This is because the SMI2 provides the theoretical foundation to select metrics of other (future) media channels that have similar functionality.

15.3 Results of the Pilot Study During Local Municipal Elections in the Netherlands

Within the Netherlands, the elections are to a large extent based on votes on individual political candidates. These candidates are at the same time representatives of political parties. These political parties present themselves as collectives. However,

Table 15.5 Selected municipalities and number of citizens

Municipality	Number of citizens in 2014[a]
Zwolle	123,159
Kampen	51,092
Hengelo	80,957
Hardenberg	59,577
Enschede	158,586
Deventer	98,322
Almelo	72,459

[a]overijssel.databank.nl

the voting system is based on preference votes for specific candidates of these political parties. Voters elect candidates for the council of municipalities or Houses of parliament. As our qualitative interviews with politicians earlier in 2012 suggested, voters are increasingly making choices for certain politicians instead of their parties. The personal campaigns of politicians are therefore becoming more relevant. Voters can give exactly one preference vote to the candidate of their choice. This situation is different from many other countries. As a result, the focus in this study was on individual politicians of parties and not the parties as groups.

It was decided to collect SMI2 data for the seven largest municipalities of the province of Overijssel during the campaign period of the municipal elections of March 19, 2014. The data collection method was based on the framework and scoring instructions as presented above. The threshold for selection was that the municipality should have more than 45,000 citizens in order to limit the number of subject in this pilot study. Table 15.5 shows the included 7 municipalities of the total of 25 municipalities of Overijssel that were included in this pilot study. The province of Overijssel in the Netherlands has 1,139,697 citizens in total (overijssel.databank.nl).

A software tool was developed (based on Java and APIs) to automatically retrieve the metrics and scores based on the framework and algorithm. Real world empirical data was gathered by applying the tool during the campaign period of the local (municipal) elections in the Netherlands held on March 19th, 2014. The data is primarily used to evaluate the feasibility of the framework and its algorithm.

The empirical results consist of a state of the field for a specific local area (Europe, Netherlands, Overijssel), a comparison of scores for a sample of individual politicians ($n = 202$), and its overarching political parties. In addition, to evaluate the usefulness of the SMI2 measure, correlations are calculated between the social media scores of the political parties (based on scores of individual candidates) with the election outcome (based on individual preference votes).

We have collected data for the political candidates and their parties in a predefined period, from March 5 to March 17, which preceded the elections on March 19. We followed the SMI2 framework and developed software with connections to the APIs[2] of Twitter, Facebook, and YouTube to retrieve the appropriate metrics. The software included the metric for both the social media channels Facebook and

[2]Application Programming Interfaces.

Table 15.6 Selected politicians as subjects

Municipality	Selected politicians in this study
Zwolle	37
Kampen	24
Hengelo	20
Hardenberg	14
Enschede	47
Deventer	30
Almelo	30

Twitter. YouTube, LinkedIn, and Google Plus were not yet included in this pilot study due to time constraints for software developing. Nevertheless, the included social media channels already provide us with data for the purposes of this pilot study. Furthermore, as our first exploratory observations and prior research made clear, channels such as Google Plus are still scarcely used in the Netherlands by political candidates in the province of Overijssel. Nevertheless, future versions of the software will be extended with all listed social media channels of the framework. We have focused on retrieving data from the politicians who had the highest positions on their party lists. The reason was that collecting and entering the "urls" for all members on the list would be impractical and time-consuming. We limited the selection to the top five members of each party in all municipalities. As a result, the number of included subjects was 202 ($n = 202$). A more detailed overview of the number of included political party candidates is displayed in Table 15.6.

Below, in Table 15.7, we present the top 10 candidates with the highest SMI2 scores in a Table.

Of each political party that was active in more than one municipality, we could calculate the total SMI2 scores within the entire province of Overijssel. The top 10 of that ordered list is displayed below:

1. CDA
2. PvdA
3. D66
4. VVD
5. GroenLinks
6. Enschede Solidair
7. Swollwacht
8. SP
9. ProHengelo
10. ChristenUnie

In order to evaluate the usefulness and feasibility of the SMI2 scores, we have made a comparison with an independent variable. In this case, we compare the social media scores with the number of preference votes in the voting outcome. We have used SPSS to calculate Spearman's rho correlations to explore potential relationships between the variables. Although there are many other factors that influence

Table 15.7 Top 10 political candidates with highest SMI2 scores

Name	Political party	Municipality	Contribution score (*C*)	Participation score (*P*)	Total SMI2 score
Hilde Palland Mulder	CDA	Kampen	2,081	9,586,964	9,589,045
Ronald Klappe	PVDA	Kampen	4,977	2,111,572	2,116,549
Jan Brink	D66	Zwolle	5,650	1,626,871	1,632,521
Elske Mooijman	Groenlinks	Hengelo	2,157	589,127	591,284
Ayfer Koç	CDA	Enschede	7,585	475,922	483,507
Wim van der Noordt	Enschede Solidair	Enschede	629	407,097	407,726
Martin Ekker	VVD	Kampen	3,421	404,186	407,607
Silvia Bruggenkamp	Swollwacht	Zwolle	1,171	390,759	391,930
Niels Jeurink	Groenlinks	Kampen	962	150,715	151,677
Leo Janssen	Pro Hengelo	Hengelo	3,545	146,636	150,181

Table 15.8 SMI contribution scores (*C*) related to preferential votes

Municipality	Spearman's rho correlation
Almelo	−.036
Deventer	.391
Enschede	.245
Hardenberg	.679
Hengelo	.050
Kampen	.517
Zwolle	.345

the number of preferential votes, these calculations could reveal whether a higher social media influence score could be associated with obtaining more votes.

Table 15.8 presents the Contribution scores in relationship to voting outcome and the correlations.

In four of the seven municipalities, we could reveal a positive relationship (Spearman's rho>.3) between the scores for Contribution (*C*) and the individual preference votes. In three municipalities, such evidence could not be found.

The SMI2 consists also of a score for engagement: the Participation score. Table 15.9 presents the Participation scores of political parties and its members in relationship to voting outcome.

In four of the seven municipalities, we could not reveal a significant positive relationship between the political party's scores for Participation (*P*) and their party members' individual preference votes. On the other hand, however, within three municipalities there was a positive relationship revealed between the Participation score of the political parties and the votes.

There are only a few minor differences between the SMI2 score calculations and the Participation score calculations, as a comparison between Tables 15.9 and 15.10 makes clear. The weight of the participation score in the total SMI2 score is very

Table 15.9 SMI participation scores (*P*) related to preferential votes

Municipality	Spearman's rho correlation
Almelo	.670
Deventer	.518
Enschede	−.100
Hardenberg	−.286
Hengelo	.267
Kampen	.383
Zwolle	−.200

Table 15.10 SMI2 total scores (SMI2) related to preferential votes

Municipality	Spearman's rho correlation
Almelo	.610
Deventer	.473
Enschede	−.191
Hardenberg	−.286
Hengelo	.267
Kampen	.383
Zwolle	−.200

dominant. Therefore, the scoring algorithm for the Participations should be revisited and improved to resolve this issue.

In the end, the pilot test showed that we were capable to retrieve and compare social media influence scores of a large number of political candidates during the 2014 local elections. The Infographic as displayed in Fig. 15.1 shows an example of how the result of a SMI2 study can be presented to a broader audience of practitioners.

15.4 Discussion

More studies and further refinement of the measure are still necessary. Especially the algorithm to calculate the participation score has to be refined to limit its weight in the total SMI2 scores. The scoring algorithm has shown to be a feasible approach for comparing social media influence scores, especially when the Participation score algorithm is adjusted.

Five limitations have to be taken into account. First, the challenge remains in how to deal with members who have more than one affiliation in their social media profiles. For example, a local politician could use his or her social media profiles for more than one affiliation. A politician could have a large network of relationships based on his daytime job. It might be justified to exclude certain members in studies where the other affiliations are expected to cause a bias in the results.

Second, because of privacy settings, it remains challenging to obtain all relevant data from the social media databases. Moreover, it could be a difficult task to keep

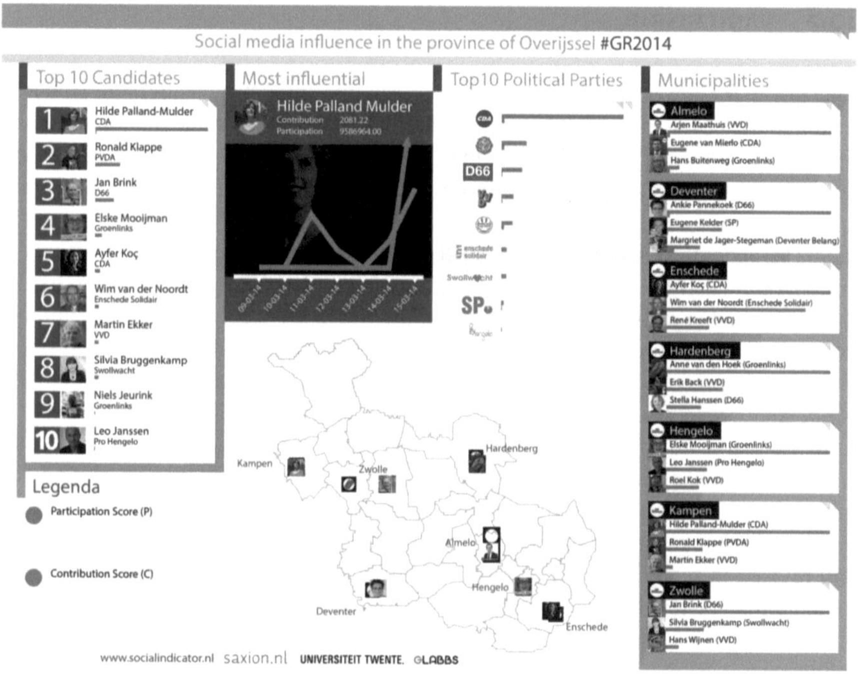

Fig. 15.1 Infographic of the social media influence in Overijssel

the software up to date and to stay connected to the Application Programming Interfaces of these included social media channels. For example, the API of Facebook will change in 2015, which will have consequences for the data collection in the software.

Third, as became apparent in this pilot test, not many politicians had a Facebook Page (which is most appropriate for public persons such as politicians). Most of them created a personal/private Facebook profile instead. Due to privacy settings of the Facebook API, we were not allowed to take data from these personal profiles. As a result, the scores in this pilot study were predominantly based on Twitter activities of the candidates.

Fourth, an already existing large offline network size of a politician can influence the SMI score because the network size is often mirrored in online connections. Someone with a rich social life in the offline world tends to have more online connections as well.

Finally, the scores as provided with the SMI2 only indicate the influence, and due to advanced algorithms and advertising programs of Facebook (Edgerank) and Twitter, the order and relevance of posts and comments are continuously influenced by these companies. As a result, the real number of followers reached by each post is smaller than the total size of the network. Future version could integrate these kinds of factors in the scoring algorithm.

15.5 Conclusion

The SMI2 framework contributes to more reliable impact measurement of social media in the political field. It was useful to collect and compare social media scores of a large number of politicians during the local elections in the Netherlands. In a first pilot test, the scoring algorithm for the Contribution score (C) seems to be quite appropriate to compare influence scores. We were already able to relate the social media contribution scores to preference votes and reveal positive correlations in certain municipalities. A positive correlation makes clear that politicians and parties that had a higher influence score based on the SMI2 also received more preference votes during elections. Our measure can potentially have predicting value in future elections. However, other factors influence voting outcome as well and social media is not solely responsible for the voting outcome. For example, some parties were in a losing spiral during these elections in the Netherlands and using social media seems not to change public sentiment. When the public sentiment regarding a certain party is negative, social media does not help greatly to change that.

The SMI2 measure comprises of a set of social media metrics that can be used and revised in many types of research where it is important to compare the social media influence levels of politicians. The scoring algorithm and metrics of the SMI2 can be revised in future studies to relate the independent variable of social media influence to various dependent variables. The SMI2 can be adjusted to specific situations in various countries and can be updated quite easily as social media channels change in popularity over time.

Software companies can apply the SMI2 measure in new software solutions to monitor and measure both the impact and interaction caused by social media use. This provides them with new business opportunities. This contributes to more justified solutions in the field of social media analytics. In preparation of this research, a consortium was initiated to develop a software tool for this end. The open and scientific approach of measuring and comparing use levels of social media can provide politicians with a more reliable approach to social media monitoring tools and social dashboards. This can help to gain knowledge about effective social media campaigns and strategies.

Acknowledgments The research projects mentioned in this chapter are initiated, supported, and funded by the Social Indicator Consortium as a collaborative project from Saxion University of Applied Sciences, University of Twente and eLabbs in Enschede, The Netherlands.

References

Bayraktutan, G., Binark, M., Çomu, T., Doğu, B., İslamoğlu, G., & Telli Aydemir, A. (2014). The use of Facebook by political parties and leaders in the 2011 Turkish general elections. In B. Pătruţ & M. Pătruţ (Eds.), *Social media in politics* (Vol. 13, pp. 165–199). New York: Springer.

Berthon, P. R., Pitt, L. F., Plangger, K., & Shapiro, D. (2012). Marketing meets Web 2.0, social media, and creative consumers: Implications for international marketing strategy. *Business Horizons, 55*(3), 261–271.

Bonsón, E., Torres, L., Royo, S., & Flores, F. (2012). Local e-government 2.0: Social media and corporate transparency in municipalities. *Government Information Quarterly, 29*(2), 123–132.

Bottles, K., & Sherlock, T. (2011). Who should manage your social media strategy? *Physician Executive, 37*(2), 68–72.

Boyd, D. M., & Ellison, N. B. (2008). Social network sites: Definition, history, and scholarship. *Journal of Computer-Mediated Communication, 13*(1), 210–230.

Christakis, N. A., & Fowler, J. H. (2009). *Connected: The surprising power of our social networks and how they shape our lives*. New York: Little Brown and Company.

D'heer, E., & Verdegem, P. (2014). An intermedia understanding of the networked twitter ecology. In B. Pătruţ & M. Pătruţ (Eds.), *Social media in politics* (Vol. 13, pp. 81–96). New York: Springer.

Deželan, T., Vobič, I., & Maksuti, A. (2014). Twitter campaigning in the 2011 national election in Slovenia. In B. Pătruţ & M. Pătruţ (Eds.), *Social media in politics* (Vol. 13, pp. 141–163). New York: Springer.

Di Fraia, G., & Missaglia, M. (2014). The use of Twitter in 2013 Italian political election. In B. Pătruţ & M. Pătruţ (Eds.), *Social media in politics* (Vol. 13, pp. 63–77). New York: Springer.

Dylko, I., & McCluskey, M. (2012). Media effects in an era of rapid technological transformation: A case of user-generated content and political participation. *Communication Theory, 22*(3), 250–278.

Edwards, C., Spence, P. R., Gentile, C. J., Edwards, A., & Edwards, A. (2013). How much Klout do you have. A test of system generated cues on source credibility. *Computers in Human Behavior, 29*(5), A12–A16.

Effing, R., Van Hillegersberg, J., & Huibers, T. W. C. (2011). Social media and political participation: Are Facebook, Twitter and YouTube democratizing our political systems? In *Electronic participation: Proceedings of the Third IFIF WG 8.5 International Conference ePart 2011* (Vol. 6847, pp. 25–35). Delft, The Netherlands: Springer.

Effing, R., Van Hillegersberg, J., & Huibers, T. W. C. (2013). Social media participation and local politics: A case study of the Enschede council in the Netherlands. In *Proceedings of Electronic Participation, ePart 2013* (pp. 57–68). Koblenz, Germany: Springer.

Goode, P. (2013). *The value of data in an evolving digital world.* Retrieved from http://www.comscore.com/Insights/Presentations_and_Whitepapers/2013/The_value_of_data_in_an_evolving_digital_world

Grönlund, Å. (2009). ICT is not participation is not democracy—eParticipation development models revisited. In A. Macintosh & E. Tambouris (Eds.), *Electronic participation: First international conference, ePart 2009* (pp. 12–23). Berlin, Germany: Springer.

Hoffman, D., & Fodor, M. (2010). Can you measure the ROI of your social media marketing? *MITSLoan Management Review, 52*(1), 41–49. Retrieved November 6, 2013, from http://www.emarketingtravel.net/resources/can you measure the ROI of your Social media marketing.pdf

Jungherr, A. (2012). Online campaigning in Germany: The CDU online campaign for the general election 2009 in Germany. *German Politics, 21*(3), 317–340.

Kaplan, A. M., & Haenlein, M. (2010). Users of the world, unite! The challenges and opportunities of social media. *Business Horizons, 53*, 59–68.

Lipsman, A., Lella, A., & Dreyer, K. (2014). *U.S. digital future in focus 2014.* Whitepaper comScore, comScore. Retrieved from http://www.comscore.com/dut/Insights/Press-Releases/2014/4/comScores-Latest-White-Paper-2014-US-Digital-Future-in-Focus-Available-for-Download

Macintosh, A., & Smith, E. (2002). Citizen participation in public affairs. In R. Traunmueller & K. Lenk (Eds.), *Proceedings of Electronic Government* (pp. 256–263). Berlin, Germany: Springer.

Medaglia, R. (2007). Measuring the diffusion of eParticipation: A survey on Italian local government. *Information Polity, 12*, 265–280.

Montero, M. D. (2009). Political e-mobilisation and participation in the election campaigns of Ségolène Royal (2007) and Barack Obama (2008). *Quaderns del CAC, 33*, 27–34.

Nielsen. (2012). *State of the media: The social media report 2012* (Public report Nielsen, New York). Retrieved from http://www.nielsen.com/us/en/insights/reports/2012/state-of-the-media-the-social-media-report-2012.html

Peters, K., Chen, Y., Kaplan, A. M., Ognibeni, B., & Pauwels, K. (2013). Social media metrics—A framework and guidelines for managing social media. *Journal of Interactive Marketing, 27*(4), 281–298.

Ren, J., & Meister, H. P. (2010). Drawing lessons from Obama for the European context. *The International Journal of Public Participation, 4*(1), 12–30.

Rustad, E., & Sæbø, Ø. (2013). How, why and with whom do local politicians engage on Facebook? In M. A. Wimmer, E. Tambouris, & A. Macintosh (Eds.), *Electronic participation: 5th IFIP WG 8.5 International Conference, ePart 2013* (pp. 69–79). Berlin, Germany: Springer. Retrieved June 18, 2014, from http://link.springer.com/chapter/10.1007/978-3-642-40346-0_7

Sommer, L., & Cullen, R. (2009). Participation 2.0: A case study of e-participation within the New Zealand Government. In R. H. Sprague (Ed.), *Proceeding of 42nd Hawaii International Conference on System Sciences* 2009 (pp. 1–9). Piscataway, NJ: IEEE.

Spierings, N., & Jacobs, K. (2012). Marginal, but significant: The impact of social media on preferential voting. In *ECPR Joint Sessions Workshop Parties and Campaigning in the Digital Era, 10–15 April 2012, Antwerp.*

Sponder, M. (2012). *Social media analytics: Effective tools for building, interpreting, and using metrics*. New York: McGraw-Hill.

Štětka, V., Macková, A., & Fialová, M. (2014). A winding road from "Likes" to votes. In B. Pătruţ & M. Pătruţ (Eds.), *Social media in politics* (Vol. 13, pp. 225–244). New York: Springer.

Stieglitz, S., & Dang-Xuan, L. (2012). Social media and political communication: A social media analytics framework. *Social Network Analysis and Mining, 3*(4), 1277–1291.

Van der Veer, N., & Boekkee, S. (2014). *Social media in perspectief: Whitepaper nationale social media onderzoek 2014.* Public whitepaper. Enschede, The Netherlands: Newcom. Retrieved from http://www.newcom.nl/socialmedia

Vitak, J. (2012). The impact of context collapse and privacy on social network site disclosures. *Journal of Broadcasting & Electronic Media, 56*(4), 451–470. Retrieved November 6, 2013, from http://www.tandfonline.com/doi/abs/10.1080/08838151.2012.732140

Withaar, R. J., Ribeiro, G. F., & Effing, R. (2013). The social media indicator 2: Towards a software tool for measuring the influence of social media. In M. A. Wimmer, M. Janssen, A. Macintosh, H. J. Scholl, & E. Tambouris (Eds.), *Joint Proceedings of Ongoing Research of IFIP EGOV and IFIP ePart 2013: Lecture Notes in Informatics (LNI), Koblenz, Germany* (pp. 200–207).

Part VI
Emerging Issues

Chapter 16
Branding Cities in the Age of Social Media: A Comparative Assessment of Local Government Performance

Efe Sevin

Abstract This chapter is a comparative study of how three local governments—Cape Town (South Africa), Philadelphia (Pennsylvania, USA), and Myrtle Beach (South Carolina, USA)—use social media platforms in their city branding attempts. Theoretical arguments in the fields of corporate and city branding point out the potential of these new communication platforms to change how brand-related content is created and shared with target audiences. However, the practice is understudied. The study first explains the potential of social media in branding through media ecology, city brand communication, and brand co-creation theories. Second, the performance of the aforementioned three cities on social media is evaluated by analyzing their Twitter and Facebook presence. The findings suggest that there is room for improvement for local governments in their employment of social media for city branding campaigns. The chapter concludes with recommendations for practitioners.

16.1 Introduction

This chapter sheds light on the use of social media by local governments in their attempts to influence how they are perceived by publics, or in other words, to build and promote their place brands (Lucarelli and Berg 2011). Social media, despite their short history as an electronic communication method, emerged as a viable platform to disseminate messages and create relationships with target audiences (Jansen et al. 2009). Following an "engage or die" understanding, various corporations and organizations have integrated social media into their overall branding

E. Sevin (✉)
Department of Public Relations and Information, Kadir Has University, Kadir Has Caddesi, Cibali, Istanbul 34200, Turkey
e-mail: efe.sevin@khas.edu.tr

M.Z. Sobaci (ed.), *Social Media and Local Governments*, Public Administration and Information Technology 15, DOI 10.1007/978-3-319-17722-9_16

strategies (Solis 2011). The main puzzle in this research is articulated around the aspiration to determine whether the local governments have shown similar incentives to increase their activities online.

Social media—regardless of the specific platform in question—have the potential to bring two important changes to the practice of place and destination branding. First, local governments are able to create multimedia content with relatively smaller budgets compared to traditional media platforms such as print or television (Mendes 2013). Consequently, during the last couple of years, there have been various digital communication campaigns in place branding—from a stone skipping robot controlled by internet users[1] to citizens acting as the spokespersons for their country.[2] Second, social media platforms gave the local governments a virtual office (Auer et al. 2012). Cities started to enjoy a digital embodiment. For instance, through Twitter, individual users can directly talk to and interact with places such as San Francisco (@onlyinSF)[3] and Paris (@Parisjecoute) (Sevin 2013).

Within this context, the objective of this research is to assess whether local governments have been able to benefit from the possible changes introduced by social media platforms. There are two research questions asked: (1) *What is the content shared by local governments on social media for place branding purposes*? and (2) *What is the role of digital "engagement" or "two-way communication" in social media branding campaigns*? The former question is posed at the content of the messages disseminated, whereas the latter inquires about the relationships created with the target audiences. The answers to the research questions are given by an analysis of social media communication practices of three cities that have been deemed as prominent adopters of new media technology in their marketing and branding attempts: Cape Town (South Africa), Philadelphia (Pennsylvania, USA), and Myrtle Beach (South Caroline, USA) on Twitter and Facebook.[4]

The existing research on the implications of social media on the specific practices of city and place branding is limited. With certain exceptions (such as Björner 2013; Braun et al. 2013; Sevin 2013), the main foci of these studies have been on the role of individuals in contributing to the branding processes and the changing definitions of brands accordingly. Building on these approaches, this chapter highlights

---

[1] Information about Sun Valley's *Skippy the Stone Skipping Robot* can be found here http://skiptown.visitsunvalley.com/

[2] The first country to launch a country Twitter account controlled by its citizens was Sweden. Information about Sweden's *Curators of Sweden* can be found here http://curatorsofsweden.com

[3] "@" in front of a word denotes a Twitter username. The exact URL for the webpage is http://www.twitter.com/username (e.g. http://www.twitter.com/parisjecoute).

[4] Given the fact that place branding is predominantly driven by practice (Lucarelli and Berg 2011), my case selection follows the innovation and best practice awards given in the field. All three cities' use of social media has won numerous awards and have been recognized as the best uses of social media by Travel + Leisure Magazine in 2012 and 2013. This chapter sees the industry awards and praises as determinants of "best case" status and subsequently argues that these three cities represent the desired employment of social media tools in branding, in other words, are "typical cases" (Gerring 2009). This case selection is appropriate for an explanatory research that aims to identify and analyze expected social behavior (Seawright and Gerring 2008).

the role of the primary responsible users—local governments—in digital branding campaigns. Furthermore, the performance of local governments is evaluated to assess whether the potential of social media platforms is realized in the case of city branding.

The chapter is structured as follows. First, the arguments presented in the introduction part, specifically the two potential changes brought in by social media, are substantiated theoretically through city brand communication (Kavaratzis 2004), media ecology (Postman 2000), and brand-co creation (Hatch and Schultz 2010; Potts et al. 2008) studies. Respectively, these theories present frameworks to study the different levels through which places communicate with these stakeholders, the impact of the specific media platform/technology on the communication platforms, and the involvement of stakeholders in brand creation. Second, the methodology for the empirical study is shared. Subsequently, the findings of the analysis are introduced. The chapter is concluded by introducing recommendations to practitioners based on these findings.

16.2 Branding Places in a Digital Environment

Michael Porter (1990) is one of the first scholars to argue for the importance of certain characteristics of nations—such as domestic competition and labor market—for economic success. Porter (1990) posited that despite the scholarly discussions on homogenization of global markets, the differences between nations constitute the basis of their competitive advantages. It is possible for countries to establish more supportive business environments and thus help their own companies prosper in international markets (Marmier and Fetscherin 2010). In addition to organizational and structural changes, the success of these nations in international markets also depends on "softer" factors such as culture and values (Porter 1990). In other words, the key to national advantages is in accepting and creating national differences (Aronczyk 2013).

This newly found appreciation for the unique identities of countries entered a new era when Simon Anholt, an advertising professional and a policy advisor, argued that the perception of countries might also be influential in their success in global economy. Anholt (1998) proposed a novel concept that drastically altered the way national identity and reputation are understood: *nation brands*. The concept practically argues that the perceptions of a given country by the rest of the world have political, social, and economic impacts (Anholt 2007). The same branding understanding has been applied to regions, cities, towns, and other places of different sizes, thus helping Anholt's insightful proposition pave way to a new field of study and practice generally known as place branding.[5]

[5] Place branding is used as an umbrella concept that covers branding activities of various administrative regions including but not limited to cities and nations.

16.2.1 Moving from Spaces to Places

Place branding literature has welcomed contributions from a variety of disciplines ranging from public relations (Szondi 2010) to international relations (Van Ham 2001) and marketing (cf. Kavaratzis 2005). Unsurprisingly, there is a plethora of definition of place branding. The academic consensus argues that place branding goes beyond establishing a visual brand identity (Kavaratzis and Ashworth 2006). In other words, it is widely accepted that even though creating new logos stays as an inherent part of campaigns (Fan 2010), place branding goes beyond introducing these elements. Fundamentally, studies are based on the assumption that when a place is named, several associated concepts are invoked in individuals' minds (Kavaratzis 2004). It is further argued that even the concept of "place" itself is a social construction of a space by individuals and societies by assigning meanings to a specific geographic area (Boisen et al. 2011:137). Place branding, thus, refers to the attempts to monitor and manipulate these meanings and associations.

The different approaches to the study of place branding can be categorized under three broad categories: production, appropriation, and critical studies (Lucarelli and Berg 2011). Production studies analyze the processes through which brands are created and managed. Appropriation studies look at how brands are perceived and consumed by target audiences. Critical studies argue for the impacts of branding processes on the existing social, economic, and cultural environments. As a whole, place branding—and city branding in the case of this research—covers the entire process in which brands are managed, received by audiences, and influence the existing structures. The brand of a city, on the other hand, is "a network of associations in the consumer's mind based on the visual, verbal, and behavio[.]ral expression of a place" (Zenker and Braun 2010:5).

There are two main obstacles in the process of creating and managing the brand of a place. First, as Anholt (2010) argues that places lead individuals' perceptions through providing high-quality products and caliber services. In order to establish a new brand, it might be necessary to implement structural and policy changes. Yet, it should be noted that individuals can interact with a place through various channels such as direct and indirect experiences, mediated messages (Govers 2011). Kavaratzis (2004) combines all these interaction channels and introduces three methods through which places can communicate their brands to target audiences. The primary method of communication is closer to Anholt's arguments and is carried out by implementing policies in the fields of landscape, infrastructure, and bureaucratic structures (Kavaratzis 2004). By changing its behavior, a place can create a new image for itself in the minds of target audiences. The secondary communication is the formal, e.g. marketing, communication geared towards changing the perceptions (Kavaratzis 2004). Places can disseminate their messages through various media platforms with the intention of raising their profiles. The last area of communication refers to the "word of mouth" (Kavaratzis 2004). It is carried out by consumers, competitors, and other stakeholders that articulate their views about a given place. Even though local governments might attempt to control the first two, tertiary communication is beyond their direct reach.

The second obstacle stems from the process through which a place brand is created. A place is not owned by a specific entity; therefore, any stakeholder might claim responsibility for its branding process (Braun 2011). The administrative body of a place does not necessarily have the legitimacy or the capability to single-handedly spearhead its branding attempts (as seen in the cases of Finland in Hakala and Lemmetyinen 2011 and; of Ankara in Hayden and Sevin 2012). Therefore, a place brand is best understood as a "dialogue, debate, and contestation" (Kavaratzis and Hatch 2013:82) among parties and is the outcome of a negotiation and deliberation process between various stakeholders, including but not limited to citizens, civil society groups, bureaucrats, and target audiences (Sevin 2011). This approach to place branding is closer to the "brand co-creation" understanding of the corporate studies where external stakeholders, including consumers, are seen as having control over the meaning of brands, in addition to the companies who own the brands (Hatch and Schultz 2010). The ownership of place brands and the responsibility of creating and managing these brands are determined through the interaction between stakeholders (Aitken and Campelo 2011).

When the concept of "co-creation" was introduced around a decade ago (Prahalad and Ramaswamy 2004), it was perceived as a novel and a critical argument (Hatch and Schultz 2010). The concept practically argues that the company-centric value creation understanding is outdated and needs to be replaced (Prahalad and Ramaswamy 2004). This understanding represents the traditional business transactions where companies are responsible for creating a product, a service, or a value in general while customers passively consume. Co-creation defines a more active role for the customers who interact with the companies and create their own experiences (Prahalad and Ramaswamy 2004). In the case of branding and place branding, co-creation argues that target audiences need to be presented with ample opportunities to interact with companies and places to create their own experiences (Hatch and Schultz 2010; Kavaratzis and Hatch 2013). Such experiences become an important—if not the most important—aspect of brands.

To sum up, the brand of a place can be seen as the meaning given to a specific geographic space by relevant stakeholders, while place branding refers to the attempts to influence these meanings. Co-creation in place branding posits that audiences actively take part in establishing brands. Place branding practice and study are influenced by corporate branding, yet are distinct due to the unorthodox nature of communicative aspects of branding and the ownership of brands. The next section builds on these premises and outlines the changes brought to place brand communication and co-creation within a new media ecology: social media.

16.2.2 Place Branding and Social Media

Social media have been influential in place branding and well-adopted (Braun et al. 2013; Yan 2011). The relatively low cost of operating on this new medium was particularly encouraging for cities and other local governments that do not necessarily have the means to promote themselves in traditional media platforms (Sevin 2013). Besides their financial advantages, these platforms also became relevant advertising venues. Over 70 % of the internet users have accounts and actively monitor social media (Pew Research Center 2013), making digital engagement a high priority for place branding. Last but not the least, social media also allow the employment of different content forms, such as video and audio, simultaneously and encourage innovative place branding projects.

The experience of Iceland and its *Iceland Naturally* branding campaign is an illustrative case of place branding in social media. The campaign started out as a pilot project in the United States to increase the brand presence of Iceland among American audiences and to position the country as a pure and unspoiled natural environment (Gudjonsson 2005:293). Apart from its offline activities, *Iceland Naturally* engaged with target audiences through social media, primarily through Facebook and Twitter. Both platforms are used to disseminate messages and interact with users. Additionally, the branding campaign hosts trivia games and sweepstakes to grab audience attention. *Follow the Fish* was such a campaign where individuals could enter to win a round-trip ticket to Iceland to visit the country's sustainable fisheries through Facebook.[6] Similarly, the city of Sun Valley in Idaho created "Skippy," a stone skipping robot. Internet users could remotely control the robot to skip stones at a lake in Sun Valley to win a week-long trip. The project attracted the attention of thousands of internet users (Skip Town with Sun Valley 2012).

The impacts of a new medium should not be solely deduced to its logistical and financial aspects. The school of media ecology argues that in order to understand communication processes taking place in a new medium, it is necessary to study the medium (McLuhan 1967). As summarized in the quote by Marshall McLuhan (1964), one of the most prominent figures in media ecology field, "the medium is the message". Content studies cannot be separated from medium studies as the medium has a considerable impact on how individuals interact with each other (Strate 2008). When local governments employ social media in their attempts to engage in place branding campaigns, they should be aware of the impacts of this particular medium on the entire process: namely communication and co-creation aspects.

In the case of place branding, social media presents opportunities for secondary and tertiary communication processes (Kavaratzis 2005). Digital communication takes places between the branding campaigns and the target audiences as well as among the individual users interested in the place. Looking at the medium as the message, it is important to understand the changes brought in by the peculiarities of these new platforms to the practice of place branding (McLuhan 1967). As argued above, first and foremost of all, place branding campaigns make use of Twitter, Facebook, and other similar platforms to disseminate their formal messages (Fouts 2010; Go and Govers 2010). Equivalently, individuals also make use of social media platforms to gather information about given places and make informed decisions

[6]More information about the sweepstakes can be found here http://www.icelandnaturally.com/boeing2013/

(Munar 2011). For instance, travellers have started to use social media search results before they settle on their final destinations (Xiang and Gretzel 2010). In the lack of direct experience, individuals need to rely on indirect resources. In other words, if a given individual has not visited a place, his or her impression is going to be based on the information relayed from other resources. During the last decade, social media platforms emerged as a highly sought-after information source (Gretzel and Yoo 2008). The reputation—and brand—of a place is influenced by the online word-of-mouth created in social media platforms (Litvin et al. 2008).

As argued before, co-creation theory in place branding assumes that place brands "are co-created by a multitude of people who encounter and appropriate them" (Kavaratzis and Hatch 2013:72). A brand is not necessarily a combination of the products and services combined by a place and its strategic communication activities. The involvement of various stakeholders, including target audiences, and the interaction between them also contribute to a brand. Social media facilitates both the practice and the study of such interactions and contributions. For instance, Twitter enables users to communicate directly with each other as well as indirectly as a group. As the social media traffic is publicly available and observable, research can use data generated in these platforms to examine the place branding processes.

In this section, theoretical underpinnings that encouraged the two research questions posed by this chapter are explained. Succinctly stated, social media is a new platform through which the perception of a brand can be changed (Jansen et al. 2009) and the behaviors of individuals can be affected (Fischer and Reuber 2011). Moreover, the individuals also have the opportunity to contribute to the branding process by actively generating content and sharing their impressions (Yan 2011). Thus, place branding is co-created by various stakeholders through content generation and engagement. In order to assess whether local governments are able to make use of new communication technologies, the first research question is posed at the content of the messages shared. The second research question investigates the relationships between local governments and other stakeholders in digital platforms to present a complete picture of place branding processes. The next section explains the research methodology in more detail.

16.3 Methodology

In order to understand how local governments make use of the unique opportunities of social media in place branding, this research asks two questions:

1. *What is the content shared by local governments on social media for place branding purposes?*
2. *What is the role of digital "engagement" or "two-way communication" in social media branding campaigns?*

The answers to these questions are given primarily by analyzing the content and behavior of these three cities' official marketing accounts on Twitter for all three cities: @capetowntourism for Cape Town, @visitphilly for Philadelphia, and @ myrtlebeach for Myrtle Beach. The majority of the Twitter-based data gathering and analysis was carried out within the *R* environment (R Core Team 2014).[7]

Data collection took place in August and September 2014 by scrapping individual tweets sent by the aforementioned accounts. Data was gathered by using the *twitteR: R based Twitter client* package (Gentry 2013). This particular package enables the users to access the web application programming interface of Twitter. In other words, *twitteR* functions as a tool to get data from Twitter. The package was used at three different times to scrap the most recent tweets sent. A separate dataset was created for each of the three accounts. Subsequently, the datasets were manually cleaned by identifying duplicate entries. The final datasets included the most recent 3,200 tweets sent by all three cities, summing up to 9,600 tweets.[8]

In order to answer the research questions, there is a need to analyze both the content produced on social media and the usage patterns. This is why tweets were divided into three parts. The first part included the text of the tweets and used for content analysis. The second part included descriptive indicators about the tweets and the account, such as the number of tweets sent and number of links sent. The third and last part examined the relationships between users by looking at the inclusion of other users in a tweet in the forms of *retweets* and *replies*. Thus, the first part is used to answer content-related questions, whereas the latter two provided information about the usage patterns.

The content was analyzed by using *tm* package in the R environment (Feinerer et al. 2008). The software was used for two different purposes. First, *tm* was instrumental in identifying the most frequently used terms, and the relationship between these terms. Basically, the software counts the number of times a given word was used in all the tweets sent by the city and calculates the physical proximity of these words to each other. If a given set of words is used frequently together, these words were grouped together. Second, *tm* was also used to uncover the association between the city's name and other terms. The software calculated which terms were used most frequently and physically close to the name of the city. The findings were visualized with *igraph* (Csardi and Nepusz 2006) and *wordcloud* (Fellows 2014) packages. Both packages are visualization tools in the R environment, with the former being used to create cluster dendrograms or tree graphs showing the relationship between the words (cf. Fig. 16.1). The latter is used to represent the frequency counts of words by creating a geometric shape of all the words and assigning sizes based on frequencies (cf. Fig. 16.2).

---

[7] R is an open-source software and a programming language used for a variety of research methods. There are individual "packages," or software add-ons that can be installed to carry out specific research methods. Further information about R can be accessed at http://www.r-project.org/

[8] Twitter allows the researchers to scrap the most recent 3,200 at each request. After requesting the tweets at three different times, I ended up with different number of tweets per account based on their daily tweet volumes. In order to create comparable datasets, I decided to limit each dataset to 3,200 tweets.

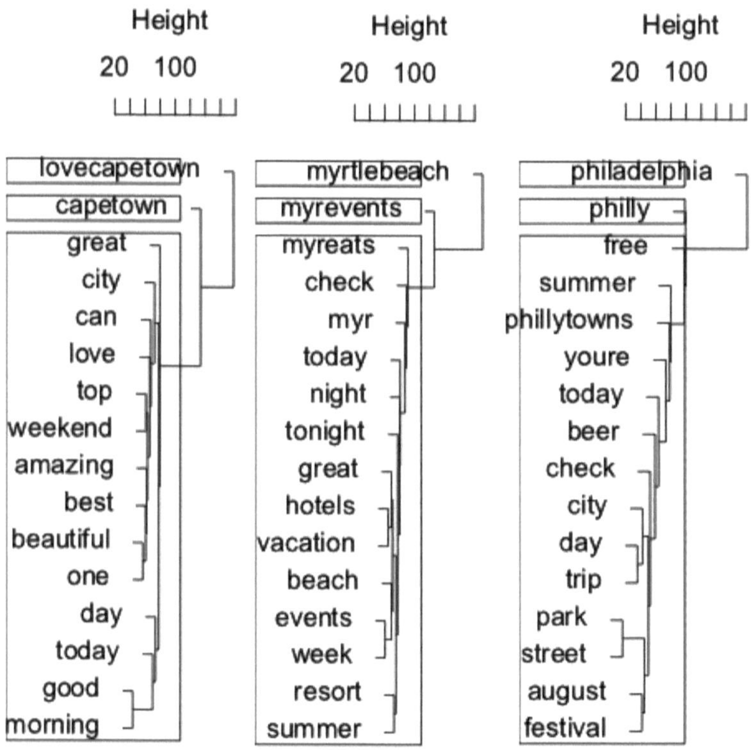

Fig. 16.1 Word dendrograms

Fig. 16.2 Word cloud

The second part, descriptive data, was analyzed to establish the background information for the content of the tweets and the interaction between the users. Additionally, at the *followers* and *following* figures—respectively number of users subscribe to the Twitter updates coming from the city's account, and of other accounts the city subscribes—were manually gathered by visiting the account pages on Twitter.

The third part was used to understand the relationship between the cities and other users and was conceptualized as an egocentric network (Wasserman and Faust 1998) with the official Twitter account of the cities being at the center. An egocentric network puts one user in the center of the network and analyzes its interactions with other users (Wasserman and Faust 1998). Within the framework of this research, the Twitter accounts of all three cities are put in the center of a social network that is composed of all other users the cities interact. The analysis focused on identifying the frequency of interactions between the cities and other Twitter users. Network analysis and visualization were done in *gephi*, a network analysis software used to explore and visual social networks (Bastian et al. 2009).

The analysis is triangulated by an impressionistic study of the activity on the Facebook accounts of three cities: *CapeTown.Travel*, *VisitPhilly*, and *myrtlebeach.*[9] The content and interactions on Facebook are analyzed in order to assess the similarities and/or differences between the two popular platforms. It should be noted that Facebook analysis was carried out following the Twitter analysis with the sole intention to assess whether the findings on Twitter were solely platform-specific or were also observed on other popular social media platforms.

16.4 Findings

All three cities have been actively using Twitter as part of their communication strategies. Table 16.1 shows the level of activities for each account. VisitPhilly account is older and has generated a larger volume of tweets than the other two combined. The accounts all have a positive follower to following ratio. In other words, more users subscribe to the updates of the cities than the cities do. The same behavior is observed in most of the popular Twitter accounts (twittercounter 2014). However, it should be noted that there is not necessarily a golden ratio follower/following ratio on Twitter.

VisitPhilly has generated significantly a higher volume of tweets than the other two accounts. The same pattern was also observed within the period included in this research. MyrtleBeach and CapeTownTourism had an average of 10.6 and 11.7 tweets per day, respectively, while VisitPhilly sent out 21.2 tweets a day.

Table 16.2 shows the summary of the structure of the tweets. The first two columns look at the relationship between the content and outside in content. *Outside links* column shows the frequency of the tweets that included a hyperlink that forward users to an outside resource. *Hashtag* refers to the tweets using Twitter's proposed way of categorizing subjects by using a # symbol followed by a word—also known as hashtagging. All three accounts use Twitter to disseminate information available on non-Twitter platforms through links. MyrtleBeach has the highest

[9] The names given here are Facebook handles. The actual pages can be visited at the URL www.facebook.com/handle, e.g. http://www.facebook.com/CapeTown.Travel Please note that Facebook handles are case sensitive.

Table 16.1 Descriptive statistics[a]

	Active since	Tweets	Followers	Following	Follower/ following ratio
VisitPhilly	2008	31,327	78,734	3,098	2,541/1
MyrtleBeach	2009	14,004	14,552	551	2,641/1
CapeTownTourism	2009	17,342	54,868	9,762	562/1

[a]Up-to-date figures as of September 15, 2014

Table 16.2 Number of tweets with links, references, and hashtags

	Tweets with/out of 3,200			
	Outside links	Hashtags	Other users	Retweet
VisitPhilly	2,110	1,015	2,223	116
MyrtleBeach	3,075	1,964	1,274	130
CapeTownTourism	1,950	2,221	2,350	946

number, with 96 % of its tweets including an outside link. This high number is caused by the fact that the account uses Twitter to forward its followers to its own website—myrtlebeach.com—and the content available over there.

Hashtags indicate that the accounts attempt to affiliate the content they share with other shared content by labeling them. Yet, the most frequent hashtags used by the accounts tend to be the ones they establish. Except for two hashtags used by VisitPhilly, the top five hashtags refer to the projects and slogans created by the accounts. For instance, MyrtleBeach uses *#myrevents* and *#myreats* to categorize its events- and restaurant-related content. CapeTownTourism labels most of its tweets with *#lovecapetown* and *#welovecapetown* hashtags. VisitPhilly, in addition to its own hashtags, uses *#free* and *#twchats*. The former hashtag indicates promotional campaigns and giveaways. The latter stands for "travel weekly chats" and is used by avid travellers to share information with each other.

The tweets also include references to other tweets. Moreover, these references are predominantly not *retweets* or the sharing of a content that was previously shared by another users. The non-retweet references to another user indicate that the accounts attempt to directly include certain users in their conversations. Table 16.3 shows the users with the ten highest interaction levels.[10]

VisitPhilly predominantly interacts with local attractions and other officials. Similarly, MyrtleBeach uses Twitter to communicate with the landmarks, movie theaters, events, and other attractions in the city. CapeTownTourism differs from the first two as it communicates with non-official city marketing campaigns, as well as its own employees, frequently.

In terms of content shared by the accounts, the research focused on word frequencies and affiliations. Figure 16.1 shows the most frequently used words,

[10]In the cases where two or more users are tied for the tenth place, they were all included in the list.

Table 16.3 Users with highest interactions

VisitPhilly		MyrtleBeach		CapeTownTourism	
Saxbys	Local at.	brookgreensc	Local at.	cityofct	Official
Philamuseum	Local at.	alabamatheatre	Local at.	vandawaterfront	Local at.
Pennslanding	Local at.	broadwayatbeach	Local at.	capetown	Marketing
Visitbuckspa	Local at.	thecarolinaopry	Local at.	gotosouthafrica	Official
Thebarnes	Local at.	medievaltimes	Local at.	wdc2014	Local at.
Franklinsqr	Local at.	pelicanbaseball	Local at.	48hrsincapetown	Marketing
Theovalphl	Local at.	palacetheatremb	Local at.	ctcarnival	Local at.
july4thphilly	Local at.	marketcommon	Local at.	tablemountainca	Local at.
Pafacademy	Local at.	ripleysaquamb	Local at.	fazielahw	Employee
Dibrunobros	Local at.	legends_mbsc	Local at.	enverduminy	Employee
phlvisitorcntr	Official			futurecapetown	Local group
				wtmafrica	Local group

Table 16.4 Word associations

Philadelphia	Myrtle Beach[a]	Capetown
Top	Blog	Stadium
Picks	Events	Outside
Ale	Resorts	Photograph
Festivals	Things	South Africa
Koozies	Hotels	Canon

[a]The list for Myrtle Beach is edited to exclude names of months from association list

grouped together based on their proximities to each other. The dendrograms are drawn in three clusters.

In each case, the first two clusters solely include one word, which is closely related to the city's name. The last clusters include 14 words that are affiliated with the other two clusters. The branches within the clusters show which word pairs or groups have been used together more frequently.

The third clusters essentially are composed of generic concepts or touristic aspects. Apart from minor exceptions—such as phillytowns and myreats—the concepts do not necessarily give us an idea about the main characteristics, peculiarities, or identities of the cities. It is even difficult to use these concepts to determine to which city the graph belongs.

The further analysis of word association reveals similar results. Table 16.4 lists the five words most closely associated with the city's names. The associations are based on generic concepts or events that are promoted. In the case of Philadelphia, the concepts predominantly revolve around a highly promoted beer festival. Myrtle Beach associations are relevant to the content on myrtlebeach.com—an event calendar and a hotel finder. Cape Town lists photography-related concepts as it shares content from photo-sharing websites.

Table 16.5 Facebook pages[a]

	Active since	Likes
VisitPhilly	2009	404,670
MyrtleBeach	2010	569,953
CapeTownTourism	2009	333,254

[a]Up-to-date figures as of September 15, 2014

Following the aforementioned findings on Twitter, the research focus shifted to Facebook. As Table 16.5 shows, all three cities enjoy a higher number of users subscribing to their accounts. Users interact with the content published by the cities by "sharing," "liking," or "commenting." Users also post their own content to the pages.

The messages revolve around marketing campaigns. During the time covered in this research, VisitPhilly shared content about the summer festivals, MyrtleBeach about summer deals, and CapeTownTourism about its Table Mountain promotion campaign. The interactions between the cities and other Facebook users were observed to be limited to local attractions, officials, and other marketing platforms. There has been little to no interaction with "ordinary" individuals. In rare occasions, the cities replied back to the questions coming from individuals.

16.5 Discussion

This chapter attempted to assess whether local governments were able to realize the potential and unique capabilities of social media platforms in their place branding attempts. The activities of three cities on Twitter and Facebook were analyzed to answer two research questions focusing respectively on the content of the messages and the nature of interaction between users.

Theoretical works in the field of communication and branding argue that organizations need to be aware of the characteristics of social media and can innovatively produce platform-specific content and promote a two-way communication between places and target audiences, rather than a message exposure. The academic literature also presents numerous successful examples of such usage from the corporate world. The findings of this research, though, argue local governments are not using social media platforms as effectively as they could.

Social media enable the local governments to promote the unique characteristics of their cities in a relatively less costly platform. The concepts of place brands and place branding are based on an assumption that cities have unique characteristics that they can promote (Anholt 2007). However, Twitter and Facebook presence of Philadelphia, Myrtle Beach, and Cape Town suggests that the cities tend to market short-term events rather than work towards establishing a brand (Govers 2011; Pike 2008). Social media is more likely to be used as a marketing and an advertising outlet. As Fig. 16.2—as well as the text analysis—shows, the content shared by three cities include event-based and generic concepts.

One of the most important—and unique—possibilities provided by social media in the field of branding in general and place branding in specific is brand co-creation. Yet, as it was apparent especially in Twitter analysis, social media is used to disseminate content created by the cities. Evident in the Twitter following/follower ratios, the cities are more interested in establishing an audience base that subscribes to their updates, rather than engaging in genuine conversation.

The ego-centric network shows limited interaction with other users. In all three networks, the official Twitter accounts of the city are placed in the middle and their relations with other users are shown. The smaller unlabeled dots are the other users that the city has interacted with at least once. The labeled dots are the ones with the highest interaction frequency (cf. Fig. 16.3). Thus, there is not necessarily a network, but rather the city interacting infrequently with various users. Therefore, it is not possible to argue that the Twitter accounts became digital offices or virtual platforms where stakeholders negotiated the meaning of brand identity.

Succinctly stated, social media presents various opportunities for especially smaller cities to brand themselves. Moreover, given the fact that there are ample opportunities for negotiating the meaning of brands (Andéhn et al. 2014) and for co-creating brands (Kavaratzis and Hatch 2013), place branding on social media has the potential to be more persuasive. Based on the findings of this research, it should be argued that there is room for improvement in the use of social media by local governments to brand their cities.

The originality of this research stems from its methodology and its findings. Prior research in place branding argues that audience participation is necessary for a successful branding campaign (Lucarelli and Berg 2011; Zenker and Erfgen 2014). It is also argued that social media is an inherent part of place branding (Fouts 2010). Even in the case of teaching place branding, faculty members acknowledge the importance of social media and encourage students to employ these platforms during their in-class branding campaigns (Alon and Herath 2014). Similar to corporate branding, the lines between brand managers and audiences are getting blurry in place branding where internet users can be seen as content creators and distributors (Ketter and Avraham 2012). This particular research aimed to see whether the potential changes in the new media ecology are observed in the practice. The findings do not provide substantial evidence to argue that local governments are successfully utilizing social media platforms.

It should be noted that this study is not with its limitations. The findings and discussions are based predominantly on the analysis of Twitter usage and limited to the most recent 3,200 tweets per account. A longer study should be carried out to increase the confidence in the findings by assessing whether they are observed across time. Secondly, Facebook study was done in an impressionistic way to assess the findings of the initial analyses. A larger netnographic study (Kozinets 2002) might shed light on how and why people are more active and engaging on Facebook and present lessons for local governments. Last but not the least, case selection limits the generalizability of the findings. As an explanatory study, the case selection focused on introducing the best practices as typical cases of social media and place branding (Seawright and Gerring 2008). Future research should increase the diversity of the cases both in terms of the practitioner actor and social media platform.

Fig. 16.3 Network maps

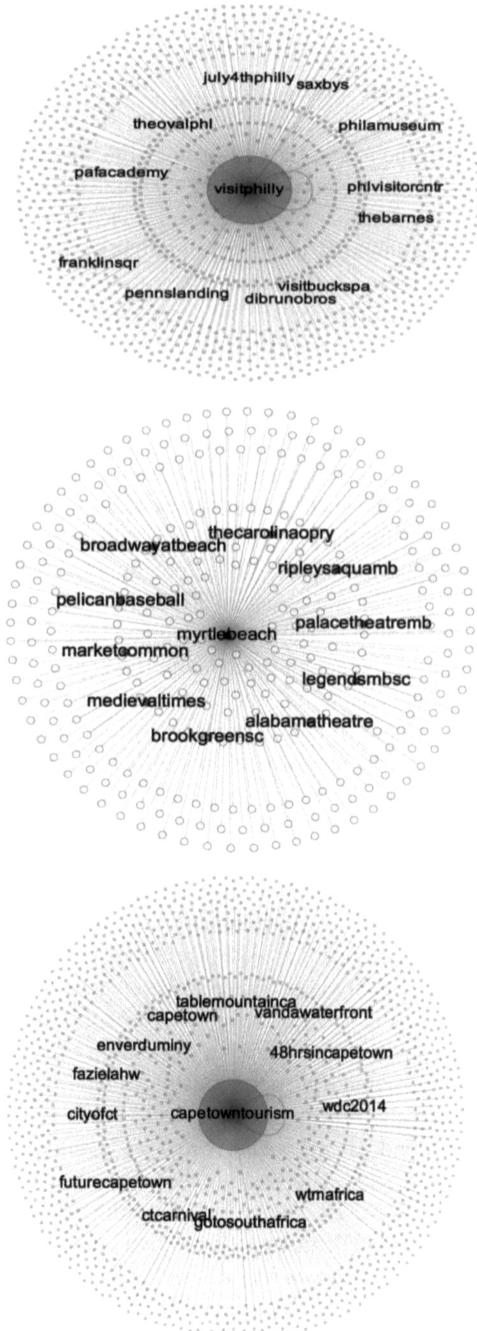

16.6 Conclusions and Recommendations

This chapter started out with an attempt to combine three separate theoretical strains to establish a research framework. *Media ecology* is introduced to choose the subject of the study. Instead of focusing solely on the messages disseminated on new platforms, social media is conceptualized as a system that affects both the content and the relations between users. Place branding communication justifies the focus on the content as secondary communication and the social networks as tertiary communication. Lastly, brand co-creation sets the borders of this research and provides further justification for the augmented role of relation and interactions in branding and of social networks in communication.

Social media has proved itself to be an indispensable communication platform. Particular social media websites—such as MySpace and ICQ—might lose their popularity in time and be replaced by new ones—such as Vine and Tumblr. Some might be popular only in certain regions—such as Orkut in India and Brazil. Yet, the fundamental idea is with us to stay: users are actively creating content and relations online. In line with the earlier research, this chapter started with the argument that social media has an unprecedented potential to change place branding (Björner and Sevin 2013; Ketter and Avraham 2012; Yan 2011; Zavattaro 2014). Yet, at the end, it is up to the local governments, city managers, and other destination branding officials to fulfill this potential. In line with the field of place branding and the objective of this book, the chapter is concluded with three recommendations to the practitioners.

First and foremost of all, *it is time to monitor and engage with the audiences*. Social media platforms do not follow the one-way and one-to-many communication understandings of traditional media (Smith 2013), but is based on a two-way and one-to-one communication understanding. It is indeed a new ecology. The "social" aspect of social media shows that the structure of communication is changing. Mass media communication theories used to argue that information would flow from media outlets to the audiences. However, social media information flow depends on the characteristics of social relations between users, rather than media outlets. The brand of a city is expected to be created, negotiated, and changed in a social environment. Therefore, being aware of the ideas of target audiences is an important component of contemporary branding communication. Local governments should invest in identifying the existing relations and in creating new social networks to effectively disseminate messages.

Second, *social media is fast but branding takes time*. A tweet can be sent relatively quickly, and various messages might be disseminated easily to online audiences. However, a place brand requires tedious work and long-term communication campaigns. The fast pace of digital communications does not change the fact that it takes time to create brand identities.

Last but not the least, practitioners should *get ready for the next platform: Web 3.0*. The digital landscape is always changing with new tools emerging everyday. Talks about a new web paradigm, Web 3.0, have already started (Hendler 2009). Practitioners should be ready for the next paradigm.

Successful incorporation of efficient social media use has the potential to transform place branding. Brands can no longer be created behind closed doors and then shared with audiences. On the contrary, failure to include audiences in brand creation processes is likely to damage the credibility of the messages. Through engaging the audiences and monitoring conversations taking place in the social media ecology, local governments can carry out important parts of their secondary and tertiary communication online.

In summary, local governments are yet to fully embrace the possibilities brought in by social media in the field of place branding. Currently, social media platforms are seen as relatively affordable outlets for direct dissemination of messages en masse. But as argued theoretically and observed in the corporate world, it is possible to use social media for stronger brands through engagement and brand co-creation.

References

Aitken, R., & Campelo, A. (2011). The four Rs of place branding. *Journal of Marketing Management, 27*(9–10), 913–933. doi:10.1080/0267257X.2011.560718.

Alon, I., & Herath, R. K. (2014). Teaching international business via socil media projects. *Journal of Teaching in International Business, 25*(1), 44–59.

Andéhn, M., Kazeminia, A., Lucarelli, A., & Sevin, E. (2014). User-generated place brand equity on Twitter: The dynamics of brand associations in social media. *Place Branding and Public Diplomacy, 10*(2), 132–144. doi:10.1057/pb.2014.8.

Anholt, S. (1998). Nation-brands of the twenty-first century. *Brand Management, 5*(6), 395–417.

Anholt, S. (2007). *Competitive identity: The new brand management for nations, cities and regions*. Basingstoke, England: Palgrave Macmillan.

Anholt, S. (2010). Definitions of place branding—Working towards a resolution. *Place Branding and Public Diplomacy, 6*(1), 1–10. doi:10.1057/pb.2010.3.

Aronczyk, M. (2013). *Branding the nation: The global business of national identity*. New York: Oxford University Press.

Auer, C., Srugies, A., & Loffelholz, M. (2012). *The role of social media in public diplomacy: Potentials and reality*. Paper presented at the International Studies Association, San Diego, CA.

Bastian, M., Heymann, S., & Jacomy, M. (2009). *Gephi: an open source software for exploring and manipulating networks*. Paper presented at the International AAAI Conference on Weblogs and Social Media.

Björner, E. (2013). International positioning through online city branding: The case of Chengdu. *Journal of Place Management and Development, 6*(3), 203–226. doi:10.1108/JPMD-03-2013-0006.

Björner, E., & Sevin, E. (2013). *A new China: Portrayal of Chinese cities in the international arena*. Paper presented at the City Branding Symposium 2013: Positioning Cities: Innovative and Sustainable Strategies for City Development and Transformation, 23–15 October, 2013, Beijing.

Boisen, M., Terlouw, K., & van Gorp, B. (2011). The selective nature of place branding and the layering of spatial identities. *Journal of Place Management and Development, 4*, 135–147. doi:10.1108/17538331111153151.

Braun, E. (2011). Putting city branding into practice. *Journal of Brand Management, 19*, 257–267.

Braun, E., Kavaratzis, M., & Zenker, S. (2013). My city: My brand—The different roles of residents in place branding. *Journal of Place Management and Development, 6*(1), 18–28. doi:10.1108/17538331311306087.

Csardi, G., & Nepusz, T. (2006). The igraph software package for complex network research. *InterJournal Complex Systems, 1695.*
Fan, Y. (2010). Branding the nation: Towards a better understanding. *Place Branding and Public Diplomacy, 6*(2), 97–103. doi:10.1057/pb.2010.16.
Feinerer, I., Hornik, K., & Meyer, D. (2008). Text mining infrastructure in R. *Journal of Statistical Software, 25*(5), 1–54.
Fellows, I. (2014). *wordcloud: Word clouds*. Retrieved from http://CRAN.R-project.org/package=wordcloud
Fischer, E., & Reuber, A. R. (2011). Social interaction via new social media: (How) can interactions on Twitter affect effectual thinking and behavior? *Journal of Business Venturing, 26*(1), 1–18. doi:10.1016/j.jbusvent.2010.09.002.
Fouts, J. S. (2010). Social media and immersive worlds: Why international place branding doesn't get weekends off. In F. M. Go & R. Govers (Eds.), *International place branding yearbook 2010 place branding in the new age of innovation* (pp. 113–120). Basingstoke, England: Palgrave Macmillan.
Gentry, J. (2013). *twitteR: R based Twitter client*. Retrieved from http://CRAN.R-project.org/package=twitteR
Gerring, J. (2009). Case selection for case-study analysis: Qualitative and quantitative techniques. In J. M. Box-Steffensmeier, H. E. Brady, & D. Collier (Eds.), *The Oxford handbook of political methodology* (1st ed., Vol. 1, pp. 645–685). Oxford, England: Oxford University Press.
Go, F. M., & Govers, R. (2010). The e-branding of places. In F. M. Go & R. Govers (Eds.), *International place branding yearbook 2010 place branding in the new age of innovation* (pp. 121–131). Basingstoke, England: Palgrave Macmillan.
Govers, R. (2011). From place marketing to place branding and back. *Place Branding and Public Diplomacy, 7*(4), 227–231. doi:10.1057/pb.2011.28.
Gretzel, U., & Yoo, K. H. (2008). Use and impact of online travel reviews. In P. O'Connor, W. Höpken, & U. Gretzel (Eds.), *Information and communication technologies in tourism 2008* (pp. 35–46). Vienna, Austria: Springer.
Gudjonsson, H. (2005). Nation branding. *Place Branding, 1*(3), 283–298. doi:10.1057/palgrave.pb.5990029.
Hakala, U., & Lemmetyinen, A. (2011). Co-creating a nation brand "bottom up.". *Tourism Review, 66*(3), 14–24. doi:10.1108/16605371111175294.
Hatch, M. J., & Schultz, M. (2010). Toward a theory of brand co-creation with implications for brand governance. *Journal of Brand Management, 17*(8), 590–604. doi:10.1057/bm.2010.14.
Hayden, C., & Sevin, E. (2012). The politics of meaning and the city brand: The controversy over the branding of Ankara. *Place Branding and Public Diplomacy, 8*(2), 133–146. doi:10.1057/pb.2012.8.
Hendler, J. (2009). Web 3.0 emerging. *Computer, 42*(1), 111–113. doi:10.1109/MC.2009.30.
Jansen, B. J., Zhang, M., Sobel, K., & Chowdury, A. (2009). Twitter power: Tweets as electronic word of mouth. *Journal of the American Society for Information Science and Technology, 60*(11), 2169–2188. doi:10.1002/asi.21149.
Kavaratzis, M. (2004). From city marketing to city branding: Towards a theoretical framework for developing city brands. *Place Branding, 1*(1), 58–73. doi:10.1057/palgrave.pb.5990005.
Kavaratzis, M. (2005). Place branding: A review of trends and conceptual models. *The Marketing Review, 5*(4), 329–342. doi:10.1362/146934705775186854.
Kavaratzis, M., & Ashworth, G. (2006). City branding: An effective assertion of identity or a transitory marketing trick? *Place Branding, 2*(3), 183–194. doi:10.1057/palgrave.pb.5990056.
Kavaratzis, M., & Hatch, M. J. (2013). The dynamics of place brands: An identity-based approach to place branding theory. *Marketing Theory, 13*(1), 69–86. doi:10.1177/1470593112467268.
Ketter, E., & Avraham, E. (2012). The social revolution of place marketing: The growing power of users in social media campaigns. *Place Branding and Public Diplomacy, 8*(4), 285–294. doi:10.1057/pb.2012.20.
Kozinets, R. V. (2002). The field behind the screen: Using netnography for marketing research in online communities. *Journal of Marketing Research, 39*(1), 61–72. doi:10.2307/1558584.

Litvin, S. W., Goldsmith, R. E., & Pan, B. (2008). Electronic word-of-mouth in hospitality and tourism management. *Tourism Management, 29*(3), 458–468. doi:10.1016/j.tourman.2007.05.011.

Lucarelli, A., & Berg, P. O. (2011). City branding: A state-of-the-art review of the research domain. *Journal of Place Management and Development, 4*(1), 9–27. doi:10.1108/17538331111117133.

Marmier, P., & Fetscherin, M. (2010). Public-private partnership to foster science, higher education, and innovation: The case of Switzerland with swissnex Boston. In F. M. Go & R. Govers (Eds.), *International place branding yearbook 2010 place branding in the new age of innovation* (pp. 97–112). Basingstoke, England: Palgrave Macmillan.

McLuhan, M. (1964). *Understanding media: The extensions of man*. New York: McGraw-Hill.

McLuhan, M. (1967). *The medium is the message: An inventory of effects*. London: Penguin.

Mendes, A. (2013). *International broadcasting and social media*. Washington, DC: Public Diplomacy Council.

Munar, A. M. (2011). Tourist-created content: Rethinking destination branding. *International Journal of Culture, Tourism and Hospitality Research, 5*(3), 291–305. doi:10.1108/1750618 1111156989.

Pew Research Center. (2013). *Social networking fact sheet*. Retrieved from http://www.pewinternet.org/fact-sheets/social-networking-fact-sheet/

Pike, S. (2008). *Destination marketing: An integrated marketing communication approach*. Amsterdam: Butterworth-Heinemann.

Porter, M. (1990). *The competitive advantage of nations*. New York: Free Press.

Postman, N. (2000). *The humanism of media ecology*. Keynote address presented at the Inaugural Media Ecology Association Convention, New York.

Potts, J., Hartley, J., Banks, J., Burgess, J., Cobcroft, R., Cunningham, S., et al. (2008). Consumer co-creation and situated creativity. *Industry & Innovation, 15*(5), 459–474. doi:10.1080/1366 2710802373783.

Prahalad, C. K., & Ramaswamy, V. (2004). *The future of competition: Co-creating unique value with customers*. Boston: Harvard Business School.

R Core Team. (2014). *R: A language and environment for statistical computing*. Vienna, Austria: R Foundation for Statistical Computing. Retrieved from http://www.R-project.org/

Seawright, J., & Gerring, J. (2008). Case selection techniques in case study research: A menu of qualitative and quantitative options. *Political Research Quarterly, 61*(2), 294–308. doi:10.1177/1065912907313077.

Sevin, E. (2011). Thinking about place branding: Ethics of concept. *Place Branding and Public Diplomacy, 7*(3), 155–164. doi:10.1057/pb.2011.15.

Sevin, E. (2013). Places going viral: Twitter usage patterns in destination marketing and place branding. *Journal of Place Management and Development, 6*(3), 227–239. doi:10.1108/JPMD-10-2012-0037.

Skip Town with Sun Valley. (2012). Retrieved October 30, 2014, from http://stoneskippingrobot.com/

Smith, W. (2013). *Brands must get social media right*. Retrieved from http://www.brandingstrategyinsider.com/2013/03/brands-must-get-social-media-right.html#.VCAz4L65LG6

Solis, B. (2011). *Engage! The complete guide for brands and businesses to build, cultivate, and measure success in the new web, revised and updated*. Hoboken, NJ: Wiley.

Strate, L. (2008). Studying media as media: McLuhan and the media ecology approach. *MediaTropes eJournal, 1*, 127–142.

Szondi, G. (2010). From image management to relationship building: A public relations approach to nation branding. *Place Branding and Public Diplomacy, 6*(4), 333–343. doi:10.1057/pb.2010.32.

twittercounter. (2014). *Twitter top 100 most followers*. Retrieved from http://twittercounter.com/pages/100

Van Ham, P. (2001). The rise of the brand state. *Foreign Affairs, 80*(5), 2–8.

Wasserman, S., & Faust, K. (1998). *Social network analysis: Methods and applications*. Cambridge, England: Cambridge University Press.

Xiang, Z., & Gretzel, U. (2010). Role of social media in online travel information search. *Tourism Management, 31*(2), 179–188. doi:10.1016/j.tourman.2009.02.016.

Yan, J. (2011). Social media in branding: Fulfilling a need. *Journal of Brand Management, 18*(9), 688–696. doi:10.1057/bm.2011.19.

Zavattaro, S. M. (2014). *Place branding through phases of the image: Balancing image and substance*. Retrieved from http://www.palgraveconnect.com/doifinder/10.1057/9781137394514

Zenker, S., & Braun, E. (2010). *Towards an integrated approach for place brand management*. Paper presented at the 50th European Regional Science Association Congress, 19–23 August 2010, Jönköping, Sweden.

Zenker, S., & Erfgen, C. (2014). Let them do the work: a participatory place branding approach. *Journal of Place Management and Development, 7*(3), 225–234. http://doi.org/10.1108/JPMD-06-2013-0016.

Chapter 17
Social Media Use in Crisis Communication Management: An Opportunity for Local Communities?

Rocio Zamora Medina and Jose Carlos Losada Diaz

Abstract Social media has changed the way public administrations face their strategic communications, to the point that social media networks are considered even more effective tools for managing a risk or a crisis than traditional media. This chapter reflects on the opportunity Twitter presents for local governments facing critical scenarios, according to the main principles of the theory of Crisis Communication Management. A qualitative analysis from this perspective of how the Madrid city government faced the Madrid Arena tragedy lets us learn from the city government's main mistakes, allowing us to think about the opportunity that social media presents local communities.

17.1 Introduction

Social networks have become essential for every organization facing a critical scenario for strategic communication. New practices have recently been analyzed that can help communicators better manage a risk or a crisis using these new tools (Veil et al. 2011). Though much research has investigated crisis communication and social media separately, very little study has been done of the effects of social media on crisis communication.

Compared to traditional media, social networks are agile and provide feedback information, both considered key elements of a correct institutional answer or reaction to serious situations (Sandman 2006; Gonzalez-Herrero and Smith 2010; Keller 2011). Social media networks are increasingly essential tools that public institutions must use to target messages strategically, appropriately, and very directly and quickly. They provide first-hand information about what is happening

R.Z. Medina (✉) • J.C.L. Diaz
Facultad de Comunicación y Documentación, Universidad de Murcia,
Campus Universitario de Espinardo, Murcia 30100, Spain
e-mail: rzamoramedina@um.es; jclosada@um.es

M.Z. Sobaci (ed.), *Social Media and Local Governments*, Public Administration and Information Technology 15, DOI 10.1007/978-3-319-17722-9_17

moment-by-moment and also provide insight into the opinion-shaping process. They also allow the possibility of individualized guidance messages, which build emotional links between the institution and its publics that are crucial for crisis-management success.

In the context of local government, proximity can make social media even more influential and consequential on the public interest. With its enormous mobilization capability, social media offers a new and broader perspective for institutional communication in local contexts, but it also offers new risks and challenges. For instance, any demand, event, or complaint against the local government on social media can be amplified into viral content and spread quickly to a large number of people, causing a reputational crisis. For that reason, social networks should be considered not only as a place to broadcast important information about the community, but also as a new place where public judgments about what is going on are expressed, which can be used to understand social concerns that point towards the best way to manage critical situations (Stephens et al. 2005; Reynolds and Seeger 2005).

This chapter considers how local governments are using social networks (Twitter) to complement traditional media in facing critical scenarios according to the main principles of the theory of Crisis Communication Management. An analysis of how the Madrid city government faced the Madrid Arena tragedy from the perspective of crisis communication management will be useful in evaluating these practices. This exploratory study will lead to better understanding of this new practice as an opportunity (Kim and Liu 2012), while at the same time measuring the risks from managing crises through social media and learning about the major mistakes involved with or poor uses of these new tools.

17.2 Crisis Management: From Traditional to Social Media

In recent years, the functions, resources, and budgets for communication in public administrations have significantly increased. This growth in action around public communication includes the increased use of traditional tools (in particular, relationships with media) alongside the use of digital tools that allow direct access and closer relationships with citizens. The recent European Communication Monitor report underscores that, for 88 % of communication managers interviewed in 42 European countries, on-line communication is an increasingly strategic consideration in 85 % of cases, while social media is a consideration in 62 % and mobile communication is a concern in nearly 51 % of cases (Zerfass et al. 2014). According to the European Communication Monitor (Zerfass et al. 2013), seven out of ten communication professionals in Europe faced crisis-communication situations during the last year. In the case of public institutions, 45 % have suffered several crises, and 20 % have faced at least one.

In urgent crisis situations, the purpose of communication is always the same: “to influence the public’s perception of the organization and to maintain a positive image or restore a damaged image among stakeholders" (Ray 1999:75). But everything becomes more difficult in a global and more technologized world. As Lerbinger (1997:172) points out, "the number of crisis incidents and their severity is rising along with the growing complexity of technology and society."

In large part, we can say that crises were much more controllable in a non-digital world because there were standardized conflict-resolution patterns affecting institutions or public personalities. These patterns were applied by communication consultants who held undisputed domain over the most important elements of crisis management: newsworthy values, mass media control, and enough economic resources, which secured influence on public opinion.

Everything has now become much more complex. Gonzalez-Herrero and Smith (2010) summarized the former panorama as:

> A very complex discipline, since (a) any organization is facing today many more potential crisis scenarios than ever before (a fact that has clear implications for issues management, crisis planning, and resource assignment, among others); and (b) crisis situations spread today in a viral way, breaking geographical and time barriers in a matter of seconds.

Rules of Public Communication have changed and, suddenly, multiple players, especially using social networks, have joined the "public" game with voice and enough authority to question official versions and to destroy any controlled or planned messages that affect public perceptions of the facts. Coombs (2013) sums up the role of social media in a crisis as follows: "Social media potential increases the various stakeholders to request information about the crisis." Weller et al. (2014:374) underline how social media can be used in several ways "(...) to disseminate breaking news, coordinate responses, monitor new developments, and express sympathy; news and emergency organizations around the world are now regularly incorporating social media into their crisis activities."

Under these new circumstances, any informed actor, by questioning the official version and mobilizing the affected community with wide resonance in the online and offline world, can cause irreparable damage to organizational reputation and destroy institutional handling of a crisis. From self-organizing and self-governing theory, Elinor Ostrom (1990) pointed out that when public authorities take no responsibility, people find a way to organize themselves, looking for and taking advantage of whatever communication resources they may reach. Ostrom believed in the power and intelligence of ordinary people to collectively solve their own problems, so long as higher-level governments did not interfere. Rather than starting from the assumption that users of common resources are helpless without an outside authority intervening to protect them from themselves, Ostrom (1990:160) assumes that "the capacity of individuals to extricate themselves from various types of dilemma situations *varies* from situation to situation," adopting the empirical approach of surveying "both successful and unsuccessful efforts to escape tragic outcomes." The consequence of those assumptions is that, when public authorities are out of sight, people tend to use social media more frequently to "solve" or "face" a critical situation. In a networked society, people interact with each other under what has been called a "mass self-communication" model (Castells 2009).

Those who do not understand or underestimate the importance of the digital version of facts themselves for stakeholders hopelessly lose the battle of public perceptions. For this reason, Wendling et al. (2013:10) suggests, "organizations that choose not to use social media during a crisis may be taken as disorganized by the public or even sending a signal of disinterest or disdain." Public institutions cannot miss the enormous capacity of these tools to be incorporated into crisis-communication planning. As Freberg (2012:416) points out:

> Contemporary public relations practice, and crisis communications in particular, is being challenged by the emergence of social media. Although many of the best practices used in traditional media are likely to remain effective in the domain of social media, some may require adaptation.

17.3 Social Media Offer New Tools for Crisis Communication Management

Social media offers clear advantages in the management of institutional conflicts. This need to incorporate social media into crisis management has led researchers to develop theories and approaches that match and are responsive to the Social Media Crisis Communication Model (SMCC) of Jin and Liu (2010).

From a broad perspective, scholars have underlined the key factors in any crisis management situation. One of the first has to do with the need for a fast response. Utz et al. (2013:40) have explained how "social media might be especially useful during organizational crises, because concerned publics can be informed quickly and directly, and because organizations can engage in a dialog with them."

Time is always a critical factor in how an institution is positioned with respect to the facts. Therefore, the ability of an organization to be visible, fast, and to provide (and receive) information is key. Stephens et al. (2005:390) explain this need, writing, "the organization must respond immediately to protect itself and others, as well as to regain control." It is essential to follow the evolution of the crisis as such in order that communication not seem outdated or decontextualized, something that has harmful results for organizational credibility.

Social media have other, distinct advantages. There are no middlemen, no brokers. This fact means that mass media, opinion leaders, or other actors cannot alter the literalness of an organization's message; its own opinion, its position, and its explanations are easily visible and impossible to spin.

Similarly, social media allows direct and immediate access to any actor involved or affected by a crisis or by its direct or indirect consequences. Ulmer and Sellnow (2000) underline the importance of identifying the most strategic publics in critical situations; as they explain, depending on the context or situation, organizations need to identify the identity of all involved stakeholders, especially because a crisis can expand the number of salient stakeholders.

Social media also provides feedback from all social actors who may be in contact. As Currye (2010) reminds us, "remember that social media is not just about you talking to the public; it is also about them talking to you and to each other." An organization can learn first-hand about doubts, worries, or even fundamental criticism from those in the network, making it possible to guide communication strategy towards the most sensitive issues, as well as to deeply analyze certain data, reorient priorities, or marginalize ineffective messages.

Social media has great power to actually monitor the real-time social debate, to detect rumors, and to identify the most concerning topics, even before the outbreak of a crisis, making an organization better able to intervene effectively if a crisis comes. Freberg (2012:420) underlines that "(…) constant monitoring of age cohorts' use of social media by researchers should assist professionals seeking to reach the most people in the shortest amount of time."

Furthermore, it appears there is increasingly overwhelming evidence that social networks are a particularly "human" channel, to the extent that these networks are simple, friendly, and part of the most citizens' day-to-day. For this reason, their use as an information source may be part of the "natural" management of information through which average individuals collect and generate their opinions about a fact.

Another important advantage of social media in crisis scenarios is its capacity to generate emotions, mostly among those directly or indirectly implicated in events. As some scholars have shown, emotional factors are key to the success or failure of crisis management. Following the suggestions of Utz et al. (2013:45), "organizations and PR departments should not only focus on rationalizations, but also address emotions." Stephens et al. (2005:410) underline that "audiences also use social media for emotional support and recovery from crises."

All these ideas regarding the advantages of using social media in crisis management scenarios have undoubtedly influenced active, open, and positive crisis management, but they should not enable us to forget that we should be careful in building and including content, because the mistakes that we make in this new medium are now more visible than ever. Their impact, therefore, is harder and harder to repair.

17.4 The Use of Social Media in Local Communities Facing Crisis Scenarios

Although crises have no geographical or skill limits in terms of how to manage them, when they arise in local or regional contexts, we should consider that organizational resources facing the crisis are smaller than those available on a national level. As O'Leary writes (2004:1), "virtually all disasters are experienced at the local level, where many communities can expect to be 'on their own' for the first 72 h after disaster impact." Local phenomena have certain distinctive features that should be recognized in order to generate an appropriate crisis communication strategy.

One of the first things to assess is, undoubtedly, the set of personal implications posed by local events—something explained by family or neighborhood proximity—which ultimately affects crisis management. Normally, this "personal" approach to the consequences of a crisis is even more important than in a national context, where an approach involving organizational or institutional reputation is more important.

Second, the management of a crisis in a local environment is more direct, closer, and especially more immediate. This is because the consequences of the crisis are more visible for citizens, who perceive them more directly. There is a much higher chance than in national contexts for stakeholders to contrast data about what is happening related to an emergency fact or event with the information disseminated from an organization.

Third, in terms of communication resources, most local institutions and organizations have public communication strategies that depend on traditional, local media in a highly controlled communication system. Since traditional messaging by organizations attempts to be scripted, controlled, and one-way—particularly crisis communications—the nature of social media would appear, on the surface, to be at odds with this fundamental goal.

Finally, local anticipation of and preparation for a crisis is not a routine matter. Local public institutions are far from understanding communication from a sufficiently broad perspective and often do not understand the need for professionals, instruments, and strategies tailored to potential crisis situations. In fact, few local organizations are professionally prepared for a crisis situation.

Though social media presents a challenge to managing communication in local contexts (Zhang et al. 2010), organizations and local governments are experimenting with social media to communicate with their constituents and stakeholders. Informing citizens about what governments are doing can encourage transparency and accountability (Chun et al. 2010; Cromer 2010) as well as trust and democracy, making social media a source of legitimization and credibility. Many analysts see in these media a powerful set of tools to reinvent government–citizen relationships, creating a more open government and facilitating openness, transparency, and democratization (Lathrop and Ruma 2010).

Although most local governments are using Web 2.0 and social media tools to enhance transparency, approximately half of local governments have no active presence in any social networks at all; they are mere passive onlookers, if that (Bonson et al. 2012). At the same time, local contexts are normally not prepared to face unexpected crises. The most frequent initial reaction is silence or communication that undermines the dimensions of the crisis. Silence, however, rarely works. It makes an organization appear guilty or supports the perception that it is actively hiding unpleasant facts. To the contrary, organizations should assume a proactive role, spreading relevant information widely while keeping an open dialogue with their stakeholders and expressing empathy with the main victims. As Syme (2011) suggests, "if information is transparent, honest and empathetic, sentiment will eventually sway in favor of an organization."

17.5 Twitter as a Tool for Crisis Management in the Local Context

Although sometimes criticized as trivial, Twitter is developing a growing reputation as being a key channel for communication during crises and emergencies. In fact, "tweets communicate messages in ways that organizations cannot" (Smith 2010:332). This is especially true during the first moments of any critical situations because, as some scholars suggest (Weller et al. 2014:381), "[tweets] may also play an important role in the early detection of crisis situations." From that initial moment, and during the different phases of any crisis, research into the motives of users who follow politicians and organizations on Twitter indicates that Twitter serves as a channel for getting political information and interacting with political elites.

Twitter is also considered a good platform for expressing political convictions as well as exchanging information about political topics (Parmelee and Bichard 2012). Because Twitter enables the real-time propagation of information to any number of users, the platform presents an ideal environment for the dissemination of breaking news directly from the news source and/or from the geographical point of interest. In this respect, Weller et al. (2014:380) distinguished two main areas of activity:

> On the one hand, emergency services are interested in using twitter as an additional means to communicate their messages; on the other hand, they are also exploring the potential to monitor valuable situational information from directly affected locals in crisis-affected areas.

Message diffusion on Twitter is heavily dependent on retweets, which, besides spreading information, appear to help form a collective identity by showing fast responsiveness, affirmative validation, and emotional support for others' opinions (Cha et al. 2010; Hughes and Palen 2010; Segerberg and Bennett 2011).

Social interactions occur through direct messages (DM) and mentions using the at-sign (@), and even though at-messages address specific receivers or stakeholders, they are also posted on the recipient's public page. A follower who sends an organization a direct message (DM) or mentions it (through the use of the @ character) expects direct replies as soon as possible.

To increase visibility on Twitter, it is common to include hashtags in messages. The political value of using hashtags is that all tweets that use a particular hashtag are grouped together on Twitter and can be searched by anyone, including journalists. If a crisis is followed through a specific hashtag (prefaced by the # character), an organization can monitor the hashtag closely to see what is being said, responding regularly to applicable posts. By applying the relevant hashtag to responses, those following the crisis will also see the message, not only disseminating information but also providing answers to similar questions.

In this regard, Twitter is gaining widespread acceptance as a strategic means of communication about risks and emergencies. Certain features of Twitter, including "brevity in messages, mobility, and pervasive access through various devices, and broadcast nature" (Zhao and Rosson 2009) may render it useful not only for informational use, but also for collective activism and social mobilization (Parmelee and Bichard 2012). In addressing the question of how social media is used in emergency and mass-convergence situations, Hughes and Palen (2010) claim that Twitter messages sent during such a situation contain greater information broadcasting and brokerage.

During a crisis, the public may be reacting emotionally; rapid information can ease stress and help people make informed decisions. But inaccurate messages can also be a problem with social media, given the sheer number of people disseminating information with virtually no limits. The use of first-person, eyewitness accounts, and official sources is crucial. In this sense, Van der Meer and Verhoeven (2013:231) in their study explain how "the rapid mass self-communication made possible by Twitter resulted in instant public crisis framing based on assumptions." On the other hand, official feeds were able to disseminate important information to the public as well as to address rumors that finally were not true.

Twitter also challenges traditional gatekeeping because users receive information from different sources, most of which are not traditional media organizations. For crisis communication management, this fact has implications for the flow of information and message control. Rather than the priorities of the news media becoming the agenda of the public, the priorities of the public, as expressed through Twitter, become, in many instances, the agenda of the news media. Regular microbloggers on Twitter become "new agenda-setters" at times of fast-breaking news. At the same time, many political discussions on Twitter naturally emerge in reaction to traditional media coverage, albeit in a more "affective" manner based on subjective experiences, opinions, and emotions (Papacharissi and de Fatime Oliveira 2012).

In order to face and recognize sources of unofficial information and to incorporate different sensitivities and concerns in organizations' own discourse, Schultz et al. (2011:25) suggest that "for successful crisis communication it might therefore be important to address twitter users." In fact, they particularly consider the use of Twitter as a fundamental tool in a crisis, writing that "organizations should therefore pay more attention to Twitter, and strategically reflect on their media choice and the target groups' media use" (Schultz et al. 2011:26).

However, we cannot fail to mention the limitations that Twitter can present. We recommend Twitter be used as part of a broad strategy, alongside and complementing other communication channels, including traditional media. Findings suggest professionals should be careful and deliberate in their use of social media in crisis responses, while not neglecting traditional media.

17.6 Some Lessons from the Madrid Arena Crisis as a Case Study

On the night of October 31, 2012, Sports Pavilion Arena Madrid hosted the celebration of a Halloween "Thiller Music Park," at which many well-known electronic music DJs performed. Over 16,000 people were estimated to be in the enclosure that night, the vast majority of them young. Unfortunately, after 3:30 am, and for unknown reasons, a significant number of young people streamed out of the evacuation gates of the main track. Because of the crowded flow of young people, security officials shut the doors, causing a deadly avalanche that killed five girls.

From the first moments, emergency response was activated from all stakeholders involved, including political authorities (especially the Madrid City Council, which was responsible for managing the sports pavilion), security, and health services, in order to proceed to an evacuation of injured people and restoration of normal order. In the first moments, neither the causes nor the real consequences of the event were known. However, the management of this crisis had to account for all potentially relevant communicative scenarios in order to inform young people, provide information to families, and disseminate information among the general population regarding facts that could have a social impact.

We analyze the crisis communication management developed by the main actors involved, following the messages they spread on one of the most relevant and influential social media platforms, the microblogging service Twitter. By using a qualitative analysis of tweets that were posted from the beginning of the crisis until 10 days after the tragedy, two important aspects for the management of any crisis were considered for analysis: (1) the Twitter activity of those local authorities (political, security, health services) who had a duty to provide information about the tragedy from their own institutional or personal Twitter accounts, and (2) the social conversation generated on Twitter around this crisis under the primary hashtags #madridarena, #botelladimiteya, and #tragediamadriarena.

Results of analysis of the main actors' Twitter accounts give some idea about how and to what extent each of them used the microblogging service in facing that crisis. Notably, the Madrid city Mayor, Ana Botella, had no Twitter account or personal profile, so she could not participate in the public debate aroused on social media during the tragedy, something we consider to be a big mistake. All information coming from the local government she represented was spread from the institutional Twitter account of the Madrid City Council (@Madrid). The Twitter activity of this account was quite short, beginning on November 1st itself, shortly before 5 am, and finishing on the next day, the 2nd of November, at 2 pm. Over this short period, only five tweets were posted.

The first of the tweets was related to the official statement from Madrid City Hall, which received just 17 retweets. The most retweeted tweet announced a mourning day for the victims, which got 37 retweets. There was no more feedback or any other sort of contact with families, nor any possibly pertinent personal information. The institutional Twitter profile from Madrid City Hall, closed to the victims and to public feelings, only focused on technical information regarding legal measures to avoid this type of tragedy (like a new law prohibiting large parties) and information about Mourning Day in the city. It is also important to underscore that no hashtag accompanied any of the tweets posted on this institutional account, which could have facilitated their spread by grouping their tweets together.

Concerning the City Emergency & Health Services (SAMUR), we also found very poor activity on their Twitter profile. Only one tweet was posted a few minutes after the tragedy on the Emergency Madrid account (@EmergenciasMad). That tweet said, "SAMUR_PC attends five girls with cardiac arrest in Madrid Arena Halloween party. Three have died. The other two were transferred with critical conditions." This achieved 360 retweets, and 13 followers marked it as favorite. Apart from this first, descriptive tweet, SAMUR added no other tweets to their timeline later. They also did not use any hashtags to spread their message among followers.

Other actors that could have had something to say regarding the tragedy were the Madrid Police and regional authorities. However, none of them used Twitter as a tool to communicate with the public, preferring to use only traditional media for their statements. In terms of secondary authorities, the official Twitter account of the Thriller Music Park, @ThrillerMPark, also didn't refer to what happened, nor did the main DJ Steve Aoki, @steveaoki, who was considered the party's star.

Contrary to the poor activity that characterized the public institutions responsible for communication crisis management, Madrid citizens were very active on social media in general, and particularly Twitter. There were nearly 10,000 tweets from people who attended the party showing a mix of consternation and surprise about what had happened, because they were unaware of the tragedy until they arrived home. Analysis of the public conversation generated under the main hashtags showed that the microblogging network became the main sources of information about the tragedy for many young people. Hashtags like #madridarena or #tragediamadridarena were trending topic from the first moments. Other descriptive hashtags, like #Botelladimiteya, that sought the city Mayor's resignation (Ana Botella) were also relevant over the following days.

The first tweets under these hashtags focused on a description of "what" had occurred, pointing to the deadly avalanche that killed three girls and injured two more. Social conversation even included testimony from those that were there and could even see how the girls had died. It is important to underline that, as in the first moments of any crisis, there was a need for information, so SAMUR health services and even traditional media (wire services like EFE, the newspaper *El Mundo*, or radio stations like SER) were cited as main news sources. However, the most personal and emotional tweets came from those who were there and who began to share relevant photos and videos, which were spread and retweeted very fast.

Besides their condolences for the families and friends of the girls who died, most tweets expressed surprise about "how" it had happened. The main reasons cited included over-crowding or a flare thrown to the main stage that sparked panic among those in attendance. In the middle of this debate, official authorities posted no explanation. This was a clear mistake because, considering their need for information, citizens received explanations from other sources; whether true or not, in the end, some of these explanations were perceived and accepted as valid.

Rapidly, under the main hashtags arose a stream of comments about the number of tickets that were ultimately sold, the security resources, the closed egress doors, and the flexible entry of minors (under 18 years old) to the *macro-bolletón*. Consequently, the public was interested in determining "who" was the main actor responsible for the tragedy and how it could have been avoided. One of the first names that surfaced was Ana Botella, the mayor of Madrid City, who represented and personalized the institution of the Madrid City Council, which authorized the organization of that macro-bolletón and managed the Madrid Arena sports pavilion. Although the first and only statement from that institution denied their responsibility for the occurrence and pointed responsibility directly at the party organizers and the security services, the City Council's lack of presence on social media trying to explain to young people what was going on, proactively and with transparency, was understood as strategic silence, so that many people attributed to Ana Botella's political management culpability for the tragedy. Her early and principled political decision to prohibit *macro-bolletón* in Madrid for the future also aroused a wide stream of tweets from young people who expressed their indignation with the tragedy and the lack of responsibility taken by organizers.

The crisis therefore had its guilty person, expressed in microblogging by a new hashtag: #Botelladimiteya (demanding the city Mayor's resignation). This feeling was further fed by traditional media coverage, mostly by some television programs that had special reporting on the Madrid Arena case with full, detailed testimony, but with hardly any participation from Madrid City Council staff. Reactions to those programs were frequent and substantial on Twitter.

One of the most emotive streams of tweets was linked to the later death of the fourth girl who was injured at the *macro-bolletón*. A letter from her father was spread on Twitter. Even after this unfortunate event, the official account of the Madrid City Council posted no response. The crisis became "dirtier" when relevant information about a possible, privileged deal between the Madrid City Council and party organizers was filtered out of traditional media reports. At the same time, a tweet showed that the Council already knew about security problems at the Madrid Arena some years before the tragedy and that organizers lacked an appropriate license or emergency plan. This tweet was frequently retweeted with indignation. Once more, the response from the institution headed by Ana Botella was wrong. Instead of being transparent and showing documentation in the face of those accusations, their answer was to delete information and data regarding that event from the Council website.

One week after the tragedy, any assignment of responsibility could only be assumed. However, citizens wanted justice. Their social indignation grew even further when tweets noted Ana Botella's decision stay at a spa in Portugal even as the tragedy unfolded. The families of the victims joined the stream of indignation, making a joint statement to ask for the City Council to take responsibility. Once more, they found silence and finger pointing, with the Council blaming the party organizers.

At the same moment that the fifth girl who was injured died, updated information spread on Twitter about a new *macro-bolletón* organized by the same business that worked for the Madrid Arena. Neither the official prohibition announced by the City at the beginning of the crisis management nor the size of the tragedy—with five girls dead—were enough to stop it. Definitively, people's trust in the Madrid City Council, and especially in Ana Botella, had disappeared by that time.

17.7 Discussion

The Madrid Arena crisis communication management case study shows us a recurring way that public organizations choose to manage their crisis communications today: not to be present, preferring to stay away from the digital world and continue to use traditional communications tools. Qualitative analysis of the Twitter activity of local authorities (political, security, health services) that had a duty to provide information during the tragedy showed that their use of Twitter as a social media tool was poor and negligent. They showed a complete lack of sensitivity to victims and their families, a marked institutional coldness, and a complete lack of answers to citizens' specific need for information.

Their management of this crisis had several political consequences, including the resignations of several local politicians and a loss of public confidence in the Mayor of Madrid, Ana Botella (who decided not to run for re-election), as public-opinion polls showed. There was a possible corruption scandal regarding the management authority that organized these social events.

Due to the absence of any official version of events, the emotional speech of *macro-bolletón* participants defined most messages on Twitter, conditioning public interpretations of events. Furthermore, a new wave of smears arose about the real danger and potential threat of raves, with consequent uncertainty for the families of teenagers involved. The feeling that one chose danger or risk as a result of a decision to take part in one of a *macro-bolletón* seized Madrid society, regardless of whether or not such information was entirely true. In fact, as noted Freberg (2012):

> It is not necessary to gather complete information before communicating a problem to the public. If there is a reason to believe that the public is in danger, a message stating that "we think there is a problem" and requests that the public regularly check back for further information is likely to elicit significant compliance (p. 421).

Another consequence resulting from the political mismanagement of this crisis included changes in the future behavior of Madrid society. The broad social conversation generated on Twitter around this event showed that, when public institutions are silent, people talk, especially on social networks, but mostly in a more belligerent way. In the absence of an official release, people built their own version of the story, collaboratively, through the exchange of messages on Twitter and other social networks. This case serves to demonstrate the power and intelligence of ordinary people who can collectively solve their own problems so long as higher-level government does not interfere, to build with their own resources their own public discourse, self-organizing just as Ostrom (1990) pointed out.

17.8 Conclusions

The present research has underlined the importance of social media for organizations in the context of crisis communication management. In order to better lead public efforts during crises, public institutions should consider the potential these new communication tools have to spread their strategic messages and help them listen to their stakeholders.

As this chapter explains, social media offers clear advantages for managing any institutional conflicts. In the specific case of crises in a local context, the use of social media is even more crucial, because proximity leads to direct influence on stakeholders and victims. In order to increase their visibility, local entities that face crises should consider that the task of implementing a dialogue with stakeholders is much more important than the (expected) mass distribution of messages on social media under a one-way model of communications.

But even as Twitter gains widespread acceptance as a strategic tool for communicating about risks and emergencies, some have fears and ignorance regarding how to use it properly for strategic communication. The Madrid Arena case study serves as a good example of this. Some of the lessons suggested by the literature review related to the use of social media in crisis contexts were, definitively, not followed in this case; local institutions' use of social media was a clear failure. Local politicians underestimated the importance of a "personal" approach to the crisis's consequences, as well as underestimating the specific community interests that were a priority for victim's families and required to provide proper assistance. They also forgot that, in local contexts, stakeholders are able to contrast data about what is happening related to an emergency fact or event with the information disseminated from an organization. In the Madrid Arena Tragedy, with the number of people that were inside the *macro-bolletón* or the number of tickets that were ultimately sold, people could easily determine these facts for themselves. Due to their dependency on traditional media and the lack of official messages on Twitter from the start of the tragedy, when local politicians tried to control public perceptions related to this event on social media, it was already too late. Finally, after this failure of crisis communication management, local authorities in Madrid have learned about the need to anticipate a crisis with a crisis.

We assume that the use of social media is a recent phenomenon that requires more experimentation and implementation for officials to properly use it as a communications tool. Further research should be done on similar situations in order to improve recommendations for planning future communication strategies in crisis contexts, with the goal of encouraging transparency and accountability.

References

Bonson, E., Torres, L., Royo, S., & Flores, F. (2012). Local e-government 2.0: Social media and corporate transparency in municipalities. *Government Information Quarterly, 29*, 123–132.

Castells, M. (2009). *Communication power*. New York: Oxford University Press.

Cha, M., Haddadi, H., & Benevenutoz, F. (2010). Measuring user influence in Twitter: The million follower fallacy. In *Proceedings of the Fourth International AAAI Conference on Weblogs and Social Media* (pp. 10–17). Menlo Park, CA: AAAI Press.

Chun, S., Shulman, S., Sandoval-Almazan, R., & Hovy, E. (2010). Government 2.0: Marking connections between citizens, data and government. *Information Policy, 15*, 1–9.

Coombs, T. (2013). *Crisis and crisis management en encyclopedia of public relations*. Thousand Oaks, CA: Sage.
Cromer, C. (2010). Understanding web 2.0's influences on public e-services: A protection motivation perspective. *Innovation: Management, Policy & Practice, 12*, 192–205.
Currye, D. (2010). *Expert round table on social media and risk communication during times of crisis: Strategic challenges and opportunities*. Washington, DC: American Public Health Association (APHA).
Freberg, K. (2012). Intention to comply with crisis messages communicated via social media. *Public Relations Review, 38*(2012), 416–421.
Gonzalez-Herrero, A., & Smith, S. (2010). Crisis communications management 2.0: Organizational principles to manage crisis in an online world. *Organizational Development Journal, 28*(1), 97–105.
Hughes, A. L., & Palen, L. (2010). Twitter adoption and use in mass convergence and emergency events. *International Journal of Emergency Management, 6*(3–4), 248–260.
Jin, Y., & Liu, B. F. (2010). The blog-mediated crisis communication model: Recommendations for responding to influential external blogs. *Journal of Public Relations Research, 22*(4), 429–455.
Keller, S. (2011). Adaptivity in risk communication. *Studies in Communication Sciences, 11*(1), 85–103.
Kim, S., & Liu, B. F. (2012). Are all crisis opportunities? A comparison of how corporate and government organizations responded to the 2009 flu pandemic. *Journal of Public Relations Research, 21*(1), 69–85.
Lathrop, D., & Ruma, L. (2010). *Open government: Collaboration, transparency, and participation in practice*. Sebastopol, CA: O'Reilly.
Lerbinger, O. (1997). *The crisis manager facing risk and responsibility*. Mahwah, NJ: Lawrence Erlbaum.
O'Leary, M. (Ed.). (2004). *The first 72 hours: A community approach to disaster preparedness*. New York: iUniverse.
Ostrom, E. (1990). *Governing the commons: The evolution of institutions for collective action*. New York: Cambridge University Press.
Papacharissi, Z., & de Fatime Oliveira, M. (2012). Affective news and networked publics: The rhythms of news storytelling on #Egypt. *Journal of Communication, 62*(2), 266–282.
Parmelee, J. H., & Bichard, S. L. (2012). *Politics and the Twitter revolution: How tweets influence the relationship between political leaders and the public*. Lanham, MD: Lexington Books.
Ray, S. J. (1999). *Strategic communication in crisis management lessons from the airline industry*. Westport, CT: Quorum.
Reynolds, B., & Seeger, M. (2005). Crisis and emergency risk communication as an integrative model. *Journal of Health Communication, 10*(1), 43–55.
Sandman, P. M. (2006). Crisis communication best practices: Some quibbles and additions. *Journal of Applied Communication Research, 34*, 257–262.
Schultz, F., Utz, S., & Göritz, A. (2011). Is the medium the message? Perceptions of and reactions to crisis communication via twitter, blogs and traditional media. *Public Relations Review, 37*, 20–27.
Segerberg, A., & Bennett, W. L. (2011). Social media and the organization of collective action: Using Twitter to explore the ecologies of two climate change protests. *The Communication Review, 14*(3), 197–215.
Smith, B. G. (2010). Socially distributing public relations: Twitter, Haiti, and interactivity in social media. *Public Relations Review, 36*, 329–335.
Stephens, K. K., Malone, P. C., & Bailey, C. M. (2005). Communicating with stakeholders during a crisis: Evaluating message strategies. *Journal of Business Communication, 42*(4), 390–419.
Syme, C. (2011). *Using social media in crisis: A study from Penn State [Blog]*. Retrieved from http://cksyme.org/penn-state-social-media-in-crisis
Ulmer, R., & Sellnow, T. L. (2000). Consistent question of ambiguity in organization crisis communication: Jack-in-the-Box as a case study. *Journal of Business Ethics, 25*, 143–155.

Utz, S., Schultz, F., & Glocka, S. (2013). Crisis communication online: How medium, crisis type and emotions affected public reactions in the Fukushima Daiichi nuclear disaster. *Public Relations Review, 39*, 40–46.

Van der Meer, T., & Verhoeven, P. (2013). Public framing organizational crisis situations: Social media versus news media. *Public Relations Review, 39*, 229–231.

Veil, S. R., Buehner, T., & Palenchar, M. J. (2011). A work-in-process literature review: Incorporating social media in risk and crisis communication. *Journal of Contingencies and Crisis Management, 19*(2), 110–122.

Weller, K., Bruns, A., Burgess, J., Mahrt, M., & Puschmann, C. (Eds.). (2014). *Twitter and society*. New York: Peter Lang.

Wendling, C., Radisch, J. & Jacobzone, S. (2013). *The use of social media in risk and crisis communication* (OECD Working Papers on Public Governance, No. 25). Paris: OECD Publishing. doi:10.1787/5k3v01fskp9s-en

Zerfass, A., Tench, R., Verčič, D., Verhoeven, P., & Moreno, A. (2013). *European communication monitor 2013*. Retrieved from http://www.zerfass.de/ecm/ECM2013-Results-ChartVersion.pdf

Zerfass, A., Tench, R., Verčič, D., Verhoeven, P., & Moreno, A. (2014). *European communication monitor 2014*. Retrieved from http://www.zerfass.de/ecm/ECM-2014-Results-ChartVersion.pdf

Zhang, W., Johnson, T. J., & Seltzer, T. (2010). The revolution will be networked: The influence of social networking sites on political attitudes and behavior. *Social Science Computer Review, 28*(1), 75–92.

Zhao, D., & Rosson, M. B. (2009). How and why people Twitter: The role that micro-blogging plays in informal communication at work. In *Proceedings of the ACM 2009, International Conference on Supporting Group Work* (pp. 243–252). New York: ACM.

MIX
Papier aus verantwortungsvollen Quellen
Paper from responsible sources
FSC® C105338

If you have any concerns about our products,
you can contact us on
ProductSafety@springernature.com

In case Publisher is established outside the EU,
the EU authorized representative is:
Springer Nature Customer Service Center GmbH
Europaplatz 3, 69115 Heidelberg, Germany

Printed by Libri Plureos GmbH
in Hamburg, Germany